GENESIS

Miracles and Predictions
according to Spiritism

GENESIS

MIRACLES AND PREDICTIONS
according to Spiritism

by

ALLAN KARDEC

UNITED STATES
SPIRITIST FEDERATION
NEW YORK
2020

GENESIS

MIRACLES AND PREDICTIONS
according to Spiritism

Copyright © 2020 by the United States Spiritist Council

Original Title: La genèse: les miracles et les prédictions
Translator: H. M. Monteiro
Proofreader: Jussara Korngold
Book Layout: HML
Cover Design: Paula Wienskoski Illustration (dreamstime.com@Alsusg)

ISBN: 978-1-948109-16-1 (United States Spiritist Council)
LCCN: 2019957992

LIBRARY OF CONGRESS CATALOGING-IN-PUBLICATION DATA

K145gmp
Allan Kardec, 1804-1869.
  Genesis, miracles and predictions according to Spiritism/
Allan Kardec; translated by Helton Mattar Monteiro. – New York, NY:
United States Spiritist Council, 2020.
  355 p.; 21.59 cm'
  Original title: La genèse: les miracles et les prédictions selon le spiritisme
  ISBN 978-1-948109-16-1
  1. Spirituality. 2. Spiritism. 3. Christianity. I. Title
  LCCN 2019957992

First edition: January 2020

Web site: http://www.spiritist.us   Email: info@spiritist.us
Book portal: https://is.gd/USSF1

Manufactured in the United States of America

Contents

Part one

GENESIS
according to Spiritism

Chapter I
Characteristics of the Spiritist Revelation . 17

Chapter II
God 51

Chapter III
Good and Evil 65

Chapter IV
Role of science in Genesis 79

Chapter V
Systems of the ancient and modern worlds ...87

Chapter VI
General uranography 95

Chapter VII
Geological sketch of the Earth 125

Chapter VIII
Theories of Earth history 147

Chapter IX
Transformations of the globe 153

PART TWO

MIRACLES

according to Spiritism

CHAPTER XIII

Characteristics of miracles 217

CHAPTER XIV

Fluids... 229

Chapter XV
Miracles in the Gospel............................ 257

Foreword to the English Edition

Genesis: Miracles and Predictions according to Spiritism was Kardec's last book before his untimely death on March 31, 1869. The 1st, 2nd, 3rd and 4th editions were all published in 1868 and are identical in content. That is the true original text used in this meticulous translation.

A fascinating read, this book is so rich and varied in its contents that highlighting its topics is almost impossible. By "Genesis," Kardec does not mean only the Mosaic volume, but also other ancient texts dealing with the creation of the world and a cataclysmic demise of humankind.

Furthermore, both in *Miracles* and *Predictions*, we are presented with facts and phenomena which have come a long way from the realm of superstitions and legends, to reveal themselves as perfectly explainable within the laws of Nature.

Add to that some surprising passages, such as a long and truly extraordinary essay by Galileo Galilee unfolding the Cosmos and deep apace to the reader, who then is treated to a complete treatise on obsession – one of the scourges of humankind – and the nature and methods used by obsessing spirits.

Needless to say, it also examines historical and moral facts of Christianity – specially the figure of Jesus himself – with a sharpness of focus that invites everyone to look at these matters afresh, with entirely new eyes, in the light of science and Spiritism.

All in all, Kardec's *Genesis* leads us with rare insight into a maze of interconnected topics, and an ability to make crystal clear most issues that have puzzled and troubled the human race for centuries and millennia.

United States Spiritist Federation
November 2019

INTRODUCTION

This new book is a step forward regarding the consequences and applications of Spiritism. As indicated by its title, it aims at studying three points variously interpreted and commented upon to this day: Genesis, miracles and predictions, in their relation with the new laws deriving from the observation of Spiritist phenomena.

Two elements or, if you like, two forces govern the universe: the spiritual element and the material element. From the simultaneous action of these two principles special phenomena are born which are naturally inexplicable, if one of the two is ignored, just as the formation of water would be inexplicable if one made abstraction of one of its two constituent elements: oxygen and hydrogen.

Spiritism in demonstrating the existence of the spiritual world and its relation to the material world gives the key to an array of phenomena that are misunderstood, and therefore considered inadmissible by a certain class of thinkers. These facts abound in the Scriptures, and it is for want of knowing the law which governs them, that the commentators of the two opposing camps, moving over and over in the same circle of ideas, some by abstracting from positive data offered by science, others by leaving out the spiritual principle, could not come to a rational solution.

Such a solution lies in a reciprocal action between spirit and matter. It is true that it removes the supernatural character from the majority of these facts; but would it be better to accept them as emerging from perfectly natural laws, or to reject them altogether? Their absolute rejection would entail the dismissal of the very base of the whole edifice, while their admission in this respect, which only suppresses the accessories, leaves its base intact. This is why Spiritism has brought so many people back to the belief of truths that they once considered fictional utopias.

Therefore, as said earlier, this book is a complement to applications of Spiritism from a special standpoint. Its contents were ready, or at least elaborated since a long time, but the right time to publish them had not yet come. First it was necessary that the ideas which were to form its fundamental premise would have reached maturity, and besides, taken into account the expediency of circumstances. Spiritism has neither mysteries nor secret theories; everything must be revealed in broad daylight, so that everyone can judge it knowingly; yet everything must surely come at the right time. A solution given hastily, before the complete elucidation of an issue, would be a cause of delay rather than advancement. Due to the importance of the issues dealt in this book, I made it a point to avoid rushing into conclusions.

Before tackling the main subject, it seemed necessary to clearly define the respective roles of spirits and humans in the work of the new doctrine. These preliminary considerations, which discard any idea of mysticism, are the subject of the first chapter herein, entitled "Characteristics of the Spiritist Revelation," to which I ask the reader to pay very close attention, because it represents, so to speak, the crux of the matter.

In spite of the part incumbent upon human activity in the formation of this doctrine, the initiative belongs entirely to the spirits. However it is not formed of the personal opinion of any of them in particular. It is, and could not be otherwise, *the result of their collective and concordant teaching*. On this condition alone it can be said to be the philosophical doctrine of the Spirits, or else it would be merely the doctrine *of a single spirit*, valued only as a personal opinion.

Generality and concordance in information, such is the essential character of Spiritism, the very condition of its existence. It follows that any principle that has not been acknowledged by means of generality control cannot be considered as an integral part of Spiritism, but rather as a single isolated opinion for which it cannot take any responsibility.

This concordant collectivity of the opinion expressed by the spirits, moreover passed through the criterion of logic, is what constitutes the strength of Spiritism, ensuring its perpetuity. In order for it to change, it would be necessary that the totality of spirits changed their opinion at some point in time, and started saying the opposite of what they have consistently said. Since it has its source in the teachings of the spirits, its capitulation would require that the spirits themselves ceased to exist. This is also why it will always prevail over personal systems which, unlike Spiritism, do not have their roots everywhere.

The Spirits' Book[1] has only consolidated its credibility because it is the expression of a general collective thought. Launched in the month of April, 1857, it has now completed ten years since its first publication. Meanwhile, the fundamental principles of which it has laid the foundations have been successively accomplished and developed as a result of the progressive teaching by the spirits, yet not a single one of them has been contradicted by experience. All Spiritist principles, without exception, remain standing, more alive than ever, whereas, of all the contradictory ideas that attempted to oppose to it, none prevailed, precisely because, everywhere, the opposite was taught. This is a characteristic result that I can proclaim without vanity, for I have never attributed it to myself.

The same scruples which presided over the writing of my other books, allowed me to state, in all truth, that they were *according to Spiritism*, because I was absolutely certain of their conformity with the general teachings of the spirits. The same applies to the current one, which, by similar reasons, is now offered as a complement to the preceding volumes, with the exception, however, of some new theories that are still hypothetical, which I took the care to point out as such, and which should be considered only as personal opinions, until they have been confirmed or contradicted, so as not to impose any undue responsibility on the Spiritist philosophy.

Moreover, readers of *The Spiritist Review*[2] have been able to notice, as a rough draft, most of the ideas that are developed in the current book, as I did with the previous ones. *The Spiritist Review* often serves as a testing ground for me to probe the opinions of both people and spirits concerning certain principles, before including them as constituent parts of Spiritism.

---

1 [Trans. note] A. KARDEC, *The Spirits' Book* (Trans. N. Alves, 2nd ed. New York: USSC/USSF, 2016).

2 [Trans. note] Founded and directed by A. KARDEC in 1858, *The Spiritist Review* was a monthly journal which ran for many years, now published in English by the USSC/USSF, New York (see bibliography).

Part one

Genesis
according to Spiritism

Chapter I
Characteristics of the Spiritist Revelation

1. Can we consider Spiritism as a revelation? In this case, what is its character? What is its authenticity based on? Who did it and how was it done? Is Spiritism a revelation in the liturgical sense of the word, that is to say, is it in every respect the product of an occult teaching from above? Is it absolute or susceptible of modification? By bringing to human beings a ready-made truth, would such revelation not have the effect of preventing them from making use of their faculties, since it would spare them the work of research? What can the authority of the teaching of the spirits be, if they are not infallible and superior to humanity? What is the use of the morals they preach, if this morality is none other than that of Christ, whom we know? What new truths do they bring to us? Do humans need a revelation and can they not find in themselves and in their consciousness whatever is necessary for them to behave? These are the questions on which it is important to keep focus.

2. Let us first define the meaning of the word *revelation. To reveal,* derived from the word "veil" (Latin *velum*), literally means *to remove the veil;* and figuratively, to discover, to make known something secret or unknown. In its most general, common acceptation, it refers to all unknown things that are brought to light, of any new idea that puts us on the path of what we did not know.

From this point of view, all the sciences which make known to us the mysteries of Nature are revelations, and it may be said that there is an incessant revelation. Astronomy has revealed the sidereal world, which we do not know; geology, the formation of planet Earth; chemistry, the law of affinities; physiology, the functions of the organism, and so on. Copernicus, Galileo, Newton, Laplace, Lavoisier, are all revealers.

3. Truth must be the essential character of any revelation. To reveal a secret is to make known a fact; if the thing is false, it is not a fact, and consequently there is no revelation. Every revelation contradicted by facts is not one; should it be ascribed to God. God can neither lie nor deceive, therefore it cannot emanate from It; it must be considered as the product of a human thought.

4. What is the role of the teacher vis-à-vis the students, if not that of a revealer? He/she teaches them what they do not know, what they would not have the time or the opportunity to discover for themselves, because science is the collective work of centuries by a multitude of individuals who have each brought their contingent of observations, which benefit those who come after them. Teaching is, in fact, the revelation of certain scientific or moral truths, whether physical or metaphysical, made by individuals who know them to others who do not know them, and who otherwise would have remained unaware of them.

5. However a teacher only teaches what he/she has learned: a teacher is a second-hand revealer. Conversely, individuals of genius teach what they have found themselves: he or she is the early revealer who brings the light which gradually becomes common knowledge. Where would humanity be without the revelations made by individuals of genius who appear from time to time in history?

But, after all, what are individuals of genius? Why are they individuals of genius? Where do they come from? What happens to them? It should be noted that most of them bear some transcendent faculties and innate knowledge, that a little work is enough to develop. They really belong to humanity, since they are born, live and die like all of us. So where did they draw the knowledge that they could not have acquired during a lifetime? Can anyone say with materialists that chance has given them brain matter in greater quantity and of better quality? In this case, they would not have more merit than a vegetable bigger and tastier than another.

Will anyone say, like certain Spiritualists, that God endowed them with a more favored soul than that of the common human being? Such an assumption is just as illogical, because it would taint God with partiality. The only rational solution of this problem is in the preexistence of the soul and in the plurality of existences. The individual of genius is a spirit who has lived longer and has, therefore, acquired and progressed more than those who are less advanced. By incarnating, he/she brings what he knows, and as such an individual knows much more than the others, without needing to learn, he/she is what is called a genius. But what he or she knows is none the less the result of previous work and not the result of a privilege. Before being reborn, he/she was therefore and advanced spirit. This spirit reincarnates, either to make others benefit from its knowledge or to acquire even more of it.

Undoubtedly, human beings progress by themselves and by exercising their intellectual abilities; yet, if left to their own strength, this progress would be very slow, unless they are helped by more advanced beings, as a schoolchild is helped by teachers. All nations have had their individuals of genius who have come at various times to give impetus to them and move them from their inertia.

6. Since one admits the solicitude of God for Its created beings, why not also admit that spirits capable, on account of their energy and superior knowledge, of advancing humanity, incarnate themselves by God's will to help us progress toward a definite direction. And that they all receive a mission, as an ambassador is given one by his/her sovereign? This is the role of all great geniuses. What do they come to do except teaching fellow humans truths that the latter do not know and have ignored for long periods of time, in order to give them a jump-start that can make them rise more rapidly? Those geniuses who appear throughout the centuries as shining stars, leaving after them a long luminous trail for humanity, are missionaries, or, if you will, messiahs. If they taught humans nothing but what the latter already knew, their presence would be completely useless. The new things they teach us, whether in the physical realm or the philosophical realm, are *revelations*.

If God gives rise to revelations of scientific truths, It can all the more give rise to revelations of moral truths, which are one of the essential elements of progress. Such come from the philosophers whose ideas have traversed the centuries.

7. In the specific sense of religious faith, revelation refers more particularly to spiritual things which humans cannot know for themselves, nor can they discover by means of their own senses, and whose knowledge is given to them by God or through Its messengers, either by means of direct speech or by inspiration. In this case, the revelation is always made to privileged individuals, designated by the name of prophets or *messiahs*, that is to say, *envoys*, *missionaries*, whose *mission* is to transmit it to fellow human beings. Considered from this point of view, revelation implies absolute passivity; it should be accepted without any verification or examination or argument.

8. All religions had their revealers, and though all were far from having known the whole truth, they were there for a providential reason, because they were appropriate to the time and the environment in which they lived, and to the specific traits of the peoples to whom they spoke, and to whom they were relatively superior. In spite of the errors of their doctrines, they have nonetheless stirred the minds, and by that, sown seeds of progress which blossomed later on, or will blossom some day in the sun of Christianity. It is therefore wrong to condemn them in the name of orthodoxy, for a day will come when all these beliefs, so diverse in form, but which in fact rest on the same fundamental principle of God and the immortality of the soul, will merge in a great vast unity, when reason will have triumphed over prejudices.

Unfortunately, religions have always been instruments of domination; the role of prophet has often induced secondary ambitions, giving rise to a multitude of so-called revealers or messiahs who, thanks to the prestige of this designation, have exploited credulity for the benefit of their pride, their greed, or their laziness, finding it more convenient to live at the expense of their dupes. The Christian religion has not been exempt from these parasites. In this regard, I ask the reader to pay very close attention to chapter XX of *The Gospel according to Spiritism*:[3] "For false christs and false prophets will arise."

9. Are there direct revelations of God to human beings? This is a question which we dare not resolve whether affirmatively or

---

3 [Trans. note] See bibliography at the end of the book.

negatively, in an absolute manner. The thing is not radically impossible, but nothing gives any definite proof of it. What is beyond any doubt is that the spirits closest to God for their perfection can penetrate Its thought and transmit it. As for incarnate revealers, depending on the hierarchical order to which they belong and the degree of their personal knowledge, they are able to draw their teachings from their own knowledge, or receive them from higher-order spirits, even from direct messengers of God. These latter, speaking in God's name, could sometimes be mistaken for God Itself.

Such communications are not strange to anyone who is acquainted with Spiritist phenomena and the way in which relations between the incarnate and the discarnate are established. The messages can be transmitted by various means: through pure and simple inspiration, by hearing the words, by the sight of the spirits instructors in visions and apparitions, either in dreams, or in the waking state, as shown in many examples found in the Bible, the Gospel, and in the sacred books of all peoples. It is therefore strictly accurate to say that most of the revealers are inspired, auditory, or seeing mediums; from which it does not follow that all mediums are revealers, let alone direct intermediaries of the Godhead or Its messengers.

10. Pure Spirits[4] alone can receive the word of God with the mission of transmitting it; but we now know that spirits are far from being perfect, and that there are some that assume false appearances; This is what the evangelist John said: "Do not believe every spirit, but test the spirits to see whether they are from God." (1John 4:1 esv)

Therefore there can be serious and true revelations, as well as apocryphal and false ones. The essential character of a divine revelation is that of *eternal truth*. Any revelation tainted by error or subject to change cannot emanate from God. Thus the laws of the Decalogue have all the characteristics of such origin, while the other Mosaic laws, essentially transitory, and often in contradiction with the laws obtained in the Sinai, reflect the personal and political views of the Hebrew legislator. With the softening of the manners and customs of the people, these laws have of themselves fallen into disuse, while the Decalogue remained standing as the beacon of all humanity. Christ made the Decalogue the basis of his edifice, while abolishing the other laws. If the latter had been the work of God,

---

4 [Trans. note] See A. Kardec, *The Spirits' Book*, book 2, ch. I, item 112.

he would not have touched it. Christ and Moses are the two great revealers who changed the face of the world, and there is evidence of their divine mission. A purely human work would not have such power.

11. An important revelation has now been fulfilled, namely, the one that shows us the possibility of communicating with beings of the spiritual world. This knowledge is not new, of course, but it has remained to this day a dead letter, that is to say, of no benefit to humankind. The ignorance of the laws governing these rapports had stifled it under the weight of superstition. Humans were incapable of drawing any salutary deduction from it; it was reserved to our age to rid it of its ridiculous accessories and understand its scope; and to let out the light that was to illuminate the road to the future.

12. Spiritism, having made known the invisible world which surrounds us, in the midst of which we have lived without suspecting it – together with the laws which govern it, its relations with the visible world, and the nature and state of the beings that inhabit it. Hence disclosing the destiny of humans after death – is a true revelation in the scientific sense of the word.

13. By its nature, the Spiritist revelation has a dual character: it is at once divine revelation and scientific revelation. From the first it retains the fact of being providential, and not the result of human initiative and premeditated purpose; that the fundamental points of Spiritism lie in the tenets taught by the spirits entrusted by God with enlightening humans on things they did not know and could not learn by themselves, and which are important for them to know now that they are ripe to understand them. From the second, it retains the fact that this teaching is not the privilege of any individual, but instead given to everyone through the same means; and that those who transmit it as well as those who receive it are not *passive* beings, exempt from the work of observation and research; that they should not renounce their judgment and their free will; that verification is not forbidden to them, but on the contrary recommended. Lastly, that the Spiritist doctrine *was not dictated in ts entirety, nor imposed on blind belief,* but rather deduced and mentally elaborated by humans, based on the observation of facts which the spirits put before our eyes, and from the instructions which they give us – instructions which we then study, discuss and compare, eventually drawing by ourselves their consequences and applications. In a word, *what characterizes the Spiritist revelation is that its source is divine, its initiative has come from the spirits, but its formulation is entirely the work of human beings.*

14. As its means of formulation, Spiritism proceeds in exactly the same way as the positivistic sciences, that is to say, it applies the experimental method. Facts of a new order emerge which cannot be explained by known laws; we observe them, compare them, analyze them, and by studying the effects going back to their causes; we arrive at the law which governs them. Then we infer their consequences and look for useful applications. *Spiritism does not establish any preconceived theory;* thus it posits neither the existence nor the intervention of spirits, nor the perispirit, nor reincarnation, nor any of the principles contained in its tenets. It concluded that spirits exist since this existence has been fully demonstrated by the observation of facts, and thus of other principles. It is not the facts that have come in hindsight to confirm a theory, but the theory itself which subsequently came to explain and summarize the facts. It is therefore strictly accurate to say that Spiritism is a science of observation, and not the product of imagination.

15. Let me give an example. There is a very singular fact in the world of the spirits, and which, assuredly, nobody would have experienced: it regards spirits that do not believe to be dead. Well then. Higher-order spirits, who know this fact perfectly well, have not warned in anticipation: "There are spirits that believe that they still lead an earthly life; that have preserved their tastes, their habits, and their instincts." Yet they have induced manifestation of spirits of this category to make us observe them. So, having seen spirits unaware of their state, or affirming that they were still of this world, and believing they were going to their ordinary occupations and affairs, from this example one can infer the rule. The multiplicity of analogous facts has proved that it was not an exception, but one of the phases of spirit life. It has made it possible to study all the varieties and the causes of this singular delusion; to recognize that this situation is especially peculiar to spirits that are morally little advanced, and that it is also peculiar to certain kinds of death. It is only temporary, but can last for days, months, and even years. This is how a theory is born from observation. It is the same with all the other principles of Spiritism.

16. Just as science properly speaking is concerned with the study of the laws that govern the material principle, the special object of Spiritism is the knowledge of the laws of the spiritual principle. Now, since this latter principle is one of the forces of Nature, which reacts incessantly on the material principle and vice versa, it follows that the knowledge of one cannot be complete without the knowledge of the other; that Spiritism and science complement each other; thus science without Spiritism finds itself in the powerless position of explaining certain phenomena by mere laws of matter. And it is because it has abstracted from the spiritual principle that science end up in so many dead ends; and Spiritism without science would lack support and verification control, and might fall into wishful thinking. If Spiritism had come before recent scientific discoveries would have been an unsuccessful experience, like everything that comes before its time.

17. All sciences are connected and succeed one another in a rational order; they are born of each other, as they find a point of support in previous ideas and knowledge. Astronomy, one of the first to have been developed, persisted in the errors of its infancy until the moment when physics came to reveal the law behind the forces of natural agents. Chemistry being able to do nothing without physics, was to succeed it closely, and then hand in hand with it, with one relying on the other. Anatomy, physiology, zoology, botany, and mineralogy have become serious sciences only by means of the light shed by physics and chemistry. Geology, born of yesterday, without astronomy, physics, chemistry and all the other sciences, would have missed its true elements of vitality; it could only have come after the others.

18. Modern science has done justice to the four primitive elements of the ancients, and from observation to observation it has arrived at the conception of *a single generating element* of all the transformations of matter. Yet matter, by itself, is inert; it has neither life, nor thought, nor feeling; it needs to be united with the spiritual principle. Spiritism has neither discovered nor invented this principle, but it was the first to demonstrate it with irrefutable proofs, while studying it, analyzing it, and rendering evident its action. To the *material element*, it came to add the *spiritual element*. *Material element* and *spiritual element*, these are the two principles, the two living forces of Nature. Through the indissoluble union of these two elements, a myriad of formerly inexplicable facts become easily explainable.

By its very essence, and by having as its object the study of one of the two constituent elements of the universe, Spiritism inevitably touches on most sciences. It could only come after the development of these sciences, and above all after they would have proved their impotence in explaining everything by the laws of matter alone.

19. Spiritism is accused by some of kinship with magic and witchcraft; but we forget that astronomy was preceded by mandatory astrology, which is not so far from us; and that chemistry descends from alchemy, which no sensible person would dare to practice today. No one denies, however, that in astrology and alchemy lie the germs of truth from which the current sciences have sprung. In spite of its ridiculous formulas, alchemy has set us in the way of simple bodies and of the law of affinities, while astrology relied on the position and motion of the stars it had studied – although for ignoring the true laws which govern the mechanism of the universe, the stars were, for the common people, mysterious beings to whom superstition lent a moral influence and a revelatory sense. When Galileo, Newton and Kepler made known these laws with the telescope tearing the veil, and plunging our gaze into the depths of space, an action deemed indiscreet by some people, the planets appeared to us as simple worlds similar to ours, and suddenly all the scaffolding of the marvelous crumbled down.

It is the same with Spiritism with regard to magic and witchcraft. These were also based on manifestations of the spirits, as astrology was based on the movement of the stars; but in ignorance of the laws which govern the spiritual world, they mingled ridiculous practices and beliefs with these relations to which modern Spiritism, fruit of experience and observation, has done justice. Assuredly, the distance separating Spiritism from magic and witchcraft is greater than that which exists between astronomy and astrology, chemistry and alchemy. A desire to confound them is proof positive that one knows nothing about them.

20.   The mere fact that communicating with beings of the spiritual world is indeed possible has incalculable consequences of the highest importance; it opens a whole new world to us, which gains even more importance for encompassing all human beings without exception. Such knowledge cannot fail to bring, once it becomes widespread, a profound change in the manners, character, habits, and beliefs which have such a marked influence on social relations. It is a revolution which takes place in the realm of ideas, a revolution which is all the greater and more powerful, because it is not circumscribed to one people or a caste, but touches the heart of all classes, all nationalities, all religious beliefs.

It is therefore right to consider Spiritism as the third great revelation. Let us see how they differ, and by what link they are connected to one another.

21.   MOSES, as a prophet, revealed to humans the knowledge of one God, sovereign master and creator of all things. He promulgated the law of Sinai and laid the foundation of true faith. As a human individual, he was the legislator of the people by whom this primitive faith, after being purified, was eventually spread all over the world.

22.   CHRIST, taking from the ancient law that which is eternal and divine, and discarding what was only transitory, purely disciplinary or of human conception, added the revelation of a future life of which Moses had never spoken, in which punishments and rewards awaited humans after death. (See *The Spiritist Review – 1861*, "Spiritist Teachings and Dissertations: Moses and Jesus' Laws" and "Spiritist Teachings and Dissertations: A Spirit to his Fellow Israelites.")[5]

23.   The most important part of Christ's revelation, of which he is the primary source, the cornerstone of all his tenets, is the whole new point of view in which he makes the Divinity be regarded. It is no longer the terrible, jealous, vindictive God of Moses, the cruel and unmerciful God which sprinkles the Earth with human blood, which ordains the slaughter and extermination of whole peoples, without excepting women, children and elders, and which

5   [Trans. note] See bibliography at the end of the book.

punishes those who spare the victims. It is no longer the injurious God which punishes a whole nation for their leader's fault, which takes revenge on the guilty by victimizing innocent persons, which strikes children for the fault of their parents, but instead a clement God, supremely just and good, full of meekness and mercy, which forgives the repentant sinner, and renders to each according to their deeds. This is no longer the God of one privileged people, *the God of the armies* presiding over battles to support Its own cause against the gods of other peoples, but the collective parent of all the human race, which extends Its protection over all Its children, and call them all to Itself. This is no longer the God which rewards and punishes only by the goods of the Earth, which makes glory and happiness consist in the enslavement of rival nations and in the multiplicity of offspring, but one which says to humanity: "Your true homeland is not in this world, it is in the celestial kingdom; it is there that the humble of heart will be elevated and the proud will be humbled." It is no longer the God which makes a virtue of vengeance and orders us to take "an eye for an eye, a tooth for a tooth," but the God of mercy which says: "Forgive if you would like to be forgiven; return good for evil; do not do unto others what you do not want others to do unto you." This is no longer a petty and meticulous God which imposes, under the most severe penalties, the manner in which It wishes to be adored, and which is offended by the non-observance of a single formula, but rather the great God which gives precedence to the thought and is not honored by the form or ceremony. In short, it is no longer a God which wants to be feared, but the God who wants to be loved.

24. Since God is the fulcrum of all religious beliefs, the aim of all religious denominations, *the character of all religions conforms to the idea of God offered by each of them.* Those who make God vindictive and cruel believe to honor It by acts of cruelty, by torture and burning stakes, whereas those who make It a partial and jealous God are intolerant. These will be more or less meticulous in form, depending on how much they conceive of God as being tainted with human weaknesses and pettiness.

25. The whole tenets of Christ are founded on the character which he ascribes to the Divinity. With an impartial God, sovereignly just, good and merciful, he was able to make of the love of God and charity toward the neighbor, the express condition of salvation, saying: *This is the whole law and the prophets, there is no other.*[6] On this belief alone, he was able to establish the principle of the equality of humans before God, and of universal fraternity.

This revelation of the true attributes of the Divinity, together with that of the immortality of the soul, and of a future life, profoundly affected the mutual relations of human beings, imposed on them new obligations, made them reconsider current life under a new angle. For that very reason, it would have an impact on social manners and relations. Therefore, because of its consequences, this is incontestably the most important point of Christ's revelation, whose importance we have not sufficiently understood. Although it is regrettable to say so, this is also the point from which we have distanced ourselves more and more, the one we have the most misunderstood in the interpretation of his teachings.

26.   However Christ adds: "Many of the things that I say to you, you cannot yet understand them, and I would have many others to tell you that you would not understand; therefore I speak to you in parables; but later *I will send you the Comforter, the Spirit of Truth who will restore all things and will explain them all to you.*"[7]

If Christ did not say all that he could have said, it was because he thought it better to leave some truths in shadow until humans should be capable of comprehending them. By his own confession, he admits that his teaching was incomplete, since he announces the coming of the one who should complete it. Furthermore he foresaw that his words would be misunderstood, that they would be diverted from his teaching, in short, that some people would undo what he did, therefore everything should necessarily be restored – now, only that which has been undone can be *restored.*

27.   Why does he call the new messiah *Comforter?* This meaningful and unambiguous name is itself a revelation. He foresaw, therefore, that humans would need comforting, which implies an insufficiency of the comforting they would find in the belief that

---

6 [Trans. note] cf. MATTHEW 7:11.

7 [Trans. note] Here, as elsewhere, A. KARDEC is closely paraphrasing the Gospels. *Cf.,* for example, JOHN 14:26 AKJV/PCE.

they had embraced. Never, perhaps, had Christ been more clear and explicit than in these last words, to which few seem to have been aware, perhaps because of an avoidance of bringing them into light and deepening their prophetic meaning.

28. If Christ could not develop his teaching in full, it was because people still lacked knowledge that they would only acquire in time, and without which they could not understand it. There are things which would have seemed nonsense for the state of knowledge of that time. To complete one's teaching must be understood in the sense of *explaining* and *developing* it, rather than adding new truths, for everything is already there in germ. Those people still lacked the key to grasp the full meaning of his words.

29. Yet who would dare to interpret the sacred Scriptures? Who has this right? Who has the necessary lights for such a task, if not the theologians?

Then who dares? Science first of all, which does not require anyone to make known the laws of Nature, and leaps headlong over errors and prejudices.

Who has this right? In this age of intellectual emancipation and freedom of conscience, the right of examination belongs to all, and the Scriptures are no longer the holy ark which no one dared to touch without risking being annihilated. As to possessing the necessary special lights, without challenging those of theologians as enlightened as those of the Middle Ages, and in particular the Fathers of the Church, those lights however were not sufficient, when they condemned as heresy the movement of planet Earth and the belief in the antipodes; nor did they ascend any higher when those of our day cast anathema on the geologic periods in the formation of the Earth!

Humans have been able to explain the Scriptures only by the aid of what they knew, the false or incomplete notions they had on the laws of Nature, which were later revealed by science. That is why theologians themselves were able, in very good faith, to misunderstand the meaning of certain words and facts of the Gospel. Wishing to find at all costs the confirmation of a preconceived thought, they always moved in the same circle, without abandoning their viewpoint, so that they saw only that which they wanted to see. As theologian-scholars, they could not understand the causes of laws of which they were completely unaware.

But who will be judge of the various and often contradictory interpretations given outside theology? The future, logic and common sense. Humans, as they become more and more enlightened with new facts and new laws which come to be revealed, will be able to distinguish between utopian systems and reality. Now, science makes certain laws known; Spiritism adds others; both are indispensable for understanding the sacred texts of all religions, from Confucius and Buddha to Christianity. As for theology, it is not in a position to judiciously point out the contradictions of science, while it does not always agree with itself.

30. SPIRITISM, by taking its starting point from the very words of Christ, as Christ had taken his from Moses, is a direct consequence of his doctrine,

To the vague idea of a future life, it adds the revelation of the existence of the invisible world which surrounds us and occupies space, and by this it sets a belief, giving it a body, a consistency, a reality in thought.

It defines the bonds which unite the soul to the body, and lifts the veil which concealed from human beings the mysteries of birth and death.

Through Spiritism, humans learn where they come from, where they are going, why they are on Earth, why they are temporarily suffering, and start seeing God's justice everywhere.

We learn that the soul progresses incessantly through a series of successive existences, until it has attained the degree of perfection which can bring it closer to God.

We learn that all souls, having the same point of departure, are created equal, with the same aptitude for progress by virtue of their free will; that all are of the same essence, and that there is among them only the difference of the progress achieved by each of them; that each and every one has the same destiny and will attain the same goal, more or less promptly according to their deeds and their good will.

We learn that there are no destitute beings, nor those who are more favored than others; that God did not create anyone as privileged and dispensed them from the work imposed on others to progress;

that there are no beings perpetually devoted to evil and suffering; that those designated by the name of *demons* are merely backward and imperfect spirits, that do evil in the state of spirits, just as they did in the state of humans, but that will eventually advance and improve themselves. And that angels or pure spirits are not beings outside creation, but spirits who have attained the ultimate goal, after having followed the path of progress; that thus there are no multiple creations of different categories among the intelligent beings, but that all creation springs from the great law of unity which governs the universe, and that all beings gravitate toward a common goal, which is perfection, without any of them being favored at the expense of others, since all are the outcome of their own deeds.

31. By the relations that we can now establish with those who have left the Earth, we have not only the material proof of the existence and the individuality of the soul, but can now understand the solidarity which connects the living and the dead of this world, and those of this world with those of other worlds. We become aware of their situation in the world of spirits and follow them in their migrations, as witnesses to their joys and sorrows. We know why they are happy or unhappy, and the fate that awaits them according to the good or the evil they have done. These relations initiate us in the future life which we now can observe in all its phases and vicissitudes. The future is no longer a vague hope: it is a positive fact, a mathematical certainty. Therefore death should no longer be feared, for it is deliverance, the door to real life for all of us.

32. By studying the situation of the spirits, humans learn that happiness and unhappiness in spiritual life are inherent in the degree of perfection or imperfection; that each one suffers the direct and natural consequences of his/her faults, in other words, that we are punished by where we have sinned; that these consequences will last as long as the cause which produced them; that thus the culprit would suffer eternally only if he/she persisted eternally in evil, but that suffering ceases with repentance and atonement. Now, as it depends on each one of us to improve, each one may, by virtue of his/her own free will, prolong or abridge these sufferings, just as a patient will suffer from his/her excesses as long as they do not put an end to them.

33. If reason repels, as incompatible with the goodness of God, the idea of irreparable, perpetual and absolute penalties often inflicted for a single fault; and torments of hell which cannot be softened by the most ardent and sincere repentance, it bows before the idea of a distributive and impartial justice, which takes into account everything, never closing the door of return, and constantly stretching its hand to the castaway, instead of driving him/her back into the abyss.

34. The plurality of existences, of which Christ posited the principle in the Gospel, but without defining it more than many other principles, is one of the most important laws revealed by Spiritism, in the sense that it demonstrates its reality and the need for progress. By this law, human beings can explain all the apparent anomalies that life presents; their differences in social position; premature deaths which, without reincarnation, would be useless for the souls' abridged lives; the inequality of intellectual and moral aptitudes, now explained by the different ages of spirits, that have lived for longer or shorter periods, having learned and progressed more or less, and that brings with themselves, through rebirths, what they have acquired in former existences. (See item no. **5** above.)

35. With the doctrine that preaches the creation of a new soul at each birth, we fall back into the system of privileged creations; humans are foreign to each other, nothing connects them, family ties are purely carnal; they cannot be in solidarity with a past in which they did not exist. With nothingness after death, all relationships would cease with life; therefore, they are not in solidarity with the future either. Conversely, by reincarnation, they are in solidarity with both the past and the future; their relationships being perpetuated in the spiritual world and in the physical world; fraternity is then based on the very laws of Nature; good has a purpose, and evil its inevitable consequences.

36. With reincarnation all race and caste prejudices fall down, since the same spirit can be reborn rich or poor, a potentate or a proletarian, a master or a minion, a free person or a slave, a man or a woman. Of all the arguments invoked against the injustice of servitude and slavery, against the subjection of women to the law of the strongest, there is none that outweighs the material fact of reincarnation. If, then, reincarnation bases upon a law of Nature the principle of universal fraternity, it also bases on the same law the principle of equality of social rights, and consequently that of liberty.

Humans are born inferior and subordinate only by their bodies; by their spirits they are all equal and free. Hence the duty of treating inferiors with kindness, benevolence and humanity, because whoever is our subordinate today may have been our equal or superior, perhaps a relative or friend, and furthermore we can become in turn the subordinate of the one we now command,

37.   Take away from humans their free and independent spirit, which survive matter, you turn it into an organized machine without purpose, without responsibility, without any other restraint than civil law, and *good to exploit* like a clever animal. Waiting for nothing after death, nothing will stop him/her from increasing the enjoyments of current time. Should he or she suffer, they have only the prospect of despair and nothingness as a refuge; whereas with the certainty of a future, of finding those he/she loved, plus *the fear of seeing again those he/she once offended,* will change all his/her ideas. If Spiritism would only have drawn humans from doubt concerning the existence of a future life, it would already have done more for their moral improvement than all the disciplinary laws which sometimes bridle humans, but never change them.

38.   Without the preexistence of the soul, the ancient doctrine of original sin is not only irreconcilable with God's justice for making all humans responsible for the fault of a single one, but it would be total nonsense, and much the less justifiable that the soul did not even exist at the time when it is claimed that its responsibility is traced back. Conversely, with preexistence and reincarnation, every human being brings forth the seeds of his/her past imperfections, flaws which they have not yet corrected, and which are translated by his/her native instincts and propensities for this or that vice. There lies one's true original sin, whose consequences one naturally undergoes; but with this capital difference, namely, that it bears the penalty of one's own faults, and not that of a fault committed by another. And with this other difference: it is at once comforting, encouraging, and sovereignly equitable, that each lifetime offers this person the means of redeeming himself/herself through atonement, and to progress either by stripping themselves of some imperfection, or by acquiring new knowledge, and that until such person is sufficiently purified and no longer needs bodily life, and can lead exclusively a spiritual, eternal and blessed life.

For the same reason, the one who has progressed morally brings, in reincarnating, native qualities, like the one who has progressed intellectually, brings new ideas, and is identified with the good, practicing it effortlessly, without calculation, and, so to speak, without thinking of doing it. Those who are obliged to combat their bad tendencies are still in the struggle. The first have already won, the second are still defeating. Therefore there is *original virtue*, as there is *original knowledge*, and *original sin*, or better, *original vice*.

39. Experimental Spiritism has studied the peculiarities of spiritual fluids and their action upon matter. It has demonstrated the existence of the *perispirit*,[8] suspected since antiquity, and called *Spiritual Body* by Paul the Apostle, that is, the fluidic body of the soul after the destruction of the tangible body. We know today that this envelope is inseparable from the soul; that it is one of the constituent elements of the human being; that it is the transmitting vehicle of thought; and that, during the life of the body, it serves as a link between the spirit and matter. The perispirit plays such an important role in the organism and in an array of pathological conditions that it is closely related to physiology as well as to psychology.

40. The study of the properties of the perispirit, of spiritual fluids, and of the physiological attributes of the soul, opens new horizons to science, and gives the key to an array of phenomena not understood till then for unawareness of the law which governs them. Phenomena denied by materialism, because they are related to spirituality, described by others as miracles or spells, according to their beliefs. Such are, among others, the phenomena of second sight; remote viewing; natural and artificial somnambulism;[9] the psychical effects of catalepsy and lethargy; prescience and presentiments; apparitions and transfigurations; thought transmission; fascination; instant cures; obsessions and possessions, etc. Having

---

8 [Trans. note] *Perispirit* is a Spiritist term coined by A. KARDEC, meaning the fluidic body of the soul.

9 [Trans. note] Somnambulism was the name given by A. KARDEC and all Spiritualist and Spiritist writers at his time to *mediumistic trance*.

shown that all these phenomena are based on laws as natural as electrical phenomena, and the normal conditions in which they can be reproduced, Spiritism has destroyed the empire of the marvelous and the supernatural, and consequently the source of most superstitions. If it makes us believe in the possibility of certain facts regarded by some as chimerical, it also prevents us from believing in many other things whose impossibility and irrationality it has demonstrated.

41.　Spiritism, far from denying or destroying the Gospel; on the contrary, it confirms, explains and develops, by the new laws of Nature that it reveals, all that Christ has said and done. It sheds light on obscure points of his teaching, so that those for whom certain parts of the Gospel were unintelligible, or seemed *unacceptable*, could readily understand and admit them with the help of Spiritism. Now we can better see the full scope, and distinguish between reality and allegory. Christ emerges even greater from this: he is no longer a mere philosopher, but a divine Messiah.

42.　If we also consider the moralizing power of Spiritism by the purpose it ascribes to all actions in one's life, by the tangible consequences of good and evil which it exposes; and the moral strength, the courage, the comforting it gives in afflictions by an unwavering confidence in the future, by the thought of having close to oneself the beings one has loved, with the assurance of seeing them again and the possibility of communicating with them. And finally by the certainty that of all that one does, all that one acquires in intelligence, in science, in moral qualities *until the last hour of one's life*, nothing is lost and everything benefits our advancement, we recognize that Spiritism fulfills all the promises of Christ with regard to the announced *Comforter*. As for the *Spirit of Truth* which presides over this great movement of regeneration, the promise of his advent is likewise fulfilled because he is, in fact, the true *Comforter*.[10]

---

10 Many family parents deplore the untimely death of children for whose education they have made great sacrifices, and say that all that was in vain. With Spiritism, they will not regret these sacrifices, and will be ready to do them, even with the certainty of seeing their children die, because they know that, if their children cannot avail themselves of this education in the current existence, it will serve them later for their advancement as Spirits in a new existence; and that when they come back, they will have an intellectual background that will make them apter to acquire new knowledge. Such are the children who bring forth innate ideas from birth, who, so to speak, have knowledge without a need to learn. If, as

43.   If, to these results, we add the incredible rapidity of propagation of Spiritism, in spite of all that has been done to bring it down, one cannot dispute that its coming is providential, since it triumphs over all forces and all human bad intentions. The ease with which it has been accepted by so many, and this without any constraints, without any other means than the power of its idea, proves that it meets a need – that of believing in something, after the void left by unbelief – and also that it came at the right time.

44.   The afflicted exist in great numbers, so it is not surprising that so many people welcome a doctrine that consoles in preference to those which only offer despair; for it is to the disinherited, more than to those who are joyful in this world, that Spiritism is addressed. A patient is more pleased to see the doctor than one who feels perfectly well. Now, the afflicted are the sick, and the Comforter is their physician.

You who fight against Spiritism, if you want one to leave it to follow you, then offer more and better than it does; heal the wounds of the soul more assuredly. Give more comforting, more satisfaction to the heart, more legitimate hopes and greater certainties; paint a more rational, more seductive picture of the future; but do not expect to prevail,with your perspective of nothingness; or you, with the alternative of the flames from hell or heavenly bliss in useless and perpetual contemplation.

45.   The first revelation was personified in Moses, the second in Christ, the third in no individual. The first two are individual, the third is collective; this is an essential characteristic of capital importance. It is collective in the sense that it has not been made as a privilege of anyone; that no one, therefore, can claim to be its exclusive prophet. It has been made simultaneously all over the world, to millions of people, of all ages, at all times and conditions, from

parents, you do not have the immediate satisfaction of seeing your children benefit from an education, they will certainly enjoy it later, either as spirits or as incarnate humans. Perhaps you will again be the parents of these same children, who are said to be blessed by Nature, but who owe their aptitudes to a previous education. It is also true that if children go wrong because of negligence from their parents, these may have to suffer later in a new existence for the troubles and sorrows to which they gave rise.

(See also A. KARDEC, *The Gospel according to Spiritism*, ch. V, item 21, "The Loss of Loved Ones; Premature Deaths.")

the lowest to the highest of the scale, according to this prediction reported by the author of the Acts of the Apostles: "And in the last days it shall be, God declares, that I will pour out my Spirit on all flesh, and your sons and your daughters shall prophesy, and your young men shall see visions, and your old men shall dream dreams."[11] Spiritism did not emerge from any special worship, in order to serve one day as a universal rallying point.[12]

46. As products of a personal teaching, the first two revelations were inevitably localized, that is to say, they took place at a single point around which the idea spread from nearby. However it took many centuries for them to reach the ends of the world without completely taking it over. The third revelation is peculiar for not being personified in a single individual, since it has occurred simultaneously at thousands of different points, all of which have become centers or focal points of radiation. Once these centers are multiplied, their connections gradually meet, like the circles formed by a multitude of stones thrown onto the surface of a lake, so that in a given time they will eventually cover the entire surface of the globe.

Such is one of the causes of the rapid propagation of Spiritism. If it had arisen at a single point, if it had been the exclusive work of one individual, it would have formed a group of followers around him/her; but perhaps half a century would have to be elapsed before it could reach the limits of the country where it would have been

---

11 [Trans. note] Acts 2:17.

12 My personal role in the great movement of ideas which is being prepared by Spiritism, and which is already beginning to take place, is that of an attentive observer who studies the facts in order to seek the cause and draw the consequences. I confronted everything I could muster; I have compared and commented on instructions given by the spirits at all points of the world, and then I have methodically coordinated the whole. In a word, I have studied and offered to the public the fruit of my researches, without ascribing to my books any other value than that of a philosophical work deduced from observation and experience, without ever claiming to be the head of a doctrine, nor imposing my ideas upon anyone. In publishing them, I used a common right, and those who accepted them did so freely. If these ideas have found many adepts, it is because they have had the advantage of meeting the aspirations of a great number of people, of which I cannot boast, since their origin does not belong to me. My greatest merit is that of perseverance and dedication to the cause that I have embraced. In all this I did what others might have done in my place. That is why I have never intended to pose as a prophet or messiah, let alone to give any such impression.

originated, whereas only after ten years Spiritism already has milestones planted from one corner of the world to another.

47. This circumstance, unheard of in the history of philosophical and religious doctrines, gives it an exceptional strength and an irresistible power of action. Indeed, if it was circumscribed to point, in one country, it would be materially impossible to spread it to all points, in all countries. For any place where it will be hindered, there will be another thousand where it will flourish. Moreover, if it is struck in one individual, this cannot be perpetrated against the spirits that are its source. Now, as spirits are everywhere, and there will always be some in the impossible eventuality of it being stifled all over the globe, it would reappear some time later, because *it rests on a fact which lies in Nature itself*, and the laws of Nature cannot be suppressed. This should be enough to convince all those who dream of a general acceptance of Spiritism. (*The Spiritist Review*, Feb. 1865, "Perpetuity of Spiritism.")[13]

48. However, these scattered focal points, these centers, could have remained isolated for a long time, limited to a few in distant lands. It was necessary for them to have a link which put them in communion of thoughts with their brothers and sisters in belief, by teaching them what was being done elsewhere. This common link, which would have been lacking in earlier Spiritism, is found in publications that go everywhere, and which condense, in a single, concise and methodical manner, the teaching given everywhere in multiple ways and through a variety of languages.

49. The first two revelations could only be the result of direct teaching; they would impose themselves on the faith by the authority of the word of their master, since people were not advanced enough to contribute to their formulation.

Let us note, however, that between them there is a very noticeable nuance, due to a progress in manners, habits and ideas, notwithstanding the fact that both revelations had been made amidst the same people and in the same milieu, albeit eighteen centuries apart. The doctrine of Moses is absolute, despotic; it does not admit of argument and imposes itself on all the people by force. That of

---

13 [Trans. note] A. KARDEC, *The Spiritist Review – 1865* is scheduled to be published in English by the USSF in New York, a few years from now.

Jesus essentially recommends and advises; it is freely accepted and imposes itself only through persuasion; it was controversial even during the lifetime of its founder who does not disdain to discuss with his adversaries.

50. The third revelation comes at a time of emancipation and intellectual maturity, when the developed intelligence cannot be reduced to a passive role, when people no longer accept anything blindly, but instead wants to see where they are being led, to know the whys and hows of each thing. Such a revelation was to be at once the product of a teaching and the fruit of labor, research and free scrutiny. Spirits teach only what is needed to put us on the path of truth, but they refrain from revealing what we can find out on our own, leaving to us the discussion, verification and submission of the whole thing to the crucible of reason; even allowing us to gain experience at a cost. They give us the principle, the raw materials, for us to implement and benefit from them (see item **15** above.)

51. The elements of the Spiritist revelation having been given simultaneously in a multitude of centers, to people of all social conditions and of varied degrees of education, it is quite evident that observations could not yield the same results everywhere; that the consequences to be drawn from them, the deduction of the laws which govern this order of phenomena and, in a word, the conclusion which was to be established from the ideas, could only be derived from a sound reasonableness and correlation of facts. Now, for each isolated center, circumscribed to a restricted circle, in most cases seeing only a particular order of apparently contradictory facts. Moreover being forced by local influences and peer pressure, and usually having only a same category of communicating spirits, it was impossible to embrace the whole which, consequently, rendered them powerless to link isolated observations to a common principle. With everyone observing facts from the point of view of his/her previous knowledge and beliefs, or the particular opinion of the communicating spirits, we would soon have as many theories and systems as centers, and none of them would have been complete, for lack of comparison and elements for verification purposes. In a word, everyone would have been immobilized in his/her partial revelation, believing they had all the truth, because they did not know that in a hundred other places others were getting more or better results.

52. Furthermore, it should be remarked that nowhere has the Spiritist teaching been given in a complete manner; it touches on so many observations, on so many different subjects requiring either knowledge or special mediumistic faculties, that it would have been impossible to gather all the necessary conditions in one location. As the teaching ought to be collective and not individual, the spirits have divided the tasks by disseminating the subjects of study and observation, as in some factories where the making of each part of one same product is distributed among different workers.

Revelation has thus been made partially, in various places and by a multitude of intermediaries, and it is in this way that it is still going on at this moment, because not everything has been revealed. Each center finds in the other centers the complement of what it obtains, and it is the whole, the coordination of all the partial teachings, that constitutes the *Spiritist tenets*.

It was therefore necessary to group the scattered facts in order to see their correlation; to collect the various documents, the instructions given by the spirits on all points and subjects, so as to compare them, to analyze them, studying their analogies and differences. Since messages are given by spirits of all kinds – some more, others less enlightened – it was necessary to appraise the degree of confidence which reasoning would allow to grant them, and to distinguish individual and isolated systematic ideas from those which had the sanction of the collective intelligence of the spirits; to tell utopias from practical ideas; to prune those which were notoriously disproved by data offered by objective science and sound logic; to use the very errors, the information provided by spirits even from the lowest order, regarding knowledge of the state of the invisible world; and to form a homogeneous whole. In a word, it had to be a center of elaboration, independent of all preconceived ideas, of any sectarian prejudices, *with a firm resolve to accept any truth that had become obvious, even if it were contrary to one's personal opinions.* This center was formed by itself, by force of circumstances, and *without any premeditated purpose.*[14]

---

14 *The Spirits' Book*, which was the first work which launched Spiritism into the philosophical path, through the deduction of moral consequences from facts, by covering all the parts of the new doctrine and dealing with the most important

53. From this state of affairs, a dual stream of ideas has resulted: some going from the extremities to the center, while others part from the center up to the circumference. Thus Spiritism has promptly marched toward unity, in spite of the diversity of sources from which it has emanated. Divergent systems have gradually fallen, because of their isolation from the majority opinion, and for lack of sympathetic echoes. A communion of thoughts has since been established among the different partial centers; which now speak the same spiritual language, as they understand and sympathize with one another from one end of the world to the other.

Spiritists were stronger, fought with more courage, and advanced with steadier steps, when they were no longer isolated, when they could feel a fulcrum, a bond that connected them to the big family. The phenomena they witnessed no longer seemed strange, abnormal and contradictory, when they were able to relate them to general laws of harmony, and to embrace at a glance the whole edifice, while seeing in all this a great and humanitarian purpose.[15]

---

issues raided by it, has since become the rallying point toward which individual works have spontaneously converged. It is remarkable that, from the publication of this book, dates the beginning of the era of philosophical Spiritism, relegated until then to the domain of curious experiments. If that book has won the sympathy of the majority, it is because it was the expression of the sentiments of this same majority, and that it corresponded to its aspirations. It was also because in it everyone could find confirmation and a rational explanation for what they had been obtaining in private. If it had disagreed with the general teaching of the spirits, no credit would have been given to it, and it would have quickly faded away into oblivion. And who did it rally behind? Not behind the human being per se, which is nothing by itself, a transient prop who dies and disappears, but behind the idea that will not perish when emanating from a source above human beings.

This spontaneous concentration of scattered forces has given rise to an immense correspondence, a unique monument to the world, a living picture of the true history of modern Spiritism, in which both the unfinished works and the manifold sentiments that gave birth to the philosophical and religious doctrine are reflected. The moral outcome, the dedication and failure; all of them precious archives for posterity that will judge the individuals and things based on authentic documents. In presence of these irrefutable testimonies, what will become, in the sequence, of all false allegations and slander stemming from envy and jealousy?

15 A significant testimony, as remarkable as it is touching, of this communion of thought which has been established among spiritists by the conformity of beliefs, is the request for prayers which come to me from the most distant countries in the world, from Peru to the ends of Asia, from people of different religions and nationalities, whom I have never met. Would this not be the prelude to the

But how do we know if a principle is taught everywhere, or if it is only the result of an individual opinion? Since the isolated groups are not in a position to know what is being said elsewhere, it was necessary for a center to gather all the instructions to make a sort of vote-counting, and to bring to the attention of all the opinion of the majority.[16]

54. There is no science that has come out whole from the brain of a single individual. All without exception are the product of successive observations based on preceding observations, as from a known point to arrive at the unknown. Thus have the spirits proceeded with regard to Spiritism; that is why their teaching is gradual; they address issues only as the principles on which they are based are sufficiently developed, and general opinion is ripe to assimilate them. It is even remarkable that whenever particular centers have wanted to tackle certain issues prematurely, they have obtained only

---

great unification that is being prepared? A proof of the serious roots that grow everywhere Spiritism reaches?

It is remarkable that, of all the groups that formed with the premeditated intention of splitting by proclaiming diverging principles, as well as those who, for reasons of self-esteem or other motives, not wishing to submit themselves to the common rule,thought they were strong enough to walk alone, and to have enough light to do without advice, none of them succeeded in constituting an idea which was preponderant and viable. They are extinct or have languished in the shade. How could it be otherwise, since, in order to distinguish themselves, instead of striving to give an greater sum of satisfactory results, they rejected the principles of the doctrine which were precisely those which represent its most powerful attractions. What is there more comforting, more encouraging and more rational? Had they understood the power of the moral elements which constitute unity, they would not have been lulled by a chimerical illusion; but taking their small circle for the universe, they saw in the adherents only a coterie which could easily be overthrown by a counter-coterie. This was strangely mistaken as to the essential characteristics of the Spiritist tenets, and this error could only bring disappointments. Instead of breaking unity, they broke the bond that alone could give them strength and life. (*The Spiritist Review*, April 1866, "Spiritism without Spirits, Independent Spiritism.") — [Trans. note: Scheduled to be published in English by the USSF, a few years from now.]

16 This is the purpose of our publications, which may be considered as the result of this vote counting. All opinions are discussed, but the questions are formulated in principle only after receiving the application of all the controls which, alone, can give them the force of law, and make it possible to assert them. That is why I do not advocate any theory, and it is for that reason that the tenets proceeding from general teachings are not the product of a preconceived system;. This is also what strengthens it, ensuring its future.

inconclusive or contradictory answers. When, on the contrary, the favorable moment has emerged, the teaching is identical all along the line, in almost the totality of centers.

There is, however, a vital difference between the march of Spiritism and that of the sciences, namely, that the latter have reached the point where they arrived only after long intervals, while it was sufficient just a few years for Spiritism to do it, if not to reach its culminating point, at least to collect a sum of observations large enough to constitute a doctrine. This is due to the innumerable multitude of spirits who, by the will of God, have manifested themselves simultaneously, each bringing the range of their knowledge. It follows that all parts of Spiritism, instead of being successively developed during several centuries, have been given almost simultaneously in just a few years, and it was enough to group them to make up a whole.

God wanted it to be so; firstly, so that the edifice could arrive more quickly at the summit; secondly, in order to be able, in comparison, to have an immediate and permanent control, so to speak, in the universality of the teachings, each part having no value or *authority* than those granted by its connectivity to the whole, all parts having to harmonize, finding their place in the general ensemble, and arriving each in its own time.

By not entrusting to one single spirit with the task of promulgating the doctrine, God also desired that the smallest as well as the greatest among spirits, as among humans, each brought their stone to the edifice, in order to establish a link of cooperative solidarity among them which has failed to exist in all previous doctrines issued from a single source.

On the other hand, each spirit, as well as each human being, having only a limited sum of knowledge, they would be individually incapable of treating as an expert the innumerable issues touched by Spiritism. This is also why the Spiritist doctrine, to fulfill the views of the Creator, could not be the work of a single spirit or medium; instead it could only come out of the community from books collectively verified by one another.[17]

---

17 See A, KARDEC, *The Gospel according to Spiritism*, "Introduction"; and A. KARDEC, *The Spiritist Review*, April 1864, "Authority of the Spiritist Doctrine, Universal Control of the Teaching of Spirits," [Trans. note: Scheduled to be published in English by the USSF in a few years from now.]

55. A last characteristic of the Spiritist revelation, and which arises from the very conditions in which it has been made, is that, relying on facts, it is and can only be essentially progressive, like all scientific observation. By its essence, it is allied with science, which, being the exposition of the laws of Nature in a certain order of facts, cannot be contrary to the will of God, the author of all these laws. *The discoveries of science glorify instead of belittling God; they only destroy what humans have built on their misconceptions of God.*

Spiritism, therefore, posits as an absolute principle only what has been clearly demonstrated, or what logically emerges from observation. Affecting all branches of the social sciences, to which it lends the support of its own discoveries, it will always assimilate all progressive ideas, of whatever order they may be, when these have reached the state of *practical truths*, not belonging to the realm of utopia, otherwise it would commit suicide. If we stopped being what it is, it would entirely belie its origin and its providential purpose. *By marching with progress, Spiritism will never be supplanted, because, if new discoveries prove to it that it is in error about some issue, it will be modified on this very issue; should a new truth be revealed, it will accept it.*[18]

56. What is the use of the moral doctrine of the spirits, if it is nothing but that of Christ? Do human beings really need a revelation, and cannot they find it in themselves; even all that is necessary for them to have a good personal conduct?

From the moral point of view, God has no doubt given humans a guide in their conscience that says to them: "Do not do unto others what you do not want others to do unto you." A natural moral code is certainly inscribed in the hearts of human beings, but do they all know how to read it? Have they never misunderstood these wise precepts? What have they done with the ethics of Christ? How do those who teach it actually behave? Has it not become a dead letter, a beautiful theory, good for others but not good for oneself? Will you

---

18 In view of statements as clear and categorical such as the ones contained in this chapter, all the allegations of a tendency to absolutism and autocracy of the principles, and all the false assimilations that prejudiced or misinformed people against Spiritism crumble down. Moreover, such statements are not new; I have repeated them over and over again in my writings so as to leave no doubt in this respect. They also assign to me my true role, the only one I have aimed at: that of a fellow associate.

reproach a parent for repeating ten times, a hundred times even, the same instructions to his/her children, if they do not seem to benefit from them? Why would God do less than a parent? Why should It not occasionally send special messengers among humans to remind them of their duties, and bring them back to the good path when they go astray? To open the eyes of intelligence of those that still have them closed, like more advanced humans send missionaries to enlighten savages and barbarians?

Spirits teach no other morality than that of Christ, for the reason that there is no better one. But then again what is the good of their teaching, since they only preach what we already know? The same thing could be said about the moral precepts of Christ, which were taught five hundred years before him by Socrates and Plato, and in almost identical words, and of all the moral educators who repeat the same thing in all nuances and in all forms. Granted then, *the spirits simply increase the number of moral educators*, with the difference that they manifest themselves everywhere: they are heard in the cottage as well as in the palace, they speak both to the ignorant and to educated people.

What the teaching of the spirits adds to the morality of Christ is the knowledge of the principles that connect the deceased and the living, thus completing the vague notions he had given of the soul, of its past and of its future, and which offers as a corroboration of his doctrine the very laws of Nature. With the help of the new lights brought by Spiritism and the spirits, humans are now able to understand the solidarity that connects all beings; charity and fraternity become a social necessity; they practice them out of conviction that it is their duty to do so, and thus do it better.

When humans start practicing the moral code of Christ, only then will they be able to say that they no longer need neither incarnate nor discarnate moral educators – but then God will not send them any more.

57. One of the most important questions among those posed at the head of this chapter is this: What is the authority of the Spiritist revelation, since it emanates from beings whose lights are limited, and that are not infallible?

Now, this would be a serious objection if this revelation only existed in the teaching of spirits; if we should take it from them exclusively and accept it with closed eyes. This would be without value from the moment that humans applied their intelligence and judgment to it, since the spirits limit themselves to putting the latter on the path of conclusions which they themselves can draw from the observation of facts. Spirit manifestations in their innumerable varieties are facts; humans study them and therein seeks the law behind them. They are assisted in this task by spirits of all kinds which are rather fellow *associates* than *revealers* in the usual sense of the word. They submit their conclusions to the control of logic and common sense; in this way they avail themselves of the special knowledge they owe to their situation, without renouncing the use of their own reasoning.

Spirits being no other than the souls of departed humans, in communicating with them we do not leave humanity – a capital circumstance to be taken into consideration. Individuals of genius who have been the beacons of humanity have thus come out of the world of spirits, where they returned to when departing from Earth. Since spirits can communicate with incarnate humans, those same geniuses can give them instructions in the spiritual state, as they did while they were incarnate in bodily form. They can instruct us after their decease, as they did in their lifetime; they are invisible instead of visible, that is the difference. Their experience and knowledge should not be less; and if their word, as humans, had authority, it should not be less authoritative because they are in the spiritual world.

58.   However it is not only higher-order spirits which manifest themselves, but also spirits of all kinds. This was necessary to initiate us into the true character of the spiritual world, showing it to us in all its aspects. In this way, relations between the visible world and the invisible world are better acquainted, the connection is more evident; we see more clearly where we come from and where we are going – this is the essential purpose of these manifestations. All spirits, to whatever category they belong, teach us something; but since they are more or less enlightened, it is up to us to discern what is good or bad in them, and extract whatever is good from their messages. Yet all, regardless of who they are or claim to be, can teach us or reveal things that we do not know and which, without them, we would not be able to know.

59. The most elevated incarnate spirits are powerful individualities, without contradiction, but whose action is restricted and necessarily slow to spread. Should only one of them, even Elijah or Moses, Socrates or Plato, come in this time and age in order to reveal to humans the spiritual world, who could prove the truth of his assertions, amid so much skepticism? Would people not regard him or her as a dreamer or utopian? And even admitting that he/she was absolutely right, centuries would have elapsed before their ideas were accepted by the masses. God, in Its wisdom, did not want it to be so; the Almighty wished that the teaching should be given by *the spirits themselves*, and not by incarnate persons, in order to convince them of their existence, and that it should take place simultaneously everywhere on Earth, either to propagate it more rapidly, or in order for the proof of truth to be found in the concurrence of all teachings, thus giving each person the means of being convinced for themselves.

60. Spirits do not come to free humans from work, study, and research; they do not give us any ready-made science; on what we can find out by ourselves: they leave us to our own devices. This is something every Spiritist knows perfectly well today. For a long time, experience has shown the erroneous opinion which ascribed to the spirits all knowledge and all wisdom, and that it was enough to communicate with the first spirit that happened to manifest itself to know all things. Away from incarnate humanity, spirits are one of its facets. As on Earth, there are those that are higher and those that are lower-order ones. Scientifically and philosophically many know less than certain incarnate persons; such spirits will say what they know, neither more nor less. As among human beings, the most advanced can tell us more about things, and give us wiser advice than backward spirits. Therefore, to seek guidance from the spirits is not to consult with supernatural powers, but *individuals just like ourselves*, with those one would even have addressed during their lifetime, such as one's parents, one's friends, or individuals who are more enlightened than oneself. It is important to be convinced of this fact, although it is ignored by those who, having not studied Spiritism, have a completely false idea about the nature of the spiritual world and relations beyond the grave.

61. Then what is the utility of spirit manifestations, or, do we really need this revelation, if the spirits do not know more than ourselves, or if they do not tell us everything they know?

First, as I have said, they refrain from giving us what we can acquire through our own efforts. Then there are also things that they are not permitted to reveal because our advancement degree does not allow for it. But that apart, the conditions of their new existence extend the circle of their perceptions; they see what they did not see on while on Earth. Once freed from the impediments of matter and relieved from the cares of corporal life, they are able to judge things from a higher point, and therefore more soundly. Their insight embraces a wider horizon; they understand their mistakes, rectify their ideas and get rid of human prejudices.

It is in this that the superiority of the spirits over the incarnate humanity consists, and that their advices may be, depending on their degree of advancement, more judicious and more disinterested than those of the incarnate. The environment in which they find themselves also enables them to initiate us into details of future life which we do not know, and which we could not learn in the place where we are now. Up to this day humans have only created hypotheses about their future; that is why our beliefs on this point have been divided into so many different and divergent systems, from nihilism to some imaginary descriptions of hell and paradise. Today it is the eyewitnesses, the very actors of life beyond the grave, that come to tell us what it really is, being the only ones that could do it. These communications have thus served to make known to us the unseen world which surrounds us, whose existence we did not suspect. This knowledge alone would be of paramount importance, supposing that the spirits were incapable of teaching us anything else.

If you travel to a country which is new for you, will you reject the information of the humblest peasant that crosses your way? Will you refuse to question him or her about the state of the road because he/she is only a peasant? You will certainly not expect from him or her very far-reaching clarifications, but such as he/she is, and in their scope, they will be able to inform you on certain points better than a scientist who does not know the country. You will draw from their indications consequences that they would not be able to draw for themselves, but they will nonetheless have been useful instrument for your observations, even if serving only to make known to you the peasant manners. The same is true of our relations with spirits, where even the smallest among them can teach us something.

62. A commonplace comparison will make the situation even easier to understand.

A ship loaded with migrants leaves for a distant destination. It carries people of all conditions, relatives and friends of those who remained behind. We learn that this ship was shipwrecked; no trace has remained of it, no news has come of its fate. It is thought that all travelers have perished, which brought mourning into all families. The whole crew, however, without excluding a single person, approached an unknown land, an abundant and fertile land, where all live happily under a mild sky; but those who remained behind are not aware of this. Now, one day another ship approaches this land and finds there all the shipwrecked people safe and sound. Then the happy news spreads with the spreed of lightning; everyone says, "Our friends are not lost!" And gives thanks to God. These people cannot see each other, but they exchange correspondence, giving testimonies of affection. So now joy follows sorrow.

Such is the image of earthly life and life beyond the grave, before and after modern revelation. This latter, like the second ship, brings us the good news of the survival of those dear to us, and the certainty of joining them one day. Doubt about their fate and about ours no longer exists; discouragement is abolished, giving way to hope.

But other results have come to fertilize this revelation. God, judging humankind to have grown mature enough to delve into the mystery of its destiny, and look undauntedly at new wonders, has allowed the veil that separated the visible world from the invisible world to be lifted. The phenomenon of spirit manifestations is nothing alien to human nature; *it is the spiritual humanity which comes to talk to the incarnate humanity and to say to them:*

"We exist, therefore nothingness does not exist; this is what we are, and this is what you shall be; the future is yours as it is ours. You walked in darkness, we came to illuminate your way and clear your path. You went randomly and aimlessly, we have shown you a purpose. Earthly life was everything to you because you did not see anything beyond it; we have come to tell you, showing you the spiritual life. Earthly life is nothing. Your sight stopped at the grave, we have shown you beyond a splendid horizon. You did not know why you suffer on Earth; now, in suffering, you see the righteousness of God. Goodness seemed to bear no fruits for the future, it will now have a purpose and become a necessity. Fraternity was only a beautiful theory, it is now based on a law of Nature. Under the belief that everything ends with physical life, immensity is empty, selfishness reigns supreme among you, and your motto is: 'Each to himself/herself." But with the certainty of the future, infinite spaces are populated to infinity, voidness and solitude are nowhere, solidarity connects all beings beyond and before the grave; it is the reign of charity, with the motto: "Each to everyone and all for one another.' Finally, at the end of your life, you often bid eternal farewell to those who were dear to you, now you should say to them: 'See you soon!'"

In a nutshell, these are the results of the new revelation. It has come to fill the emptiness hollowed out by incredulity; to raise up the courage cut down by doubt or the perspective of nothingness; and to give everything its raison d'être. Is this result irrelevant, because the spirits do not come to solve the problems of science, or to give knowledge to the ignorant, or, to the lazy, the means to enrich themselves the easy way? Nevertheless, the fruits that humans must draw from spirits are not only for the future; they will also gather them on Earth through the transformation which these new beliefs will necessarily have on human character, tastes, tendencies and, consequently, on habits and social relations. By putting an end to the reign of selfishness, pride, and unbelief, they are preparing the reign of good, which is God's reign.

The object of a revelation, therefore, is to put humans in possession of certain truths which one could not acquire by oneself; and this with a view to stimulating progress. These truths are generally limited to fundamental principles intended to put us on the path of research, and not to guide us by a leading string. Those are milestones which show us the purpose: of the task of studying them and inferring their applications. Far from freeing humans from work, these are new elements supplied to our activity.

Chapter II
God

EXISTENCE OF GOD

1. God, being the first cause of all things, the starting point of everything, the pivot on which the edifice of creation rests, should be the capital point to be considered first and foremost.

It is an elementary principle that we judge a cause by its effects, even though we do not see the cause. Science goes further: it calculates the power of the cause by the power of the effect, and can even determine its nature. Thus, for example, astronomy has concluded that planets exist in certain regions of space. By the knowledge of the laws which govern the motion of the stars, we have searched for and found planets, which we can actually say that have been discovered even before being seen.

2. On a more trivial order of events, if we are plunged into a thick fog, in the diffuse light we guess that the Sun is on the horizon, although we cannot actually see the Sun. If a bird splits the air after being fatally shot, we guess that a hunter has struck it, although the latter was not seen. It is not always necessary to have seen a thing to know that it exists. In everything, it is by observing the effects that we arrive at the knowledge of causes.

3. Another equally elementary principle, elevated to the state of axiom by force of truth, is that every intelligent effect must have an intelligent cause.

If one were to ask who invented such and such ingenious mechanism, the architect of such a monument, the sculptor of such a statue, or the painter of such a picture, what would one think of those who would answer that it was made by itself? When we see a masterpiece of art or industry, we say that it must have been the product of an individual of genius, since a higher intelligence must have presided over its design. Although we believe that a human being must have done so, because we know that the thing is not above human capacity, it would not occur to anyone the thought of saying that it came out of the brain of an idiot or ignorant person, let alone that it is the work of an animal or the product of chance.

4. Everywhere we recognize the presence of humans in their works. If you approach an unknown land, even a desert, and therein discover the least vestiges of human labor, you conclude that human beings live or had lived in that region. The existence of antediluvian humans would not be proved only by human fossils, but also, and with as much certainty, by the presence in the lands of that period of artifacts worked by human beings, such as a fragment of a vase, a cut stone, a weapon, a brick, all will suffice to attest to their presence. According to the grossness or perfection of the work, the degree of intelligence and advancement of those who have accomplished it will be recognized. If then, in a land inhabited exclusively by savages, you discovered a statue worthy of Phidias, you would not hesitate to say that savages being incapable of having made it, it must be the work of an intelligence superior to that of the locals.

5. So, there! By looking around ourselves, at the works of Nature, and by observing the foresight, the wisdom, the harmony which preside over all things, we recognize that there is not a single one which does not surpass the highest flights of human intelligence, since the greatest genius on Earth is not able to create the smallest blade of grass. Therefore, human intelligence cannot produce them for they are the product of an intelligence superior to humanity. As this harmony and wisdom extends from the grain of sand and the tiniest worm up to the innumerable stars orbiting in space, we must conclude that this intelligence embraces the infinite, unless one would say that there are effects without cause.

6. To this some oppose the following reasoning:
The so-called works of Nature are the product of material forces acting mechanically, as a result of the laws of attraction and re-pulsion. The molecules of inert bodies aggregate and disintegrate under the influence of those laws. Plants are born, grow, thrive and multiply always in the same manner, each one in its species, by virtue of these same laws. Each progeny is similar to the one from which it came out; growth, flowering, fruit bearing, and coloring

are subordinated to material causes, such as heat, electricity, light, humidity, etc. The same is true of animals. The stars are formed by molecular attraction, and move perpetually in their orbits by the effect of gravitation. This mechanical regularity in the employment of natural forces does not denote the activity of free intelligence. A human being moves his/her arm when he or she wants to do it, and the way he or she wishes – for that reason, anyone moving their arms in one same direction from birth to death would be considered automatons. However, considered as a whole, the organic forces of Nature are in a sense automatic.

All this is true; yet these forces are effects which must have a cause, and no one has claimed that they constitute the Divinity. They are material and mechanical; they are not intelligent by themselves – that is also true – albeit put into practice, distributed, and made suitable for the needs of each thing by an intelligence which is not human. The useful suitability of these forces is an intelligent effect that denotes an intelligent cause. A pendulum moves with automatic regularity, and its merit lies in this regularity which renders it useful. The force which activates it is entirely material and not at all intelligent; but what would this pendulum be if an intelligence had not combined, calculated and distributed the use of this force to make it function with precision? From the fact that intelligence is not in the mechanism, and that we cannot see it, would it be rational to conclude that it does not exist? It is inferred by its effects.

The existence of a clock attests to the existence of the clockmaker. The ingenuity of the mechanism attests to the intelligence and knowledge of a clockmaker. When we see one of those complicated clocks which measure time in the main cities of the world; and register the movement of planets and stars, while also playing tunes and, in a word, seeming to speak to us so as to give the information we need; has it ever occurred to anyone to doubt or wonder, "Is this clock the product of an intelligence?'

The same applies to the mechanism of the universe, God does not show Itself, but attests Itself through Its works.

7.   The existence of God is therefore an acquired fact, not only through revelation, but by the material evidence of the facts. The most savage peoples have no revelation, and yet they instinctively believe in the existence of a superhuman power. It is because the savages themselves do not escape the logical consequences; they see things which are above human power, and they conclude that they come from a being superior to humanity.

NATURE OF GOD

8. It is not given to humans to probe into the inner nature of God. Bold would be anyone who intended to lift the veil that conceals it from our sight, for we still lack the sense which is only acquired through the complete purification of the spirit. But if we cannot penetrate God's essence, with Its existence being given only as premises, we can, through reasoning, arrive at the knowledge of Its required attributes; for, seeing what It cannot not be without ceasing to be God, we infer what It ought to be.

Without knowing God's attributes, it would be impossible to understand the work of creation: it lies at the point of departure of all religious beliefs, and it is for lack of referring to it as the beacon which could guide them, that most religions have gone astray in their dogmas. Those who have not ascribed omnipotence to God have in fact conceived of many gods. Those who have failed to ascribe to God sovereign goodness have made It a jealous, angry, partial and vindictive Divinity.

9. *God is the supreme and sovereign intelligence.* Human intelligence is limited, since human beings can neither make nor understand all that exists; whereas God's intelligence, embracing the infinite, must be infinite. If we supposed it to be finite in any way, we could conceive of a being even more intelligent, capable of understanding and doing what the other could not do, and so on to infinity.

10. *God is eternal,* that is, It had no beginning and will have no end. If It had had a beginning, that would mean that God would have come out of nothingness. Now, nothingness being nothing, can produce nothing; or else it would have been created by another previous being, and then that being would be God. If we supposed It had had a beginning or will have an end, we could conceive of a being which existed before It, or which could exist after It, and so on to infinity.

11. *God is immutable.* If it were susceptible to change, the laws governing the universe would have no stability.

12. *God is immaterial;* that is to say, its nature differs from all that we call matter; otherwise it would not be immutable, for it would be subject to the transformations of matter.

God has no appreciable form to our senses, otherwise it would be material. We say: the hand of God, the eye of God, the mouth of God, because we, humans, knowing It only through their own conceptions, take these as a term of comparison for everything that they do not understand. Images in which one represents God under the figure of an elderly man with a long beard, covered with a cloak, are quite ridiculous: they have the disadvantage of reducing the supreme being to the petty proportions of humanity. From there it takes only one step to lend It human passions and defects, turning It into an angry and jealous God.

13. *God is all-powerful.* If It did not possess supreme power, one could conceive of a being even more powerful, and so on until one found the being that no other could surpass in power, and that is the one which would be God. Thus, It would not have done all things, and those It would not have done would be the work of another god.

14. *God is supremely just and good.* The providential wisdom of God's laws is revealed in the smallest as well as in the greatest things, and this wisdom makes it impossible to doubt either Its justice or Its goodness. These two qualities imply all the others; if they were limited, even in a single aspect, one could conceive of a being which would possess them in a higher degree, thus being superior to God.

The infinite of a quality excludes the possibility of the existence of a contrary quality that would weaken or cancel it. An *infinitely good* being cannot have the smallest spot of wickedness, nor would an *infinitely bad* being have the smallest portion of goodness – just as an object cannot be an absolute jet black with the slightest hint of white, or an absolute white with the slightest black spot.

Therefore God cannot be at once good and bad, because then, by possessing neither of these qualities in the highest degree, It would not be God. All things would be subject to whim, and there would be no stability for anything. It could only be infinitely good or infinitely bad; if It were infinitely bad, It would do no good. Now, as Its works bear witness to Its wisdom, Its kindness, and Its solicitude, we must conclude that no one would be able to be both good and bad without ceasing to be God, which must necessarily be infinitely good.

Supreme goodness implies supreme justice; for if God acted unjustly or with partiality *in a single circumstance*, or with regard to *a single one of Its created beings*, It would not be supremely just, and consequently not be supremely good.

15. *God is infinitely perfect.* It is impossible to conceive of God without an infinity of perfections, otherwise It would not be God, for one could always conceive of a being possessing what It would miss. In order to be unsurpassable, God must be infinite in everything.

Being infinite, God's attributes are not susceptible to increase or diminution, otherwise they would not be infinite, and God would not be perfect. If we removed the smallest portion of one of Its attributes, we would no longer have God, since there could be a more perfect being.

16. *God is unique.* The unicity of God is the consequence of the absolute infinity of Its perfections. Another God could exist only on condition of being equally infinite in all things; for if there were the slightest difference between them, one would be inferior to the other, subordinate to the other's power, and therefore not be God. If there was absolute equality between them, it would be from all eternity the same thought, the same will, the same power, which thus blended in their identity, would be really only one God. If they each had special attributions, one would do what the other would not do, and then there would not be perfect equality between them, since neither of them would possess supreme authority.

17. It is the ignorance of the principle of the infinity of God's perfections that engendered polytheism, the worship of all primitive peoples. They attributed divine status to any power which they deemed above humanity. Later, reason led them to blend these various powers into one. Then, as humans came to understand the essence of the divine attributes, they removed from their symbols the beliefs that would spread their negation.

18. In summary. God can only be God if It is not surpassed by any other being; otherwise the being which surpassed God in any respect, even if only the thickness of a hair, would be the true God. For that reason, God must be infinite in all things.

It is thus that the existence of God, being ascertained by the fact of Its works, lead us, by simple logical deduction, to determine the attributes which characterize It.

19. Therefore God is *the supreme and sovereign intelligence. God is unique, eternal, immutable, immaterial, all-powerful, supremely just and good, infinite in all Its perfections,* and cannot be anything else.

This is the fulcrum on which rests the universal edifice. It is the lighthouse whose rays extend over the entire universe, and which alone can guide humans in the search for truth; by following it, humans will never go astray, and if they are so often misled, it is for want of having followed the road which was indicated to them.

Such is also the infallible criterion to be applied to all philosophical and religious systems. To evaluate them, we humans have a rigorously exact rule of thumb in the attributes of God, and can say with certainty that every theory, every principle, every dogma, every belief, every practice, which would be in contradiction with a single one of these attributes, and which would tend not only to cancel it, but solely to weaken it, cannot be based in truth.

In philosophy, in psychology, in morality, in religion, there is no truth except that which does not deviate one iota from the essential qualities of the Divinity. The perfect religion would be that in which no article of faith would be in opposition to those qualities, and whose dogmas could all undergo the test of this verification control, without conflicting with it in any aspect.

DIVINE PROVIDENCE

20. Providence is the solicitude of God for all Its created beings. God is everywhere, It sees everything, It presides over everything, even the smallest things. Therein lies God's providential action.

"How can God, being so great, so powerful, so superior to all things, possibly interfere with minute details, and be preoccupied with the least actions and the least thoughts of every individual?" Such is the question which an unbeliever would raise, whence it concludes that, in admitting the existence of God, Its action must extend only to the general laws of the universe; and that the universe functions for all eternity by virtue of those laws to which every created being is subject within their sphere of activity, without the need of being incessantly aided by providence."

21. At their current level of humanity, we can hardly understand the infinite God, because we ourselves are restricted and limited, which is why we regard God to be as restricted and limited as they are. Humans represent It as a circumscribed being, and make an image of it in their own image. Our pictures, which paint God as having human features, greatly contribute to maintaining this error in the minds of the masses who adore in God the form rather than the thought. It is for the majority of people a powerful sovereign, sitting on an inaccessible throne lost in the immensity of heaven; and because their faculties and perceptions are limited, they do not understand that God can or deign to intervene directly in little things.

22. In their helplessness in understanding the very essence of the Divinity, humans can only make a rough idea of It by means of comparisons which are necessarily quite imperfect, but which can at least show them the possibility of what at first seemed impossible to them.

Imagine a fluid sufficiently subtle to penetrate all bodies, it is evident that each molecule of this fluid, being in contact with each molecule of matter, will produce on the body an action identical to that which would produce the whole fluid. This is what chemistry shows every day in limited proportions.

This fluid, lacking intelligence, acts only mechanically by material forces; but if we imagine this fluid endowed with intelligence, perceptive and sensory faculties, it will act, not blindly, but with discernment, with willpower and freedom; it will see, hear and feel.

The properties of the perispiritual fluid can give us an idea of this fact. It is not intelligent by itself since it is a sort of matter, however it is the vehicle of thoughts, sensations and perceptions of the spirit. It is because of the subtlety of this fluid that spirits penetrate everywhere and are able to scrutinize our innermost thoughts. Through it they see and act at from distance. It is to this fluid, which has reached a certain degree of purification, that higher-order spirits owe the gift of ubiquity; – it suffices that a ray of their thought be directed to various points, so that they may manifest their presence simultaneously. The extension of this faculty is subordinated to the degree of elevation and purification of the spirit. It is again by means of this fluid that humans themselves can act from a distance, by using their willpower, over certain individuals. It modifies within certain limits the properties of matter, by giving inactive substances certain properties, repairing organic disorders, and operating cures through imposition of hands.

23. Yet the spirits, however higher they may be, are beings limited in their faculties, their power, and the extent of their perceptions, and cannot in this respect approach God. However, they can serve as a point of comparison. What the spirit can accomplish only to a limited extent, God, which is infinite, performs in unlimited proportions. Another difference is that a spirit's action is momentary and subordinate to circumstances, whereas God's action is permanent. A spirit's thought embraces only a circumscribed time and space, whereas that of God transcends the universe and eternity. In a word, between spirits and God, there is the distance between the finite and the infinite.

24. The perispiritual fluid is not the thought of the spirit, but the agent and intermediary of such thought, since it is the perispirit that transmits it. This fluid is somehow *impregnated* with the spirit's thought, which, due to our impossibility of isolating it, seems to be one with the fluid, as a sound seems to be one with the air, in such a way that we can, so to speak, materialize it. Just as we say that the air becomes an audible sound, we could say, by taking the effect for the cause, that the fluid becomes intelligent.

25. Whether or not it is so with the thought of God, that is to say, that God acts directly or through a fluid, for the ease of understanding for our own intelligence, we represent it under the concrete form of an intelligent fluid filling the infinite universe, penetrating all parts of creation: *the whole Nature is immersed in the divine fluid*; or, under the pretense that the parts of a whole are all of the same nature, and have the same properties as the whole, every atom of this fluid, as it were, possesses the thought, that is to say, the essential attributes of the Divinity. Since this fluid is everywhere, everything is subject to its intelligent action, its foresight, its solicitude. Every single being, however small it may be, is somehow saturated with it. We are thus constantly in the presence of the Divinity; there is not one of our actions that we can remove from God's eyes; our thought is in incessant contact with Its thought, and it is rightly said that God reads in the deepest recesses of our heart. *We are in Him, as He is in us,* according to the words of Christ.

To extend Its solicitude to all Its created beings. God does not need to look down from the depths of immensity; our prayers, to be heard by God, do not need to go beyond space, nor be said in a resounding voice, for our thoughts reverberate in God, constantly at our side. Our thoughts are like the sounds of a bell which vibrate all the molecules of the ambient air.

26. Far be from me the thought of materializing the Divinity; the image of an intelligent universal fluid is obviously only a comparison, although apt to give a more accurate idea of God than the pictures which represent It under a human similitude. The only purpose of conceiving it as a fluid is to make people understand the possibility of God being everywhere and taking care of everything.

27. We have before our eyes an example which can give us an idea of how the action of God can be exercised over the innermost parts of all beings, and consequently how the most subtle impressions of our soul go straight to God. It is taken from an communication given by a spirit on this subject.

"One of the attributes of the Divinity is infinity. The Creator cannot be represented as having a form, a limit, a boundary. If It were not infinite, one could conceive of something greater than God Itself, and then this something would be would be God instead. Being infinite. God is everywhere, for if It were not everywhere It would not be infinite – one cannot get out of this dilemma. So, if there is a God, and this is of no doubt to anyone, such God is infinite and one cannot conceive of a corner which It does not occupy. God is therefore in contact with all its created beings; it envelops them, they are all in It. It is understandable that God is directly related to each created being, and, to make you understand as materially as possible how this contact takes place universally and constantly, let us examine what happens in humans between their spirits and their bodies."

"Every human being is a small world whose director is the spirit and whose directed principle is the body. In this universe, the body will represent a creation of which the spirit is God. (Bear in mind that this is only a question of analogy and not of identity.) The limbs of this body, the various organs that compose it, together with its muscles, its nerves, and its articulations, are each material individualities, so to speak, located in specific places of the body. Although the number of these constituent parts – so varied and different in nature – is considerable, it would be inconceivable to anyone that any movement or impression could take place at any particular region, without the spirit being aware of it. Are there different sensations in several simultaneous locations of the body? The spirit feels them all, discerns them, analyzes them, assigns to each one of them its cause and place of action."

"A similar phenomenon takes place between God and the creation. God is everywhere in Nature, just like the spirit is everywhere in the body. All the elements of the creation are in constant relation with God, just like all the cells of the human body are in immediate contact with the spiritual being. Therefore there is no reason why phenomena of the same order should not occur in the same way, in both cases."

"A limb moves: the spirit feels it; a created being has a thought: God knows it. All the limbs are in movement, the different organs are put in vibration: the spirit feels each occurrence, distinguishes them and locates them. The various outputs of the creation, the different created beings, all move, think and act variously; yet God knows everything that happens, and assign to each one what is particular to them."

"We can also deduce the solidarity between matter and intelligence, the solidarity of all beings of a world among themselves, that among all worlds, and that between the creation and the Creator." (QUINEMANT, Parisian Society of Spiritist Studies , 1857.)

28. We are able to understand the effect, which is already a major achievement. From the effect we ascend to the cause, and judge of its greatness by the greatness of the effect. However its innermost essence escapes us, like that of the cause of a multitude of phenomena. We know the effects of electricity, heat, light, gravitation; we calculate them, and yet we do not know the inner nature of the principle which produces them. Is it, then, more rational to deny the divine principle, just because we do not understand it?

29.   Nothing prevents us from admitting the existence, for the principle of supreme intelligence, of a center of action, an endlessly radiating focal point flooding the universe with its emanations, like the sun of its light. But where is its core? That is what no one can say. It is probable that it is no more fixed on a determined point than its actions, and that it incessantly traverses the regions of boundless space. If mere spirits have the gift of ubiquity, this faculty must be unlimited in God. Since God fills the entire universe, we might still admit, as a hypothesis, that this core does not need to be transported, and that it is formed on every point where the sovereign will deems it fitting to occur, whence one could say that it is located everywhere and nowhere.

30.   Faced with these unfathomable problems, our reason should humble itself. God exists; we cannot doubt it; It is infinitely just and good: this is Its essence. Its solicitude extends to every single being: this we can understand. It can only want our good, which is why we must trust It. For now, this is the essential; as for the rest, let us wait until we become worthy of understanding it.

SEEING GOD

31.   Since God is everywhere, why do not we see It? Will we see It when leaving the Earth? These are questions we ask ourselves daily.

The first one is easy to answer: our material organs have limited perceptions which render them unfit for the sake of certain things, even material ones. This is how certain fluids completely escape our sight and our analytical instruments, and yet we do not doubt their existence. We see the effects of the plague, and we do not see the fluid that carries it. We see bodies moving under the influence of the force of gravitation, but we do not see this force.

32.   Things of spiritual essence cannot be perceived by material organs; it is only through spirit sight that we can see the spirits and the things of the immaterial world; therefore only our soul can have the perception of God. Does one see God immediately after death? This is what communications from beyond the grave alone can teach us. Through them we know that seeing God is the privilege of only the purest souls, and that very few possess, when leaving their earthly envelope, the necessary degree of dematerialization. Some rudimentary comparisons can make this fact easy to understand.

33. One who is at the bottom of a valley surrounded by a thick mist, cannot see the Sun. However, as I said above, in the diffuse light one can guess the presence of the sun. If one climbs the mountain, as one rises, the fog clears up, the light becomes more and more vivid, but one does not yet see the Sun. When one eventually begins to see it, it is still veiled, for the least vapor is enough to weaken its brightness. It is only after having completely risen above the misty layer that, being in perfectly pure air, one can see the Sun in all its splendor.

It is the same with one whose head is wrapped in several veils. At first one sees nothing at all, but with the removal of each veil, one starts to distinguish a gleam more and more clearly. It is only when the last veil vanishes that one can clearly perceive things.

The same is true of a beverage turbid with suspended matter: it may be cloudy at first; but, with each new distillation, its transparency increases, until, having been completely purified, it acquires a perfect limpidity and presents no obstacle to the sight.

It is likewise with the soul. The perispiritual envelope, although invisible and impalpable for us, is dense matter to the soul, still too crude for certain perceptions. This envelope becomes more spiritualized as the soul rises in morality. The imperfections of the soul are like veils obscuring its sight; with every imperfection corrected there is one less veil, but it is only after being completely purified that a soul can enjoy the fullness of its faculties.

34. Being the divine essence par excellence, God can be perceived in all its splendor only by those spirits which arrived at the highest degree of dematerialization. If imperfect spirits do not see It, it is not that they are further from God than others like them. Like all beings of nature, they are immersed in the divine fluid, since we are all in the light. Only their imperfections are veils that rob those spirits of seeing it. When the fog is dissipated, they will see the light shine; for achieving that they will not need to go up, nor to seek it in the depths of the infinite. Once the spirit sight is rid of the moral blindfolds that obscured it, they will see it wherever they may be, even on Earth, for it is everywhere.

35. The Spirit is purified only in the long run, and its different incarnations are like distilling stills at the bottom of which it deposits each time a few impurities. When leaving its bodily envelope, a soul does not instantly get rid of its imperfections. This is why there are some who, after death, do not see God any more than in their lifetime; but as they are purified they have a more distinct intuition. If they do not see it, they understand it better, the light becomes less diffuse. When, therefore, spirits say that God forbids them to answer such a question, it is not that God appears to them, or address them the word to prescribe or forbid them such or such thing, but rather, if they feel It, they receive the emanation of Its thought, as happens to the spirits that surround us with their fluid, though we do not see them.

36. No human being can see God with the eyes of the flesh. If this were a favor granted only to a few, it would only be in a state of ecstasy, while the soul is as free from the bonds of matter as it is possible during its incarnation. Besides, that of the souls of spirits of the highest order, incarnated in mission and not for *atonement*, since they shine with dazzling brightness, may possibly have led lower order spirits, whether incarnate or discarnate, struck by the splendor which surrounds them, to mistakenly think they were seeing God Itself, as one sometimes sees a mere representative taken to be the sovereign.

37. Under what appearance does God appear to those who have made themselves worthy of such favor? Is it in any form? Under a human figure, or as a luminous core? This is what human language is powerless to describe, because there is no point of comparison for us that can give an idea of it; we're like blind people to whom one would in vain try to make understand the sun's glow. Our vocabulary is limited to our needs and to the circle of our ideas. A language of savages would not be able to describe the wonders of civilization, whereas the vocabulary of the most civilized peoples is too poor to depict celestial splendors, since our intelligence is still too limited for understanding them, and our sight would be completely dazzled due to its weakness.

Chapter III
Good and Evil

SOURCE OF GOOD AND EVIL

1. God, being the principle of all things, and this principle being all wisdom, all goodness, all righteousness, then all that proceeds from it must share in these attributes, for what is infinitely wise, just and good can produce nothing unreasonable, bad and unfair. The evil we observe cannot have its source in God.

2. If evil was in the attributes of a special being, whether it is called Ahriman or Satan, one of two things would happen: either any such being would be equal to God and therefore as powerful, and from all eternity like It; or it would be inferior to God.

In the first case, there would be two rival powers, struggling incessantly, each seeking to undo what the other was doing, and thwarting each other. This hypothesis is irreconcilable with the unicity of vision which is revealed in the orderly arrangement of the universe.

In the second case, since this being is inferior to God, it would be subordinated to the latter; since it could not have been eternally like God without being Its equal. Furthermore, it would have had a beginning; and if it had been created, it could only have been created by God. Now, God would thus had created the spirit of evil, which would be the negation of Its infinite goodness.

3. According to one of those doctrines, the evil spirit, created good, would have become evil, and God, to punish it, would have condemned it to remain eternally evil, and would have given it the mission of seducing humans in order to induce them to commit evil. But can a single fall deserve the most cruel punishments for eternity, without hope of any forgiveness? There would be more than a lack of kindness, but premeditated cruelty in this, because to make seduction easier and better hide the trap, Satan would be allowed to *turn into an angel of light, and to simulate the very works of God, to the point of being mistaken for God Itself.* If this were true, there would be more iniquity and improvidence on the part of God, because with all freedom being granted to Satan to leave its empire of darkness and to indulge in worldly pleasures in order to lead humans there, the inciter of evil would actually be punished less than the victims of its ruses, who would fall into it by reason of their weakness, since, once in the abyss, they could never go out. So God refuses them a glass of water to quench their thirst, and for all eternity It hears, without being moved, together with Its angels, their moaning, while letting Satan give itself all the enjoyments it longed for.

Of all the doctrines on the theory of evil, the one above is unquestionably the most irrational and the most injurious to the Divinity. (See A. Kardec, *Heaven and Hell*, ch. IX, "Demons.")[19]

4.   Nevertheless, evil exists and has a cause. Evil can be of many kinds. First there is physical evil and moral evil, then the evils that humans can avoid and those that are beyond our control. Among the latter are the natural plagues.

Having limited faculties, humans cannot penetrate or embrace all the visions of the Creator. We judge things from the point of view of our personality, the artificial interests and conventions which we have created for ourselves, and which are not in the order of Nature. That is why we often find evil and unjust what we would find right and admirable if we could see the cause, the goal, and the final result. In seeking a reason for being and the utility of everything, we will eventually recognize that all bears the imprint of infinite wisdom, and then we will bow to that wisdom, even for things we would not understand.

5.   We humans have received intelligence by means of which we can invoke, or at least greatly mitigate, the effects of all natural evils. The more we acquire knowledge and advance in civilization, the less disastrous these calamities become. With a wise social organization humans can even neutralize the consequences, when these cannot be entirely avoided. Thus, for those same scourges which have their utility in the general order of Nature and in the future,

---

19 [Trans. note] See bibliography at the end of the book.

but which strike us in the present, God has given us, by the faculties with which It has endowed our spirit, the means of offsetting their effects.

In this way, we clean up unhealthy regions, by neutralizing plague miasmas; fertilizing uncultivated lands and striving to protect them from floods; and building healthier homes strong enough to withstand the winds so necessary to the purification of the atmosphere, that it shelters from bad weather. Finally it is thus that, little by little, necessity made us create the sciences, with whose help we improve living conditions in the whole world, increasing general welfare.

Since all human beings must progress, the evils to which we are exposed, are a stimulus for us to exercise our intelligence, all our physical and moral faculties, by inviting us to seek the means of escaping from them. If we had nothing to fear, there would be no need for us to seek for the best; we would become numb in the inactivity of our spirit; we would invent nothing and discover nothing. *Pain is the energetic stimulus that pushes humans forward on the path of progress.*

6. Yet the most numerous evils are those which humans create by their own vices; those which come from our pride, from our selfishness, from our immoderate ambition, from our greed, from our excesses in all things: this is the cause of wars, calamities, dissensions, injustices, and the oppression of the weak by the strong; finally, it is in the origin of most diseases.

God has established laws full of wisdom which aim only at goodness; humans find in themselves all that is necessary to follow such laws. Our path is traced by our conscience; God's law is engraved in our heart; and, moreover, God reminds us incessantly through Its messiahs and prophets, and by all the incarnate spirits who have received the mission of enlightening, moralizing and improving others; and lately also by a multitude of discarnate spirits which manifest themselves everywhere. *If we humans rigorously complied with God's law, there is no doubt that we would avoid the most grievous evils and live happily on Earth.* However, we do not do so because of our free will, and thus end up suffering the consequences.

7. Meanwhile God, full of goodness, has placed the remedy beside the evil, that is to say, that even evil brings out the good. There comes a time when the excess of moral evil becomes intolerable and makes humans feel the need to change course. Instructed by experience, human beings are then urged to seek a remedy in good, always by the effect of their free will. When they enter a better road, it is because of their own will and because they have recognized the disadvantages of the other road. Necessity, therefore, compels us to improve morally in order to be happier, as the same necessity has compelled us to improve the material conditions of our existence.

It can be said that *evil is the absence of good, as cold is the absence of heat.* Evil is no more a distinct attribute than cold is a special fluid; one is the negative of the other. Where good does not exist, there is necessarily evil; not to do evil is already the beginning of good. God only wants good; from humans alone comes evil. If there were in the whole creation a being charged with evil, humans would not be able to avoid it; but since every human being has the cause of evil in themselves, and have at the same time their free will and God's laws to guide them, they can avoid it if they wish to do so.

Let us take a trivial example for comparison. A landowner knows that at the end of his field there is a dangerous place where one could venture in and get hurt or perish. What does he do to prevent accidents? He places near the spot a warning sign forbidding anyone to go further because of danger. Such is the law; it is wise and forward-looking. If, in spite of this, an imprudent person does not care about it and keeps on walking anyway, who is to blame but himself/herself?

So it is with all evil. Humans would avoid it if they observed the divine laws. God, for example, has put a limit on the satisfaction of one's needs; humans are warned by satiety. If they exceed this limit, they do so voluntarily. The diseases, the infirmities, and even death which ensue from it, are the result of one's own actions and not an act of God.

8.   Since evil is the result of human imperfections, and humans were created by God, it will be said that God has nonetheless created, if not evil, at least the cause of evil. If God had made humans perfect, evil would not exist.

If humans were created perfect, they would be carried by fate to good. Now, by virtue of their free will, they are not inclined to good or evil by fate. God wanted us to be subject to the law of progress, and that this progress should be the fruit of our own work, so that we had the merit of it, just as one bears the responsibility for any evil that one willingly does. Yet the question remains, what is the source of this propensity for evil in human beings?[20]

9. If we study all the passions, and even all the vices, we see that they have their principle in the instinct of self-preservation. This instinct is found in all its force in animals and in the most primitive beings, which are the closest to animal life. It alone dominates them, because among them there is still no moral sense as a counterweight. The being is not yet born to intellectual life. Conversely, instinct weakens as intelligence grows, because it dominates matter; with reasoned intelligence free will is born which humans use as they please. Then they suddenly begin to be held responsible for their actions.

10. The spirit's destiny is spiritual life. In the first phases of its corporeal existence, it has only material needs to satisfy, and for this purpose the exercise of passions is a necessity for the preservation of the species and individuals, materially speaking. But once out of this period, it develops other needs, which at first are semi-moral and semi-material, then become exclusively moral. It is then that the spirit dominates matter. If it shakes off the yoke, it moves forward on its providential path, and gets closer to its ultimate destiny. If, on the contrary, it lets itself be dominated by matter, he lags behind by assimilating itself to the brute. In this situation, *what was once good, because it was a necessity of the individual's nature, becomes an evil, not only because it is no longer a necessity, but because it*

---

20 "The error is in claiming that the soul would come perfect out of the Creator's hands, while the Creator, on the contrary, wanted perfection to be the result of a gradual purification of the spirit by its own effort. God wanted that the soul, by virtue of its free will, would choose between good and evil, and that it accomplished its ultimate goals by an active life and resisting evil. If God had made perfect souls like Itself, and, the moment they were coming out of Its hands, had associated them with Its eternal bliss, he would have created them not in his image and likeness, but similar to Itself, as we have already said. In this way, knowing everything by virtue of their very essence and having learned nothing; furthermore moved by a sense of pride born of the awareness of their divine attributes, humans would be forced to deny their origin, disregarding the author of their existence; and would have been in a state of rebellion and revolt against their Creator" (M. BONNAMY, examining magistrate, *La Raison du Spiritisme* [Paris: Librairie Internationale, 1868], ch. VI).

becomes harmful to the spiritualization of the being itself. Evil is thus relative, and responsibility for it is proportionate to the degree of one's advancement.

Therefore all passions have their providential usefulness, otherwise God would have done something useless and harmful. Abusing them is what constitutes evil, and humans do abuse by virtue of their free will. Later, enlightened for their own benefit, they will choose freely between good and evil.

INSTINCT VERSUS INTELLIGENCE

11. What is the difference between instinct and intelligence? Where does one ends and the other begins? Is instinct a rudimentary form of intelligence, or a distinct faculty, an exclusive attribute of matter?

Instinct is the occult force that requests organic beings to perform spontaneous and involuntary acts for their preservation. In instinctive acts, there is no reflection, no combination, no premeditation. As a plant seeks air, it turns to the light, directs its roots toward the water and the nourishing earth. Like a flower opens and closes alternately according to need; like climbing plants wrap around a support or cling with their tendrils. It is by instinct that animals are warned of what is useful or harmful to them; and by which they direct themselves to different places, according to the seasons, looking for the a favorable climate. By instinct they build, without any previous lessons and more or less skillfully, depending on the species, soft layers and shelters for their offspring, gear to trap the prey on which they feed; deftly using the offensive and defensive weapons with which they are equipped. By instinct the sexes attract each other; the mother broods over her young; and these latter look for their mother's breast. In humans, instinct dominates exclusively at the beginning of life; it is by instinct that the child makes its first movements, that it seizes its food, that it cries to express its needs, that it imitates the sound of the voice, that it tries to speak and to walk. Even in adults, certain acts are instinctive; such are the spontaneous movements to ward off danger, to get out of peril, to maintain one's balance; such are also the blinking of the eyelids to temper the brightness of light, the mechanical opening of the mouth to breathe, and so on.

12. *Intelligence is revealed by voluntary, thoughtful, premeditated, combined acts, according to the expediency of circumstances.* It is unquestionably an exclusive attribute of the soul.

Every mechanical act is instinctive; he who denotes reflection and combination is intelligent; one is free, the other is not.

Instinct is a guide that never fails, whereas intelligence, due to the sole fact that it acts freely, is sometimes subject to error.

If an instinctive act does not have the character of an intelligent act, it nevertheless reveals an intelligent cause that is essentially providential. If we admit that instinct has its source in matter, we must admit that matter is intelligent, even more intelligent and foresighted than the soul, since instinct never fails, while intelligence may sometimes be mistaken.

If we consider instinct a rudimentary intelligence, how come is it that, in certain cases, it proves superior to reasoned intelligence? And that it gives the possibility of performing things that the latter cannot produce?

Now, if instinct is an attribute of a special spiritual principle, what becomes of this principle? Since instinct is erased, this principle would be annihilated? If animals are only gifted with instinct, their future leads nowhere; their sufferings have no redress. This would not be in keeping with God's justice or goodness.

13. According to another system, instinct and intelligence have one and the same principle. Having arrived at a certain degree of development, this principle, which at first would have had only the qualities of instinct, would then undergo a transformation which would give it the qualities of free intelligence. In a word, it would receive what is conventionally called the divine spark. This transformation would not occur suddenly, but gradually, so that during a certain period there would be a mixture of the two aptitudes, the first decreasing as the second increased.

14. Finally, one last hypothesis, which moreover perfectly combines with the idea of the unicity of principle, is apparent from the essentially foreseeing nature of instinct, besides being consistent with what Spiritism teaches us, concerning the relations between the spiritual world and the corporeal world.

It is now known that discarnate spirits have a mission to watch over the incarnate ones, of whom they are the protectors and guides.

We also learned that they surround the latter with their fluids, and that humans often *unconsciously* act under the influence of such emanations.

Moreover, we know that instinct, which itself produces unconscious acts, predominates in children, and generally in beings whose reason is weak. Now, according to this hypothesis, instinct is neither an attribute of the soul nor of matter; it would not belong to the living being, but rather be an effect of the direct action of the invisible protectors who would make up for the imperfections of our intelligence, by inducing in us the unconscious acts necessary for the conservation of one's being. It would be like a baby walker with which one supports the child who does not know how to walk yet. But in the same way that we gradually eliminate the use of a leading string as the child learns to walk by itself, our protector spirits leave us to ourselves as we become able to be guided by our own intelligence.

Thus instinct, far from being the product of a rudimentary and incomplete intelligence, would be the result of an extraneous intelligence in the fullness of its strength, providing for the inadequacy of a younger intelligence that it would push unconsciously, for its own good, to do what it is still unable to do by itself. This may happen to a mature intelligence momentarily hindered in the use of its virtues, as well as during our childhood, and in cases of insanity and other mental illnesses.

It is said proverbially that there is a God for all fools, lunatics, and drunkards. This saying is truer than one may think: this God is none other than the spirit protector which watches over the incarnate being unable to protect himself/herself by means of their own reasoning.

15. In this order of ideas, we can advance even further. This theory, however rational it may be, does not solve all the difficulties of the question. To look for the causes, one must study the effects, and from the nature of the effects one can deduce the nature of the cause.

If we observe the effects of instinct, we notice first of all a unity of view as a whole, a certainty of results which ceases to exist when instinct is replaced by free intelligence. Furthermore, in the constant and perfect adaptation of the instinctive faculties to the needs of each species, we can discern a profound wisdom. This uniformity of view could not exist without a uniformity of thought. Consequently with the multiplicity of acting causes and as a result of the progress which individual intelligences are incessantly making, there is among them a diversity of aptitudes and wills that is incompatible with this perfectly harmonious ensemble, which has been produced since the beginning of time and in all environments, with mathematical regularity and precision, without ever failing. This uniformity in the result of the instinctive faculties is a characteristic fact which necessarily implies a unique cause. If this cause were inherent in each individuality, there would be as many varieties of instincts as there are individuals, from plants to humans. A general effect, uniform and constant, must have a general, uniform, and constant cause. An effect which denotes wisdom and foresight, must necessarily have a wise and forward-looking cause.

Now, as a wise and forward-looking cause is necessarily intelligent, it cannot be exclusively material.

Not finding in any created beings, whether incarnate or discarnate, the qualities necessary to produce such a result, one must go higher, that is, to the Creator Itself. If we turn to the explanation given of how we can conceive of providential action (see ch. **II**, item **25** above), according to which we are all beings saturated with the supremely intelligent divine fluid, we can understand the uniform view which presides over all instinctive movements for the good of each individual being. Such solicitude is all the more active as the individual possesses fewer resources in itself and in its own intelligence. That is why it is greater and more absolute in animals and inferior beings than in humans.

If we follow this theory, we understand that instinct is always a sure guide. The maternal instinct, the noblest of all, which materialism demeans down to the level of mere attractive forces of matter, is thus exalted and ennobled. Because of its consequences, it was not necessary for it to be delegated to the capricious eventualities of intelligence and free will. *Through the mother's organism, God Itself watches over Its newly born beings.*

16. This theory in no way destroys the role of protector spirits whose aid is an established and proven fact corroborated by experience; but it should be noted that such actions are essentially individual; that they vary according to the qualities peculiar to the protector and the protected; and that nowhere do they have the uniformity and generality of instinct. God Itself, in Its wisdom, leads the blind, but entrusts to free intelligences the task of leading the sighted, thus leaving to each one the responsibility for their actions. The mission of protector spirits is a duty which they have voluntarily accepted, and which is for them a means of advancement, depending on the manner in which they fulfill it.

17.   All these ways of regarding instinct are necessarily hypothetical, and none of them has a sufficient mark of authenticity to be taken as a definitive solution. The question will certainly be solved one day, when we have gathered the elements of observation which are still lacking. Until then, we must limit ourselves to submitting various opinions, trying them in the crucible of reason and logic, and waiting for some light to be shed. The solution that is nearest to the truth will necessarily be that which best corresponds to the attributes of God, namely, Its supreme goodness and supreme justice (see ch. **II**, item **19** above).

18.   Instinct being the guide, and passions being the motivating drive of souls in the first phase of their development, are sometimes mixed up in their effects, and especially in human language, which does not always lend itself sufficiently to the expression of all the shades of their meanings. There are, however, differences between these two principles which are essential to consider.

Instinct is a sure guide, always good; in time it may become useless, but never harmful. It is weakened by the predominance of intelligence.

Passions, when the soul is giving its first steps, have that in common with instinct, namely, that beings are aroused by an equally unconscious force. They are born more particularly of bodily needs, and depend more on the organism than instinct does. Above all, what distinguishes them from instinct is that they are individual and do not produce general and uniform effects like the latter. On the contrary, they vary in intensity and nature according to the individual. They are useful as stimuli, until the emergence of the moral sense, which, from a passive being, turns one into a rational being. At this moment they become, not only useless, but harmful to the advancement of the spirit, whose dematerialization they retard. Passions are weakened with the development of reason.

19.   A human being who would act constantly only by instinct could be very good, but would let his/her intelligence slumber. Such a person would be like a child who would not quit the baby walker, and unable to properly use his/her limbs. Whoever does not control his/her passions, can be very intelligent, but at the same time a very bad person. *Instinct annihilates itself; passions are tamed only by the effort of one's will.*

All humans have passed through the path of passions; those who have none, who by their nature are neither proud nor ambitious, nor selfish, nor hateful, nor vindictive, nor cruel, or angry, or sensual; who do good without effort, without premeditation and, in a manner of speaking, involuntarily; do so because they have progressed in the course of their previous lives in which they purged themselves of the dross. It is wrong to say that they have less merit to do good than those who have to struggle against their own tendencies. For the former, victory is won; for the latter it is has not been achieved yet – and when it will be, they will be like the others: in their turn, doing good without thinking, like children who read fluently without needing to spell anymore. They are like two patients, one of whom is cured and full of energy, while the other is only convalescing and still stumbles while walking. Actually, they are like two runners, one of whom is closer to the final stretch than the other.

MUTUAL DESTRUCTION OF LIVING BEINGS

20.   The mutual destruction of living beings is one of the laws of Nature which, at first sight, seems totally irreconcilable to the goodness of God. One wonders why God has made it a necessity to destroy one another so as to feed oneself at the expense of one another.

For those who see nothing but matter, thus limiting their sight to current life, it indeed appears to be an imperfection in the divine work; hence the conclusion held by unbelievers that since God is not perfect, there is no God. This happens because they judge the perfection of God from their own point of view, making their personal judgment the measure of God's wisdom. In this way, they think that God could not do any better than what they themselves would have done. Their inability to see beyond their narrow horizon does not allow them to judge of the whole; they do not understand that genuine good can come out of an apparent evil. Knowledge of the spiritual principle, considered in its true essence, and of the great law of unity which constitutes the harmony of creation, can alone give humans the key to this mystery, and show the wisdom of providence and harmony precisely where those individuals saw only an anomaly and a contradiction. The depths of this truth along with a multitude of others can only be probed by humans when their spirit has reached a sufficient degree of maturity.

21.   The true life, both of animals and humans, is not found more in one's physical body than it would be in one's clothing. Instead, it is in the intelligent principle that preexists and survives the body. This principle needs a body to develop itself through the work it must perform on brute matter. The body is used in this work, but the spirit never wears out; on the contrary, it comes out each time stronger, more lucid and more capable. What does it matter, then, that the spirit changes more or less often of physical envelope? It is not less spirit for that; it is like a person who would change his/her clothing a hundred times a year; yet still remain the same individual.

By means of the incessant spectacle of destruction, God teaches humans the little importance they should accord to their material envelope, while arousing in them the idea of spiritual life by making them long for it as recompense.

But God, some will say, could not obtain the same result by other means, without compelling living beings to destroy one another? Well, bold indeed whoever pretends to penetrate God's designs! If all is wisdom in God's work, we must suppose that such wisdom would not be lacking in this point as it is ever present in all the others. If we fail to comprehend it, this must be due to our little progress. However, we can try to seek for the reason, taking as compass the following principle: *God must necessarily be infinitely just and wise.* Let us therefore seek in all Its justice and wisdom, while bowing down before what is beyond our comprehension.

22. A peculiar usefulness which presents itself out of this destruction – purely physical, it should be noted – is as follows: organic bodies are only maintained by means of organic matter, whose materials contain only the nourishing elements necessary for their transformation. Because these bodies, instruments of action of the intelligent principle, have to be incessantly renewed, Providence makes them serve for their mutual sustenance; that is why beings feed on other. So the body is nourished by the body, but the spirit is neither annihilated nor altered as a result: it is only stripped of its envelope.

23. In addition, there are moral considerations of a higher order.

Struggles are necessary for the development of the spirit. It is in the struggle that the spirit exercises its faculties. Those that attack to get their food, and those that defend themselves to preserve their lives, have to resort to cunning and intelligence, and thus increase, by this very fact, their intellectual forces. One of them succumbs; but what has the strongest or the most adroit removed from the weakest in reality? Its garment of flesh, nothing else. The spirit, which has not died, will take a new body later on.

24. In the lower beings of creation, in those where the moral sense does not exist, and in which intelligence has not yet replaced instinct, the struggle can only have the motive of satisfying a material need. Now, one of the most imperative material needs is that of food; these beings struggle only to live, that is to say, to either take prey or defend themselves as prey, because they cannot be aroused by a higher motive. It is in this first phase that the soul develops itself and learns to live. When it has reached the degree of maturity necessary for its transformation, it receives new faculties: from God, namely, free will and the moral sense. In a word, the divine spark, which gives a new course to its ideas, endows it with new skills and new perceptions.

But the new moral faculties with which it is endowed develop only gradually, for nothing is abrupt in Nature. There is a period of transition when a human being is barely distinguishable from the brute. In the initial stages, animal instinct dominates, and the struggle still has the motive of satisfying one's material needs. Later, the animal instinct and the moral sense counterbalance each other;

the humans struggle, no longer to feed themselves, but to satisfy their ambition, their pride, their need to dominate. For that, they must still destroy. But as the moral sense takes over, sensibility develops and the urge for destruction diminishes, even fading away and becoming repulsive, as humans detest bloodshed.

However, struggle is always necessary for the development of the spirit, for even after having reached that point which seems culminating to us, humans are far from perfect; it is only through their own efforts and deeds that they acquire knowledge, experience, and get rid of the last vestiges of animality. It is then that the struggle, bloody and brutal as it was, becomes purely intellectual: humans struggle against difficulties and no longer against one another.[21]

---

21 This issues is related to the no less serious one of relations between animality and humanity, which will be dealt with further on. I have only wished to demonstrate by this explanation that the mutual destruction of living beings does not undermine in any way the divine wisdom, and that everything is bound and connected in the laws of Nature. This bond and interrelation would be broken if one abstracted from the spiritual principle. That is why so many questions remain unsolvable, if one considers only matter.

Chapter IV
Role of science in Genesis

1. The history of the origin of almost all the ancient civilizations is merged with that of their religion. That is why their first books were religious books; and since all religions are related to the principle of things – which is also that of humanity – they all gave explanations on the formation and arrangement of the universe according to the state of knowledge at the time, and their founders. As a result, the first sacred books were at the same time the first books of science, as well as the only code of civil laws for a long time.

2. In ancient times, religion had a powerful effect in restraining the population, governing the people who would willingly bend under the invisible potencies whereby they felt subjugated, and whose rulers claimed they held their power, should the people not give themselves entirely to the so-called equals of such potencies.

To give more strength to religion, it had to be presented as absolute, infallible and immutable, otherwise it would have lost its ascendancy over an almost brute population barely born to reason. At the time, religion needed not to be discussed, no more than the orders of the sovereign. Hence the principle of blind faith and passive obedience which thus originally had their reason for being and their utility. The reverence for sacred books, almost always supposedly descended from heaven, or inspired by the Divinity, forbade any scrutiny.

3. In primitive times, when means of observation were inevitably quite imperfect, the first theories on the world's system were to be tainted with gross mistakes. But if these means had been as complete as they are today, we humans would not have known how to use them. They could only emerge as the outcome of the development of our intelligence and the increasing knowledge of the laws of Nature. As human beings have advanced in the knowledge of these laws, they penetrated the mysteries of creation, and rectified their ideas about the origin of things.

4. Just like we, in order to understand and define the correlative movement of the hands of a clock, have to know the laws that govern its mechanism, it is necessary to learn the laws which govern all the forces that are put into action in the universe, besides evaluating the nature of materials and calculating the power of acting forces, before we can understand the mechanism that governs its vast whole.

Humans had been powerless to solve the problem of creation until the key was been given to them by science. It was necessary for astronomy to open the gates of infinite space, and allow us to delve into it, before, by using the power of calculation, we could determine with rigorous precision the motion, the position, the volume, the nature, and the role of the celestial bodies. Then physics revealed to us the laws of gravitation, heat, light, and electricity; the power of these agents over the whole Nature; and the cause of innumerable phenomena that flow from them. Meanwhile, chemistry taught us the transformations of matter; mineralogy the matters which form the crust of the planet; whereas geology taught us to read in the earthly layers the gradual formation of the latter. Botany, zoology, paleontology, and anthropology were to introduce us to the origins and succession of organized beings, while archeology enabled us to trace back the footsteps of humanity through the ages. In short, by complementing each other, all sciences were to furnish their indispensable contribution for the knowledge of the history of the world. In their absence, we would have no guide but our early hypotheses.

Thus, before humans were in possession of these elements of evaluation, all commentators of Genesis, whose reason was confronted with material impossibilities, moved over and over in the same circle without being able to get out of it. They were only able to do so when science opened the way, breaching the edifice of old beliefs, and then everything changed. Once the thread was found, difficulties were quickly resolved. Instead of an imaginary Genesis, we had a positive and somewhat experimental Genesis; the field offered by the universe has spread to infinity; we have seen the earth and the stars forming gradually according to eternal and immutable laws, which testify much better to the greatness and wisdom of God than a miraculous creation suddenly emerging from nothingness, like a change in view, with the sudden idea of a divinity after an eternity of inaction.

Since it is impossible to conceive of Genesis without the data provided by science, we can say in all truth that *it is science which must be invoked to constitute the true Genesis according to the laws of Nature.*

5. At the point where it arrived in the 19th century, has science solved all the difficulties contained in the problem of Genesis?

Certainly not; but it is indisputable that it has unerringly destroyed all the capital mistakes, and has done that by laying the most essential foundations on irrefutable data. Points that remain uncertain are, strictly speaking, only questions of detail, the solution of which, whatever it may be in the future, will not be prejudicial to the whole. Moreover, despite all the resources available to it, it has missed until now an important element without which the work could never be complete.

6. Of all the ancient Geneses, the one which most closely resembles modern scientific data despite the mistakes that it contains – and which are today clearly demonstrated – is incontestably that of Moses. Some of those mistakes are even more apparent than real, and come either from the misinterpretation of certain words whose original meaning has been lost in passing from language to language through translation, or whose meaning has changed with the manners and habits of people, also regarding the allegorical forms peculiar to the Eastern style, which have been interpreted by their literal sense instead of seeking for their inner meaning.

7. Of course, the Bible contains facts that reason developed by science cannot accept today, and others that seem strange and repugnant because they are related to moral conventions that are no longer ours. But apart from that, one would be biased not to acknowledge that it contains great beautiful things. Allegory holds a considerable place in human thought, and under this veil it hides sublime truths which reveal themselves if one seeks the depths of thought – then what is apparently absurd disappears.

Then why did humans not lift this veil sooner? Because, on the one hand, there was a lack of enlightenment which science and a healthy philosophy alone could provide; and on the other, because of the belief in the perennial immutability of faith, the consequence

GENESIS, MIRACLES AND PREDICTIONS

of an excessive, blind respect to the letter, under which reason was forced to bow; and consequently the fear of compromising the scaffolding of beliefs built only on literal sense. Since these beliefs departed from a primitive point, it was feared that, if the first link of the chain would break, all the other meshes of the net would end up separating. That is why people kept their eyes shut anyway. Yet to overlook a danger is not to avoid it. When a building falters, is it not more prudent to replace the bad stones with good ones immediately, instead of waiting, out of respect for the antiquity of the building, that the problem is beyond remedy, leaving no alternative but to rebuild it from top to bottom?

8. Science, in carrying out its investigations even into the bowels of the Earth and the depths of the sky, has therefore demonstrated in an irrefutable way the mistakes contained in the Mosaic Genesis if taken literally, and the material impossibility that things have happened, as they are textually reported. It has, by this very fact, carried a profound attack on secular beliefs. The orthodox faith was stirred by it, because it thought to see its fundamental stone removed; but which should be right: science, which walks cautiously and progressively on the solid ground of numbers and observation, without asserting anything before having the proof in hand; or a written account made at a time when means of observation were absolutely lacking? Which of them would ultimately prevail, those who say 2 and 2 are 5, and refuse to check, or those who say 2 and 2 are 4, and prove it?

9. But then, it is said, if the Bible is a divine revelation, does that mean that God was wrong? In case it is not a divine revelation, it has no authority any longer, and religion completely crumbles for lack of basis.

Of two things one is certain: either science is wrong, or it is right. If it is right, it cannot make an opposite opinion true; there is no revelation that can override the authority of facts.

Unquestionably God, which is all truth, cannot mislead humans, whether knowingly or unknowingly, otherwise It would not be God. If, therefore, the facts contradict the words attributed to God, it must logically be concluded that God has not pronounced them, or that they have been taken the wrong way.

82

If religion suffers, in some aspects, from such contradictions, the fault is not with science, which cannot agree with untrue statements, but with humans who have prematurely established absolute dogmas, of which they have made a matter of life and death, based on hypotheses that were liable to be contradicted by experience.

We should resign ourselves to the sacrifice of certain things, whether we like it or not, when we cannot do otherwise. When the world moves on, the will of some individuals cannot deter it. The wisest will try to follow it, and adapt themselves to the new state of things, instead of clinging to the past that is collapsing, the risk of falling with it.

10. Can anyone, out of respect for texts regarded as sacred, impose silence on science? This would be as impossible as preventing the Earth from turning. Religions, whatever they may be, have never gained anything by supporting manifest errors. The mission of science is to discover the laws of Nature. Now, as these laws are the work of God, they cannot be contrary to any religion based on truth. Science accomplishes its mission by the very force of things, and as a natural consequence of the development of human intelligence, which is a divine work as well, and advances only with God's permission, under the laws It has established. Therefore, to pronounce anathema against progress as an offense to religion is to go against the will of God; which more useless trouble, since all the anathemas in the world will not prevent science from moving on, and truth from coming into our understanding. *If religion refuses to walk hand in hand with science, then science will walk on alone.*

11. Only stationary religions can fear the discoveries of science, These discoveries are fatal only to those which are left behind by innovative ideas, while immobilizing themselves in the absolutism of their beliefs. As a rule, they make so petty an idea of the Divinity, that they do not understand that, actually, to assimilate the laws of Nature revealed by science is to glorify God in Its works. Nevertheless, in their blindness, they prefer to pay homage to the spirit of evil. *Any religion that would in no way be in contradiction with the laws of Nature, would be invulnerable and have nothing to fear from progress.*

12.   Genesis consists of two parts; the history of the formation of the material world, and that of humanity considered in its twofold corporeal and spiritual principle. Science has confined itself to seeking the laws that govern matter; in humans themselves it has studied only the bodily envelope. In this respect, it has come to realize with unquestionable precision the principal parts of the mechanism of the universe and the human organism. On this vital point it was able to complete Moses' Genesis and rectify its defective parts.

But the human history, considered from its spiritual aspect, is connected with a special order of ideas which does not fall within the realm of science proper, and which, for this reason, has not been made the subject of its researches. Philosophy, which more particularly has this kind of study in its attributions, has formulated on this point only contradictory systems, from pure spirituality to the negation of the spiritual altogether, and even of the principle of God. Based solely on the personal ideas of their authors, it left the question unsolved for lack of sufficient verification.

13.   For humans, however, this is the most important question, because it entails the problem of our past and future, since the problem of the material world affects us only indirectly. What is important for us to know is where we come from, where we go after this lifetime, and whether we will ever live again, and what fate is reserved for us.

On all these questions science is silent. Philosophy gives only opinions that come to diametrically opposite conclusions, but at least it allows discussion, which makes many people take its side in preference to religion which allows no discussion at all.

14.   All religions are in agreement with the principle of the existence of the soul, albeit without demonstrating it. However, they do not agree on its origin, its past, its future, or especially, on that which is essential: the conditions upon which the soul's future happiness depend. For the most part, they depict the soul's future based on ideas imposed on the their followers' faith, which can only be accepted by blind faith, but do not stand serious scrutiny. The destiny they portray to the soul is linked, in their dogmas, to ideas of the material world and in primitive concepts about the mechanism of the universe; and is irreconcilable with the current state of knowledge. As examination and discussion would only bring loss to them, they find it easier to proscribe both.

15. From these divergences concerning the future of human beings, doubts and unbelief were born. It could not be otherwise, with each religion claiming to possess the whole truth, one pointing to one way and the other to another way, without giving sufficient proof of their assertions in order to rally the majority. Faced with so much indecision, people took refuge in the present. On the other hand, unbelief leaves a painful void: humans start anxiously contemplating the unknown, where each of them must sooner or later fatally enter. The idea of nothingness freezes them, their conscience tells them that there must be something beyond the present: but what? Their developed reasoning no longer allows them to accept the tales which were told to them in infancy – to take an allegory for reality, what is the meaning of such an allegory? Science has lifted part of the veil, but it has not revealed the most important detail for us to know. We interrogate in vain, nothing answers us in a peremptory and suitable manner to calm our apprehensions. Everywhere we find affirmations colliding with negations, without more positive proofs on one side than on the other. Hence this uncertainty; and *uncertainty about a future life, make humans throw themselves with a sort of frenzy into material life.*

Such is the inevitable effect of transition periods: the edifice of the past collapses, and that of the future has not yet been built. The human being are like the adolescent who no longer has the naive beliefs of his/her early years, but does not yet have the knowledge of mature age. We have only vague aspirations which we do not yet know how to define.

16. If the question of human spirituality has remained in the state of theory until today, it is because we have lacked the means of direct observation through which we had to ascertain the state of the material world, and the field remained open to conceptions of the human spirit. As long as humans have not known the laws governing matter, and have not been able to apply the experimental method, they have wandered from system to system regarding the mechanism of the universe and of the formation of the planet Earth. This applies to the moral as well as to the physical order. To establish our ideas the essential element has escaped us, namely, the knowledge of the laws governing the spiritual principle. This knowledge was reserved for our time, as the knowledge of the laws of matter has been the work of the past two centuries.

17. Until now the study of the spiritual principle, as part of metaphysics, had been purely speculative and theoretical. In Spiritism it is entirely based on experimentation. With the aid of mediumistic faculties, which are more developed today, and above all generalized and better studied, humans found themselves in possession of a new instrument of observation. Mediumship has been for the spiritual world, what the telescope has been for the astronomical world and the microscope for the world of the infinitely small. It has made it possible to explore, to study with one's own eyes, so to speak, its relations with the corporeal world; to isolate, in living humans, the intelligent being from the material being, and see them act separately. Once in contact with the inhabitants of this world, we were able to follow the discarnate soul in its ascending march, in its migrations, in its transformations, thus finally being able to study the spiritual element. This is what was lacking in the early commentators of Genesis for understanding and rectifying errors.

18. Being in incessant contact, the spiritual world and the material world act in solidarity with each other; both have their share of action in Genesis. Without the knowledge of the laws which govern the first, it would be as impossible to constitute a complete Genesis, as it is to a sculptor to give life to a statue. Only nowadays, although neither material science nor spiritual science has said their last word, humans have both elements to shed light on this immense problem. These two keys were absolutely necessary to arrive at an approximate solution. As for the final solution, it may never be given to humans to find it on Earth, because there are things that belong to the secrets of God.

Chapter V
Systems of the ancient and modern worlds

1. The first idea that humans were made from earth, of the movement of the stars, and of the constitution of the universe, must have been, in the beginning, solely based on the testimony of the senses. In ignorance of the most elementary laws of physics and the forces of Nature, and having only their limited view as a means of observation, they could only judge on appearances.

On seeing the Sun appear in the morning on one side of the horizon and disappearing in the evening on the opposite side, it is naturally concluded that it was turning around the Earth, while it remained motionless. If humans would have been told then that the opposite was actually happening, they would have answered that this could not possibly be because, while we see the Sun changing places, we do not feel the Earth moving.

2. The small extent of the voyages, which at the time seldom went beyond the limits of the tribe or the valley, could not permit us to observe the sphericity of the Earth. Moreover, how could one suppose that the Earth had the form of a ball? In this way, we humans could have kept themselves only at the highest point of the globe, and, supposing we inhabited all over its surface, how could we have lived in the opposite hemisphere, head down and feet up? The thing would have seemed even less likely with a movement of rotation. When one still sees today, when most of us know the law of gravitation, relatively enlightened people still unable to realize this phenomenon, no one should be surprised that humans in ancient times did not even suspect it.

Therefore the Earth was for them a flat, circular surface like a millstone, extending as far as the eye could see in horizontal direction; hence the expression still used today: Go to the end of the world. Its limits, its thickness, its interior, its lower face, whatever lies below, was the unknown.[22]

3. The sky seemed to be concave, and was, according to vulgar belief, a real vault, with its lower edges resting on Earth, and marking its borders; a vast dome whose air filled all the capacity. Without any notion of the infinity of space, incapable even of conceiving it, humans imagined this vault to be formed of solid matter; hence the term firmament which has survived the belief itself, and which means *firm, resistant* (from Latin *firmamentum*, derived from *firmus*, and from Greek *herma, hermatos*, firm, support, supporting point),

4. The stars, of which they could not suspect the nature, were simple luminous points, being more or less big, and attached to the vault like suspended lamps, arranged on a single surface, and consequently all at the same distance from the Earth. In the same way they are represented in the interior of certain domes painted in blue to represent the azure of the skies.

Although today our ideas are quite different, the use of old expressions has been preserved; we still say, by comparison, the starry vault, under the sky's vault.

5. The formation of clouds by the evaporation of waters from earth was also unknown in ancient times. They could not arrive at the thought that the rain falling from the sky had its origin on the

---

22 "Hindu mythology taught that the star of the day stripped the night of its light, and passed through the night sky with a dark face. Greek mythology depicted Apollo's four-horse chariot. Anaximander of Millet argued, according to Plutarch, that the Sun was a cart full of very blazing fire that would have escaped through a circular opening. It seems that Epicurus was of the opinion that the Sun lighted up in the morning and extinguished at night in the waters of the ocean. Others thought that this star was made of a pumice stone heated to the point of incandescence. Anaxagoras regarded it as a piece of red hot iron as big as the Peloponnese – what a singular remark! The ancients were so irresistibly prone to regard the apparent immensity of this star as real, that they persecuted this reckless philosopher for attributing such specific volume to the shiny star of the day, which required all the authority of Pericles to save him from a death sentence, who sent him into exile instead." C. FLAMMARION, *Études et Lectures sur l'Astronomie* (Paris: Gauthier-Villars, in various volumes).

When one sees the sort of ideas which emanated in the 5th century BC, the most flourishing period of Ancient Greece, one cannot be astonished at those issued by humans even earlier, about the system of the world.

earth from which one could not see the water rising. There was a belief in the existence of *upper and lower waters*, celestial sources and terrestrial sources, reservoirs placed in the high regions, an assumption which was in perfect accord with the idea of a solid vault capable of keeping them. The upper waters escaping through the cracks of the vault fell in form of rain; and depending on the width of such openings, which could be wider or narrower, the rain was soft or torrential and diluvial.

6. A complete ignorance of the whole universe and the laws which govern it; and of the nature, constitution, and destination of the stars, which seemed so small compared to Earth; must necessarily have made Earth be considered as the main thing, the unique purpose of creation, with the stars as accessories created solely for the benefit of its inhabitants. This prejudice has persisted to this day, in spite of the scientific discoveries which have totally changed, for humans, the aspect of the world. How many people still believe that stars are ornaments in the sky to entertain the view of the inhabitants of the Earth!

7. Not before long, humans perceived the apparent motion of the stars, moving in mass from east to west, rising in the evening and setting in the morning, and preserving their respective positions. This observation had for a long time no other consequence than to confirm the idea of a solid vault involving the stars in its rotational movement.

Throughout the centuries, these early, naive ideas formed the background of religious beliefs, and have served as a basis for all ancient cosmogonies.

8. Later on, by the direction of the motion of the stars and their periodic return to the same order, it was understood that the celestial vault could not be simply a half-sphere placed on Earth, but rather a whole hollow sphere, in the center of which was the Earth – always flat, or at most convex – inhabited only on its upper face. That was already a progress.

But what was the Earth resting on? It would be pointless to report all the ridiculous suppositions produced by imagination, like that of the Hindus who said that the Earth was borne by four white elephants, which stood on the wings of an immense vulture. Meanwhile, the wisest individuals admitted that they knew nothing.

9.   However, an opinion generally prevalent in the pagan theogonies placed in *lower places*, that is to say, in the depths of the Earth, or beneath – that was not very clear – the region where the reprobate stayed, called hell, the *infernal region*, that is to say, the *nether region*. And the *higher places*, beyond the region of the stars, was the abode of the blessed. The word *inferno* (in the sense of hell) has been preserved to this day, although it has lost its etymological meaning since geology has dislodged the place of eternal torments from the bowels of the Earth, and astronomy has shown that it does not exist. There is neither high nor low in infinite space.

10.   Under the clear skies of Chaldea, India and Egypt, cradle of the most ancient civilizations, the movement of the stars could be observed with as much precision as the absence of special instruments permitted. At first, humans saw that certain stars had their own motion independent from the mass of stars, which contradicted the idea that they were attached to the sky vault. These were called wandering stars or planets to distinguish them from fixed stars. Their movements and their periodic returns were measured and calculated.

In the diurnal motion of the starry sphere, we noticed the immobility of the polar star, around which the others described, in twenty-four hours, parallel oblique circles, more or less large, according to their distance from the central star. That was the first step toward the knowledge of the obliquity of the axis of the world. Longer journeys made it possible to observe the difference of aspect of the sky according to the latitudes and the seasons; the elevation of the polar star above the horizon, varying with the latitude, put us on the path of the roundness of the Earth. It is thus that little by little we form a more just idea of the system of the world.

Around the year 600 BC, Thales of Miletus (Asia Minor) knew the sphericity of the Earth, the obliquity of the ecliptic and the cause of eclipses.

A century later, Pythagoras of Samos discovers the diurnal motion of the Earth on its axis, its annual movement around the Sun, and links the planets and comets to the solar system.

In the year 160 BC, Hipparchus of Alexandria (Egypt) invents the astrolabe, calculates and predicts eclipses, observes the Sun's spots, determines the tropical year, and the duration of the revolutions of the Moon.

However precious these discoveries may have been for the progress of science, they took nearly 2,000 years to become widely known. New ideas then, spreading only through scarce manuscripts, remained exclusive to a few philosophers who taught them to privileged disciples, while the masses, who were hardly ever thought as worth enlightening, took no advantage of them and continued to feed on old beliefs.

11. Toward the year 140 AD, Ptolemy, one of the most illustrious thinkers of the Alexandrian school, by combining his own ideas with common beliefs and some of the most recent astronomical discoveries, composed a system that may be called mixed, which bears its name, and which, for nearly fifteen centuries, was adopted alone in the civilized world.

According to Ptolemy's system, the Earth is a sphere in the center of the universe; it consisted of the four elements: earth, water, air, and fire. It was the first region, called *elementary*. The second region, called the ethereal one, consisted of eleven heavens, or concentric spheres, circling the Earth, namely the heaven of the Moon, and those of Mercury, Venus, the Sun, Mars, Jupiter, Saturn, the fixed stars, the first crystalline transparent solid sphere, the second crystalline sphere, and finally of the first mobile sphere, which imparted motion to all the lower heavens, and made them complete a revolution in twenty-four hours. Beyond the eleven heavens was the *Empyrean* (or *Empyreal*), the sojourn of the blessed, so called because of the Greek term *pyr* or *pur*, which means *fire*, because it was believed that this region was resplendent with light like fire.

Belief in many superimposed heavens had long prevailed, yet with varying numbers. The seventh was generally regarded as the highest one; hence the expression: To be delighted in the seventh heaven. The Apostle Paul said that he was raised to the third heaven.

Independently of the collective motion, each star had, according to Ptolemy, its own peculiar movements, more or less great according to their distance from the center. Fixed stars completed a revolution in 25,816 years. This last calculation denotes a knowledge of the precession of the equinoxes which in fact is accomplished in about 25,000 years.

12.   At the beginning of the 16th century AD, Copernicus, a famous astronomer born in Thorn (Prussia)[23] in 1472 and deceased in 1543, took up Pythagoras' ideas. He published a system which, confirmed every day by new observations, was favorably received, and soon overthrew that of Ptolemy. According to this system, the Sun is in the center, the planets describe circular orbs around this star, and the Moon is a satellite of the Earth.

A century later, in 1609, Galileo, born in Florence (Italy), invented the telescope. In 1610, he discovers the four satellites of Jupiter and calculates their revolutions. He recognizes that the planets have no light like the stars, but that they are illuminated by the Sun, and that they are spheres similar to Earth. He also observes their phases and determines the duration of their rotation on their axis; which thus provides, by material evidence, a definitive corroboration of Copernicus' system.

From then on, the scaffolding of superimposed heavens collapsed; the planets were recognized as worlds similar to Earth, and no doubt inhabited as the latter. The Sun was identified as a star, the center of a whirlwind of planets that are subject to it; and the stars were seen as being innumerable other suns, and probably centers of as many planetary systems.

The stars are no longer confined in an area of the celestial sphere, but irregularly scattered in boundless space. Those which seem to be touching are in fact at immeasurable distances from one another, whereas those which are apparently the smallest are the farthest from us; and the largest, are only the nearest, although still hundreds of billions of miles away.

The groups to which we have given the name of *constellations* are only apparent assemblages caused by distance and the effects of perspective, as form, in one's sight as he/she is placed at a fixed point, like lights scattered in a vast plain, or the trees of a forest, whose assemblages do not exist in reality. If one could move into the region of one of these constellations, as one got nearer, the form would disappear and new groups would emerge at sight.

Since these groups exist only in appearance, the meaning which a vulgar superstitious belief attributes to them is illusory, and their influence can exist only in one's imagination.

---

23 [Trans. note] Now Toruń, Poland.

To distinguish the constellations, they have been given names, such as Leo, Taurus, Gemini, Virgo, Libra, Capricorn, Cancer, Orion, Hercules, Ursa Major (Great Bear) or David's Chariot, Ursa Minor, Lyra, and so on; and they have been represented by figures which recall these names, most of them fanciful, but which in any case have nothing to do with the apparent shape of the star group. In vain would one seek these figures in the sky.

The belief in the influence of constellations, especially those which constitute the twelve signs of the zodiac, comes from the idea attached to the names they bear. If a constellation was called *lion* or *sheep*, it would certainly have been ascribed a different influence.

13.   Starting from Copernicus and Galileo, old cosmogonies were forever destroyed; and ever since, astronomy could only advance and not retreat. History tells us of the struggles these individuals of genius had to sustain against prejudices, and above all against the sectarian spirit of some who were interested in maintaining the errors on which they had been grounded in unwavering beliefs. The invention of an optical instrument was enough to overturn the scaffolding of ideas held for many thousands of years, since nothing can prevail against a fact proved to be true. Thanks to printing, the general public, new to such ideas, began to no longer fall for illusions and started taking part in the struggle; it was no longer against a few individuals that antagonists had to fight, but against general opinion which took action and sided with the truth.

How vast is the universe compared to the petty proportions assigned to it by our ancestors! How sublime is God's work when we see it accomplished according to the eternal laws of Nature! But also by the passing of time, by the efforts of genius, by all discoveries that were necessary in order to open our eyes and finally tear the blindfold of ignorance!

14.   The way was now open to numerous illustrious scientists to complete the sketched work. Kepler, in Germany, discovered the famous laws which bear his name, and with which he recognizes that the planets describe, not circular orbits, but elliptical ones, in which the Sun occupies one of the focal centers. Newton, in England, discovered the law of universal gravitation. Laplace, in France, invented celestial mechanics. Finally, astronomy became no longer a system founded on conjectures or probabilities, but a science established on the most regular bases of calculation and geometry. Thus is laid down one of the fundamental stones of Genesis

Chapter VI
General uranography[24]

SPACE AND TIME

1. Several definitions of space have been given, of which the main one is as follows: space is the expanse that separates two bodies. Hence some sophists have deduced that where there was no body, there was no space. It is on this concept that theological doctors have based their theories to establish that space was necessarily finite, alleging that limited bodies in certain numbers cannot form an infinite series; and where bodies ceased, space would also cease. Space has also been defined as the place where the worlds move, the void where matter acts, etc. Let us leave in the treaties where they belong all these definitions which define absolutely nothing.

Space is one of those words that represent a primitive and axiomatic idea, which is self-evident, and that the various definitions that can be given, serve only to obscure. We all know what space is, and I want only to establish its infinity, so that our ulterior studies present no barrier opposing the investigations of our views.

Now, I say that space is infinite, for this reason, that it is impossible to suppose any limit to it, and that, despite the difficulty we have in conceiving of the infinite, it is nevertheless easier for us to go eternally in thought through space, than to stop at some place beyond which we would no longer find any remaining expanse to go farther.

24 This chapter was textually excerpted from a series of spirit communications dictated at the Spiritist Society of Paris, in the years 1862 and 1863, under the title "Uranographic studies," and signed Galileo, through the medium M. C. F—. [Trans. note: *uranography* was the name formerly given to the branch of astronomy concerned with describing and mapping the stars].

To represent to ourselves the infinity of space, as much as possible within our limited faculties, suppose that, starting from planet Earth lost in the middle of the infinite, up to any point of the universe, and at the prodigious speed of an electric spark traveling *thousands of miles per second*, once we have scarcely left this globe, having already traveled millions of miles, we find ourselves in a place from which the Earth appears to us only as a tiny pale star. A moment later, always following the same direction, we reach the distant stars, which you can barely distinguish from your earthly abode. From there, not only the Earth completely disappears from sight in the depths of space, but even the Sun itself, in its splendor, is eclipsed by the expanse that separates us from it. Always animated by the same speed of light, we cross planetary systems with every step we take in the expanse, islands of ethereal light, stellar paths, sumptuous places where God has sown worlds with the same profusion with which It sowed plants in the earthly meadows.

Although we have been moving for only a few minutes, already hundreds of millions of miles separate us from Earth, billions of worlds have passed under our gaze, and yet, listen! We have not actually taken a single step into the universe.

If we continue for years, centuries, thousands of centuries, millions of periods lasting hundreds of centuries, and incessantly at the same lightning speed, we will not have advanced ant farther! And that regardless of the direction we went, and to whatever point we went, from that invisible grain that we have left and which is called the Earth.

This is what space is!

2. Time, like space, is a word defined by itself; we may have a more accurate idea of it by establishing its relationship with the infinite whole.

Time is the succession of things; it is related to eternity in the same way that these things are bound to infinity. Let us suppose ourselves at the origin of our world, at this primitive time when the Earth was not yet ruled by the divine impulsion, in a word, in the beginning of Genesis. Time has not yet come out of the mysterious cradle of Nature, and no one can say in what epoch of the ages we are, since the pendulum of the centuries has not yet been set in motion.

But hush! The first hour of the isolated Earth rings with an eternal timbre, the planet moves in space, and from then on there is *evening and morning*. Beyond Earth, eternity remains impassive and motionless, although time goes on for many other worlds. On Earth, time replaces it, and during a definite sequence of generations, years and centuries are counted.

Let us now move on to the very last day of this world, at the hour when, bowed under the weight of its dilapidated state, Earth will be erased from the book of life to no longer reappear: at this point the succession of events stops; the earthly movements that measured time are interrupted; and time itself ends with them.

This simple explanation of the natural things that give birth to time, nourish it and set it off, is enough to show that, from the point where we must place ourselves for our studies, time is a drop of water falling from a cloud into the sea, and whose falling can be measured.

So many worlds in the vast expanse, so many different and incompatible times. Outside of the worlds, eternity alone replaces these ephemeral successions, and peacefully fills the immensity of the heavens with its immobile light. Unlimited immensity and boundless eternity are the two major properties of universal Nature.

The eye of the observer who crosses, without ever stopping, the immeasurable distances of space, and that of the geologist who goes back beyond the limits of the ages, or who descends into the depths of the gaping eternity where they will lose themselves one day, act in concert, each in their way, to acquire this dual notion of the infinite: extension and duration.

Now, while keeping in mind this order of ideas, it will be easy for us to conceive of time as being only the relation of transitory things, and depending only on things that can be measured. If, taking earthly ages as units, we pile them up, thousands upon thousands, to form a colossal number, this number will never represent but one point in eternity; as thousands of miles joined to thousands of miles are but a mere dot in the whole extent.

Thus, for example, since the centuries are outside the ethereal life of the soul, we could write a number as long as the earthly equator, and suppose to be aged this number of centuries, without actually our soul counting a single extra day; and, by adding to this indefinable number of ages, a series as long as from here to the Sun, of similar numbers – or still larger – and imagining ourselves living during the prodigious succession of secular periods represented by the addition of such numbers; when we would reach the end, the incomprehensible accumulation of ages that weighs on our heads would be as if they had never been. Before us, there would always remain the whole eternity.

Time is only a relative measurement of the succession of transient things. Eternity is not susceptible of any measurement from a duration point of view, for it has neither beginning nor end; everything is in the present for eternity.

If centuries after centuries are less than a second in relation to eternity, what is the duration of human life?

MATTER

3.   At first sight, nothing seems so deeply diverse, so essentially distinct, as these various substances that make up the world. Among the objects that art or Nature makes daily under our eyes, are there two that would be perfectly identical, or only a parity of composition? There is so much dissimilarity from the point of view of solidity, compressibility, weight and multiple properties of the bodies, between the atmospheric gases and a thread of gold; between the aqueous molecule of a cloud and that of the mineral which form the sturdy framework of the globe! What a diversity between the chemical tissue of the various plants which decorate the plant kingdom, and that of the no less numerous representatives of animal species on Earth!

However, we can posit as being an absolute principle, that all known and unknown substances, however dissimilar they may seem to be, either from the point of view of their inner constitution or in relation to their reciprocal action, are in fact only variations under which matter presents itself, and that such varieties in which it has been transformed due to the direction of innumerable forces that govern it.

4.   Chemistry, whose progress has been so rapid since my epoch – when its followers themselves still relegated it to the secret domain of magic – as a new science which can rightly be considered as the child of the century of observation, since it is solely based, much more firmly than its older siblings, on the experimental method; chemistry, I say, has had fair play with the four primitive elements which the ancients had agreed to recognize in Nature. It has shown that the earthly element is only a combination of various substances infinitely varied; that air and water are also decomposable, being the product of a certain number of equivalents of gas; and that fire, far from being one of the main element, is only a state of matter resulting from the universal movement to which it is subjected, and of a sensible or latent combustion.

On the other hand, it has found a considerable number of principles hitherto unknown, which appeared to form, by their definite combinations, the various substances, the various bodies which it has studied, and which act simultaneously according to certain laws, and certain proportions, in the works operated at the large laboratory of Nature. These principles were denominated *simple bodies*, thereby indicating that it regards them as primitive and indecomposable, and that no operation, up to this day, can reduce them into relatively simpler parts than themselves.[25]

5. But where human appreciations stop, even helped by their most improbable artificial senses, the work of Nature continues; where the vulgar takes appearance for reality, the practitioner raises the veil and discern the beginning of things, the eye of the one who has grasped Nature's mode of action can see under the materials that constitute the world, that the primitive *cosmic matter*, simple and single, has diversified in certain regions at the time of their birth, then divided into solidary bodies during their life, and one day will be dismembered and assimilated in the receptacle of life's immensity by decomposing.

6. These are the questions that we ourselves, spirits that love of science, cannot deepen, and about which we could only issue more or less conjectural, personal opinions. About these questions I will keep quiet or justify my way of thinking; but the one at hand is

---

25 The main simple bodies are: among non-metallic bodies, oxygen, hydrogen, nitrogen, chlorine, carbon, phosphorus, sulfur, iodine; and among metal bodies, gold, silver, platinum, mercury, lead, tin, zinc, iron, copper, arsenic, sodium, potassium, calcium, aluminum, etc.

not of this number. To those who would be tempted to see in my words only a risky theory, I will say: Embrace, if it is possible, in an inquiring glance, the multiplicity of the operations of Nature, and you will recognize that, if one does not admit the unicity of matter, it is impossible to explain – I will not say only suns and spheres, but without going so far – the germination of a tiny seed underground, or the production of a single insect.

7.   If one observes such a diversity in matter, it is because the forces which presided over its transformations and the conditions in which they occurred, being unlimited in number, the varied combinations of matter could only be limitless themselves.

Therefore, whether the substance we are considering belongs, properly speaking, to fluids – that is to say, to imponderable bodies – or whether it is clothed with the ordinary characters and properties of matter, there is in all the universe only one primitive substance: the *cosmos* or *cosmic matter* of uranographers.

LAWS AND FORCES

8.   If any of those unknown beings that spend their ephemeral existence at the bottom of the dark regions of the ocean; if any of these polygastric animals, of these sea nymphs – miserable animalcules, which know of Nature only ichthyophagous fish and underwater forests – suddenly received the gift of intelligence, the faculty of studying their world, and to establish upon their appreciations a conjectural reasoning extended to the universality of things, what idea would they form of the living nature which develops in their midst, and of the earthly world which does not belong to the field of their observations?

If, now, by a marvelous effect of its new power, this same being could rise above its eternal darkness, on the surface of the sea, not far from the opulent shores of an island of splendid vegetation bathed in the fertile Sun, the dispenser of beneficent warmth, what judgment would that tiny creature make of its anticipated theory of universal creation, a theory which it would soon erase by a wider appreciation, but relatively still as incomplete as the first? Thus is, O humans! the image of all your speculative sciences.[26]

---

26 Such is also the situation of the deniers of the spiritual world, when, after being stripped of their carnal envelope, the horizons of the world beyond unfold

9. Therefore, when I come here to deal with the question of the laws and forces that govern the universe – I who, like you, am only a relatively ignorant being regarding real science – and in spite of the apparent superiority given to me over my earthly siblings in this opportunity that I have taken to study questions about Nature which are beyond limits to them in their current position, my goal is only to draft a general notion of the universal laws, without explaining in detail the mode of action and the nature of the special forces that depend on it.

10. There is an ethereal fluid that fills space and penetrates the bodies. This fluid is the ether or primordial cosmic matter, generator of the world and its beings. In ether are inherent the forces which preside over the metamorphoses of matter, the immutable and necessary laws which govern the world. These multiple forces, indefinitely varied according to the combinations of matter, allocated according to the masses, diversified in their modes of action according to circumstances and environments, are known on Earth under the names of *weight, cohesion, affinity, attraction, magnetism, and active electricity.* The vibratory movements of the agents under those are called *sound, heat, light,* etc. In other worlds, they present themselves in other aspects, offer other characteristics unknown to this one; and in the immense expanse of heavens, an indefinite number of forces has developed in an unimaginable scale, of which we are as little capable of evaluating the magnitude as the crustacean at the bottom of the ocean is of encompassing the universality of earthly phenomena.[27]

---

before their eyes. They then understand the emptiness of theories by which they claimed to explain everything by matter alone. However, these horizons still have for them mysteries which are revealed only successively, as they rise through purification. But from their first steps in this new world, they are forced to recognize their blindness, and how far they are from the truth.

27 We relate everything to what we know, and we do not understand what escapes the perception of our senses any more than those born blind are unable to understand the effects of light and the utility of the eyes. So it may be that, in other environments, the cosmic fluid has properties, combinations of which we have no idea, effects which are adequate to needs unknown to us, giving rise to new perceptions or to other modes of perception. We do not understand, for example, that one can see without the eyes of the body and without light; but who can assure us that there are no agents other than light to which special organs are assigned? The somnambulic (i.e., entranced) sight, which is not stopped by distance, nor by material obstacles, nor by obscurity, is a good example. Suppose that, in any

Now, just as there is only one simple, primitive substance, generative of all the bodies, but diversified in its combinations, as all these forces depend on a universal law diversified in its effects, which we find at their origin, and which by eternal decrees have been sovereignly imposed upon creation to constitute its permanent harmony and stability.

11. Nature is never opposed to itself. The crest of the universe has only one motto: $\frac{\text{UNITY}}{\text{VARIETY}}$. Going up the ladder of worlds, one finds the unity of harmony and creation, as well as an infinite variety in this immense bed of stars. By traversing the degrees of life, from the lesser of beings up to God, the great law of continuity is recognized. Considering the forces in themselves, we can form a series of which the consequent result, blending with the generator itself, is the universal law.

You will not be able to appreciate this law in all its extent, since the forces which represent it in the field of your observations are restricted and limited, However, gravitation and electricity can be regarded as a broad application of the primordial law which reigns beyond the heavens.

All these forces are as eternal – I will explain this word – and universal as creation; Being inherent in the cosmic fluid, they necessarily act upon everything and everywhere, modifying their action by their simultaneity or their succession; predominant here, fading away elsewhere; powerful and active in some points, latent or secret in others; but ultimately preparing, directing, preserving, and destroying worlds in their various periods of life, governing the wonderful labors of Nature at whatever point they execute them, forever assuring the eternal splendor of creation.

FIRST CREATION

12. After having considered the universe under the general points of view of its composition, its laws and its properties, I can carry our studies on the mode of formation which gives rise to the

---

world, beings are normally what our entranced mediums are only exceptionally: they will need neither our light nor our eyes, and yet they will see what we are not able to see. It is the same with all other sensations. The conditions of viability and perceptibility, the sensations and the needs, vary according to the environment.

worlds and the beings. I will then descend to the creation of the Earth in particular, and to its current state in the universality of things, and from there, taking this globe as a point of departure and for relative unity, I shall proceed to our planetary and sidereal studies.

13. If we have understood the relation, or rather the opposition of eternity to time, if we have become familiar with the idea that time is only a relative measure of the succession of transient things; while eternity is essentially one, immovable and permanent, and that it is not susceptible of any measure from the point of view of duration; we will then understand that for it there is neither beginning nor end.

On the other hand, if we make a just – albeit necessarily weak – idea of the infinity of divine power, we will understand how it is possible that the universe has always been and always is. From the moment God was, Its eternal perfections have spoken. Before time was born, immeasurable eternity received the divine word and fertilized the eternal space as it did.

14. God being by nature from all eternity, has created from all eternity, and it could not be otherwise; for, at some distant epoch, from which our imagination recoils due to supposed limits of creation, eternity will always remain beyond such limits – I entreat you to weigh well this thought – an eternity during which the divine hypostases, the infinite vaults, would supposedly have been buried in mute inactivity and infertile lethargy, an eternity of apparent death for the eternal Creator which gives life to all beings, an indifferent mutism for the verb that governs them, a cold and selfish sterility for the spirit of love and of vivification.

Let us better understand the greatness of the divine action and its perpetuity under the hand of the absolute being! God is the sun of all beings; it is the light of the world. Now, the appearance of the sun instantly gives rise to streams of light which spread everywhere over the expanse; so the universe, born of the supreme God, goes back to the unimaginable periods of infinite duration, to the *Fiat lux! of the beginning.*

15. The absolute beginning of things therefore goes back to God; their successive appearances in the domain of existence constitute the order of perpetual creation.

Which immortal would be able to tell the unknown and superbly veiled magnificences under the night of the ages which developed in those ancient times when none of the wonders of the present universe existed? At that primitive time when the voice of God supreme was heard, the materials which were to be assembled in the future symmetrically and of themselves to form the temple of Nature, suddenly found themselves in the infinite void; when, with the mysterious voice that every created being venerates and cherishes like that of a mother, harmoniously varied notes have been produced to vibrate together and modulate the concert of the immense heavens!

The world at its cradle was not established in its vitality and plenitude of life. No, the creative power never contradicts itself, and, like all things, the universe was born an infant. Covered with the laws mentioned above, and with the initial impulsion inherent in its very formation, the primitive cosmic matter gave rise in turn to vortexes, to agglomerations of this diffuse fluid, to clusters of nebulous matter which were divided and infinitely modulated to give birth, in the incommensurable regions of the expanse, to various centers of simultaneous or successive creations.

Because of the forces that prevailed in one or another, and the subsequent circumstances that presided over their development, these primitive centers became the focal points of a special life. Those less scattered in space and richer in principles and action forces, therefore began their particular astral life, whereas others, occupying an unlimited extent, grew only with extreme slowness, or again divided themselves into other secondary centers.

16. Referring to only a few millions of centuries before current times, our Earth did not yet exist, our solar system itself had not yet begun its planetary life evolutions; and yet, already splendid suns illuminated deep space. Already inhabited planets gave life and existence to a multitude of beings that preceded us in the human trail. Opulent productions of unknown nature, and marvelous phenomena of the sky, developed under other eyes images of immense creation. What am I saying! Already splendors are no longer that once made the heart of other mortals beat under the thought of the infinite potency, and we, poor little beings who come after an eternity of life, think ourselves to be contemporaries of creation.

Once again, better understand Nature. Let us know that eternity is behind us as before, that space is the theater of a succession and an unimaginable simultaneity of creations. Such nebulae, which we scarcely distinguish from the distance in the sky, are agglomerations of suns in the process of formation; others are milky ways of inhabited worlds; others, finally, besieged by catastrophes or decay. Let us know that, just as we are placed in the midst of an infinity of worlds, so are we in the midst of a dual infinity of earlier and later durations. And that universal creation is not for us, and that we must reserve this word only when referring to the formation of our tiny little globe.

UNIVERSAL CREATION

17. After ascending, as much as it is possible in our weakness, toward the hidden source from which the worlds flow like drops of water of a river, let us consider the course of successive creations and their serial developments.

Primitive cosmic matter contained the material, fluidic, and vital elements of all the universes that unfold their magnificence throughout eternity. It is the fertile mother of all things, the first grandmother, and, what is more, the eternal generator. It has not disappeared, that substance whence come the sidereal spheres is not dead. This power incessantly gives birth to new creations, and incessantly receives the reconstituted principles of worlds that have been effaced from the eternal book.

Ethereal matter, more or less rarefied, which descends among interplanetary spaces; this cosmic fluid which fills the world, more or less rarefied in the immense regions, rich in agglomerations of stars, more or less condensed where the astral sky does not shine yet, more or less modified by various combinations according to the places in the expanse, is nothing other than the primitive substance in which the universal forces reside, whence Nature has drawn all things.[28]

---

28 If we ask what is the principle of these forces, and how they can be in the very substance that produces them, we would reply that mechanics gives us numerous examples of them. Is it not the elasticity that makes a spring relax in the spring itself, and does it not depend on the mode of aggregation of its molecules? The body which obeys the centrifugal force receives its impulsion from the primitive movement which has been impressed upon it.

18. This fluid penetrates the bodies like an immense ocean. It is in it that resides the vital principle that gives birth to the life of beings and perpetuates them on each globe according to their condition; a principle in latent state that remains dormant where the voice of a being does not call it. Every mineral, plant, animal, or other created being – for there are many other natural kingdoms whose existence you do not even suspect – knows, by virtue of this universal vital principle, how to take possession of the conditions of its existence, and of its duration.

The molecules of minerals have their share of this life, as well as the seeds and the embryos, and are grouped, as in the organism, into symmetrical figures which constitute the individuals.

It is very important to penetrate this notion: that the primitive cosmic matter was clothed, not only with the laws which assure the stability of the worlds, but also with the universal vital principle which forms spontaneous generations on every world, as the conditions of the successive existence of beings, and when the time for the appearance of the offspring of life during the creative period begins.

This is universal creation. It is therefore true to say that, since the operations of Nature are the expression of the divine will, God has always created, creates without ceasing, and will always create.

19. But so far we have passed in silence over the *spiritual world* which is also part of creation and fulfills its destinies according to the venerable prescriptions of the Master.

I can only give a very limited teaching on the subject of how spirits were created, in view of my own ignorance; and I must still keep silent on questions which I have been allowed to examine.

To those who are religiously desirous of knowing, and who are humble before God, I will say, begging them not to base any premature system on my words: The spirit cannot receive the divine illumination which gives, at the same time as free will and conscience, the notion of its high destinies, without having passed through the divinely fateful series of inferior beings among which the work of its individuality is slowly developed. It is only from the day when God supreme imprints on a spirit's forehead Its august seal, that the spirit is ranked among humans beings.

Again, do not build your reasonings upon my words, which became sadly notorious in the history of metaphysics: I would prefer a thousand times to keep silent on questions so elevated, above our ordinary meditations, rather than expose you to adulterate the meaning of my teaching, and to plunge you, through my fault, into the inextricable labyrinths of deism or fatalism.

SUNS AND PLANETS

20. Now it happened that at one point of the universe, lost among the myriad of worlds, cosmic matter condensed in the form of an immense nebula. This nebula was animated by the universal laws which govern matter. By virtue of these laws, and especially of the molecular force of attraction, it took the form of a spheroid, the only one that a mass of matter isolated in space could primitively take.

The circular motion, produced by the rigorously equal gravitation of all the molecular zones toward the center, soon modified the primitive sphere to lead it, from motion to motion, toward the lenticular form – here I am referring to the whole nebula.

21. New forces emerged as a result of this rotational movement: the centripetal force and the centrifugal force; the first tending to gather all contrary parts, the second tending to drive them away. Now, with this motion accelerating as the nebula is condensed, and with its radius increasing as it approaches lenticular form, the centrifugal force, incessantly developed by these two causes, soon prevails over the central attraction.

Just as a too rapid movement of a slingshot can brake the rope and let the projectile escape, so the predominance of the centrifugal force detached the equatorial circle from the nebula; and from this ring thus formed a new mass isolated from the first one, albeit remaining subject to its power. This mass has preserved its equatorial motion which, modified, became its translational movement around the solar star. In addition, its new state gives it a rotational movement around its own axis.

22. The generating nebula that gave birth to this new world, condensed and resumed the spherical form; but since the primitive heat developed by its various motions, is weakened only with extreme slowness, the phenomenon which we have just described will often be repeated for a long time, as long as this nebula has not become sufficiently dense, sufficiently solid to oppose an effective resistance to changes of shape successively imparted on its rotational movement.

It will not have given birth to a single star, but to hundreds of worlds detached from the central core, stemming from it by the mode of formation mentioned above. Now, each of these worlds, clothed as the primitive world of the natural forces that preside over the creation of universes, will engender in this sequence new globes which revolve around it, as it gravitates concurrently with its siblings around the core of their existence and of their life. Each of these worlds will be a sun, center of a whirlwind of planets successively escaped from its equator. These planets will receive a special life peculiar to each one, although dependent on their generating star.

23.   The planets are thus formed of masses of condensed matter, but not yet solidified; detached from the central mass by the action of the centrifugal force, and taking, by virtue of the laws of motion, a more or less elliptical spheroidal form, according to the degree of fluidity that they have preserved. One of these planets will be the Earth which, before being cooled down and covered with a solid crust, will give birth to the Moon, by the same mode of astral formation to which it owes its own existence. The earth, henceforth inscribed in the book of life, cradle of beings whose weakness is protected under the wing of Divine Providence, becomes a new chord on the infinite harp which must vibrate in its place, in the universal concert of the worlds.

SATELLITES

24.   Before the planetary masses have reached a degree of sufficient cooling to solidify themselves, smaller masses, some liquid globules have detached from the equatorial plane; a plane in which the centrifugal force is the strongest, and which by virtue of the same laws have acquired a translational movement around their generating planet, such as it was around their central generating star.

That is how the Earth gave birth to the Moon whose smaller mass had to undergo a quicker cooling. Now, the laws and forces that presided over its detachment from the earthly equator, and its translational movement on the same plane, acted in such a way that this world, instead of assuming an spheroidal shape, took the ovoid shape of a globe, that is to say, having the elongated form of an egg, whose center of gravity would be fixed at the bottom.

25. The conditions in which the detachment of the Moon was made scarcely allowed it to move away from Earth, and compelled it to remain perpetually suspended in the latter's sky, like an ovoid figure whose heavier parts formed the underside toward the earth, and whose least dense parts occupied the summit – if we can designate by this word the side turned to the opposite the Earth and rising towards the sky. This is what makes this satellite continually present the same face to us. It may be assimilated, in order to better understand its geological state, to the image of a crescent globe whose base turned towards the Earth would be made of lead.

Hence, there are two essentially distinct natures on the surface of the lunar world: one, without any possible analogy with ours, because the fluid and ethereal bodies are unknown to our world; the other, light in relation to the Earth, since all the least dense substances were carried on this hemisphere. The first, perpetually turned towards the Earth, without water and without atmosphere, if it is not sometimes at the limits of its subterranean hemisphere; the other, rich in fluids, perpetually opposite to the one we see from our world.[29]

---

29 This theory about the Moon, entirely new, explains by the law of gravitation the reason why this orb always presents the same face to Earth. Its counterweight, instead of being in the center of the sphere, lies in one of the points of its surface, and consequently attracted to the Earth by a force greater than the lighter parts. Thus the Moon would produce the effect of a French humpty-dumpty toy called *poussah*, which once struck always returns back to its standing position, whereas the planets, whose center of gravity is equidistant from the surface, rotate regularly on their axis. The vivifying, gaseous, or liquid fluids, owing to their specific lightness, would be accumulated in the upper hemisphere constantly opposite to Earth. The lower hemisphere, the only one visible to us, would be deprived of those, and consequently unfit for life, while still reigning over the other. If, therefore, the upper hemisphere would be inhabited, its inhabitants would never see the Earth, unless there were excursions to the other hemisphere.

26. The number and condition of the satellites of each planet have varied according to the special conditions in which they have formed. Some have given birth to no secondary orbs, as is the case of Mercury, Venus, and Mars, while others have formed one or more, such as planets Earth, Jupiter, Saturn, and so on.

27. In addition to its satellites or moons, the planet of Saturn presents the special phenomenon of a ring which, seen from afar, seems to surround it like a white halo. This formation is for us a new proof of the universality of the laws of Nature. This ring is indeed the result of a separation that occurred at primitive times in the equator of Saturn, just like an equatorial zone escaped from Earth to form its satellite. The difference lies in the fact that the ring of Saturn was formed, in all its parts, of homogeneous molecules, probably already in a certain state of condensation, and thus could continue their rotational movement in the same direction and in a time roughly equal to that which animates the planet. If one of the points of this ring had been denser than any other, one or more agglomerations of substance would have suddenly operated, and Saturn would have counted several more satellites. Since the time of its formation this ring has solidified as well as the other planetary bodies.

COMETS

28. As wandering celestial objects, even more than the planets which have retained their etymological denomination, the comets will be the guides that will help us cross the limits of the system to which the Earth belongs, in order to reach the distant regions of sidereal space.

But before exploring the heavenly realms with the aid of these voyagers of the universe, it will be useful to make known as far as possible their intrinsic nature and their role in the planetary economy.

29. In these haloed celestial objects, we have often seen nascent worlds, elaborating in their primitive chaos the conditions of life and existence which are shared with the inhabited lands. Others

---

No matter how rational and scientific this opinion may be, as it has not yet been confirmed by any direct observation, it can only be accepted as a hypothesis, and as an idea which may serve as a milestone for science.

have imagined in these extraordinary bodies worlds in the state of destruction, and their singular appearance was for many the subject of erroneous assessments of their nature. Even official astrology would teach that they carried omens of coming disasters, and that they were messengers decreed by divine providence to warn an astonished and trembling Earth.

30. The law of variety is applied with so great profusion in the works of Nature, that one wonders how naturalists, astronomers or philosophers have raised so many systems to assimilate comets to planetary bodies, and to see in them only celestial objects in a greater or lesser degree of development or obsolescence. Yet the settings offered by Nature were amply sufficient to remove from the observer the care of checking it against relations which do not exist, and to leave to comets the modest but useful role of wandering celestial bodies as scouts for solar empires. The celestial bodies in question are quite different from the planetary bodies, and are not, like them, destined to serve as a residence for any humanity. They successively move from suns to suns, sometimes enriching them-selves in their course with planetary fragments reduced to the state of vapors, draining from their homes the vivifying and renovating principles which they pour onto other worlds.

31. If, when one of these celestial objects approaches our lit-tle globe, to cross the orbit and return to its apogee located at an immeasurable distance from the Sun, we could follow it with our thought, to visit with it the sidereal regions, we would cross this prodigious expanse of ethereal matter, which separates the Sun from the nearest stars; and by observing the combined movements of that comet, which is thought to have been lost in the desert of the infinite, we would find, again, an eloquent proof of the universality of the laws of Nature, which operate at distances of which the most active imagination can hardly conceive.

There, the elliptical form takes a parabolic form, and the march slows down to the point of traversing only a few meters at one time, while at its perigee it traversed several thousand miles. Perhaps a more powerful sun, more important than the one it has just left behind, will use this comet with a preponderant attraction, and will receive it in the rank of its own subjects. Then the astonished children of your little planet will have waited in vain for the return they had predicted by incomplete calculations, in which case we, whose thought has followed the wandering comet into these unknown regions, will then meet a new orb not found in earthly glances, unimaginable to the spirits which inhabit Earth, inconceivable even to their thought, because it will be the stage of unexplored wonders.

We have reached the astral world, In this world, dazzling with vast suns that radiate in infinite space, and which are the glowing flowers of the magnificent firmament of creation. Until we arrive there, we can never know what Earth really is.

THE MILKY WAY

32. During beautiful starry and moonless nights, everyone has been able to notice a whitish glow which crosses the sky from one end to the other, and which the ancients had dubbed the *Milky Way*, because of its milky appearance. This diffuse glow has been explored for a long time by the eye of the telescope in modern times, and this path of golden powder, or the stream of milk of ancient mythology, has turned into a vast field of unknown wonders. The researches conducted by observers have brought knowledge of its nature, and have shown, where the unaided vision could discern only a feeble light, millions of suns brighter and more important than that which illuminates us.

33. Actually, the Milky Way is a separate field of solar or planetary flowers which shine in its vast expanse. Our Sun and all the bodies that accompany it are part of those radiant globes of which the Milky Way is composed; but, in spite of its gigantic dimensions relative to Earth and the greatness of its empire, it nevertheless occupies only an inappreciable place in the immensity of creation. We can count about thirty millions suns, similar to ours, which gravitate in this vast region, each separated from one another by more than a hundred thousand times the radius of the Earth's orbit.[30]

34. By this approximation, we can make an idea of the extent of this sidereal region, and the relation which unites our system with

---

30 [Trans. note] The Milky Way is about 1,000,000,000,000,000,000 km (about 100,000 light years or about 30 kpc) across.

the universality of all the systems which occupy it. We can also judge of the smallness of the solar system, and a fortiori the nothingness, the relative unimportance of our little Earth. What then should the beings that populate it be considered to be!

I use the term nothingness, for my assertions should apply not only to the material, physical extent of the bodies which are the object of this study – this would not be enough – but also, and above all, to their moral state, to the degree that they occupy in the universal hierarchy of beings. Creation appears in all its majesty, creating and propagating all around the solar world, and granting each the systems that surround them on all sides, the manifestations of life and intelligence.

35. Thus the position occupied by our Sun or the Earth in the world of stars becomes known. These considerations will gain even greater weight if we reflect on the very state of the Milky Way, which, in the immensity of the sidereal creations, itself represents only a minuscule and inappreciable point seen from a distance; for it is nothing more than a stellar nebula, like thousands of others in space. If it appears to us more vast and richer than others, it is for the reason alone that it surrounds us and expands to its full extent before our eyes; while other galaxies, lost in unfathomable depths, can scarcely be glimpsed.

36. Now, if we know that the Earth is relatively nothing, or almost nothing in the solar system, this one nothing or almost nothing in the Milky Way, which in turn is nothing or almost nothing in the universality of nebulae – and this universality itself very little in the midst of the infinite immensity – we will begin to understand what our planet is.

FIXED STARS

37. The so-called fixed stars, constituting the two hemispheres of the firmament, are not isolated from all external attraction, as is generally supposed. Far from it, they all belong to the same agglomeration of stellar bodies. This agglomeration is none other than the great nebula of which we are part, and whose equatorial plane which projects in the sky has received the name of *Milky Way*. All the suns that compose it are solidary; their multiple influences perpetually react one upon the other, and universal gravitation brings them all together into one big family.

38. Of these various suns, most are, like ours, surrounded by secondary worlds, which they illuminate and fertilize by the same laws which preside over life on our planetary system. Some, like Sirius, are thousands of times more magnificent in size and wealth than ours, and their role is more important in the universe, as well as the planets surrounding it, in greater numbers, and much superior than ours. Others are very dissimilar in their astral functions. Thus, a certain number of these suns, veritable twins in the sidereal order, are accompanied by their siblings of the same age, and form, in space, binary systems to which nature has given quite different functions, from those that belong to our Sun. There the years are not measured by the same periods, nor days by the same sun, and these worlds illuminated by a double torch have received in common conditions of existence unimaginable for those who have not left our little inhabited world.

Other stars without retinue, deprived of planets, have received the best elements of habitability which are given to any of them. The laws of nature are diversified in their immensity, and if unity is the great word of the universe, infinite variety is nonetheless its eternal attribute.

39. Despite the prodigious number of these stars and their systems, and despite the immeasurable distances that separate them, they all belong to the same stellar nebula that the eyes of the most powerful telescopes can barely reach, and that the most daring conceptions of imagination can scarcely penetrate. Nevertheless, this nebula is only a unit in the multitude of nebulae which make up the astral world.

40. The so-called fixed stars do not stand motionless in space. The constellations that we have figured on the vault of the firmament are not real symbolic creations. The distance from the Earth and the perspective under which the universe is measured from here are the two causes of this double optical illusion.

41. As we have seen, the totality of the celestial bodies sparkling in the azure dome is enclosed in the same cosmic agglomeration, in the same nebula which you call the *Milky Way*. Yet, although they all belong to the same group, these stars are each animated with its own translational movement in space. Absolute rest exists nowhere; they are governed by the universal laws of gravitation, and roll in space under the incessant impulsion of this immense force. They roll, not according to paths traced by chance, but in closed orbits, the center of which is occupied by an upper star. To make my words more understandable by an example, I will now talk especially about your Sun.

42. It is known from modern observations that the Sun is not fixed or central, as was believed in the early days of new astronomy, but that it rather advances in space, carrying with it its vast system of planets, satellites and comets.

Now, this march is not fortuitous, and it does not go astray, wandering in the infinite voids, away from the regions assigned to it, its offspring and its subjects. Instead, its orbit is measured, and concurrent to other suns of the same order as itself, and surrounded like it by a certain number of inhabited globes. It revolves around a central sun. Its gravitational motion, like that of the other suns, its sibling stars, is invaluable to annual observations, since secular periods in great numbers could scarcely mark the time of one of these astral years.

43. This central sun of which I have just spoken is itself a secondary globe relative to another still more important, around which it perpetuates a slow and measured march in company of other suns of the same order.

We could go on following this successive subordination of suns to other suns until our imagination would become tired of climbing such a hierarchy; for, let us not forget, we can count in round numbers about thirty millions of suns in the Milky Way, subordinated to each other like gigantic gears of an immense system.

44. And these suns, in innumerable numbers, each live a life of solidarity; just as nothing is isolated in the economy of your little earthly world, nothing is isolated in the immeasurable universe.

These systems upon systems would appear from afar, to the inquiring eye of the philosopher who would know how to embrace the picture developed by space and time, a dust of gold pearls raised in whirlwinds under the divine breath which makes the sidereal worlds fly in both, like grains of sand through the desert.

More stillness, more silence, more night! The great spectacle that would thus unfold under our gaze would be the real creation, immense and full of ethereal life, which the all-seeing Creator thoroughly encompasses in Its infinite vision.

But so far I have only spoken of a nebula, whose millions of suns and millions of inhabited orbs form, as I have said, only one island in an infinite archipelago.

THE DESERTS OF SPACE

45. An immense desert, without boundaries, extends beyond the agglomeration of stars of which we have just spoken, and envelops it. Solitudes follow solitudes, and immeasurable areas of emptiness extend far and wide. The clusters of cosmic matter being isolated in space like the floating islands of an immense archipelago. In order to appreciate, in some way, the enormous distance which separates the cluster of stars, of which we form a part, from the agglomerations nearest to them, it is necessary to bear in mind that these stellar islands are disseminated sparsely in the vast ocean of heavens; and that the extent of space dividing them is immeasurably larger than the agglomerations themselves with their respective dimensions.

Now, it should be remembered that the stellar nebula measures, in round numbers, a thousand times the distance of the nearest stars taken as a unity; that is to say, over three hundred thousand trillion miles. Since the distance extending between them is much larger, it cannot be expressed by numbers within the comprehension of our minds. Imagination alone, in its higher conceptions, is capable of crossing this prodigious immensity. These mute solitudes, deprived of all appearance of life, can give us some idea, as it were, of this relative infinity.

46. However, this celestial desert, which envelops our sidereal universe, and which seems to extend as the distant confines of our astral world, is encompassed by the vision and by the infinite power of the Most High, which, beyond these heavens of our heavens, has developed the framework of Its unlimited creation.

47. Actually, beyond these vast solitudes, worlds radiate in their magnificence as well as in the regions accessible to human investigations. Beyond these deserts, splendid oases sail in the limpid Aether, and incessantly renew the admirable scenes of existence and life. Here are the distant aggregates of cosmic substance, which the deep eye of the telescope glimpses through the transparent regions of our sky. These nebulae, which you call irresoluble, appear to you like light clouds of white dust lost in an unknown point of ethereal space. Therein new worlds are revealed and developed, the varied conditions of which are foreign to those which are inherent to your globe, and give them a life that your conceptions cannot imagine, nor your studies notice. It is here that the creative power shines forth in all its fullness; those who come from the regions occupied by your system would find out that other laws are in action, whose forces govern the manifestations of life; and the new paths found in these strange countries open unknown possibilities.

ETERNAL SUCCESSION OF WORLDS

48. We have seen that only one primordial and general law has been given to the whole universe to ensure its eternal stability, and that this general law is perceptible to our senses by several particular actions which we call the guiding forces of Nature. Now I am going to show that the harmony of the whole world, considered under the dual aspect of eternity and space, is ensured by this supreme law.

49. In fact, if we go back to the primitive origin of the primitive agglomerations of cosmic substance, we will notice that already, under the influence of this law, matter undergoes the necessary transformations which lead it from the germ to the ripe fruit, and that under the impulsion of the various forces born of this law, it traverses the scale of its periodic transformations, which is also the first fluidic center of its movements. These become generator of worlds, later a central and attracting nucleus of the spheres which have originated within it.

We already know that these laws preside over the history of Cosmos. What is important to know now is that they also preside over the destruction of the stars, for death is not only a metamorphosis of our life, but also a transformation of inanimate matter; and if it is true to say, in the literal sense, that life alone is accessible to the scythe of death, it is also no less true to state that matter must, in all necessity, undergo the transformations inherent in its constitution.

50.   Here is a world which, since its primitive cradle, has traversed the whole extent of the years which its special organization allowed it to traverse; the inner core of its existence has now extinguished, its proper elements have lost their original virtue; the phenomena of its nature which claimed for their production the presence and the action of the forces devolving upon this world, cannot be presented henceforth, because this lever of their activity no longer has the fulcrum which gave it all its strength.

Now, can it be thought that this dead and lifeless Earth will continue to gravitate into celestial spaces, aimlessly, and pass like useless ashes into the whirlwind of the skies? Can it be thought that she remains inscribed in the book of universal life when it is no more than dead letter, now meaningless? No; the same laws that elevated it above the dark chaos and rewarded it with the splendors of life; the same forces that governed it during the centuries of its adolescence; which strengthened its first steps in existence, and which have led it to maturity and old age, will preside over the disintegration of its constituent elements into the laboratory where creative power constantly draws upon conditions of general stability. It will return to this common mass of the Aether to assimilate itself to other bodies, or to regenerate other suns. Such death will not be a useless event to such world nor to its siblings: other regions of other creations of a different nature will be renovated by it; and where systems of worlds have vanished, they will soon be reborn as a new bed of flowers, so to speak, brighter and even more fragrant.

51.   Thus the real and effective eternity of the universe is assured by the same laws which direct the operations of time. Thus worlds succeed to worlds and suns succeed to suns, without the immense mechanism of the vast heavens ever being affected in its gigantic resources.

Where your eyes today admire splendid stars under the vault of the nights; where your spirit contemplates magnificent radiations which shine forth from places far away; for a long time the finger of death has extinguished all those splendors, long since emptiness has succeeded these dazzlements and received new creations still unknown to us. The immense distance of these stars which make the light they send us take thousands of years to reach us, makes us only today receive the rays they sent to us long before the creation of Earth, and left behind for us to admire them again for thousands of years after their actual disappearance.

What are six thousand years of historical humanity next to the immense age of the world? Perhaps seconds in uncountable centuries? What are your astronomical observations next to the absolute state of the world? A mere shadow eclipsed by the Sun.

52. So, here as in my other studies, let me acknowledge the fact that the Earth and human beings are relatively nothing in relation to what really is, and that the most colossal operations of our thought has advanced only an insignificant extent into the immensity and eternity of a universe without an end.

And when these periods of our immortality have passed over our heads; when the current history of Earth will appear to us like a vaporous shadow in the depths of our memory. And when we will have lived during countless centuries these various degrees of our cosmological hierarchy traversed by manifold peregrinations the most distant areas of future ages, will have been traversed by countless peregrinations, we will finally have before our eyes the unlimited succession of worlds and the stillness of eternity opening wide our perspective.

UNIVERSAL LIFE

53. This immortality of souls, of which the system of the physical world is the basis, has seemed to be imaginary in the eyes of certain prejudiced thinkers. They ironically described it as a wandering immortality, and did not understand that it was true only in light of the spectacle offered by creation. However, it is possible to make all of its greatness understood – I would say almost its entire perfection.

54. That the works of God are created for thought and under-standing; and that the worlds are dwellings of beings who contemplate them and discover under their veil the power and wisdom of the

One which formed them; is no longer a doubtful fact for us. But that all the souls that populate them are solidary with one another – this is what is important for us to know.

55. Indeed, human intelligence can scarcely fathom these radiant globes which sparkle in the expanse, like simple masses of inert and lifeless matter. It is difficult to imagine that there are, in these distant regions, magnificent twilights and splendid nights, fertile suns and days full of light, valleys and mountains, where the manifold productions of Nature have developed their luxurious diversity. One can scarcely imagine, I say, that such a divine spectacle in which a soul could thrive as it does in its own environment, is stripped of existence and forever deprived of thinking and any conscious life.

56. But to this eminently accurate idea of creation, we must add that of solidary humanity, wherein lies the mystery of future eternity.

One same human family has been created in the universality of worlds, and bonds of fraternity still unappreciated on your part have been given to these worlds. If these celestial bodies which harmonize in their vast systems are inhabited by intelligences, it is not by beings unknown to one another, but by beings marked on the brow by the same destiny, who must meet momentarily following their functions in life, and meet again according to their mutual sympathies. It is the great family of spirits which inhabit the celestial lands; it is the great radiance of the Divine Spirit which embraces the immense expanse of the heavens, and which remains as the original and final type of spiritual perfection.

57. By what strange aberration could one refuse to believe in immortality and the vast regions of the Aether, confining us to an unacceptable limit and an absolute duality? Is the true system of the universe not to have precedence over any dogmatic doctrine proclaimed either by science or theology? Will such doctrines go astray as long as their basis is purely metaphysical? The answer to this question is easy and shows us that the new philosophy will sit triumphant on the ruins of the old, because its foundations will be raised victoriously over the old errors.

SCIENCE

58. Human intelligence has elevated its powerful conceptions above the limits of space and time; it has penetrated the inaccessible domain of the ancient ages, probed the mystery of unfathomable skies, explained the enigma of creation. The exterior world has unfolded under the gaze of science its splendid panorama and magnificent opulence, and studies carried out by humans have elevated it to the knowledge of truth. It has explored the universe, found the expression of the laws which govern it and the application of the forces which support it; and if looking face to face at the root cause has not been given to it, at least it has arrived at the mathematical notion of the series of secondary causes.

In this last century especially, the experimental method – the only one that is truly scientific – has been put into practice in the natural sciences, and by its aid humans have successively stripped away the prejudices of the old school and its speculative theories to dedicate themselves instead to the field of observation, and cultivating it with care and intelligence.

Indeed, human science is solid and fruitful, worthy of our homage for its difficult and long-tested past, deserving our sympathy for a future full of useful and profitable discoveries. For Nature is henceforth a book accessible to the researches of studious individuals, a world open to the investigations of thinkers, a brilliant region which the human spirit has already visited, and in which they can now boldly advance, having experience as compass.

59. An old friend in my earthly lifetime spoke to me like that before. A peregrination had brought us back to Earth, and we were morally studying this world again. My companion added that humans are today familiar with the most abstract laws of mechanics, physics, chemistry; that the effects on industry are no less remarkable than the conclusions of pure science, and that the whole of creation, skilfully studied by human beings, seems to have become its royal appanage. And as we continued our journey out of this world, I replied to him in the following terms:

60. A feeble atom lost in an imperceptible point of the infinite, the human being believed to encompass the whole universal expanse within its vision. And when humans could scarcely contemplate the region they inhabit, they thought they were studying the laws of the whole Nature. When their appreciations had barely touched on the forces in action around them, they thought they were determining the greatness of heaven; and when they consumed themselves in the determination of a speck of dust, the field of their observations being so small that, once they lose sight of a fact, the spirit can hardly find it; the sky and the ground of humans being so small, that the soul, in its development, does not have the time to deploy its wings before having reached the last places accessible to observation.

The immeasurable universe surrounds us on all sides, deploying beyond our heavens unknown riches, putting into play unappreciated forces, developing modes of existence inconceivable for us, and propagating to infinity splendor and life.

As if the wretched mite, deprived of wings and light, whose sad existence is consumed on a leaf, which the day brought to it, would pretend, because of the few steps it took on this leaf agitated by the wind, to have the right to speak about the immense tree to which it belongs – a tree by whose shadow, which the leaf has scarcely been able to perceive, it would foolishly imagine that it could reason about the whole forest of which this tree is only a part, or wisely discuss the nature of the plants which develop there, and the beings that live in it away from the distant Sun, whose rays sometimes go down there, carrying movement and life. Likewise, humans would be strangely pretentious to wish to measure infinite greatness at the foot of their infinite littleness!

So one must be well aware of this idea: that if the arid labors of past centuries have acquired one's early knowledge of things; if the progress of the spirit has placed one in the vestibule of wisdom, one has not yet done more than spelling out the first page of the book. And that humans are, like children, susceptible to be in the wrong with every word, and, far from extending their doctoral work, must content themselves with studying it more humbly, page by page, line by line. Happy are those who still manage to do it this way.

MORAL CONSIDERATIONS

61. You have followed me on these celestial excursions, and we have visited the immense regions of space. Under our eyes, suns have succeeded to suns, systems to other systems, nebulae to nebulae. The splendid panorama of the harmony of the cosmos has unfolded before our feet, and we have received a foretaste of the idea of the infinite, which we will be able to fully comprehend only according to the extent our future perfectibility. The mysteries of the Aether have unveiled their enigma so far indecipherable, and we have conceived at least of the idea of the universality of things. It is important now to pause and ponder.

62. It is no doubt beautiful to have recognized the infinity of the Earth and, at the same time, its middling importance in the hierarchy of worlds. It is beautiful to have humbled the human arrogance which is so dear to us, and to be humbled before absolute greatness; but it will be even more beautiful to interpret in a moral sense the spectacle which we have witnessed. Now I wish to speak of the infinite power of Nature, and of the idea that we must make of its mode of action in the various reaches of the vast universe.

63. Accustomed as we are to judging things by our poor little abode, we imagine that Nature could or must have acted on the other worlds only according to the rules we have noticed here below. But it is precisely in this that it is important to rectify our judgment.

Take a moment's glance at any region of your globe and on any of the productions of your Nature. Do you not recognize the seal of infinite variety and the proof of unparalleled activity? Do you fail to see in the wing of a little bird of the Canaries, in the petal of a half-opened rosebud, the prodigious fertility of this beautiful Nature?

May your studies apply to beings that hover in the air; may they descend into the violet hues of the woods; let them plunge into the depths of the ocean, into everything and everywhere you read this universal truth: The all-powerful Nature acts according to places, times and circumstances; it is one in its general harmony, but manifold in its productions; it plays with the Sun like a drop of water; it brings to life an immense world with the same ease as it hatches the tiny egg laid by an autumn butterfly.

64. Now, if such is the variety that Nature has been able to display to us in all places on this small world, so narrow, so limited, how much bigger should our conception of this mode of action be, when thinking from the perspectives of vast worlds? How much more do we have to develop our perception until we can recognize the powerful extent of Nature by applying it to those wonderful worlds which, far more than the Earth, bear witness to its unknowable perfection?

Can you not see, then, around each of the suns in space, systems similar to your own planetary system? Do you not see on these supposed planets the three kingdoms of Nature that shine all around you? Yet bear in mind that, just as no human face is identical to another one in the entire human race, so a prodigious, truly unimaginable, diversity has been widespread in the ethereal abodes that sail in deep space.

Since our animated Nature begins with the zoophyte and ends with the human being; since the atmosphere feeds earthly life; since the liquid element renews it incessantly; and since your seasons are succeeded in this life by phenomena which divide them; this is no reason to conclude that the millions of millions of worlds which sail in the universal expanse are in any way similar to it. Actually, far from it, they differ according to the different conditions which have been devolved upon them, and vary according to their respective roles on the world stage: they are like variegated jewels from one immense mosaic, the diversified flowers of an admirable firmament.

Chapter VII
Geological sketch of the Earth

GEOLOGICAL PERIODS · PRIMEVAL STATE OF THE EARTH · PRIMEVAL PERIOD ·
TRANSITION PERIOD · SECONDARY PERIOD · TERTIARY PERIOD · DILUVIAL
PERIOD · POST-DILUVIAL OR CURRENT PERIOD · BIRTH OF THE HUMAN RACE

GEOLOGICAL PERIODS

1. The Earth bears in itself obvious traces of its formation. We
have been able to follow its phases with mathematical precision in
the different terrains that make up its framework. All of these studies
constitute a science called geology, born in the 19th century, which
shed light on the controversial question of its origin and that of the
living beings which inhabit it. Here there is no hypothesis; it is the
rigorous result of the observation of facts, and in presence of facts
doubt is not allowed. The history of the formation of the globe is
written in geological layers in a much more ascertained way than
in preconceived books, because it is Nature itself which speaks, uncovering and revealing itself, and not human imagination creating
systems. Where we see traces of fire, we can say with certainty that
fire has existed there; where we see vestiges of water, we can say
with no less certainty that water has once flew there; where we see
traces left by animals, we say that animals once lived in that place.

Geology is therefore a science of observation; it draws consequence
only from what it sees; on dubious points it will assert nothing,
emitting instead only arguable opinions, whose final solution awaits
more thorough observations. Without the discoveries of geology, as
without those of astronomy, the Genesis of the world would still lie
in the darkness of legends. Today, thanks to it, humans know the
story of their planet, and the scaffolding of fables that surrounded
its cradle has collapsed once and for all.

2. Wherever there are trenches, natural or man-made excava-
tions, we notice so-called *stratifications*, that is to say, superimposed

layers. Land that has this provision is referred to as a *stratified terrains*. These layers, of very variable thickness, from a few centimeters up to 100 meters and more, are distinguished by the color and the nature of the substances of which they are composed. Works of art, the drilling of wells, quarrying and especially mining have allowed to observe them in great depth.

3. The layers are generally homogeneous, that is, each is formed of the same substance, or various substances that have existed together, forming a compact whole. The line of separation which isolates them from each other is always clearly defined. As in the seated parts of a building, nowhere do we see them intermingle and lose themselves into one another at their respective limits, as it happens, for example, with the colors of the prism or the rainbow.

Because of these characteristics, we recognize that they have been formed successively, deposited one upon the other under different conditions and causes. The deepest ones were obviously formed first, and the most superficial ones later on. The last of all, the one on the surface, is the layer of topsoil that owes its properties to detritus of organic matter from plants and animals.

The lower layers, placed beneath the vegetal layer, have in geology the name of rocks, a word which, in this sense, does not always imply the idea of a stony substance, but signifies a bed or bench of any mineral substance. Some are made of sand, clay or loam, marl, or rolled pebbles. Others of stones proper, more or less hard, such as sandstones, marbles, chalk, limestones or lime, millstones, coals, bituminous pitch, etc. It is said that a rock is more or less strong depending on the degree of its thickness.

4. By the inspection of the nature of these rocks or layers, we can recognize through certain signs that some come from melted matter, sometimes vitrified by the action of fire. Other earthy substances were deposited by water; some of these substances have remained disintegrated like sands, while others, at first in a pasty state, under the action of certain chemical agents or other causes, have hardened and in the long run acquired the consistency of stone. Banks of stacked stones announce successive deposits. Fire and water have had their share of action in the formation of materials that make up the solid framework of our globe.

5. The normal position of earthy or stony layers from aqueous deposits is horizontal. When one sees these immense plains which sometimes extend as far as the eye can see, of perfect horizontality, united as if they had been leveled with a roller; or these bottoms of valleys as flat as the surface of a lake; one can be certain that, at a more or less remote period, these places had long been covered by still waters which, in retreating, have left dry the lands they had deposited during their stay. After the gradual retreating of the waters, these lands were covered with vegetation. If instead of greasy, silty, clayey or marly soils, suitable for assimilating the nutritive principles, the waters deposited only siliceous sands, without aggregation, we would have those sandy and arid plains which constitute certain terrains and the deserts. Deposits left by partial floods, and those which form the alluvium at the mouths of rivers, may give us an idea of this in smaller scale.

6. Although horizontal is the normal and most general position of aqueous formations, hard rocks are often found in relatively large areas in mountainous regions, whose nature indicates to have been formed by the waters in an inclined position and sometimes even in vertical position. Now, according to the laws of equilibrium of liquids and the laws of gravity, aqueous deposits can only be formed in horizontal planes, since those which take place on inclined planes are carried into the shallows by the currents and their own weight. Therefore, it remains evident that these deposits had to be raised by some force, after their solidification or transformation into stones.

From these considerations it can be concluded with certainty that all the stony layers from aqueous deposits in a perfectly horizontal position have been formed after centuries by still waters, and that whenever they have an inclined position, it is because the soil has been disturbed and dislocated later on by general or partial upheavals, on a more or less considerable scale.

7. A characteristic fact of the highest importance, by the irrefutable testimony it provides, consists in the fossil remains of animals and plants, which are found in innumerable quantities in different layers; and as these remains are found even in the hardest stones, we must conclude that the existence of these beings preceded the formation of these same stones. Now, if we consider the prodigious number of ages that it took for hardening and bring them to the state where they are from time immemorial, we arrive at this compulsory consequence, namely, that the emergence of organic beings on Earth is lost in the mists of time and is much earlier than the date assigned in Moses' Genesis.[31]

8.   Among these remains of plants and animals, there are some which have been penetrated in all parts of their substance, without their shape being altered, with siliceous or calcareous materials which have transformed them into stones, some of which have the hardness of marble. These are, properly speaking, personification. Others have been simply enveloped by matter in their state of softness: they are found intact, some in their entirety, within the hardest stones. Others have left only imprints, but with perfect sharpness and delicacy of details. In the interior of certain stones even footprints were found; and by the shape of the foot, toes and nails, the kind of animal from which they came from could be identified.

9.   Animal fossils can be hard to be understood. While it is easy to imagine them through solid and resistant parts, such as bones, scales, and horns – and sometimes there are complete skeletons – most often they are only detached parts, whose origin may nevertheless be relatively easy to recognize. While inspecting a jaw or a tooth, we see immediately if it belongs to a herbivorous or carnivorous animal. As all parts of the animal have a necessary correlation, the shape of the head, scapula, leg bone, foot, is sufficient to determine the size, the general shape, and the way of life of the animal.[32] Terrestrial animals

31 *Fossil*, from Latin *fossilia, fossilis*, derived from *fossa*, pit, and *fodere*, digging the earth. This word is said to represent, in geology, bodies or remains of organized bodies, coming from beings who lived before historical times. By extension, it is also said of mineral substances bearing traces of presence of organized beings, such as footprints of plants or animals.

The word *fossil*, of a more general meaning, has substituted for *petrification*, which applied only to bodies transformed into stone by the infiltration of siliceous matter or calcareous matter into the organic tissues. All petrifactions are necessarily fossils, although not all fossils are petrifactions

Objects that are covered with a stony layer, when immersed in certain waters laden with calcareous substances, are not petrifactions, but mere encrustations.

Monuments, inscriptions and objects of human manufacture belong to archeology..

32 Given the point up to which Georges Cuvier carried paleontology, a single bone is often sufficient to determine the genus, species, and form of an animal,

have an organization that does not allow them to be confused with aquatic animals. Fossil fish and shells are exceedingly numerous; the shells alone sometimes form whole benches of great thickness. Their nature is easily recognized whether as marine or freshwater animals.

10. Rolled pebbles, which in some places are powerful rocks, offer an unequivocal indication of their origin. They are rounded like the pebbles of the seashore, a sign of the friction they have undergone by the action of the waters. Regions where they are found buried in considerable masses have undoubtedly been occupied by the ocean, or by violent waters.

11. Terrains of various formations are further characterized by the very nature of the fossils they contain. The oldest contain animal and vegetal species that have entirely disappeared from the surface of the globe. Some newer species have also disappeared, but have retained their analogues which differ from their strains only in size and some aspects of form. Finally, others whose last representatives we see, are obviously bound to disappear in a more or less distant future, such as elephants, rhinos, hippopotamuses, etc. Thus, as the Earth's layers approach our times, animal and plant species are also closer to those that exist today.

Turbulences and cataclysms which have taken place on Earth since its origin, have changed its life conditions, thus making whole generations of living beings disappear.

12. By inquiring the nature of the geological strata, we know most positively whether, at the time of their formation, the terrain which encloses them was occupied by the sea, by lakes, or by forests and plains populated by terrestrial animals. If, then, in the same terrain, we find a series of superimposed layers, alternately containing marine, terrestrial and freshwater fossils, several times repeated, this is irrefutable proof that this same terrain has been invaded several times by the sea, covered with lakes and dried off.

And certainly how many centuries, perhaps thousands of centuries, has each period taken to fulfill itself! What powerful force was required to move and relocate the ocean, and lift whole mountains! How many physical transformations and violent turbulences did the Earth have to undergo before becoming what we have seen

---

together with its habits; and to reconstruct it entirely.

since historical times! And yet, some would like to believe that such work took less time to be accomplished than it takes to grow a single plant!

13. The study of geological strata attests, as has been said, to successive formations, which have changed the aspect of the globe, and divide its history into several epochs. These epochs constitute what are called *geological periods*, the knowledge of which is essential for the establishment of Genesis. There are six major periods that are referred to as primeval, transition, secondary, tertiary, diluvial, and post-diluvial or current periods. The lands formed during the duration of each period are also called: primeval, transition, secondary terrains, and so on. It is said that this or that layer or rock, this or that fossil, are found in terrains of such and such period.

14. It is essential to note that the number of these periods is not absolute and depends on classification systems. The six main ones as mentioned above are understood to mean only those which are marked by a perceptible and general change in the state of the globe. However, observations have proved that several successive formations have been made during the time span of each, which is why they are divided into sub-periods characterized by the nature of the terrain, and which bring the number of general formations up to twenty-six, well characterized ones, not counting those resulting from changes due to purely local causes.

PRIMEVAL STATE OF THE EARTH

15. The flattening of the poles and other conclusive facts are sure signs that the Earth must have been, in its origin, in a state of fluidity or softness. This condition could be caused by matter being liquefied by fire, or waterlogged.

It is said proverbially, "There is no smoke without fire." This rigorously true proposition is an application of the principle: There is no effect without a cause. By the same reason we can say: There is no fire without a source. Now, by the facts that take place before our eyes, it is not only smoke that is produced, but a real fire which must have a source. Since this fire comes from within the Earth and not from above, the source must be interior; the fire being permanent, its source must be it as well.

The heat which increases as one enters the interior of the Earth; and which, at a certain distance from the surface, reaches a very high temperature; thermal springs all the warmer because they come from a greater depth; the fires and masses of molten and glowing matter escaping from volcanoes, as if by vast vents, or by crevasses produced in certain earthquakes, can leave no doubt as to the existence of a fiery core.

16. Experience shows that the temperature rises one degree every thirty meters deep; from which it follows that at a depth of 300 meters the increase will be 10 degrees; at 3,000 meters; and 100 degrees, the temperature of boiling water. At 30,000 meters, or about 25 miles; rising to 1,000 degrees; and over 3,300 degrees at about 86 miles deep, at which temperature no known material is resistant to melting. From there to the center of the Earth there is still a distance of more than 4,800 miles, with a diameter of about 9,700 miles, which would be occupied by molten matter.

Although this is only a conjecture, in judging the cause by the effect, it has all the characteristics of probability, and we arrive at this conclusion, that the Earth is still an incandescent mass covered with a solid crust not more than 86 miles thick, which is hardly the 120th part of its diameter. Proportionally it would be much less than the thickness of the thinnest orange peel.

Moreover, the thickness of the Earth's crust varies widely, because there are regions, especially in volcanic soils, where the heat and the flexibility of the soil indicate that it is very thin. The high temperature of thermal waters also indicates the vicinity of the central fire.

17. From this it is evident that the primeval state of fluidity or softness of the Earth must have been caused by the action of heat, and not of water. The Earth was therefore, at its origin, an incandescent mass. As a result of the radiation of the caloric,[33] all the molten matter has gradually cooled, and the cooling has naturally begun by the surface which has hardened, while the interior has remained fluid. It is thus possible to compare the Earth with a block of charcoal coming out of a furnace, whose surface is extinguished and cooled in contact with the air, whereas, if it is broken, the core is still glowing.

33 [Trans. note] Up to the 19th century, *caloric* was the name given to a hypothetical fluid substance that was thought to be responsible for the phenomena of heat.

18. At the time when the Earth was an incandescent mass, it did not contain an atom more or less than today; except that, under the influence of high temperatures, most of the substances which compose it, and which we see in the form of liquids or solids, earths, stones, metals, and crystals, were in quite a different state. They only underwent a transformation. As a result of cooling and mixing, the elements formed new combinations. The air, considerably dilated, was to extend at an immeasurable distance; all the water, necessarily reduced to vapor, was mixed with the air; all the substances liable to volatilize, such as metals, sulfur, and carbon, were there in the state of gas. The state of the atmosphere at that time had nothing to compare it with what it is today; the density of all these vapors gave it an opacity which could not be traversed by any ray of the Sun. If a living being could have existed on the surface of the globe at that time, it would have been illuminated only by the sinister brilliancy of the furnace placed under its feet and the burning atmosphere.

19. The first effect of the cooling was to solidify the outer surface of the molten mass, and to form a resistant crust, which, thin at first, then thickened slightly. This crust constitutes the stone known as *granite*, of extreme hardness, so called from its granular aspect. Three main substances are found there, namely, feldspar, quartz or rock crystal, and mica – the latter having metallic brilliance, although it is not a metal.

The granite layer is therefore the first that has formed on the globe which it envelops in its entirety, and of which it constitutes in a way the bone structure, It is the direct product of the consolidated molten material. It was on it, and in the cavities presented by its tormented surface, that the layers of the other terrains formed later were successively deposited. What distinguishes it from these is the absence of any stratification, that is to say, it forms a compact and uniform mass throughout its thickness, not arranged in layers. The effervescence of the incandescent matter was destined to produce numerous deep crevices through which such matter flowed.

20. The second effect of the cooling was to liquefy some of the substances contained in the air which were in a state of vapor, and which then precipitated over the surface of the soil. Rains and lakes of sulfur and bitumen came after that, veritable brooks of iron, lead, and other molten metals, seeping into the fissures, and which now constitute the veins and seams of metal.

Under the influence of various agents, the granitic surface experienced alternating decompositions; blends were formed which formed the primitive so-called lands, distinct from the granitic rock, but in confused masses, and without regular stratifications.

Then came the waters which, falling on a scorching ground, vaporized again, fell again in torrential rains, and so on, until the temperature allowed them to remain on the ground in liquid state.

It is with the formation of granitic soils that the series of geological periods begins. To the six main periods, it would be advisable to add that of the primeval state of incandescence of the globe.

21.   This was the aspect of this first period, a veritable chaos of all the elements combined, seeking their place, where no living being could exist. Also, one of its distinctive characteristics of its geology is the absence of any trace of plant and animal life.

It is impossible to assign a fixed duration to this first period, nor to the following one; yet, according to the time required for a ball of a certain volume, heated to red heat, then cooled down enough for a drop of water to remain in the liquid state on its surface, it can be calculated that if this ball had the size of the Earth, the cooling would take more than a million years.

TRANSITION PERIOD

20.   ([34]) At the beginning of the transition period, the granitic solid crust was still of little thickness and offered only a slight resistance to the effervescence of the burning materials which it covered and compressed. There was blistering and many cracks through which the inner lava flowed. The soil presented only slight relief inequalities.

Shallow waters covered almost the entire surface of the globe, with the exception of the raised parts forming terrains that were frequently submerged.

---

34 [Trans. note] This inconsistency in item numbering (number **20** where **22** was expected), found in all four editions of A. KARDEC's *Genesis* of the 1868 original, was preserved in this translation for consistency with that historical edition.

The air had gradually been drained of the heavier matter, which was momentarily in a gaseous state, and which, condensing by the cooling action, was precipitated onto the surface of the ground, and then driven and dissolved by the water.

When we speak of cooling at that time, we must understand this word in a relative sense, that is, in relation to the primeval state, for the temperature must still have been hot.

Thick aqueous vapors rising from all over the vast liquid surface, fell in heavy, hot rains, obscuring the air. However, the rays of the sun were beginning to appear through this murky atmosphere.

One of the last substances whose air must have been purged, because it is naturally found in the gaseous state, is carbonic acid which then formed one of its constituent parts.

21.   ([35]) At this time the layers of sedimentary ground began to form, deposited by the waters laden with silt and various materials peculiar to organic life.

Then the first living beings of the vegetal and animal kingdoms appeared. At first in small numbers, we find traces of them more and more frequently as we go up in the layers of this formation. It is remarkable that everywhere life manifests itself as soon as conditions are propitious to it; and that each species is born as soon as the conditions peculiar to its existence occur. It seems that the germs of life were latent and only waiting for favorable conditions to hatch.

22.   The first organic organisms to have appeared on Earth are plants of the least complicated organization, designated in botanical terms by the names of cryptogams, acotyledons, and monocotyledons; or, in other words, lichens, mushrooms, mosses, ferns, and herbaceous plants. We do not yet see trees with woody stems, but those of the palm-like genus whose spongy stem is analogous to that of grasses.

The animals of this period, which came after the first plants, are exclusively marine. They are, first of all, polyparia, radiata and zoophytes; that is, animals whose simple and, as it were, rudimentary organization, comes closest to plants. Later come crustaceans and fish whose species no longer exist today.

---

35 [Trans. note] See footnote 34 above.

23.   Under the influence of heat and humidity, and as a consequence of the excess of carbonic acid diffused in the air – a gas unfit for the respiration of terrestrial animals, but necessary for plants – the open fields are quickly covered with exuberant vegetation at the same time as aquatic plants multiplied in the swamps. Plants of the kind which, in our day, are mere grasses of a few inches, reached a prodigious height and size at that time. Thus, there were forests of tree ferns eight to ten meters high, and of adequate size; lycopods (i.e., wolf's foot, a type of moss) of the same size; horsetails[36] four to five meters long, which barely reach one meter today. At the end of this period some trees of the coniferous type, or pines, begin to appear.

24.   As a result of the displacement of waters, the soils which produced these masses of vegetation were repeatedly submerged, covered with new earthy sediments, while those which were dried up were in turn adorned with similar vegetation. Thus there were several generations of plants alternately annihilated and renewed. It was not the same with animals, which, being all aquatic, could hardly suffer from these alternatives.

These debris, accumulated during a long series of centuries, formed layers of great thickness. Under the action of heat and moisture, the pressure exerted by later earth deposits, and undoubtedly also by various chemical agents, gases, acids and salts produced by the combination of primitive elements, these vegetal materials underwent fermentation which converted them into coal. Coal mines are therefore the direct product of the decomposition of accumulated clumps of vegetation during the transition period. That is why we find them in almost every country.[37]

25.   The fossil remains of the powerful vegetation of this period being nowadays under the ice of the polar lands as well as in the torrid zone, it was necessary to conclude that, since the vegetation was uniform, the temperature should be too. The poles were not covered with ice like now. It was because the Earth was drawing its heat from itself, from the central fire, which warmed in an equal manner

---

36 Popular name of a flowerless plant of the *Equisetum* genus.

37 Peat was formed in the same manner, by the decomposition of heaps of vegetation in marshy ground, but with this difference, that being much more recent, and undoubtedly in other conditions, it did not have time to char.

all the solid layer still not very thick. This heat was much greater than that which could be given by the solar rays, which moreover would have been weakened by the density of the atmosphere. Only later, when the central heat could exert on the outer surface of the globe only a weak action or no action at all, did the heat of the sun become preponderant, and the polar regions receiving only oblique rays giving very little heat, were covered in ice. We understand that at the time we are talking about, and still for a long time after that, ice was unknown on Earth.

This period must have been very long, judging by the number and thickness of the coal beds.[38]

SECONDARY PERIOD

26. With the transition period the colossal vegetation disappeared, and so did the animals that characterized that epoch, either because the weather was no longer the same, or because of a series of cataclysms which destroyed everything that was alive on Earth. It is likely that both causes contributed to this change, because on the one hand the study of the lands marking the end of this period attests to great upheavals caused by the turbulences and eruptions which poured on the ground large quantities of lava; and on the other hand, notable changes took place in Nature's three kingdoms.

27. The secondary period is characterized, in the mineral realm, by numerous and powerful layers which attest to a slow formation within the waters, and mark different well-defined periods.

The vegetation is slower to grow and less colossal than in the previous period, probably as a result of the decrease in heat and humidity, and changes in the constituent elements of the atmosphere. Herbaceous and pulpy plants were joined by woody stems and the first trees, properly speaking.

---

38 In the Bay of Fundy, Nova Scotia, Sir Charles Lyell found, on a thickness of 400 meters of coal, 68 different levels, showing obvious traces of several soils of forests whose tree trunks still had their roots. (L. Figuier)

Assuming a thousand years for the formation of each of these levels, it would already have taken 68,000 years for this single coal layer to form.

28. Animals are still aquatic, or at most amphibious; animal life on Earth makes little progress. A prodigious quantity of shelled animals develop in the seas as a result of the formation of calcareous matter; new fish, of a more perfected organization than in the preceding period, are born; the first cetaceans appear. The most characteristic animals of this period are the monstrous reptiles among which the following should be highlighted:

Ichthyosaur – A species of fish-lizard that was up to ten meters long, and whose wonderfully elongated jaws were armed with one hundred and eighty teeth. Its general shape is somewhat reminiscent of that of the crocodile, but without a scaly armor; its eyes had the volume of a human head; it had fins like a whale, and it discharged water through vents like whales.

Plesiosaur – Another marine reptile, as large as the ichthyosaur, whose excessively long neck fell back like that of a swan, and gave it the appearance of an enormous serpent attached to a turtle's body. It had the head of a lizard and the teeth of a crocodile; its skin must have been smooth like that of the preceding one, for no trace of scales or carapace was found.[39]

Teleosaur – Closer to current crocodiles, which appear to be its smaller cousins. Like the latter, it had a scaly cuirass, and lived both in water and on land. It measured about ten meters, of which three or four for the head alone; its huge mouth being two meters wide.

Megalosaur – A large lizard, a kind of crocodile 14 to 15 meters long, essentially carnivorous, feeding on reptiles, small crocodiles and turtles.

Its formidable jaw was armed with teeth in the shape of a double-edged pruning blade, bent backwards, so that once the prey entered, it was impossible for it to disengage.

Iguanodon – The largest of the lizards[40] that have appeared on the Earth; it was 20 to 25 meters from head to tail. Its muzzle was surmounted by a bone horn similar to that of the modern iguana from which it appears to differ only in size, the latter being barely one meter long. The shape of its teeth proves that it was herbivorous, and that of its feet that it was a terrestrial animal.

---

39 The first fossil of this animal was discovered in 1823.

40 [Trans. note] The author frequently uses the term lizard instead of dinosaur.

Pterodactyl – A bizarre animal the size of a swan, having character-istics both of a reptile by its body, and bird by its head, and the bat by the fleshy membrane which connected its fingers of a prodigious length and served as a parachute when it rushed upon its prey from the top of a tree or a rock. It had no horny beak like the birds, but the bones of its jaws, as long as half its body and lined with teeth, ended in a point like a bill.

29. During this period, which must have been very long, as attested by the number and importance of its geological strata, animal life took an immense development in the waters, as the vegetation had done in the preceding period. A purer and more breathable air begins to allow some animals to live upon earth. The sea has been displaced several times, but seemingly without violent jarring. With this period, those species of gigantic aquatic animals disappeared in their turn, replaced later by analogous species, less disproportionate in their forms, and infinitely smaller in size.

30. Pride has made humans say that all animals were created for themselves and for their needs. But what is the number of those who serve humans directly, which the latter have been able to subjugate, compared to the incalculable number of those with which they have never had and will never have any contact or relation? How to sustain such a thesis in presence of those innumerable species which alone populated the Earth thousands and thousands of centuries before humans came into existence, and which have since disappeared? Can we say that they were created for our benefit? However, these species all had their reason for being, their utility. God would not create them by a caprice of Its will, and then give Itself the pleasure of annihilating them; for all those species had life, instincts, and feelings of pain and well-being. For what purpose did God do it? This goal must have been supremely wise, although we do not un-derstand it yet. Perhaps one day it will be given to humans to know it and thus confound their pride; yet, in the meantime, how many ideas will grow in presence of these new horizons in which humans are now allowed to plunge their gaze, and unfold before them the imposing spectacle of this creation, so majestic in its slowness, so admirable in its foresight, so punctual, so precise and so invariable in its results.

TERTIARY PERIOD

31.   With the tertiary period begins a new order of things for the Earth. The state of its surface changes completely; life conditions are profoundly modified and approach the current state. The early days of this period are signaled by a halt in plant and animal production; everything bears the marks of an almost general destruction of living beings. Then new species appear successively whose organization is better adapted to the nature of the environment in which they are called to live.

32.   During the preceding periods, because of its small thickness, the solid crust of the globe presented, as said above, a rather weak resistance to the action of the internal fire. This envelope, easily torn apart, allowed molten materials to freely expand to the surface of the ground. It was not the same when the crust had acquired a certain thickness; the burning materials compressed on all sides, like boiling water in a closed container, and ended up by bursting in a sort of explosion. The granite mass violently broken on a multitude of points, was furrowed with cracks like a *cracked vase*. *Along these crevasses* the solid crust raised upright, forming peaks, mountain ranges and their ramifications. Parts of the envelope that were not torn apart were simply raised, while at other points there was heaving and excavating.

The ground surface then became very unequal; the waters, which up to that time covered it in an almost uniform manner over most of its range, were pushed back into the lowest parts, leaving vast continents or mountain tops dry and isolated, which formed islands.

This is the great phenomenon that has taken place in the tertiary period, transforming the appearance of the globe. It did not happen instantly or simultaneously on all points, but successively and at more or less distant epochs.

33.   One of the first consequences of these turbulences has been, as said above, the inclination of the primitively horizontal sediment layers, which have remained in this position wherever the soil has not been upset. It is therefore on the flanks and in the vicinity of mountains that these inclinations are most pronounced.

34. In terrains where the layers of sediment have preserved their horizontality, it is necessary to cross all the others in order to reach those of the first formation, often to a considerable depth at the end of which one inevitably finds granitic rock. But when these layers were raised in mountains, they were raised above their normal level, and sometimes at very great height, so that if one makes a vertical trench on the side of these mountains, they are consistent throughout their thickness, and superimposed as the foundations of a building.

Thus, at great elevations, there are considerable banks of shells originally formed at the bottom of the seas. It is perfectly recognized today that at no time has the sea reached such a height, for all the water that exist on Earth would not be enough, even if their volume was a hundred times bigger. We should therefore assume that the total amount of water has decreased; and then we would wonder what has become of the missing portion. Turbulences that are today an indisputable fact demonstrated by science, explain in a logical and rigorous way the marine deposits that we encounter on certain mountains. These lands have obviously been submerged for a long succession of centuries, but at their original level and not at the place they occupy today.

It is absolutely as if a portion of the bottom of a lake were raised twenty-five or thirty meters above the surface of the water; the summit of this elevation would carry the remains of the plants and animals that once lay at the bottom of the water, which would in no way imply that the waters of the lake were raised to this height.

35. In places where the rising of the original rock has produced a complete tearing of the ground, either due to its rapidity, or shape, height and volume of the lifted mass, the granite has been exposed *like a tooth piercing the gum.* The layers that covered them, raised, broken, straightened, were exposed; it is thus that lands belonging to the oldest formations, and which were in their primitive position at great depths, now form the soil of certain regions.

36. The granite mass, dislocated by the effect of turbulences, has left in some places cracks through which the internal fire escapes and molten matter flows: it is the volcanoes. Volcanoes are like the chimneys of an immense furnace, or better still, they are relief valves which, by giving a solution to the overflow of igneous matter, prevent much more formidable shocks; hence it can be said that the number of active volcanoes is *like a safety valve* for the whole surface of the globe.

One can get an idea of the intensity of this fire, by remembering that volcanoes open in the very heart of the sea, and that the mass of water that covers and penetrates them is not enough to extinguish them.

37. These upheavings of the solid mass necessarily displaced the waters, which were pushed back into the hollow parts, which became deeper by the rising of emerged rocks, and by depressions. But these same lowlands, raised in their turn, sometimes in one place, sometimes in another, driving the waters, which flowed elsewhere, and so on, until they could take a more stable resting place.

Successive displacements of this liquid mass inevitably plowed and altered the surface of the soil. The waters, as they flowed, carried part of former formations exposed by the upheavals, and denuded certain mountains which were covered with them, also exposing their granitic or calcareous base. Deep valleys were dug while others were filled.

Therefore there are mountains formed directly by the action of the central fire;. These are mainly granite mountains, whereas others are due to the action of the waters, which, by carrying along loose earth and soluble matter, dug valleys around a resistant base, calcareous or made of other material.

Substances carried along by the water stream formed the layers of the tertiary period, which are easily distinguished from the preceding ones, less by their composition, which is nearly the same, than by their arrangement.

The layers of the primeval, transition, and secondary periods, formed on a rough surface, are nearly uniform throughout the Earth. Those of the tertiary period, on the contrary, formed on a very uneven base, and by the carrying action of waters, have a more local character. Everywhere, by digging to a certain depth, one finds all the previous layers, in the order of their formation, while one does not find everywhere tertiary soil, nor all the layers that formed it.

38.   During the Earth upheavings that took place at the beginning of this period, it is understandable that organic life had to undergo a downtime, which is recognized by the inspection of certain terrains of fossils. But as soon as a calmer state came, plants and animals reappeared. With life conditions now changed, and the atmosphere becoming more refined, new species of a more perfect organization were formed. Plants, in terms of their structure, differ little from those of today.

39.   During the two preceding periods, land not covered by water was of little extent, and was still marshy and frequently submerged. That is why it had only aquatic or amphibious animals. The tertiary period, which has seen the formation of vast continents, is characterized by the emergence of terrestrial animals.

Just as the transition period saw the birth of a colossal vegetation, the secondary period saw that of monstrous reptiles, gigantic mammals such as the elephant, the rhinoceros, the hippopotamus, the palaeotherium, the megatherium, the deinotherium, the mastodon, the mammoth, etc. It has also seen the birth of birds, as well as most species that still live today. Some of the species of this period survived later cataclysms; others, which are designated by the generic qualification of antediluvial animals, have completely disappeared, or have been replaced by analogous species, of less heavy and less massive forms, of which the first types have been like sketches, such as the *felis spelaea* (or *panthera spelaea*), a carnivorous animal the size of a bull, having the anatomical traits of the tiger and the lion; the *cervus megaceros*, a variety of deer, whose antlers, three meters in length, were spaced from three to four meters at their extremities.

40.   For a long time it was supposed that the monkey and the various varieties of quadrumanous primates, animals which come closest to humans in physical conformation, did not yet exist; but recent discoveries seem to leave no doubt about the presence of these animals, at least toward the end of the period.

DILUVIAL PERIOD

41.   This period is marked by one of the greatest cataclysms that has upset the globe, again changing the appearance of its surface, and destroyed without return an entire host of living species of which we find only remains. Everywhere it left traces that attest to its global reach. The waters, violently driven from their beds, invaded the continents, carrying with them the lands and the rocks, denuding the mountains, uprooting the old forests. The new deposits they have thus formed are designated in geology as *diluvial soils* (flood formations).

42. One of the most significant traces of this huge catastrophe are rocks called *erratic blocks*. Granitic rocks, which are isolated in the plains, rest on tertiary soils and in the midst of the torrential ground, sometimes several hundred miles from the mountains from where they were torn. It is evident that they could not be transported over so large distances by other means but the violence of currents.[41]

43. A fact no less characteristic, and of which we cannot yet explain the cause, is that it is in diluvial soils that we find the first *aerolites*;[42] it was only then that they began to fall on Earth. The cause that produced them did not exist previously.

44. It is around this time that the poles begin to be covered in ice, and that the glaciers of the mountains are formed, which indicates a noticeable change in the temperature of the globe. This change must have been sudden, for if animals such as elephants, which today live only in hot climates and which are found in such large numbers in the fossil polar lands, would have had time to gradually withdraw to more temperate regions. Everything proves, on the contrary, that they must have been seized abruptly by a great cold and enveloped by ice.

45. Therefore this was the true universal deluge. Opinions are divided as to the causes which may have produced it, but whatever the cause, the fact remains that it did happen.

It is quite generally supposed that a *sudden* change took place in the position of the axis of the Earth, in consequence of which the poles have been displaced. Hence a general projection of waters surging

---

41 Judging by its composition, it is obviously one of these blocks, from the mountains of Norway, that has served as a pedestal for the statue of Peter the Great in St. Petersburg.

42 A stony meteorite.

on the surface. If this change had been slow, the waters would have shifted gradually, without disturbance, whereas everything indicated a violent and sudden upheaving. Due to our current ignorance of the true cause, we can only make hypotheses.

The sudden displacement of the waters may also have been occasioned by the rising of certain parts of the solid crust and the formation of new mountains within the seas, as recorded at the beginning of the tertiary period. Yet, besides that, this cataclysm would not have been general, it would not explain the sudden change in the temperature of the poles.

46. In the turmoil caused by the upheaving of waters, many animals perished; others, to escape the flood, have retreated to heights, into caves and crevasses, where they perished in mass, either by hunger or by devouring each other, or perhaps by the irruption of the waters into places where they had taken refuge, and from which they had not been able to escape. This explains the great quantity of bones of various animals, carnivorous and others, which are found pell-mell in certain caves, called for this reason *bony caverns*. They are most often found under stalagmites. In some of them the bones would seem to have been carried along by water currents.[43]

POST-DILUVIAL OR CURRENT PERIOD ·
BIRTH OF THE HUMAN RACE

47. Once balance was restored to the surface of the globe, animal and vegetal life has promptly resumed its course. Firm ground had taken a more stable consistency; the more refined air suited more delicate organs. The Sun, shining in all its splendor through a limpid atmosphere, diffused with its light, a less suffocating and more invigorating heat than that of Earth's interior furnace. The land was inhabited by less savage and more sociable animals; more succulent plants offered a less coarse diet; and finally, all was prepared on Earth for the new host who was to populate it. It was then that

---

43 A great number of similar caves are known, some of which have a considerable extent. There are some in Mexico which measure several miles; and that of Edelsberg in Carniola (Austria) is about nine miles long. One of the most remarkable is that of Gaillenreuth, in Württemberg (Germany). There are several others in France, England, Germany, Sicily, and other parts of Europe.

human beings came into existence, the last beings of creation, the ones whose intelligence would henceforth contribute to general progress, while itself evolving.

48. Have humans really existed on Earth since the diluvial period, or did they appear before that time? This question is very controversial today, but its solution, whatever it may be, is only of secondary importance, because it would not change "the whole ensemble of established facts.

What made us think that the emergence of humans is posterior to the flood is that no authentic trace of their existence had been found during the previous period. The bones discovered in various places, which made believe in the existence of an alleged race of antediluvian giants, have lately been identified as elephant bones.

There is no doubt that humans did not exist in the primeval period, in the transition period, or in the secondary period, not only because vestiges or remains of their presence were nowhere to be found, but mainly because life conditions for their existence were not present. If humans appeared in the tertiary period, it could only have happened toward the end, and even so it must have been scarce; otherwise, since we find the most delicate remains of so many animals that lived at that time, it would be difficult to admit that humans had left no indication of their presence, either by bodily remains or by any work.

Moreover, the diluvial period, besides being short, did not bring any notable changes in climatic and atmospheric conditions; animals and plants were also the same before and after. There is no material impossibility, therefore, that the emergence of human beings preceded this great cataclysm. The presence of monkeys at this time adds to the probability of the fact that recent discoveries seem to confirm.[44]

Be that as it may, whether or not humans appeared before the great universal flood, it is certain that their humanitarian role did not begin to take shape until the post-diluvial period. We can therefore consider it as characterized by human presence.

---

44 See the writings of French archaeologist Jacques Boucher de Crèvecœur de PERTHES.

Chapter VIII
Theories of Earth history

THE PROJECTION THEORY · THE CONDENSATION THEORY ·
THE INCRUSTATION THEORY

THE PROJECTION THEORY

1. Of all the theories concerning the origin of the Earth, the one that has had the most credit in the 18th and 19th centuries is that of Georges-Louis Leclerc, Comte de Buffon, either because of his position in scholarly circles, or because nobody was better informed at that time.

Seeing that all the planets move in the same direction, from west to east, and on the same plane; and traverse orbits whose inclination does not exceed seven degrees and a half; Buffon concluded from such uniformity that they had to be set in motion by one same cause.

According to him, because the Sun is an incandescent mass in fusion, he supposed that a comet having struck it obliquely, while shaving its surface, had detached a portion which, projected into space by the violence of the shock, was divided into several fragments. These fragments formed the planets which have continued to move circularly by the combination of centripetal and centrifugal forces, following the direction of the original shock, that is, on the plane of the ecliptic.

The planets would thus be parts of the Sun's incandescent substance, and would therefore have been incandescent in their origin. They began to cool down and consolidate in a time proportional to their volume; and when the temperature allowed it, life was born on their surface.

As a result of the gradual lowering of the core heat, the Earth would arrive, in a given time, at a complete state of cooling. The liquid mass would be entirely frozen, and the air, more and more condensed, would eventually disappear. The lowering of the temperature, rendering life impossible, would bring about the reduction and the disappearance of all organized beings. The cooling, which began with the poles, would successively gain all the lands up to the equator.

Such, according to Buffon, is the current state of the Moon, which, smaller than the Earth, would be today an extinct world, from which life is henceforth excluded. The Sun itself would one day have the same fate. According to his calculation, the Earth would have taken about 74,000 years to reach its present temperature, and in 93,000 years it would see the end of existence of organized nature.

2. Buffon's theory, contradicted by new discoveries of science, is today almost completely abandoned for the following reasons:

1ST) For a long time it was believed that comets were solid bodies whose encounter with a planet could bring about the destruction of such planet. In this hypothesis, Bulfon's supposition was not improbable. But it is now known that they are formed of condensed gaseous matter, which is rarefied enough, however, to allow stars of less magnitude to be visible through their nucleus.. In this state, offering less resistance than the Sun, a violent shock capable of throwing off a portion of its mass would be impossible,

2ND) The incandescent nature of the Sun is also a hypothesis which nothing has so far confirmed, and which, on the contrary, seems to be refuted. Although we have not yet fully established its nature, the improved means of observation available today have made it possible to study it better. It is now generally accepted by science that the Sun is a globe composed of solid matter, surrounded by a luminous atmosphere which is not in contact with its surface.[45]

3RD) In Buffon's time, only the six planets registered by the ancients were known: Mercury, Venus, Earth, Mars, Jupiter and Saturn. Since then, a large number have been discovered, three of which, mainly Juno, Ceres, and Pallas,[46] have their inclined orbits

---

45 A complete and modern dissertation on the nature of the sun and comets can be found in *Études et Lectures sur l'Astronomie* [*Studies and Readings on Astronomy*] by Camille FLAMMARION.

46 [Trans. note] Later debunked as being mere fragments, etc. They were believed to be planets in the 19th century

of 13, 10 and 34 degrees, which does not agree with the hypothesis of a single projection movement.

4TH) Buffon's calculations on cooling have been found completely inaccurate since the discovery of the law of heat reduction by Joseph Fourier. It is not 74,000 years that the Earth has taken to reach its present temperature, but millions of years.

5TH) Buffon considered only the core heat of the globe, without taking into account that of the solar rays. Nowadays it is recognized by means of scientifically accurate data, based on experiments, that because of the thickness of the Earth's crust, the internal heat of the globe was for a long time only an insignificant part of the temperature of the outer surface. The variations which our atmosphere undergoes are periodic and due to the preponderating action of solar heat (see chapter **VII**, item **25** above). Since the effect of this cause is permanent, that of the core heat is nil or almost none. The latter's reduction cannot cause any significant modifications in the surface of the Earth. To render the Earth uninhabitable by general cooling, it would be necessary to extinguish the Sun.[47]

THE CONDENSATION THEORY

3.   The theory of Earth's formation by the condensation of cosmic matter is the one prevailing today in science, as being the one best justified by observation, and which solves the greatest number of difficulties, besides supporting, more than all the others, the great principle of universal unity. It is the one described above, in chapter **VI**, "General uranography."

These two theories, as we cam see, lead to the same result: the primeval state of incandescence of the globe, the formation of a solid crust by cooling, the existence of the core fire, and the appearance of organic life as soon as temperatures make it possible. They differ in the way they conceive of the formation of the Earth, and it is probable that if Buffon had lived today, he would have had different ideas. These are two different paths leading to the same goal.

---

47 For more details on this subject, and for the law of heat reduction, see *Lettres sur les Révolutions du Globe* [*Letters on the Transformations of the globe*] by Alexandre BERTRAND, pp. 19 and 307.

Geology takes Earth to a point where direct observation is possible. Its previous state having escaped experimentation could only be conjectural. Now, between these two hypotheses, common sense says that we must choose the one corroborated by logic and which best accords with the observed facts.

THE INCRUSTATION THEORY

4. We are mentioning this theory only for the sake of remembrance, since it is not scientific; in fact, only because it has had some influence in recent times, and has seduced a few people. It is summarized in the following letter:

"God, according to the Bible, created the world in six days, four thousand years before the Christian era. This is what geologists are challenging by the study of fossils and the thousands of undeniable characters of antiquity that show the origin of the Earth going back millions of years ago, and yet the Scripture has told the truth and geologists as well – and it is a simple peasant[48] that make them agree by telling us that Earth is a very recently *incrustated* planet, composed of very ancient materials."

"After the removal of the *unknown planet*, mature or in harmony with the one that existed in the place we occupy today, the soul of the Earth was ordered to gather its satellites to form our present globe according to the rules of progress in everything and for everything. Only four of these celestial objects consented to the association proposed to them; the Moon alone persisted in its autonomy, because globes also have their free will. To carry out this fusion, the soul of the Earth directed toward the satellites an attracting magnetic ray that put all their vegetal, animal and human contingents in a cataleptic state, and then brought them to the new environment. This operation was witnessed only by the Earth and the great heavenly messengers who helped it in this great work, opening these globes to put their entrails together. Once the welding was done, the waters flowed into the voids left by the absence of the Moon. Atmospheres were mingled, and the awakening or resurrection of the *germs in cataleptic state* began. Humans were finally drawn from their hypnotic state, and found themselves surrounded by the luxuriant vegetation

---

48 Michel of Figagnères (Var), author of *La Clef de la Vie* [*The Key of Life*].

of the earthly paradise and animals that grazed peacefully around them. All this could be done in six days with workers as powerful as those whom God had charged with this task. Planet *Asia* brought us the yellow race, the oldest civilized race; *Africa*, the black race; *Europe*, the white race, and *America*, the red race. The Moon might have brought us the green or blue race."

"Thus, some animals, of which we only find remains, would never have lived on our present Earth but would have been brought from other worlds dislocated due to their old age. The fossils that one encounters in climates where they could not exist here below probably lived in very different zones, on the globes where they were born. Such remains are found in our poles where they lived at the equator of their home planets."

5. This theory has against it the most unequivocal data of experimental science, besides leaving open the whole question of origin which it claims to solve. It says how the Earth would be formed, but it does not say how the so-called four worlds were formed to constitute it.

If things had really occurred this way, how could it be possible that traces of these immense welds were nowhere to be found, going as far as the entrails of the Earth? Each of these worlds bringing its own materials, Asia, Africa, Europe, America would each have a different geology, *which is definitely not the case here*. On the contrary, we see, first of all, a uniform granite nucleus of a homogeneous composition in all parts of the globe, *without any discontinuity*. Then, the geological layers of the same formation, identical in their constitution, everywhere superimposed in the same order, continuing without interruption from one side of the seas to the other, from Europe to Asia, to Africa, to America, and vice versa. These layers, witnesses of the transformations of the globe, testify that these transformations were accomplished on all its surface, and not on any isolated part of it. They show us the periods of appearance, existence and disappearance of the same animal and vegetal species also in different parts of the world; the fauna and flora of these remote periods walking everywhere simultaneously under the influence of a uniform temperature; changing everywhere in character as the temperature changes. Such a state of things is irreconcilable with the formation of the Earth by an alleged addition of several different worlds.

If this system had been conceived a century ago, it could have conquered a provisional place in purely imaginary speculative cosmogonies, founded without the experimental method. Yet today it has no vitality, and it does not even stand scrutiny, because it is contradicted by concrete facts.

Without discussing here the alleged free will attributed to the planets, nor the question of their souls, one wonders what would have become of the sea, which occupies the void left by the Moon, if it had not been unwilling to meet with its sibling planets. And what would become of present Earth, if one day it took fancy for the Moon to come and take its place, thus expelling the sea.

6. The system described above seduced some people, because it seemed to explain the presence of different human races on Earth, and their respective locations. But since these races might allegedly have sprouted upon separate worlds, why could they not have done so on different points of the same globe? This is like wishing to solve a difficulty by a much greater difficulty. Indeed, due to the speed and *dexterity* that the *operation* was made, this addition could not be done without violent jolts; the faster it has been, the more disastrous the cataclysms must have been. It seems impossible, therefore, for beings *simply asleep in a cataleptic state* to be able to survive it, and then to wake up quietly. If they were only embryonic germs, what did they consist of? How would fully formed beings have been reduced to the state of germs? There would always remain the question of how these germs have developed again. All in all, it would still be planet Earth formed miraculously, but by another process less poetic and less grandiose than the first; whereas natural laws give a far more complete explanation of its formation, and above all a more rational one, deduced from experiments and observation.[49]

---

49 When such a system defines a whole cosmogony, one can only ask on what rational basis can sustain all the rest.

The concordance between biblical Genesis and science, which is supposed to be established by this system, is altogether illusory, since it is contradicted by science itself. On the other hand, all beliefs stemming from the biblical texts have as a cornerstone the creation of a unique couple from which all humans are born. Take away this stone, and all that is built on it crumbles. Now, this system, by giving to humanity a multiple origin, is the negation of the doctrine which gives humans a common parent.

Chapter IX
Transformations of the globe

GENERAL OR PARTIAL TRANSFORMATIONS

1.   The geological periods mark the phases of the general aspect of the globe, as a result of its transformations; but, if we except the diluvial period, which bears the characteristics of a sudden upheaving, all the others have been accomplished slowly and without abrupt transition. During the whole time that the constituent elements of the globe were realigning themselves and seeking their position, changes must have been general. Once the base was consolidated, only partial changes in certain areas occurred.

2.   In addition to general transformations, the Earth has experienced a great number of local turbulences which have changed the appearance of certain regions. As for the others, two causes contributed to them: fire and water.

Fire: Either by volcanic eruptions which have buried the surrounding lands under thick layers of ashes and lava, making cities and their inhabitants disappear; or by earthquakes, by the solid crust pushing the waters downwards; or by the subsidence of this same crust in certain places, to a more or less large extent, where the waters have precipitated, leaving other terrains uncovered. It is thus that islands have arisen in the ocean, while others have disappeared; and that portions of continents have been separated, forming islands; and that dry sea-arms have united islands with continents.

Water: Either by the irruption or retreat of the sea on certain coasts; or by scree, which, by stopping the rivers, formed lakes; or by overflows and floods; or finally by landings formed at the mouth

---

The author of the above letter, a man of great knowledge, for a moment seduced by this theory, soon saw its vulnerable sides, and decided to combat it with the weapons of science.

of the rivers. These landings, by driving back the sea, created new lands. Such is the origin of the delta of the Nile or Lower Egypt, the delta of the Rhône or the Camargue, and so many others.

BIBLICAL FLOOD

3. Through inspecting the lands torn by the rising of mountains and the layers which form the buttresses, one can determine their geological age. By geological age of the mountains, we must not understand the number of years of their existence, but the period during which they were formed, and consequently their relative antiquity. It would be a mistake to believe that this antiquity is due to their elevation or their exclusively granitic nature, since the mass of granite, when rising, may have perforated and separated the superimposed layers.

It has thus been found, through observation, that the mountains of Vosges, Brittany and Côte-d'Or, in France, which are not very high, belong to the oldest formations and date from the transition period, being earlier than the coal deposits. The Jura was formed around the middle of the secondary period; it is contemporary with gigantic reptiles. The Pyrenees were formed later, at the beginning of the tertiary period. Mont Blanc and the group of the Western Alps are later than the Pyrenees, and date from the middle of the tertiary period. The Eastern Alps, which include the Tyrol mountains, are even more recent, seeing that they were formed only around the end of the tertiary period. Some mountains of Asia came after the diluvial period, or are contemporary to it.

These upheavals must have caused great local turbulences and larger or minor floods by the displacement of the waters, with the interruption and the change in course of the rivers.[50]

---

50 The 18th century offers a remarkable example of a phenomenon of this kind. Six days' march from Mexico City there was, in the year 1750, a fertile and well-cultivated area. Rice, maize and bananas were growing in abundance. Then, in the month of June, frightful earthquakes shook the ground; and these tremors were constantly renewed for two whole months. In the night of September 28 through September 29, the soil was violently convulsed; a terrain of several miles in extent gradually rose, and finally reached a height of 500 feet over an area of 30 square miles. The ground undulated like the waves of the sea under the winds of a the storm; thousands of mounds rose and fell in turn. Finally a gulf of nearly

4. The Biblical Flood, also known as the Great Asian Flood, is a fact whose existence cannot be disputed. It must have been caused by the upheavals of a part of the mountains of that region, like that in Mexico. What supports this view is the existence of an inland sea that once stretched from the Black Sea to the Boreal Ocean, attested by geological observations. The Sea of Azoff, the Caspian Sea, whose waters are salty, though not communicating with any other sea; Lake Aral and the innumerable lakes spread over the vast plains of Tartary and the steppes of Russia appear to be remnants of this ancient sea. During the upheavals of the Caucasus mountains, some of these waters were pushed back to the north, toward the Boreal ocean; others to the south, to the Indian Ocean. These flooded and ravaged precisely the Mesopotamia and all the land inhabited by the ancestors of the Hebrew people. Although this deluge has spread over a fairly large area, a point made today is that it was only local; that it could not be caused by the rain, for, abundant and continuous as it had been for forty days, calculations proves that the quantity of water that fell could not be large enough to cover all the Earth, even over the highest mountains.

For the humans of that time, who knew only a very limited extent of the surface of the globe and who had no idea of its configuration, from the moment that the flood had invaded their known regions, for them it was like covering all the Earth. If, to this belief, we add the peculiar, hyperbolic form typical of the Eastern style, we shall not be surprised at the exaggeration of the biblical narrative.

5. The Asiatic deluge came evidently after the appearance of humans on Earth, since memory has been preserved by tradition among all the peoples of this part of the world, who have consecrated it in their theogonies.

---

nine miles opened in the place; smoke, fire, burning stones, ashes were thrown to a prodigious height. Six mountains rose out of this gaping chasm, among which the volcano, to which the name of Jorullo has been given, now rises above the old plain. At the moment when the ground was beginning to shake, the two rivers of Cuitimba and San Pedro, ebbing backwards, flooded all the plain occupied today by the Jorullo; but in the ground that was always rising, a gulf opened and swallowed them up. They reappeared in the west, on a point far removed from their old bed. (Louis FIGUIER, *La Terre avant le Déluge* [*The Earth before the Deluge*], page 370).

It also came after the great universal deluge that marked the current geological period; and when we refer to antediluvial humans and animals, this was actually the first cataclysm.

PERIODIC TRANSFORMATIONS

6. In addition to its annual movement around the Sun, which produces the seasons;, and its movement of rotation around itself in 24 hours, which produces the day and the night; the Earth has a third movement which is accomplished every 25,000 years approximately (or, more exactly, every 25,868 years) which produces the phenomenon designated in astronomy by the name of *precession of the equinoxes.*

This motion, which would be impossible to explain in just a few words without illustrations and without a geometrical demonstration, consists in a sort of circular sway that has been compared to that of a dying spinning top, as a result of which the Earth's axis, changing inclination, describes a double cone whose summit is at the center of the Earth, and the bases embrace the surface circumscribed by the polar circles, that is, with a radius of 23 degrees and a half amplitude.[51]

7. The equinox is the moment when the Sun, passing from one hemisphere to the other, is perpendicular to the equator, which happens twice a year, on March 20, when the Sun returns to the northern hemisphere, and September 22, when it returns to the southern hemisphere.

But as a result of the gradual change in the obliquity of the axis, which leads one to the obliquity of the equator on the ecliptic, the moment of the equinox is found each year advanced in some minutes (25 min. 7 sec.). It is this advance that is called *precession of the equinoxes* (from Latin *præcedere*, precede, formed of *præ*, before, and *cedere*, go).

These few minutes, in the long run, become hours, days, months, and years. It follows that the Spring equinox, which now arrives

---

51 An hourglass composed of two conical glasses, turning on itself in an inclined position; or else, two cross-shaped sticks in the shape of an X, turned on their point of intersection; can give an approximate idea of the figure formed by this movement of the axis.

in March, will someday arrive in a given time in February, then in January. Then it will be in December, and then the month of December will have the temperature of March, and March that of June, and so on until, returning in March, things are found in the current state, which will take place in 25,868 years, to start the same transformation all over again indefinitely.[52]

8. It results from this conical movement of the axis, that the poles of the Earth do not look constantly at the same points of the sky; that the polar star will not always be polar star; that the poles are gradually more or less inclined toward the Sun, and receive more or less direct rays; whence it follows that Iceland and Lapland, for instance, which are under the polar circle, may in a given time, receive the solar rays as if they were at the latitude of Spain and Italy; and that, at the extreme opposite, Spain and Italy may someday have the temperature of Iceland and Lapland (Finland), and so on, at each renewal of the period of 25,000 years.

9. The consequences of this movement could not yet be determined with precision, because only a very small part of its transformation could be observed. There are, then, only conjectures of which some have a certain probability.

These consequences are as follows:

1ST) The alternating warming and cooling of the poles, and consequently the melting of the polar ice during half of the period of 25,000 years, and their formation again during the other half of this period. Whence it follows that the poles are not destined to perpetual sterility, but would, in turn, enjoy the benefits of fertility.

---

52 The precession of the equinoxes brings another change, that which takes place in the position of the signs of the zodiac.

As the Earth turns around the Sun in one year, as it moves forward, the Sun is every month in front of a new constellation. These constellations are twelve in number, namely: *Aries, Taurus, Gemini, Crayfish, Leo, Virgo, Libra, Scorpio, Sagittarius, Capricorn, Aquarius, Pisces.* They are called zodiacal constellations or signs of the zodiac, and they form a circle in the plane of the Earth's equator. According to the month of the birth of an individual, it was said that he was born under such sign; of it the prognostics of astrology. But as a result of the precession of the equinoxes, it happens that the naked months correspond more to the same constellations than 2000 years ago: therefore anyone born in the month of July, is no longer in the sign of Leo but in that of the Crayfish. Thus crumbles the superstitious idea attached to the influence of the zodiac signs (see chapter **V**, item **12** above).

2ND) A slow and steady displacement of the sea gradually invades the land, while uncovering others, to abandon them again and return to its former bed. This periodic movement, renewed indefinitely, would constitute a veritable universal tide every 25,000 years.

The slowness with which this movement of the sea operates makes it almost imperceptible for each generation; but it is noticeable after a few centuries. It cannot cause any sudden cataclysm, because humans retreat, from generation to generation, as the sea advances, and humans advance into lands from which the sea retreats. This is more than likely the cause to which some scholars attribute the retreat of the sea from certain coasts and its invasion upon others.

10. The slow, gradual and periodic movement of the sea is a fact observed from experience, and attested by numerous examples on all points of the globe. It results in the maintenance of the productive forces of the Earth. This long immersion is a time of rest during which the submerged lands recover vital principles exhausted by a production which was no less long. The immense deposits of organic matter formed by the dwelling of water for centuries and centuries, are periodically renewed natural fertilizers; and generations succeed one to another without perceiving these changes.[53]

---

53 Among the most difficult facts which prove the displacement of the sea, the following ones can be cited:

In the Bay of Biscay, between the old Soulac and the tower of Cordouan in France, when the sea is calm, one discerns at the bottom of the sea sections of a wall; they are the remains of the old and great city of Noviomagus, invaded by the waves in 580. The rock of Cordouan, which was then connected to the shore, is now twelve kilometers away.

In the English Channel sea, on the coast of Le Havre, the sea gains ground every day and undermines the cliffs of Sainte-Adresse, which are collapsing little by little. At two kilometers from the coast, between Sainte-Adresse and the cape of La Hève, there exists the Eclat Bank, formerly uncovered and united to the mainland. Ancient documents show that on this site, where we sail today, there was the village of Saint-Denis-Chef-de-Canx. The sea having invaded the land in the 14th century, its church was engulfed in 1378. It is claimed that one is able to see its remains at the bottom of the sea, on a calm day.

Certainly almost throughout the whole extent of the coast of Holland, the sea is only retained by the strength of dikes, which break from time to time. The old river Flero was joined to the sea in 1225, and is now the Zuiderzee gulf. This irruption of the ocean engulfed several villages.

FUTURE CATACLYSMS

11. The great upheavings of the Earth took place at a time when the solid crust, by its slight thickness, offered only a feeble resistance to the effervescence of incandescent matter from within. They have been reduced in intensity and general range in the extent that the crust has been consolidated. Many volcanoes are now extinct, others have been covered by later formations.

Surely local turbulences may still occur as a result of volcanic eruptions, the opening of a few new volcanoes, the flooding of certain regions. Some islands may emerge from the sea, and others may be submerged; but the time of general cataclysms, like those which marked the great geological periods, is gone. The Earth has now taken a resting place that, without being highly invariable, is now shielding the human race from general upheavals – except for unknown causes, foreign to our globe, which could not possibly be foreseen.

12. As for comets, we are now fully reassured of their influence, more salutary than harmful, in that they seem destined to supply, if we may so express their action, the worlds, by bringing to them the vital principles that they, the comets, have collected during their orbit through space, and in the neighborhood of suns. They should thus be regarded as sources of prosperity rather than messengers of misfortune.

Because of their fluidic nature, now well established (see chapter **VI**, items **28** *et seq.* above), a violent shock is not to be feared, since, in the event that one comet would shock with the Earth, the latter would pass through the comet as through a fog.

According to this, the region of Paris and France would once again be occupied by the sea, as it had already been several times, as proved by geological observations. The mountainous parts would then form islands, as are now Jersey, Guernsey and England, formerly contiguous to the continent.

Someday, we will sail over the countries we travel today on the railroad. Ships will board at Montmartre, at Mount Valérien, at the slopes of Saint-Cloud and Meudon. The woods and forests where we walk will be buried under water, covered with silt, and populated with fish instead of birds.

The biblical flood would not have any part in this, since the invasion of the waters was sudden and their stay of short duration, while otherwise it would have lasted several thousand years, and would last up to this day, without humans being able even to notice it.

A comet's tail is not more formidable; it is only a reflection of the sunlight in the immense atmosphere which surrounds it, since it is constantly directed towards the opposite side of the Sun, and changes direction according to the position of this star. This gaseous matter could also, as a result of the rapidity of its pace, form a sort of hair trailing out like the wake following a ship, or the smoke of a locomotive. For the rest, several comets have already approached the Earth without causing any injury; and because of their respective densities, the Earth would exert on the comet an attraction greater than the comet on the Earth. Only a remnant of old prejudices could inspire fears about their presence.[54]

13. It is also necessary to relegate to chimerical hypotheses the possibility of an encounter of the Earth with another planet. The regularity and invariability of the laws which preside over the movements of celestial bodies make such an encounter highly improbable.

The Earth will however come to an end. How? It is impossible to foresee; but, as it is still far from the perfection which it can achieve, and of the dilapidation which would be a sign of decline, its current inhabitants may rest assured that it will not happen in their time (see chapter **VI**, items **48** *et seq.* above).

14. Physically, it passed through the convulsions of its childhood. It has now entered a period of relative stability, a period of peaceful progress, which is accomplished by the regular return of the same physical phenomena, and the intelligent contribution of humans. But *it is still right in the middle of the birth of moral progress.* This will be the cause of its biggest commotions. *Until humankind has sufficiently grown in perfection through their intelligence and the practice of divine laws, the greatest disturbances will be caused by humans rather than by Nature; in other words, it will be more moral and social than physical.*

---

54 The comet of the year 1861 crossed Earth's path twenty hours ahead of it, which must have made it immerse in the latter's atmosphere, without any accidents.

Chapter X
Organic genesis

FIRST FORMATION OF LIVING BEINGS

1. There was a time when animals did not exist, an then a time when they began to appear. Every species came into being as the globe acquired the conditions necessary for its existence – this fact is positively known. How were the first individuals of each species formed? We understand that a first couple being given, the individuals are then multiplied; but this first couple, where did it come from? This is one of those mysteries which depend on the principle of things and about which we can only make hypotheses. If science cannot solve the problem completely, it can at least put it on a path of being solved.

2. A first question that comes to mind is the following: Has each animal species emerged from a *first couple* or from several couples created or, if you will, simultaneously *germinated* at different places?

This last supposition is the most probable. One can even say that it results from observation. In fact, there exists in the same species an infinite variety of genera, distinguished by more or less distinct traits. It was necessary, at any rate, at least one type for each variety, appropriate to the environment in which it was called to live, since each reproduces itself identically.

On the other hand, the life of an individual, especially of an incipient individual, is subject to so many eventualities that a whole creation could have been compromised without a plurality of primeval types, which would not have been in accordance with divine foresight. Moreover, if a type could be formed at a point, there is no reason for it to have formed at several points by the same cause.

Lastly, observation of the geological layers attests to the presence, in the same formations, and in enormous proportions, of the same species on the farthest points of the globe. This multiplication, so general and in a certain way dating from the same time, would have been impossible with a single primeval type.

Therefore all evidence combines to prove that there has been simultaneous and multiple creation of the first pairs of each animal and vegetal species.

3. The formation of the first living beings can be deduced, by analogy, from the same law according to which inorganic bodies have been formed and are formed daily. As one delves deeper into the laws of Nature, one sees the cogs, which, at first sight, seem so complicated, to be simplified and to blend into the great law of unity which presides over the whole work of creation. It becomes better understood when the formation of the inorganic bodies, which is the first degree, is realized.

4. Chemistry considers as elementary a number of substances, such as: oxygen, hydrogen, nitrogen, carbon, chlorine, iodine, fluorine, sulfur, phosphorus, and all metals. By their combination they form compounds: the oxides, the acids, the alkalis, the salts, and the innumerable varieties which result from the combination of these.

The combination of two component bodies to form a third requires a special set of circumstances: either a certain degree of heat, drought, or humidity; or motion or repose, or an electric current, etc. If these conditions do not exist, the combination will not take place.

5. When combined, the component bodies lose their characteristic properties, while the resulting compound possesses new ones, different from those of the former. Thus, for example, oxygen and hydrogen, which are invisible gases, being chemically combined, form water which is liquid, solid or vaporous, according to the temperature. In water there is no longer oxygen and hydrogen, properly speaking, but a new body; this water being decomposed, the two gases, once again free, recover their properties, and then there is no water anymore. The same amount of water can thus be alternately decomposed and recomposed indefinitely.

In a simple mixture there is no production of a new body, and the mixed principles retain their intrinsic properties which are merely weakened, as is mingling wine with water. Thus, a mixture of 21 parts of oxygen and 79 parts of nitrogen forms the air, while a chemical combination of 5 parts of oxygen over 2 of nitrogen produces nitric acid.

6. Composition and decomposition of bodies take place as a result of the degree of affinity which the elementary principles have for one another. The formation of water, for example, results from the mutual affinity of oxygen and hydrogen; but if we put in contact with water a body having more affinity for oxygen than this one has for hydrogen, the water decomposes; the oxygen is absorbed, the hydrogen becomes free, and there is no water anymore.

7. Compound bodies are always formed in definite proportions, that is, by the combination of a fixed quantity of its constituent principles. Thus, to form water it requires one part of oxygen and two of hydrogen. Even if, under the same conditions, a greater proportion of one or the other of the two gases were placed, there would still be only the desired quantity of absorbed matter, and the surplus would remain free. If, under other conditions, there are two parts of oxygen combined with two of hydrogen instead of water, we obtain hydrogen deutoxide, a corrosive liquid formed however of the same elements as water, but in a different ratio.

8. Such is, in a few words, the law which governs the formation of all the bodies of Nature. The innumerable variety of these bodies results from a very small number of elementary principles combined in different ratios.

Thus oxygen, combined in certain proportions with carbon, sulfur, and phosphorus, forms the carbonic, sulfuric, and phosphoric acids. Oxygen and iron form iron oxide or rust. Oxygen and lead, both harmless, give rise to the oxides of phosphorus, such as litharge, white lead, and minium, which are poisonous. Oxygen, with metals called calcium, sodium, potassium, form lime, soda, and potash. Lime combined with carbonic acid forms the carbonates of lime or calcareous stones, such as marble, chalk, building stone, and stalactites in caves; combined with sulfuric acid, it forms sulphate of lime or plaster, and alabaster; with phosphoric acid, it forms phosphate of lime, the solid base of bones. Hydrogen and chlorine form hydrochloric acid; hydrochloric acid and soda form the hydrochloric acid of soda or marine salt.

9. While these combinations, and thousands of others, are obtained artificially in small groups in chemistry laboratories; they take place spontaneously in the big laboratory of Nature.

The Earth, in principle, did not contain these combined bodies, but only their constituent elements volatilized. When limestone and other soils, which in the long run became stony, were deposited on its surface, those combined bodies did not all exist yet, but all the primeval substances were in the air in a gaseous state. Such substances, precipitated by the effect of cooling, and under the influence of favorable circumstances, were combined according to the degree of their molecular affinity. It is then that different varieties of carbonates, sulphates, etc., are formed, first dissolved in the waters, then deposited on the surface of the soil.

Suppose that, by some cause whatever, the Earth would return to its primitive state of incandescence: all this would decompose; the elements would separate; all fusible substances would melt; all those which are volatile would volatilize. Then a second cooling would bring a new precipitation, and the old combinations would be formed again.

10. These considerations show how much chemistry was necessary for comprehending Genesis. Before the knowledge of the laws of molecular affinity, it was impossible to understand the formation of the Earth. Chemistry has shed a whole new light on this question, just as astronomy and geology have done likewise in other ways.

11. In the formation of solid bodies, one of the most remarkable phenomena is that of crystallization, which consists in the regular form which certain substances take on when passing from the liquid or gaseous state to the solid state. This form, which varies according to the nature of the substance, is generally that of geometric solids, such as the prism, the rhomboid, the cube, and the pyramid. Everyone knows that candy sugar crystals, rock crystals, or crystalline silica, are hexagonal prisms ending in an equally hexagonal pyramid. Diamond are pure carbon or crystallized coal. The contours that occur on windows in winter are due to the crystallization of water vapor in the form of prismatic needles.

The regular disposition of the crystals holds the particular form of the molecules of each body; these particles, infinitely small for us, but which nevertheless occupy a certain space, solicited from one another by molecular attraction, arrange and juxtapose themselves according to the requirements of their form, so that each takes its place around the nucleus or first center of attraction, thus forming a symmetrical set.

Crystallization takes place only under the influence of certain favorable circumstances beyond which it cannot occur. The amount of temperature and rest are essential conditions. It is understandable that too great a heat, keeping the molecules apart, would not allow them to condense; and that any agitation opposing their symmetrical arrangement, would cause them to form only a confused and irregular mass, and consequently preventing crystallization itself.

12. The law that governs the formation of minerals naturally leads to the formation of organic bodies.

Chemical analysis shows us all vegetal and animal substances to be composed of the same elements as the inorganic bodies. Those of these elements which play the main part are oxygen, hydrogen, nitrogen, and carbon; others are there only incidentally. As in the mineral kingdom, the difference in ratios in the combination of these elements produces all the varieties of organic substances and their various properties, such as muscles, bones, blood, bile, nerves, cerebral matter, and gum, in animals; and sap, wood, leaves, fruits, essences, oils, resins, etc., in plants. Thus, in the formation of animals and plants, there is no special body that cannot also be found in the mineral kingdom.[55]

---

55 The following table, displaying the analysis of some substances, shows the difference of properties which results from the difference in ratios of the constituent elements. Out of 100 parts:

	Carbon	Hydrogen	Oxygen	Nitrogen
Sugar cane......................	42.470	6.900	50.530	--
Grape sugar....................	36.710	6.780	56.510	--
Alcohol...........................	51.980	13.700	34.320	--
Olive oil........................	77.210	13.360	9.430	--

13. Some common examples will explain the transformations that take place in the organic kingdom by the sole modification of constituent elements.

In grape juice, there is still no wine or alcohol, but only water and sugar. When this juice has reached maturity and is placed under favorable circumstances, an inner work is produced, which is called fermentation. In this work a part of the sugar decomposes; oxygen, hydrogen, and carbon separate and combine in the proper ratios so as to make alcohol. Therefore when drinking grape juice, one really does not drink alcohol, since it does not exist yet.

In the bread and vegetables that we eat, there is certainly no flesh, no blood, no bone, no bile, no cerebral matter, and yet these same foods will produce, by decomposing and recomposing themselves through the work digestion, these different substances by the mere transmutation of their constituent elements.

In the seed of a tree, there is no wood, no leaves, no flowers, no fruit, and it is a childish mistake to believe that the whole tree, in microscopic form, is in the seed. In it, there is not even the amount of oxygen, hydrogen and carbon necessary to form a single leaf of the tree. The seed contains a germ that hatches when it encounters favorable conditions. This germ grows by absorbing the juices it draws from the soil, and the gases it sucks from the air. These juices, which are neither wood, nor leaves, nor flowers, nor fruits, by penetrating into the plant, form its sap; as food, in animals, they form the blood. This sap, carried by the circulation through all parts of the plant, according to the organs where it ends and where it undergoes a special formulation, is transformed into wood, leaves, fruits, as the blood is transformed into flesh, bone, bile, and so on; and yet they are always the same elements: oxygen, hydrogen, nitrogen, and carbon, variously combined.

14. The different combinations of the elements for the formation of mineral, vegetal and animal substances can only take place in suitable environments and circumstances. Outside these circumstances, the elementary principles are in a sort of inertia.

Oil of nuts......................	79.774	10.570	9.122	0.534
Fat................................	78.996	11.700	9.304	--
Fibrin.............................	53.360	7.021	19.685	19.934

However, as soon as the circumstances are favorable, a work of formulation begins; the molecules start moving. As they move, they attract one another, drawing near and separating by virtue of the law of affinities; and through their multiple combinations, they compose the infinite variety of substances. Whenever these conditions cease, the work suddenly comes to a halt, to start again when favorable conditions come back. That is how the vegetation activates, slows down, ceases and resumes, depending on the action of heat, light, humidity, cold, and drought. That is why such a plant thrives in one climate or in a field, but withers away or perishes in another.

15. What happens daily before our eyes can put us on the path of what happened at the beginning of time, because the laws of Nature have always been the same.

Since the constituent elements of organic beings and inorganic beings are the same; and that we see them incessantly under the influence of certain circumstances, to form stones, plants, and fruits, we may conclude that the bodies of the first living beings were formed as the first stones, by the combination of elementary molecules by virtue of the law of affinities, as the conditions of Earth's vitality have been favorable to such and such species.

The similarity of form and color in the reproduction of individuals of each species may be compared to the similarity of form of each species of crystal. Molecules, juxtaposed under the same law, produce analogous wholes.

THE VITAL PRINCIPLE

16. By saying that plants and animals are formed of the same constituent principles as minerals, we must understand it exclusively in the   material sense, since this is not only a matter of physical bodies.

Without discussing the intelligent principle, which requires a separate question, there is in organic matter a special, elusive principle which has not yet been defined: it is the vital principle. This principle, which is active in all living beings, is extinguished with the death of the being, but it nevertheless gives to the substance characteristic properties which distinguish it from the inorganic substances. Chemistry, which decomposes and recomposes the majority of inorganic bodies, has also been able to decompose organic bodies, but never managed to reconstitute even a dead leaf, an obvious proof that therein lies something that does not exist in others.

17. Is the vital principle something distinct, having an existence of its own? Or, to enter into the system of the unity of the generating element, is it only a particular state, one of the modifications of the universal cosmic fluid which becomes the principle of life, just like it becomes light, fire, heat, and electricity? It is in this last sense that the question is solved by spirit communications reported above (see chapter **VI**, "General Uranography").

Yet, whatever the opinion about the nature of the vital principle may be, it does exist, since we see its effects. We can therefore logically admit that, by their formation, organic beings have assimilated the vital principle which was necessary for their purpose; or, if one wishes, that this principle has developed in every individual through the very effect of the combination of elements, just like one can see, under the influence of certain circumstances, heat, light, and electricity develop themselves.

18. Oxygen, hydrogen, nitrogen, and carbon, by combining without the vital principle, would have formed only a mineral or an inorganic body. The vital principle, by modifying the molecular constitution of such a body, gives it special properties. Thus instead of a mineral molecule, we have a molecule of organic matter.

The vital principle's activity is maintained during life by the action played by the organs, as heat by the movement of rotation of a wheel. This action ceases with death, the vital principle is then *extinguished*, like a wheel, when it stops turning. But the *effect* produced on the molecular state of the body by the vital principle remains after the extinction of this principle, as the charring of the wood persists after the extinction of the heat and the cessation of the movement of the wheel. In analyzing organic bodies, chemistry is able to retrieve its constituent elements: oxygen, hydrogen, nitrogen and carbon. But it cannot reconstitute them, because the cause no longer exists; it is unable to reproduce the *effect*, as it could do if it were restoring a stone.

19. I have taken for comparison the heat produced by the movement of a wheel, because it is a commonplace effect, known to everybody, and easier to understand; yet it would have been more accurate to say that in the combination of elements to form organic bodies, *electricity* is produced. Organic bodies would thus be veritable *electric batteries* which function as long as the elements of these cells are in the conditions required to produce electricity: then it is life, which stops when these conditions end: that is death. According to this, the vital principle is none other than the particular kind of electricity designated by the name of *animal electricity*, released during life by the action of the organs, and whose production is arrested at death by the cessation of such action.

SPONTANEOUS GENERATION

20. One naturally wonders why it no longer forms living beings in the same conditions as the original ones that first appeared on Earth.

The question of spontaneous generation, which today preoccupies science, although still variously resolved, cannot fail to shed light on this subject. The problem proposed is as follows: Are organic beings spontaneously formed today by the single union of constituent elements, without embryos as prerequisite products of ordinary generation, in other words, procreated without any parenting?

Proponents of spontaneous generation respond affirmatively, and rely on direct observations that seem conclusive. Others think that all living things reproduce by one another, and are based on this fact, proved by experience, that the germs of certain vegetal and animal species, once dispersed, can preserve a latent vitality during a given period of time, actually a considerable time until circumstances are favorable for their emergence. This opinion always leaves unanswered the question of the formation of the first types of each species.

21. Without discussing the two systems above, it should be noted that the principle of spontaneous generation can obviously apply only to beings of the lowest orders of the vegetal and animal kingdom, to those where life is just beginning to appear, and whose extremely simple body is in a way rudimentary. These were the first to appear on Earth, and their generation must have been spontaneous. We would thus be witnessing a permanent creation process similar to that which took place in the early ages of the world.

22.   But then, why do we not see the formation of beings of complex organization as well? These beings have not always existed, this is a proven fact, so they had to start at some time. If moss, lichen, zoophytes, infusoria, intestinal worms and others can occur spontaneously, why are not trees, fish, dogs, horses generated in the same way?

For the moment, this is as far as investigations have gone. The thread is lost, and until it is found again, the field will remain open to hypotheses. It would therefore be imprudent and premature to present any system as the absolute truth.

23.   If the fact of spontaneous generation is demonstrated, however limited it may be, it is nonetheless a capital fact, a milestone that may lead to new discoveries. If complex organic beings do not occur in this way, who knows how they started? Who knows the secret of all transformations? When we see the oak and the acorn, who can tell if a mysterious link does not exist from the polyp to the elephant?

Let time be the bringer of light to the bottom of this abyss, if one day it can be probed. Such knowledge is interesting, no doubt, from the point of view of pure science, but it is not among those facts which affect the destinies of humankind.

SCALE OF BODILY BEINGS

24.   Between the vegetal and the animal kingdoms, there is no definite delimitation. On the borders of the two kingdoms there are the *zoophytes* or *animals-plants* whose name indicates that they belong to one and the other: they are the hyphen between the two.

Like animals, plants are born, live, grow, feed, breathe, reproduce and die. Like them, to live, they need light, heat and water; if they are deprived of them, they wither and die. The absorption of stale air and deleterious substances poisons them. Their most distinctive trait is to be attached to the ground and to draw food from it without moving.

The zoophyte has the external appearance of a plant; as a plant, it stands on the ground; as an animal, life in it is more accentuated; it draws its food from the environment.

A degree above, the animal is free to move and search for its food. First there are innumerable varieties of polyps with gelatinous bodies, without distinct organs, and which differ from plants only for having locomotion. Then come, in the order of the development of organs, vital activity and instinct: helminths or intestinal worms; mollusks, fleshy, boneless animals, some of which are bare like slugs; octopuses. Others are provided with shells like snails and oysters; crustaceans, whose skin is covered with a hard carapace like crayfish; lobsters; insects, in which life takes on a prodigious activity and manifests an industrious instinct, like the ant, the bee, and the spider. Some undergo a metamorphosis, like the caterpillar, which turns into an elegant butterfly. Then comes the order of vertebrates, animals with a bone structure, which includes fish, reptiles, birds, and finally mammals, whose organization is the most complete.

HUMAN BEINGS

25. From a corporeal and purely anatomical point of view, humans belong to the mammals class, of which they differ only by certain traits in their external form. Moreover, they share the same chemical composition as all animals, in organs, functions and modes of nutrition; in respiration, secretion, and reproduction. Humans are born, live, and die in the same conditions, and at their death their bodies decompose like those of all living beings. There is not in human blood, in human flesh, in human bones, an atom more or less than in the bodies of animals. Like these, in dying, humans return to the earth the oxygen, the hydrogen, the nitrogen, and the carbon which combined to form them, and which go on, through new combinations, to form new mineral bodies, plants and animals. The analogy is so great, that one studies the organic functions in certain animals, when the experiments can not be made on oneself.

26. In the mammals class, humans belong to the *bimanous* order. Immediately below humans come the *quadrumanous* order (four-handed animals) or monkeys, some of whom, like the orangutan, the chimpanzee, the apes, have some of the appearance of humans; so much so that they had long been referred to as "men of the woods." Like humans, they walk straight, use sticks as tools, and take food to their mouths with the hand, which are characteristic human habits.

27. As long as we observe the scale of living beings from the point of view of the organisms, we recognize that from the lichen to the tree, and from the zoophyte to the human being, there is a chain continually ascending by degrees, and of which all links have a point of contact with the preceding link. By following the series of beings step by step, it seems as if each species is an improvement, a transformation of the immediately inferior species. Since the body of human beings present conditions identical to the other bodies, both chemically and constitutionally; and that humans are born, live and die in the same manner as the other animals, it follows that humans must have been formed under the same conditions.

28. Whatever may be the cost to human pride, we must resign ourselves to seeing in our material body only the last link in the animality chain on Earth. The inexorable arguments of facts are there, against which we would protest in vain.

Yet the more our body diminishes in our eyes, the more the spiritual principle grows in importance. If the first places humans at the same level of the brute, the second raises them to an immeasurable height. We see the circle where the animal stops; however, we do not see the limit the human spirit can reach.

29. Materialism can see by this that Spiritism, far from dreading the discoveries of science and its positivism, goes ahead and encourages them, because it is certain that the spiritual principle, which has its own existence, can suffer no harm.

Chapter XI
Spiritual genesis

THE SPIRITUAL PRINCIPLE · UNION OF THE SPIRITUAL PRINCIPLE TO MATTER ·
HYPOTHESIS ON THE ORIGIN OF THE HUMAN BODY · INCARNATION OF SPIRITS ·
REINCARNATION · EMIGRATION AND IMMIGRATION OF SPIRITS ·
ADAMIC RACE · DOCTRINE OF FALLEN ANGELS

THE SPIRITUAL PRINCIPLE

1. The existence of *the spiritual principle* is a fact which has, so to speak, no more need of demonstration than the material principle. It is, in a way, a self-evident truth; it asserts itself by its own effects, like matter does it by its own.

According to the axiom, "every effect has a cause, every intelligent effect must have an intelligent cause," there is no one who would fail to see the difference between the mechanical movement of a bell agitated by the wind, and the movement of the same bell intended to give a signal, a warning, and attesting by that even a thought, an intention. Now, since it would not occur to anyone to attribute thought to the matter which forms a bell, we must therefore conclude that it is moved by an intelligence to which it serves as an instrument for manifesting itself.

For the same reason, no one would have the idea of attributing thought to the body of a dead person. If the living person thinks, then there is something in him/her that is no longer there after death. The difference between the living person and the bell is that the intelligence that moves the latter is outside of it, whereas the one that makes humans act is in themselves.

2. The spiritual principle is the corollary of God's existence. Without this principle, God would have no reason to be, for we would not be able to conceive of a sovereign intelligence reigning in eternity only over brute matter, more than imagining an earthly monarch reigning throughout his/her life only over rocks and stones. Since one cannot admit God without the essential attributes of divinity; namely, justice and goodness; these qualities would be useless if they were only to be exerted over matter.

3. On the other hand, one could hardly conceive of a God which is supremely just and good, creating intelligent and sensitive beings, only to devote them to nothingness after a few days of suffering without any compensation, enjoying the spectacle of an indefinite succession of beings who are born without having asked for it, endowed with the ability of thinking only to know pain, and who disappear forever after an ephemeral existence.

Without the survival of the thinking being, all life sufferings would be purposeless cruelty on God's part. This is why materialism and atheism are corollaries of each other; by denying the cause, the effect cannot be admitted; denying the effect, the cause cannot be admitted. Materialism is therefore consistent with itself, if not with reason.

4. The idea of perpetuity of the spiritual being is innate in humans; it lies in us in the state of intuition and aspiration. We understand that in survival there can be compensation for the miseries of life. That is why there has always been and always will be more spiritualists than materialists, and more deists than atheists.

To the intuitive idea and to the power of reasoning, Spiritism has added the corroboration of facts, the material proof of the existence of the spiritual being, of its survival, of its immortality, and of its individuality. It specifies and defines what used to be vague and abstract in this thought. It shows us the intelligent being acting outside matter, either after or during the life of the body.

5. Is the spiritual principle and the vital principle one and the same thing?

Hence, as always, from the observation of facts, we will say that if the vital principle were inseparable from the intelligent principle, there would be some reason to confuse them; but as we see beings that live but do not think, such as plants; human bodies may still be animated by organic life whereas there is no longer any manifestation of thought. And that vital movements, independent of any act of willpower, are produced in a living being. And have, during sleep, its organic life in full activity, while its intellectual life is not manifested by any external sign. It is necessary to admit that the organic life resides in a principle inherent in matter, independent of the spiritual life that is inherent in the spirit. Since matter has a vitality independent of the spirit, and the spirit has a vitality independent of matter, it remains evident that this dual vitality rests on two different principles.

6. Should the spiritual principle have its source in the universal cosmic element? Is it only a transformation, a mode of existence of this element, such as light, electricity, heat, etc.?

If it were so, the spiritual principle would suffer the vicissitudes of matter; it would be extinguished by disintegration as the vital principle; the intelligent being would only have a momentary existence like the body, and at death it would return to nothingness, or whatever would be the same, in the universal whole. This would be, in a word, the corroboration of materialistic doctrines.

The unique properties recognized in the spiritual principle prove that it has its own, independent existence, since if it had its origin in matter, it would not possess these properties. Since intelligence and thought cannot be attributes of matter, we come to the conclusion, going back from the effects to causes, that the material element and the spiritual element are the two constituent principles of the universe. The individualized spiritual element constitutes the beings denominated *spirits*, as the individualized material element constitutes the different bodies of Nature, both organic and inorganic.

7. Since the existence of the spiritual being is admitted, and its source cannot be in matter, what is its origin, its point of departure?

Means of investigation are absolutely lacking in this, as in everything that comes from the principle of things. Humans can only find what exists; on all the rest they can only issue hypotheses. Whether this knowledge is beyond the reach of their current intelligence, whether it is useless or inconvenient for them to possess it for the time being, God does not give it to humans, even by revelation.

What God has made known through its messengers, and what humans could deduce themselves from the principle of supreme justice, which is one of the essential attributes of the Divinity, is that all beings have the same point of departure; that all are created simple and ignorant, with equal aptitude for progress through their individual activity; that all will attain the degree of perfection compatible with the created being through their personal efforts; that all, being the children of the same Parent, are the object of equal solicitude; that no one is more favored or gifted than the others, and exempted from the work that would be imposed on others to achieve the ultimate goal.

8.　At the same time that God created material worlds from all eternity, It also created spiritual beings from all eternity, otherwise the material worlds would have been without purpose. We would rather conceive of spiritual beings without material worlds, than the latter without spiritual beings. It is the material worlds that were to provide spiritual beings with elements of activity for the development of their intelligence.

9.　Progress is the normal condition of all spiritual beings, and relative perfection the goal they must attain. Now, God, having created them from all eternity, and by creating without ceasing, also from all eternity there have been those who reached the highest step of the ladder.

Before Earth existed, worlds had succeeded to worlds; and when Earth came out of the chaos of the elements, space was already peopled with spiritual beings at all stages of advancement, from those who were just born to life, to those who from all eternity had ranked among the pure spirits, commonly called angels.

UNION OF THE SPIRITUAL PRINCIPLE TO MATTER

10.　In order to become the object of the work of the spirit for the development of the latter's faculties, the spirit had to be able to act upon matter. That is why the spirit came to live in it, just as the woodcutter lives in the forest. The latter, being at once the goal and the instrument of work, God, instead of uniting it with rigid stone, created and organized for the spirit's use flexible bodies capable of receiving all the impulsions of its will, and to lend itself to all its movements.

The body is thus at the same time the envelope and the instrument of the spirit, and as it acquires new aptitudes, it puts on an envelope appropriate to the new kind of work that it is called to perform, just like it is given to a worker less coarse tools as he/she becomes able to do a more meticulous job.

11. To be more exact, it must be said that it is the spirit itself that shapes its envelope and adapts it to its new needs. It perfects, develops and completes the organism as it feels the need to manifest new faculties; in a word, it puts it at the height of its intelligence. God provides the spirit with the materials, for it to implement them. It is thus that advanced races have an organism, or, if you will, a tool more perfected than primitive races. This also explains the special traits that the character of a spirit imprints on the countenance features and on the looks of the body.

12. As soon as a spirit is born to spiritual life, it must, for its advancement, make use of its faculties, at first in a rudimentary way. That is why it puts on a body envelope appropriate to its state of intellectual infancy, an envelope which it leaves to put on another as its forces grow. Now, as at all times, there have been worlds, and these worlds have given birth to organized bodies suitable to receive spirits. Spirits have always found, whatever their degree of advancement, the necessary elements for their corporeal life.

13. The body, being exclusively material, undergoes the vicissitudes of matter. After having worked for some time, it disorganizes and breaks down; the vital principle, finding no more support to its activity, is extinguished and the body dies. The spirit, to which the body deprived of life is now useless, leaves it, as one leaves a house in ruins, or an old garment unfit for wearing.

14. The body is therefore only an envelope destined to receive the spirit, regardless of its origin and the materials of which it is built. Whether the body of a human being is a special creation or not, it is nonetheless formed of the same elements as that of animals and animated by the same vital principle. In other words, since it is heated by the same fire, enlightened by the same light, subject to the same vicissitudes and having the same needs, this is a point about which there can be no dispute.

If one considers only matter, abstracting from the spirit, humans have nothing that distinguishes them from animal. But everything changes if one is able to distinguish the difference between *the dwelling and the dweller.*

A great lord, under his own roof or clothed in peasant's clothes, is no less a great lord. It is the same with humans: it is not their garment of flesh that raises them above the brute and set them apart; it is their spiritual being, their spirit.

HYPOTHESIS ON THE ORIGIN OF THE HUMAN BODY

15. From the similarity of external forms which exists between the human body and that of the monkey, certain physiologists have concluded that the former was only a transformation of the second. About this there is nothing impossible, unless, if it is so, the dignity of humans might suffer a blow. The bodies of monkeys may very well have been used as clothing for the first human spirits that came to incarnate on Earth, who were necessarily little advanced. These fleshly envelopes would have been the most appropriate to their needs, and more suitable to exercising their faculties than the bodies of any other animal. Instead of a special garment being made for the spirit, it would then have found a ready made one. The human spirit was able to dress in the skin of the monkey, without ceasing to be a human spirit, same as a human sometimes puts on the skin of certain animals without ceasing to be a human being.

It is understood that this is only a hypothesis which is in no way posited as a principle, but given only to show that the origin of the body in no way detracts from the spirit which is the main being; and that the similarity between the human body and the body of a monkey does not imply a parity between the human spirit and that of the monkey.

16. If one admits this hypothesis, it may be said that under the influence, and by the effect, of the intellectual activity of its new inhabitant, the envelope has been modified, embellished in detail, while preserving the general form of the original. Improved bodies, by procreating themselves, have reproduced under the same conditions. Such as grafted trees, they gave birth to a new species which gradually moved away from the primitive type as the spirit evolved. The monkey spirit, which has not been annihilated, has continued to procreate monkey bodies for its use, as the offspring of the savage reproduces savages, so did the human spirit procreate the bodies of humans, variants of the first mold where it had settled. The trunk has forked; it has produced an offshoot, and this offshoot became a trunk.

Since there are no abrupt transitions in Nature, it is probable that the first humans to appear on Earth must have differed slightly from the monkey as to their external form, and undoubtedly not much more intelligent either. There are still savages nowadays who, by the length of their arms and feet, and the conformation of the head, are so much like the monkey, that should they also be hairy all over their bodies, the resemblance would be complete.

INCARNATION OF SPIRITS

17. Spiritism teaches us how the union of the spirit to the body takes place in incarnation. The spirit, by its spiritual essence, is an indefinite, abstract being, which cannot exert a direct action upon matter. It needs an intermediary; this intermediary is in the fluidic envelope which is in some way an integral part of the spirit; that is to say, a semi-material envelope holding matter by its origin and spirituality by its ethereal nature. Like all matter, it is drawn from the universal cosmic fluid, which undergoes in this circumstance a special modification. This envelope, designated under the name of *perispirit*, makes the spirit, which is an abstract being, a concrete, definite being, seizable by thought. It makes it capable of acting on tangible matter, as well as all the imponderable substances which are, as we know, the most powerful engines.

The perispiritual fluid is therefore the link between the spirit and matter. During its union with the body, it is the vehicle of its thought to transmit movement to the different parts of the body that act under the impulsion of its will, and to reflect in the spirit the sensations produced by external agents. Its connecting wires are the nerves; as in a telegraph, the electric fluid has the wires as its conductor.

18. When a spirit is about to incarnate in a human body, during the process of the latter's formation, a spiritual link, which is nothing other than an expansion of its perispirit, links it to the seed to which it is attracted by an irresistible force from the moment of conception. As the embryonic germ grows, the bond tightens; under the influence of *the germ's material vital principle*, the perispirit, which possesses certain properties of matter, unites *molecule by molecule* with the body which is being formed. Hence we can say that the spirit, through its perispirit, is in some way rooted in this germ, like a plant in the earth. When the germ is fully developed, the union is complete, and then it is born to outer life

Conversely, this union of the perispirit and the corporeal matter, which was accomplished under the influence of the germ's vital principle, at the time this principle ceases to act as a result of a disorganization of the body – which causes death – the union, which was maintained only by an active force, ceases when this force by its turn ceases to act. Then the perispirit releases itself *molecule by molecule*, as it had been united, and the spirit regains its freedom. *Therefore it is not the departure of the spirit that causes the death of the body, but the death of the body that causes the departure of the spirit.*

19.   Spiritism teaches us, through the facts which it enables us to observe, the phenomena which accompany this separation: it is sometimes rapid, easy, gentle and insensible. At other times it is very slow, laborious, horribly painful, depending on the moral state of the spirit, and can last for whole months

20.   A particular phenomenon, also highlighted by observation, always accompanies the incarnation of a spirit. As soon as the latter is seized by the fluidic link which connects it to the embryonic germ, trouble takes possession of it. This disturbance grows as the bond tightens, and in the last moments the spirit loses all consciousness of itself, so that it is never a conscious witness of its own birth. The moment when the newborn breathes, the spirit begins to recover its faculties, which develop as the organs that are to serve its manifestation are formed and consolidated. Here again the wisdom that presides over all parts of the work of creation is evident. If faculties were too active, they would use and break delicate organs barely outlined; this is why their energy is proportional to the strength of resistance of these organs.

21.   However, at the same time that the spirit recovers the consciousness of itself, it loses the memory of its past, without losing the faculties, qualities and aptitudes acquired previously; aptitudes which were momentarily latent, and which, taking up the spirit's activity, will help it to do more and better than it has done before. It is reborn from what it did with its previous work; it is for it a new point of departure, a new step to climb. Here again the supreme goodness of the Creator manifests itself, for the memory of a past, often painful or humiliating, adding to the bitterness of its new existence, might disturb and hinder the spirit. It remembers only what it has learned, because this is useful. If at times it retains a vague intuition of past events, it is like the memory of a fleeting dream. Therefore the spirit is a new human being, regardless of how old its spirit might be. It comes across new mistakes helped by what it has acquired in previous lifetimes. When it returns to the spiritual world, its past unfolds before it, and it can judge whether it has spent its time well or badly.

22. There is no interruption in the spiritual life. In spite of forgetting the past, the spirit is always *itself*, before, during and after its incarnation. The incarnation is only a special phase in its existence. This forgetfulness has occurred only during the external life of relations; during sleep, the spirit, partially freed from corporeal bonds, is restored to freedom and spiritual life, and then it remembers; with its spiritual sight no longer obscured by matter.

23. When taking humanity to its lowest degree on the intellectual ladder, among the most backward savages, one wonders if this is the point of departure of the human soul.

According to the opinion of some spiritualist philosophers, the intelligent principle, distinct from the material principle, becomes individualized and is formulated by passing through the various degrees of animality. It is there that the soul experiences life and develops its first faculties through practice. This would be, so to speak, its incubation period. Once it arrives at the stage of development that includes this state, it receives the special faculties that constitute the human soul. In this way, there would be spiritual filiation, as there is corporeal filiation.

This system, founded on the great law of unity which presides over creation, addresses, it must be admitted, the issues of injustice and the goodness of the Creator; it gives a way out, an end, a destiny for animals, who are no longer disinherited beings, but which find, in the future reserved for them, a compensation for their sufferings. What constitutes the spiritual human being lies not in its origin, but in the special attributes with which it is endowed upon its entry into humanity – attributes which transform it and make it a distinct being, as the tasty fruit is distinct from the bitter root from which it came out. For having passed through the animality chain, humans would be no less humans; and they would not be more animal than the fruit is root, than the scientist is the formless fetus through which he/she began in this world.

However this system raises many questions, and it would not be opportune to discuss their pros and cons here, nor to examine the various hypotheses issued on this subject. Thus, without seeking the origin of the soul, and the chains through which it has been able to pass, we take it at its *entry into humanity*, to the point where, endowed with moral sense and free will, it begins to incur the responsibility for its actions.

24. The obligation of the incarnate spirit to provide for the nourishment of its body, for its safety, for its wellbeing, compels it to apply its faculties to research, to exercise them and to develop them. Its union with matter is therefore useful for its advancement – that is why incarnation is necessary. Besides, because of the intelligent work that it does for its advantage over matter, it helps the transformation and material progress of the globe that the spirit inhabits. Thus, while itself evolving, it contributes to the work of the Creator of which it is the unconscious agent.

25. But the incarnation of the spirit is neither constant nor perpetual, it is only transitory. When leaving a body, it does not take another one instantly; for a longer or shorter period of time, it lives the spiritual life, which is its normal life. Therefore the sum of time spent in different incarnations is little compared with the time it spends in the state of free spirit.

In the interval between its incarnations, the spirit also evolves, in the sense that it makes use for its advancement of the knowledge and experience acquired during its bodily life. I am referring to the spirit having arrived at the state of human soul, having freedom of action, and being aware of its acts. The spirit examines what it has done during its earthly stay, reviews what it has learned, acknowledges its mistakes, draws up its plans, and makes resolutions according to which it intends to guide itself in a new existence by striving to do better. This is how each existence is a step forward in the path of progress, a sort of practical school.

Incarnation is therefore not normally a punishment for the spirit, as some have thought, but a condition inherent in the inferiority of the spirit, and a means of progress.

As the spirit progresses morally, it becomes dematerialized, that is to say, it evades the influence of matter, it purifies itself. Its life becomes spiritualized, its faculties and perceptions expand; its happiness comes from the progress made. But, since it acts by virtue of its free will, it may, by negligence or ill-will, delay its advancement. Thus a spirit may prolong, the duration of its material incarnations which then become for it a punishment, in view of the fact that, by its own fault, it remains in the lower ranks, obliged to repeat the same task. It is therefore up to the spirit to abbreviate, through a work of purification of itself, the duration of the period of incarnations.

26. The material progress of a planet follows the moral progress of its inhabitants; Now, as the creation of worlds and spirits is incessant, because of the fact that some progress more or less rapidly than others by virtue of their free will, it follows that there are younger or older worlds, at different degrees of physical and moral advancement, where incarnation is more or less material, and where, consequently, work for the spirits is more or less harsh. From this point of view, the Earth is one of the least advanced, inhabited by comparatively inferior spirits, and where bodily life is more painful than in others. Conversely, in more backward planets, life is more painful than on Earth, which in this case would be a relatively happy world.

27. When spirits have achieved on a world the amount of progress that the state of such world entails, they leave it to incarnate themselves in another, more advanced one where they acquire new knowledge, and so on, until the incarnation in a material body is no longer useful to them, Then they live exclusively from spiritual life, in which they progress in another direction and in other ways. Arrived at the culminating point of progress, they enjoy supreme bliss and are admitted into the counsels of the Almighty. They have Its thoughts, and become Its messengers, Its direct ministers for the government of the worlds, having under their orders spirits at different degrees of advancement.

Thus all spirits, incarnate or discarnate, regardless of the degree of hierarchy they belong, from the least to the highest, have their attributions in the great mechanism of the universe. Each one of them is useful to the whole, and at the same time useful to themselves. To the less advanced, as to simple operations, it is a material task, at first unconscious, then gradually becoming intelligent tasks. There is activity everywhere in the spiritual world; nowhere lies in idleness.

The community of spirits is in a sense the soul of the universe; it is the spiritual element that acts in everything and everywhere, under the impulsion of God's thought. Without this element there would be only inert matter, without purpose, without intelligence, without any other motor than the material forces which leave a multitude of insoluble problems. By the action of the *individualized* spiritual element, everything has a purpose, a reason for existence; everything is explained. That is why, without spirituality, we encounter insurmountable difficulties.

28. When the Earth was in a climatic conditions proper to the existence of the human species, spirits came to incarnate on the planet; and it is admitted that they have found ready-made physical envelopes which they had only to appropriate for their use. It is better understood that they could have originated simultaneously in several points of the globe.

29. Although the first spirits that came to Earth had to be little advanced – due to the fact that they had to incarnate in very imperfect bodies – there must have been marked differences in their characters and aptitudes, according to their moral and intellectual development. Akin spirits naturally grouped themselves by analogy and mutual sympathy. The Earth has thus been peopled with different categories of spirits, more or less apt or rebellious to progress. The bodies receiving the imprint of the character of the spirit, and procreating themselves according to their respective types, have resulted in different races, both physically and morally. Similar spirits, still incarnating among their fellow beings, have perpetuated the distinctive physical and moral character of races and peoples, which in the long run is lost only through miscegenation and the progress of spirits (see *The Spiritist Review – 1860*, July, "Phrenology and Physiognomy")[56].

30. We can compare the spirits that came to populate the Earth, to these groups of emigrants of various origins who come to settle on virgin land. There, they find wood and stone to build their dwellings, and each gives to their own a different character, according to their degree of knowledge and intelligence. They group themselves by analogy of origins and tastes. These groups end up forming tribes, then nations, each having its own manners and habits.

31. Progress has not been uniform throughout the whole human race; the most intelligent races have naturally advanced before others, without taking into account spirits newly born to spiritual life, who, having come to incarnate on Earth since the first arrivals, render the difference in progress more sensible. Indeed, it would be impossible to attribute the same antiquity of creation to savages, who scarcely distinguish themselves from the apes, as that of the Chinese, and even less to civilized Europeans.

These savage spirits, however, also belong to humanity; they will one day reach the level of their elders, but it will certainly not be in the bodies of the same physical race, unfit for a certain intellectual and moral development. When the instrument is no longer related to their development, they will emigrate from this environment to incarnate in a higher degree, and so on, until they have conquered all the earthly ranks, after which they will leave the Earth to move into increasingly advanced worlds.[57]

REINCARNATION

32. The principle of reincarnation is an inevitable consequence of the law of progress. Without reincarnation, how can one explain the difference between the current social state and that of barbarism?

---

56 [Trans. note] See bibliography at the end of this book.

57 [Trans. note] At this point A. KARDEC had inserted a reference note pointing to an article formerly published in *The Spiritist Review – 1862*, April, footnote 12 (New York: USSF, 2019).

If souls were created at the same time as their bodies, those born today would be just as new and just as primitive as those that lived thousands of years ago. Let me add that between them there is no connection, no necessary relation; that they are completely independent of each other. Why, then, should the souls of today be better endowed by God than their predecessors? Why do they understand better? Why do they have purer instincts, mellower manners? Why can they intuit certain things without having learned them? I challenge anyone to deny the concept of reincarnation, unless one admits that God has created souls of different quality levels, according to times and places; a hypothesis irreconcilable with the idea of supreme justice.

Let us say, on the contrary, that the souls of today have already lived in ancient times; that they may have been as barbarous as their century, but have since progressed; that with each new existence, they bring the knowledge of previous existences, and that, therefore, the souls of civilized times are not created more perfect, but have perfected themselves over time; and you will have the only plausible explanation for the cause of social progress. (*cf.* A. KARDEC, *The Spirits' Book*, chapters IV and V).[58]

---

58 Some people think that the different existences of the soul are fulfilled from world to world, and not on the same globe where each spirit would appear only once.

This doctrine would be admissible if all the inhabitants of the Earth were at exactly the same intellectual and moral level. They could then only advance by going to another world, and their reincarnation on Earth would be useless – God, however, does nothing useless. From the moment that one finds on Earth all different degrees of intelligence and morality, from the savagery which verges on animality to the most advanced civilizations, it is clear that it offers a vast field to progress. One would wonder why savages would be obliged to look elsewhere for the degree above their own when they can find it right beside them. Likewise, why advanced human beings could have taken their first steps only in inferior worlds, when the analogues of all these worlds are right here around them, where there are different degrees of advancement, not only from people to people, but within the same people, and in the same family? If it were so, God would have done something useless by placing ignorance and knowledge side by side, barbarism and civilization, good and evil, while it is precisely this contact that is advancing the latecomers.

There is, therefore, no more need for humans to change their world at each stage, than for a pupil to change schools when he/she changes class. Far from being an advantage for progress, it would be a hindrance, for the spirit would be deprived of the example offered by the sight of higher degrees, and of the possibility of repairing his/her wrongs in the same environment and witnessed, at the same time, by those that he/she has offended – a possibility which is for the spirit the

186

EMIGRATION AND IMMIGRATION OF SPIRITS

33. In the intervening time of their bodily existences, the spirits are in the state of *erraticity*,[59] and compose the spiritual population of the globe. By deaths and births, these two populations flow incessantly into one another. So there are daily emigrations from the corporeal world to the spiritual world, and immigrations from the spiritual world into the corporeal world: this is the normal state of affairs.

34. At certain times, regulated by the divine wisdom, these emigrations and immigrations take place in greater or lesser masses because of major transformations which at the same time leave innumerable amount of deaths that are soon replaced by a proportional amount of incarnations. It is therefore necessary to consider the destructive scourges and cataclysms as occasions of collective arrivals and departures, providential means of renewing the corporeal population of the globe, of reinvigorating it by the introduction of new, more refined spiritual elements. If in these catastrophes there is the destruction of a great number of bodies, only the *torn physical garments* are destroyed, yet no spirit perishes; they only change of

---

most powerful means of moral advancement, dispersing and becoming strangers after living only a short time together, family ties and friendship bonds would be broken, for not having had enough time to be consolidated.

That the spirits leave for a more advanced world once that on which they live can no longer teach it anything, is an inescapable fact, and therein lies a principle. If one would leave a world before that, it is undoubtedly by individual reasons that God has weighed in Its wisdom.

Everything has a purpose in creation, otherwise God would be neither prudent nor wise. However, if the Earth were to be only once, the single stage for the progress of each individual, what use would it be for children, who die at an early age, to come and spend a few years, a few months, a few hours, during which time they cannot acquire anything? It is the same for the mentally handicapped and the mentally challenged. A theory is good only on the condition of solving all the questions that affect it. The question of premature deaths has been a stumbling block for all philosophical and religious doctrines, except for Spiritism, which alone has solved it in a rational way.

For those who lead a normal course of life on Earth, there is a real advantage for their progress in finding themselves again in the same environment, in order to resume what they have left unfinished, often in the same family or in contact with the same persons, to repair the harm they have done, or to suffer the punishment of retaliation.

59 [Trans. note] *Erraticity* or *errant state* is an early Spiritist terminology used to refer generically to the period a spirit "wanders" in between incarnations.

environment. Instead of leaving Earth individually, they leave it in numbers; that is the only difference. Because, inevitably, despite leaving by one cause or another, they would nonetheless have to leave Earth sooner or later.

The rapid, almost instantaneous renovations which take place in the spiritual element of the population, as a result of destructive plagues and other scourges, hasten social progress. Without the emigrations and immigrations which happen from time to time to give the human race a violent impulsion, it would advance with extreme slowness.

It is remarkable that all the great calamities which decimate populations are always followed by an epoch of progress in the physical, intellectual or moral orders, and consequently in the social state of the nations in which they are accomplished. The reason is that they are intended to bring about a reshuffling of the spiritual population, which is the normal active population of the globe.

35.   This transfusion which takes place between the incarnate population and the discarnate population of a globe, also takes place between different worlds, either individually under normal conditions, or by masses in special circumstances. There are emigrations and collective immigrations from one world to another. The result is the introduction into the population of a globe of entirely new elements. New groups of spirits, mingling with existing groups, constitute new human races. Now, as spirits never lose what they have acquired, they bring with them the intellectual skills and intuition of the knowledge they possess. Therefore they imprint their character upon the bodily race they come to animate. For this they do not need new bodies to be specially created for their use, since the corporeal species already exists. They find everything ready to receive them, as they are simply new inhabitants; when they arrive on Earth. They form the first part of their spiritual population, which then incarnate like the others.

ADAMIC RACE

36.   According to the teaching of the spirits, it was one of those great immigrations, or, if you like, one of those colonies of spirits from another sphere, which gave birth to the race symbolized in the person of Adam, and, for this reason, named Adamic race. When it arrived, the Earth was already populated from time immemorial, *like America when the Europeans came there.*

The Adamic race, more advanced than those who had preceded it on Earth, was indeed the most intelligent; it has been the one that drove all others to progress. The Mosaic Genesis shows them, since their beginnings, as industrious, fit for the arts and sciences, without having passed through intellectual infancy, which is not peculiar to primitive peoples, but which accords with public opinion that it consisted of already evolved spirits. Everything proves that it is not old on Earth, and nothing prevents it from being here only for a few thousand years, which would be in contradiction neither with geological facts, nor with anthropological observations, tending on the contrary, to confirm them.

37. The doctrine that has claimed that the whole human race has derived from a single individuality six thousand years ago is not admissible in the current state of knowledge. The principal considerations which contradict it, of physical and moral orders, can be summed up as follows;

38. From the physiological point of view, certain races have particular characteristics which do not allow them to be assigned a common origin. There are differences which are obviously not the effect of the climate, since whites breeding in lands originally inhabited by blacks (such as Africa) do not become black as a result, and vice versa. Although the heat of the Sun increases, tanning the epidermis, it has never transformed a an individual of one race into another, nor has it changed the shape of the features of anyone's physiognomy, nor has it turned silky hair into frizzy and woolly hair. For instance, it is now known that the color of the so-called black race comes from a particular subcutaneous tissue that belongs to that species.

We must therefore consider that the Black, Mongolian and Caucasian races; each having their own origin, and having originated simultaneously or successively in different parts of the globe; produced secondary mixed breeds with their miscegenation. The physiological traits of the primitive races are an obvious indication that they come from specific types. The same considerations therefore exist for humans as for animals, as regards their numerous varieties.

39. Adam and his descendants are represented in Genesis as essentially intelligent humans, since, from the second generation, they built cities, cultivated the soil, and worked metals. Their progress in the arts and sciences is fast and consistently sustained. It would not be conceivable, therefore, that this stock would have given birth to so many backward nations; so rudimentary in their intelligence, that even today they still verge on animality; as if having lost all trace and even a hint of traditional memory of what their ancestors did. Such a radical difference in intellectual aptitude and moral development attests, with no less obviousness, to a difference of origin.

40. Independently of geological facts, the proof of the existence of humans on Earth before the time fixed by Genesis is obtained from the own population of the globe.

Without mentioning the Chinese chronology, which goes back, it is said, thirty thousand years, other authentic documents attest that Egypt, India and other countries were populated and flourishing at least three thousand years BC – therefore a thousand years after the creation of the first human being, according to biblical chronology. Recent documents and observations seem to leave no doubt today about relations which have existed between America and the ancient Egyptians; from which it must be concluded that the American continent was already populated at that time. Therefore, it would have to be admitted that in just a thousand years the posterity of a single individual could have covered most of the Earth; but such fertility would be contrary to all anthropological laws. Genesis itself does not attribute to the first descendants of Adam an abnormal fecundity, since it gives the nominal enumeration descendants up to Noah.

41. This impossibility becomes even more evident if one admits, with Genesis, that the deluge destroyed *the entire human race*, with the exception of Noah and his family, which was not numerous, in the year of the world. 1656, or 2348 BC. It would in fact be only from Noah that the settlement of the whole globe would date; now, about this time, history designates Menes as king of Egypt. When the Hebrews settled in Egypt, 642 years after the flood, that nation was already a powerful empire which would have been populated, not to mention the other countries, in less than six centuries, only by the descendants of Noah, which is not admissible.

Note, by the way, that the Egyptians welcomed the Hebrews as strangers. It would be surprising if they had lost the memory of a common origin so close in time, since they religiously preserved all monuments of their history.

A rigorous logic, corroborated by facts, thus demonstrates in the most peremptory way that human beings have been on Earth for an indeterminate time, well before the time assigned by Genesis. The same is true of the diversity of primitive progeny, since the impossibility of a proposition being demonstrated, its contrary proposition is necessarily demonstrated as well. If geology discovers authentic traces of the presence of humans before the great diluvial period, such demonstration will be even more absolute.

DOCTRINE OF FALLEN ANGELS AND A LOST PARADISE[60]

42. The word *angel*, like many others, has several meanings: it is taken indifferently in a good or bad sense, since one says the good and the bad angels, the angel of light and the angel of darkness; from which it follows that, in its general meaning, it simply means *spirit*.

Angels are not beings apart from humanity, created perfect, but spirits that have arrived at perfection, like all created beings, through their efforts and merit. If angels were beings created perfect, rebellion against God being a sign of inferiority, those which rebelled could not be angels. Rebellion against God would not be conceived on the part of beings created perfect, whereas it is conceived on the part of beings that are still backward.

By its etymology, the word angel (from Greek *angelos*) means an *envoy*, a *messenger*; but it is not rational to suppose that God has picked up Its messengers among beings who are imperfect enough to rebel against It.

60 When, in *The Spiritist Review – 1862*, January, I published an "Essay about the Interpretation of the Doctrine of the Fallen Angels," I presented this theory only as a hypothesis, with only the authority of a controversial personal opinion, because then I lacked elements which would be complete enough for an absolute statement. I gave it on a trial basis, in order to encourage its examination, always determined to abandon it or to modify it if necessary. Today, this theory has undergone the test of universal control. Not only has it been accepted by the great majority of Spiritists as the most rational and the most consistent with the supreme justice of God, but has also been confirmed by the communications given by the spirits on this subject. The same is true as regards the origin of the Adamic race.

43. Until they have reached a certain degree of perfection, spirits are susceptible to fail while they are incarnate or discarnate. To fail is to break God's law, although this law is written in the hearts of all souls, so that they do not need revelation to know their duties. The spirit understands it only gradually, as its intelligence grows. Those who break this law by ignorance and lack of experience, which is acquired only with time, incur only a relative responsibility; but in those whose intelligence is already developed, and who, despite having all the means to enlighten themselves, choose to violate the law voluntarily and knowingly do harm, this is a revolt, a rebellion against the author of the law.

44. The worlds progress physically through the development of matter, and morally by the purification of the spirits which inhabit them. Happiness is there when good prevails over evil, and the predominance of good is the result of the moral advancement of spirits. Intellectual progress is not enough, since with intelligence they still can do evil.

So when a world has arrived at one of its periods of transformation which should elevate it in the hierarchy, mutations take place in its incarnate and discarnate population. It is then that the great emigrations and immigrations take place. Those who, despite their intelligence and knowledge, have persevered in evil, in their rebellion against God and Its laws, would henceforth be a hindrance to further moral progress and a permanent cause of trouble for the rest, by preventing the happiness of the good ones. That is why they are excluded and sent to less advanced worlds; where they will apply their intelligence and the intuition of their acquired knowledge to the progress of those among whom they are called to live, at the same time that they will atone, in a series of painful lives and hard work, for their past faults and their voluntary hardening.

What will they be taken for among these tribes new to them, still in the infancy of barbarism, if not as angels or fallen spirits sent to atone themselves? Is not the abode from which they were expelled a lost paradise for them? Was it not a place of delight for them in comparison with the inhospitable environment in which they are to be relegated for thousands of centuries until the day when they have deserved their deliverance? The vague, intuitive recollection they maintain is for them like a distant mirage that reminds them of what they *lost by their own fault.*

45. But at the same time that the wicked leave the world they lived in, they are replaced by better spirits, either from the erraticity of that same world or from a less advanced world if they have deserved to come, and for which their new stay is a reward. The spiritual population being thus renewed while purged of its worst elements, after a while, the moral state of that world is improved.

These mutations are sometimes partial, that is to say, limited to a people, to a race; at other times they are general, when the period of renovation has arrived for the globe.

46. The Adamic race has all the characteristics of a proscribed race. The spirits which are part of it have been exiled to Earth, which was already populated, but of primitive human beings, still immersed in ignorance, and whose mission it was to advance by bringing among the latter the lights of a developed intelligence. Is it not this the role that this so-called Adamic race has filled to this day? Their intellectual superiority proves that the world from which they came was more advanced than Earth. But that superior world had to enter a new phase of progress, and these spirits, on account of their obstinacy, not having been able to rise to that height, would have been displaced there and would have become an obstacle to the providential march of things. That is why they were excluded, while others deserved to replace them.

By relegating this race to Earth, a planet of labor and suffering, God was right to say to them: "By the sweat of your face you shall eat bread (Genesis 3:19)." In his leniency, God promised humans that It would send them a *Savior*, in other words, the one who would enlighten them on the path to follow in order to get out of this place of misery, of this *hell*, and arrive at the happiness of the elect. This Savior was sent to us in the person of Christ, who taught the law of love and charity unknown to us, and who was to be our true anchor of salvation. Christ not only taught the law, but he gave the example by practicing this law, by his meekness, his humility, his patience to suffer without murmuring the most ignominious mistreatment and the greatest pains. For such a mission to be accomplished without deviations, a spirit above human frailties was required.

It is also with a view to advancing humanity in a definite direction, that higher-order spirits, without having the qualities of Christ, may incarnate from time to time on Earth to perform special missions that benefit their personal advancement, if they fulfill them according to the Creator's views.

47. Without reincarnation, Christ's mission would be nonsense, as well as the promise made by God. Suppose, indeed, that the soul of every human being is created at the birth of his/her body, and that it only appears and disappears on Earth: there would be no relation between those who have come from Adam to Jesus Christ, or among those who have come since. They all would be strangers to one another. The promise of a Savior made by God could not apply to the descendants of Adam, if their souls were not yet created. In order that the mission of Christ could be connected with the words of God, they must be referring to the same souls. If these souls are new, they cannot be tainted by the fault of the first ancestor, who is only the carnal parent and not the spiritual parent; otherwise God would have created souls tainted by a fault which they would not have committed. Thus the usual concept of original sin implies the necessity of a relation between the souls of the time of Christ and those of the time of Adam, and consequently of reincarnation.

Now suppose that all these souls were part of the colony of spirits exiled to planet Earth in Adam's time; and that they were tainted with the fault that had excluded them from a better world; and then you will have the only rational interpretation for the original sin, a sin peculiar to each individual, and not the result of taking responsibility for the fault of another, whom one has never known. Imagine that these souls or spirits are reborn to corporeal life at various times on Earth, in order to evolve and purify themselves; that Christ has come to enlighten these same souls not only for their past lives, but for their subsequent lives; and only then you can give to his mission a real serious purpose acceptable to reason.

48. A familiar example, striking by its analogy, will give a better understanding of the principles which have just been exposed.

On May 24, 1861, the frigate Iphigenia brought to New Caledonia a disciplinary company composed of 291 men. The commander of the colony sent them, on their arrival, an order in the following terms:

"By setting foot on this distant land, you have already understood the role that is reserved for you.

"At the example of our brave soldiers of the Navy serving before your eyes, you will help us carry with brilliance, among the wild tribes of New Caledonia, the torch of civilization. Is this not a beautiful and noble mission that I ask from you? You shall fulfill it with dignity."

"Listen to the voice and advice of your leaders. I am at the helm; may my words be well understood."

"The choice of your commander, your officers, your non-commissioned officers and corporals is a sure guarantee of all the efforts that will be made to make you excellent soldiers; and I add: to raise you to the level of good citizens and turn you into honorable settlers, if you wish."

"Your discipline will be severe; as it must be. Placed in my hands, let it be known, it will be firm and inflexible, as well as fair and paternal. It will be able to distinguish the error of vice and degradation ..."

Therefore this is a case of individuals expelled, for bad behavior, from a civilized country, and sent away, as punishment, to live among barbarians.

What does the chief commander tell them? "You have broken the laws of your country; you have been a cause of trouble and scandal, so you have been driven out. We sent you here, but you can redeem your past; you can, through work, earn an honorable position, and become honest citizens. You have a beautiful mission to fulfill, that of bringing civilization among these savage tribes. The discipline will be severe, but fair, and I will be able to distinguish those who behave well."

To these men relegated to savage place, would not the motherland be a paradise lost by their fault and their rebellion to the law? In this distant land, are they not fallen angels? Is this not the language of the leader whom God spoke to, when addressing the spirits exiled on Earth? "You have disobeyed my laws, and that is why I drove you out of the world where you could live happily and peacefully. Here you will be condemned to work, but you will be able, by your good conduct, to deserve forgiveness and reconquer the homeland that you have lost through your fault, in a word, heaven."

49. At first sight, the idea of decline seems to be in contradiction with the principle that spirits cannot retrogress; but we must take into consideration that it is not a question of returning to the primitive state. The spirit, though in an inferior position, loses nothing of what it has acquired; its moral and intellectual development is the same, whatever the environment in which it is placed. It is in the same position of the man of the world condemned to the galleys for his misdeeds; it has fallen from the social point of view, but it becomes neither more stupid nor more ignorant as a result.

50. Do we now believe that these individuals sent to New Caledonia will suddenly become models of virtue? That they will suddenly abjure their past mistakes? We should not know human nature to suppose it. For the same reason, the spirits of the Adamic race, once transplanted to the planet of exile, did not instantly give up their pride and bad instincts. For a long time they have retained the tendencies of their origin, a remnant of the old leaven, so to speak. Now, is this not the original sin? The task they bring with them in being born is one of a culpable race of guilty spirits to which they belong, but which they can erase through repentance, atonement, and the renovation of their moral being. Original sin, considered as the responsibility of a fault committed by another, is nonsense and the negation of God's justice. Considered, on the contrary, as a consequence and a remnant of a primary imperfection of the individual, not only can reason admit it, but we find in all fairness the responsibility which results from it.

Chapter XII
Mosaic Genesis

THE SIX DAYS · PARADISE LOST

THE SIX DAYS[61]

Chapter One

1. 1. In the beginning, God created the heavens and the earth. 2. The earth was without form and void, and darkness was over the face of the deep. And the Spirit of God was hovering over the face of the waters. 3. And God said, "Let there be light," and there was light. 4. And God saw that the light was good. And God separated the light from the darkness. 5. God called the light Day, and the darkness he called Night. And there was evening and there was morning, the first day.

6. And God said, "Let there be an expanse in the midst of the waters, and let it separate the waters from the waters." 7. And God made the expanse and separated the waters that were under the expanse from the waters that were above the expanse. And it was so. 8. And God called the expanse Heaven. And there was evening and there was morning, the second day.

9. And God said, "Let the waters under the heavens be gathered together into one place, and let the dry land appear." And it was so. 10. God called the dry land Earth,4 and the waters that were gathered together he called Seas. And God saw that it was good. 11. And God said, "Let the earth sprout vegetation, plants yielding seed, and fruit trees bearing fruit in which is their seed, each according to its kind, on the earth." And it was so. 12. The earth brought forth vegetation, plants yielding seed according to their own kinds, and trees bearing fruit in which is their seed, each according to its kind.

---

61 [Trans. note] All biblical citations extracted from the *Holy Bible, English Standard Version (ESV)*.

And God saw that it was good. 13. And there was evening and there was morning, the third day.

14. And God said, "Let there be lights in the expanse of the heavens to separate the day from the night. And let them be for signs and for seasons, and for days and years, 15. and let them be lights in the expanse of the heavens to give light upon the earth." And it was so. 16. And God made the two great lights – the greater light to rule the day and the lesser light to rule the night – and the stars. 17. And God set them in the expanse of the heavens to give light on the earth, 18. to rule over the day and over the night, and to separate the light from the darkness. And God saw that it was good. 19. And there was evening and there was morning, the fourth day.

20. And God said, "Let the waters swarm with swarms of living creatures, and let birds fly above the earth across the expanse of the heavens." 21. So God created the great sea creatures and every living creature that moves, with which the waters swarm, according to their kinds, and every winged bird according to its kind. And God saw that it was good. 22. And God blessed them, saying, "Be fruitful and multiply and fill the waters in the seas, and let birds multiply on the earth." 23. And there was evening and there was morning, the fifth day.

24. And God said, "Let the earth bring forth living creatures according to their kinds – livestock and creeping things and beasts of the earth according to their kinds." And it was so. 25. And God made the beasts of the earth according to their kinds and the livestock according to their kinds, and everything that creeps on the ground according to its kind. And God saw that it was good.

26. Then God said, "Let us make man in our image, after our likeness. And let them have dominion over the fish of the sea and over the birds of the heavens and over the livestock and over all the earth and over every creeping thing that creeps on the earth." 27. So God created man in his own image, in the image of God he created him; male and female he created them. 28. And God blessed them. And God said to them, "Be fruitful and multiply and fill the earth and subdue it and have dominion over the fish of the sea and over the birds of the heavens and over every living thing that moves on the earth." 29. And God said, "Behold, I have given you every plant yielding seed that is on the face of all the earth, and every tree with

seed in its fruit. You shall have them for food. 30. And to every beast of the earth and to every bird of the heavens and to everything that creeps on the earth, everything that has the breath of life, I have given every green plant for food." And it was so. 31. And God saw everything that he had made, and behold, it was very good. And there was evening and there was morning, the sixth day.[62]

Chapter Two

1. Thus the heavens and the earth were finished, and all the host of them. 2. And on the seventh day God finished his work that he had done, and he rested on the seventh day from all his work that he had done. 3. So God blessed the seventh day and made it holy, because on it God rested from all his work that he had done in creation. 4. These are the generations of the heavens and the earth when they were created, in the day that the LORD God made the earth and the heavens. 5. When no bush of the field was yet in the land and no small plant of the field had yet sprung up – for the LORD God had not caused it to rain on the land, and there was no man to work the ground, 6. and a mist was going up from the land and was watering the whole face of the ground –

7. then the LORD God formed the man of dust from the ground and breathed into his nostrils the breath of life, and the man became a living creature.

---

2. After the developments contained in the preceding chapters about the origin and constitution of the universe, according to the data provided by science for the material part, and according to Spiritism for the spiritual part, it would be useful to put the texts in parallel, even Moses' Genesis, so that everyone could make a comparison and arrive at an informed judgment. A few additional explanations will suffice to better understand the parts wherever they need special clarifications.

3. On some points, there is certainly a remarkable concordance between the Genesis of Moses and science; but it would be a mistake to believe that it suffices to substitute for the six days of twenty-four hours of creation, six indeterminate time periods to find a complete

---

62 [Trans. note] The French Bible used by KARDEC goes up to number 32, whereas the English Bible finishes at number 31, with no text missing between them.

analogy. Moreover, it would be an equally great mistake to believe that, except for the allegorical meaning of a few words, Genesis and science follow each other step by step and are only the paraphrase of each other.

4. Let us first remark, as has already been said (see chapter **VII**, item **14** above), that the number of six geological periods is arbitrary, since there are more than twenty-five well-characterized formations. This number marks only the great general phases; it was adopted, in principle, only to refer back, as much as possible, to the biblical text at a time – not far removed from the rest, where it was believed that science should be controlled by the Bible. This is why the authors of most cosmogonic theories, in order to be more easily accepted, have endeavored to agree with the sacred scriptures. When science relied on the experimental method, it felt stronger and emancipated itself; so today, the Bible is controlled by science.

On the other hand, geology, taking its point of departure only at the formation of granitic soils, does not include in the number of its periods the primordial state of the Earth. Nor does it deal with the Sun, the Moon, the stars, or the whole universe, which belong to astronomy. To enter into the framework of Genesis, it is therefore necessary to add a first period embracing this order of phenomena, that we could call *astronomical period.*

Moreover, the diluvial period is not considered by all geologists as a distinct period, but as a transient and momentary fact which has not markedly changed the climatic state of the globe, nor marked a new phase in the vegetal and animal species, since, with few exceptions, the same species are found before and after the deluge. We can therefore abstract from it without departing from the truth.

5. The following comparative table, in which are summed up the phenomena which characterize each of the six periods, makes it possible to embrace the whole, and to reduce the relations and the differences which exist between them and Biblical Genesis:

SCIENCE	GENESIS
I. *Astronomical period*	*1st day*
Agglomeration of universal cosmic matter in a point of space into a nebula which has given birth, by the condensation of matter on various points, to the stars, the Sun, the Earth, the Moon, and all planets.	The sky and the earth. – The light.
Fluidic and incandescent primitive state of the Earth. – Huge atmosphere charged with all the water in steam, and with all the volatilizable matters.	
II. *Primeval or primary period*	*2nd day*
Hardening of the surface of the Earth by cooling; formation of granitic layers. – A thick and burning atmosphere, impenetrable to the Sun's rays. – Gradual precipitation of water and volatilized solids in the air. Absence of all organic life	The firmament. - Separation of the waters that are under the firmament from those that are above.
III. *Transition period*	*3rd day*
The waters cover the entire surface of the globe. – First deposits of sediment formed by water. – Moist heat. – The Sun begins to pierce the misty atmosphere. – First organized beings of a most rudimentary constitution. – Lichens, mosses, ferns, lycopods, herbaceous plants. Colossal vegetation. – First marine animals: zoophytes, polyps, crustaceans. – Coal deposits.	The waters under the firmament gather together; the arid element appears.– The land and the seas.– Plants.
IV. *Secondary period*	*4th day*
Surface of the ground slightly uneven; shallow and swampy waters. – Less scalding temperature; more refined atmosphere. – Considerable deposits of limestone by water. – Less colossal vegetation; new species; woody plants; first trees. – Fishes; cetaceans; shelled animals; large aquatic reptiles and amphibians.	The Sun, the Moon, and the stars.

V. *Tertiary period*	*5th day*
Great upheavals of the solid crust; formation of the continents. Retreat of waters in low places; sea formation. – Atmosphere purified; current temperature by solar heat. – Gigantic terrestrial animals. Current plants and animals. Birds.	Fishes and birds.

UNIVERSAL FLOOD

VI. *Quaternary or post-diluvial period*	*6th day*
Alluvial land. – Current plants and animals. – Human beings.	Terrestrial animals – Human beings.

6. A first fact which emerges from the comparative table above is that the work of each of the six days does not correspond rigorously, as many believe, to each of the six geological periods. The most remarkable concordance is that of the succession of organic beings, which is almost the same, and in the emergence of humans last. This is an important fact.

There is also coincidence, not with the numerical order of the periods, but for the fact, in the passage where it is said, on the third day: "Let the waters under the heavens be gathered together into one place, and let the dry land appear." This is the expression of what took place in the tertiary period, when the upheavals of the solid crust exposed the continents, and held back the waters which formed the seas. Only then did the terrestrial animals appear, both according to geology and according to Moses.

7. When Moses said that creation was done in six days, did he want to talk about days of twenty-four hours, or did he understand that word in the sense of: period, duration, indefinite space of time? Did the Hebrew word translated as *day* have this double meaning? The first hypothesis is the most probable, if one refers to the text itself. The evening and morning specification, which limits each of the six days, gives every reason to suppose that he wanted to refer to ordinary days. One cannot even conceive of any doubt in this respect, when he says in verse 5: "God called the light Day, and the darkness he called Night. And there was evening and there was morning, the first day." This, of course, can only apply to the day of twenty-four hours, divided by light and darkness. The meaning is even more precise when he says, in verses 17–19, speaking of the Sun, the Moon and the stars: "And God set them in the expanse of the heavens to give light on the earth, to rule over the day and over the night, and to separate the light from the darkness.... And there was evening and there was morning, the fourth day."

Moreover, everything in creation was miraculous, and since we are all in the way of miracles, we can perfectly believe that the Earth was made in six times twenty-four hours, especially when we ignore the first natural laws. This belief has been shared by all civilized peoples until the time when geology came, pieces in hand, demonstrating the impossibility of such feat.

8. One of the most criticized points in Genesis is the creation of the Sun after the light. It has been sought to explain it even according to the data furnished by geology, by saying that, in the first stages of its formation, Earth's atmosphere, being charged with dense and opaque vapors, did not allow the sun to be seen, which consequently did not exist for the Earth at the time. This reasoning would perhaps be acceptable if, at that time, there had been human inhabitants to judge of the presence or absence of the Sun; however, according to Moses, there were still only plants, which, by the way, could not have grown and multiplied without the action of solar heat.

There is, of course, an anachronism in the chronological order assigned by Moses to the creation of the Sun; but, involuntarily or not, he was not wrong in saying that light had preceded the Sun.

The Sun is not the principle of universal light, but a concentration of the luminous element on a point; in other words, a fluid which, under given circumstances, acquires luminous properties. This fluid, which is the cause, must necessarily exist before the Sun, which is only an effect. The Sun is a *cause* for the light it spreads, but it is just an *effect* in relation to that which it has received.

In a dark room, a lighted candle is a small sun. What did we do to light the candle? The lighting property of the luminous fluid has been sparked, and this fluid has been concentrated on one point. The candle is the cause of the light scattered in the room, but if the light principle had not existed before the candle, it could not be lit.

It is the same with the Sun. The error comes from the misconception that the Sun has been a long time, since the entire universe began, with Earth; and we do not understand how the Sun could have been created after light. Now we know that before our Sun and our Earth, millions of suns and planets existed, which consequently enjoyed light. The assertion of Moses is therefore perfectly correct in principle; it is false in that it causes the Earth to be created before the Sun. The Earth, being subject to the Sun in its translation movement, had to be formed after it. This is something that Moses could not know, since he did not know the law of gravitation.

The same thought is found in the Genesis of ancient Persians; in the first chapter of the *Vendedad*, Ormuzd, recounting the origin of the world, says: "I created the light that went to light the Sun, the Moon and the stars, a (*Dictionnaire de Mythologie Universelle* [*Dictionary of Universal Mythology*]) The form is certainly here clearer and more scientific than in Moses, and does not need any further comment.

9. Moses obviously shared the most primitive beliefs about cosmogony. Like the people of his day, he believed the sky was solid, and in upper reservoirs for the waters. This thought is expressed without allegory or ambiguity in this passage (verses 6 *et seq.*): "And God said, 'Let there be an expanse in the midst of the waters, and let it separate the waters from the waters.' And God made the expanse and separated the waters that were under the expanse from the waters that were above the expanse." (See chapter **V** above, "Systems of the ancient and modern worlds," items **3**, **4** and **5**.)

An ancient belief made water be regarded as the principle, the primeval generating element; so Moses does not speak of the creation of the waters, which seem to have already existed. "Darkness was over the face of the deep," that is to say, the depths of space that imagination conceived as vaguely occupied by the waters and in darkness before the creation of light. That is why Moses says that "the Spirit of God was hovering over the face of the waters." The Earth being supposed to be formed in the midst of the waters, it was necessary to isolate it. It was supposed, then, that God had made the firmament,[63] a solid vault which separated the waters from above from those which remained on the earth.

---

63 [Trans. note] Firmament, translated as *expanse* in the English Bible used herein.

To understand certain parts of Genesis, it is necessary to place oneself in the point of view of the cosmogonic ideas of the time in which it was conceived and which it reflects

10.   Since the progress of physics and astronomy, such a doctrine is not sustainable.[64] Yet Moses gives these words as coming from God Itself. Now, since they express a notoriously false fact, one of two things happened: either God was been mistaken in the account It makes of Its own work, or this narrative is not a divine revelation. Since the first supposition is not admissible, it must be concluded that Moses expressed his own ideas (see chapter **I**, item **3** above).

11.   Moses is more in the truth when he says that God has formed man with the mud of the earth.[65] Science indeed shows us (see chapter **X** above) that the human body is composed of elements drawn from inorganic matter, that is, from the mud of the earth.

The woman formed of one of Adam's ribs is an allegory, childish in appearance if taken literally, but deep in meaning. Its purpose is to show that woman is of the same nature as man, therefore her equal before God, and not a being created apart, made to be enslaved and treated as an inferior being. Coming from his own flesh, the image of equality is much more striking than if she had been formed separately from the same mud; it is to say to man that she is his equal, and not his slave, and that he must love her as a part of himself.

12.   For uneducated spirits, without any idea of the general laws, unable to embrace the whole and to conceive of the infinite, this miraculous and instant creation had something fantastic that struck their imagination. The image of the universe as drawn from nothingness in a few days, by a single act of the creative will, was for them the most brilliant sign of God's power. Indeed what depiction of such power could be more sublime and more poetic than these words: "And God said, 'Let there be light,' and there was light."

---

64 However crass the error of such a belief may be, children today are still cradled in it as being a sacred truth. It is only shuddering that some schoolteachers dare to venture a timid interpretation. Then how do we want them not to grow incredulous later on?

65 The Hebrew word *haadam*, man, from which comes the name Adam, and the word *haadamah*, the earth, have the same root.

God, creating the universe by the slow and gradual fulfillment of the laws of Nature, would have seemed to them less great and less powerful; they needed something marvelous, away from ordinary ways, otherwise they would have said that God was no more able than humans. A scientific and reasoned theory of creation would have left them cold and indifferent.

Primitive humans are like children to whom one must give only the intellectual nourishment adequate to their intelligence. Today, when we are enlightened by the light of science, let us notice the material errors of the story of Moses, but not blame him for having spoken the language of his time, otherwise he would have been neither understood nor accepted.

Let us respect these depictions, which seem puerile to us today, as we respect the apologists who enlightened our early childhood and opened our minds by teaching us how to think. It is with these images that Moses inculcated the hearts of early humans with faith in God and Its power; a naive faith which was to be purified later on in the flames of science. Because today you know how to read fluently, do not despise the book where you learned to spell.

Let us not reject Moses' Genesis; instead let us study it, as we study the history of the infancy of civilizations. It is an epic, rich in allegories whose hidden meaning must be sought; and that one should necessarily comment and explain aided by the light of reason and science. While highlighting its poetic beauties, and the veiled instructions contained in its pictorial form, we must plainly prove its errors, in the interest of religion itself. It will be better respected when these errors are not imposed on faith as truths, and God will appear only greater and more powerful when Its name is not mingled with counterfeit facts.

PARADISE LOST[66]

Chapter Two

13. 8. And the LORD God planted a garden in Eden, in the east, and there he put the man whom he had formed. 9. And out

---

66 Immediately after a few verses I have placed the literal translation of the Hebrew text, which more faithfully renders the original thought. Thus the allegorical meaning comes out more clearly. [Trans. note: Textual differences between KARDEC's literal translations and the English Bible used herein are minimal, due to the greater accuracy of the *English Standard Version* vis-à-vis the old French Bible.]

of the ground the LORD God made to spring up every tree that is pleasant to the sight and good for food. The tree of life was in the midst of the garden,[67] and the tree of the knowledge of good and evil. *...(Jehovah Elohim made sprout out of the earth* [min haadamah] *every beautiful tree to see and eat, and the tree of life* [vehetz hachayim] *in the middle of the garden, and the tree of the knowledge of good and evil.)*

15. The LORD God took the man and put him in the garden of Eden to work it and keep it. 16. And the LORD God commanded the man, saying, "You may surely eat of every tree of the garden, *(Jehovah Elohim commanded to man* [haadam], *saying, from all the trees of the garden* [hagan] *you can eat)* 17. but of the tree of the knowledge of good and evil you shall not eat, for in the day that you eat of it you shall surely die." *(And from the tree of the knowledge of good and evil* [oumehetz hadaat tob vara] *you will not eat it, because the day you eat it, you will die.)*

Chapter Three

14. 1. Now the serpent was more crafty than any other beast of the field that the LORD God had made. He said to the woman, "Did God actually say, 'You shall not eat of any tree in the garden'?" *(And the serpent was more cunning than all the terrestrial animals that Jehovah Elohim had made, it said to the woman* [el haisha]: *Did Elohim say, "You shall not eat of any tree from the garden?")* 2. And the woman said to the serpent, "We may eat of the fruit of the trees in the garden, *(The woman said to the serpent, of the fruit* [miperi] *of the trees of the garden, we can eat.)* 3. but God said, 'You shall not eat of the fruit of the tree that is in the midst of the garden, neither shall you touch it, lest you die.'" 4. But the serpent said to the woman, "You will not surely die. 5. For God knows that when you eat of it your eyes will be opened, and you will be *like God,* knowing good and evil."

6. So when the woman saw that the tree was good for food, and that it was a delight to the eyes, and that the tree was to be desired to make one wise, she took of its fruit and ate, and she also gave some to her husband who was with her, and he ate.... (The woman

---

67 Garden or paradise, from Latin *paradisus*, Greek *paradeisos*, garden, orchard, place planted with trees. The Hebrew word used in Genesis is *hagan*, which has the same meaning.

saw that it was good for food, and that it was desirable for making one be able to understand [leaskil]*, and she took from its fruit, etc.)*

8. And they heard the sound of the LORD God walking in the garden in the cool of the day, and the man and his wife hid themselves from the presence of the LORD God among the trees of the garden.

9. But the LORD God called to the man and said to him, "Where are you?" 10. And he said, "I heard the sound of you in the garden, and I was afraid, because I was naked, and I hid myself." 11. He said, "Who told you that you were naked? Have you eaten of the tree of which I commanded you not to eat?" 12. The man said, "The woman whom you gave to be with me, she gave me fruit of the tree, and I ate." 13. Then the LORD God said to the woman, "What is this that you have done?" The woman said, "The serpent deceived me, and I ate."

14. The LORD God said to the serpent, "Because you have done this, cursed are you above all livestock and above all beasts of the field; on your belly you shall go, and dust you shall eat all the days of your life. 15. I will put enmity between you and the woman, and between your offspring and her offspring; he shall bruise your head, and you shall bruise his heel."

16. To the woman he said, "I will surely multiply your pain in childbearing; in pain you shall bring forth children. Your desire shall be for your husband, and he shall rule over you."

17. And to Adam he said, "Because you have listened to the voice of your wife and have eaten of the tree of which I commanded you, 'You shall not eat of it,' cursed is the ground because of you; in pain you shall eat of it all the days of your life; 18. thorns and thistles it shall bring forth for you; and you shall eat the plants of the field. 19. By the 'sweat of your face you shall eat bread, till you return to the ground, for out of it you were taken; for you are dust, and to dust you shall return."

20. The man called his wife's name Eve, because she was the mother of all living.

21. And the LORD God made for Adam and for his wife garments of skins and clothed them. 22. Then the LORD God said, "Behold, the man has become like one of us in knowing good and evil. Now, lest he reach out his hand and take also of the tree of life and eat,

and live forever" (*Jehovah Elohim said: Behold, man has been like one of us for the knowledge of good and evil, and now he can reach out and take from the tree of life* [veata pen ischlach yado velakach mehetz hachayim]; *he will eat from it and live forever.*)

23. Therefore the LORD God sent him out from the garden of Eden to work the ground from which he was taken. 24. He drove out the man, and at the east of the garden of Eden he placed the cherubim[68] and a flaming sword that turned every way to guard the way to the tree of life.

15. Under a puerile and sometimes ridiculous image, if one stops at the form, allegory often hides the greatest truths. Is a fable more absurd at first sight than that of Saturn, a god devouring stones he takes for his children? But, at the same time, what can be more profoundly philosophical and true than this figure, if one seeks the moral sense of it! Saturn is the personification of time; all things being the work of time, he is the father of all that exists, but also everything is destroyed with time. Saturn devouring stones is the emblem of the destruction by time of the hardest bodies that are his children, since they have formed over time. And who escapes this destruction according to this same allegory? Jupiter, the emblem of superior intelligence, of the spiritual principle that is indestructible. This image is even so natural that, in modern parlance, without allusion to the ancient myth, it is said of something deteriorated in the long run, that it is devoured by time, eaten away, ravaged by time.

16. All pagan mythology is, in fact, only a large allegorical picture of the various good and bad sides of humanity. For those seeking their wit, it is a complete course of the highest philosophy, like our modern fables. The absurd was to taking the form for the substance; but the pagan priests taught only the form, that some of them did not know the meaning either, or because they had an interest in maintaining the people in beliefs which, while promoting their domination, were more productive to them than philosophy. The veneration of the people for form was an inexhaustible source of riches, not just by the gifts accumulated in the temples,

---

68 From the Hebrew *cherub*, ox, *charab*, plow. Angels of the second choir of the first hierarchy, represented with four wings, four faces, and ox hooves.

the offerings and the sacrifices made in intention to the gods, but in reality for the benefit of their representatives. A less credulous people would have given less to images, statues, emblems and oracles: That is why Socrates was condemned as impious to drink hemlock for wanting to dry up this source of riches by putting the truth in the place of error. Then it was not yet in use to burn the heretics alive; and, five centuries later, Christ was condemned to an infamous death, as impious, for having, like Socrates, wished to substitute the spirit for the letter, and because his teachings, wholly spiritual, ruined the supremacy of the scribes, the Pharisees, and doctors of the law.

17. The same is true of Genesis, where we must see great moral truths in material figures of speech, which, taken literally, would be as absurd as if, in our fables, we would take literally the scenes and dialogues attributed to animals.

Adam is the personification of humanity; his fault individualizes human weakness, in whom predominate material instincts which he cannot resist.

The tree, as the tree of life, is the emblem of spiritual life; as the tree of knowledge is that of the awareness that humans acquire of good and evil through the development of their intelligence, and that of free will by virtue of which they may choose between the two. It marks the point where the human soul, ceasing to be guided by mere instincts, takes possession of its freedom and incurs responsibility for its actions.

The fruit of the tree is the emblem of the object of human material desires; it is the allegory of lust; it sums up under the same image the influences that lure toward evil; to eat of it is to succumb to temptation.[69] It lies in the middle of the garden of delights to show that seduction is at the heart of pleasures, and to recall at the same

---

69 In no original text, the fruit is specified as being an apple; this word is found only in childish versions. The word of the Hebrew text is *peri*, which has the same meanings as in French (*fruit*, in English), without specification of species, and can be taken in the material, moral, allegorical, literal or figurative sense. Among the Israelites, there is no obligatory interpretation; when a word has several meanings, everyone hears it as they wish, provided that the interpretation is not contrary to grammar. The word *peri* has been translated into Latin as *malum*, which was used for apple and all kinds of fruits. It is derived from the Greek *melon*, and participates in the verb *mé'o*, to interest, to take care, to attract.

time that if humans give preponderance to material enjoyments, they attach themselves to the earth and move away from their spiritual destiny.

The death of which Adam is threatened, if he breaks the prohibition which was made to him, is a warning of the inevitable consequences, both physical and moral, which result from the violation of the divine laws which God engraved in his conscience. It is quite obvious that this is not a matter of corporeal death, since after his fault Adam lived a very long time, but of spiritual death; in other words, of the loss of assets resulting from moral progress, a loss whose expulsion from the garden of delights is the image.

The snake is far from passing today for the archetype of trickery; it is here, in relation to its form rather than its character, an allusion to the perfidy of the bad advice which creeps like the serpent, and of which often, for this reason, one is not wary. Moreover, if the snake, for having deceived the woman, was sentenced to crawl on its belly, it would mean that before it had legs, and then it was no longer a snake. Why, then, impose on the naive and credulous faith of children, as truths, such blatant allegories, which, by falsifying their judgment, make them later look upon the Bible as a tissue of absurd fables?

18.   If Adam's fault is literally to have eaten a fruit, it cannot, by its almost childlike nature, unquestionably justify the rigor with which he has been struck. Nor can it be rationally admitted that it is generally admissible; otherwise God, considering this fact as an inalienable crime, would have condemned Its own work, since It had created humans for propagation. If Adam had taken in this sense the prohibition of touching the fruit of that tree, and if it had been scrupulously conformed to it, where would humanity be, and what would have become of the Creator's designs? If that were the case, God would have created the immense apparatus of the universe for two individuals, and the whole of humankind would have appeared against Its will and designs.

God did not create Adam and Eve to remain alone on Earth; and the proof of it is in the very words which It addresses to them immediately after their formation, while they were still in the earthly paradise: "God blessed them. And God said to them, 'Be fruitful and *multiply and fill the earth* and subdue it' (Gen 1:28 ESV)."

Since the multiplication of humans was a law from the earthly paradise, Adam and Eve's expulsion cannot have been caused by this supposed reason.

That which gave credit to this supposition is the feeling of shame that seized Adam and Eve at the sight of God, which led them to cover themselves. But this shame itself is a figure of comparison: it symbolizes the confusion that every guilty person feels in the presence of the one that he/she has offended.

19. What, then, is ultimately so great a fault that it has been able to perpetually condemn all the descendants of the one who committed it? Cain the fratricide was not treated so severely. No theologian could have defined it logically, because all of them, unable to come out of the letter of the text, got stuck in a vicious circle.

Today, we know that this fault is not an isolated personal act of an individual, but that it gathers, under a single allegorical fact, all the prevarications of which the still imperfect humanity of earth can be guilty, and which can be summed up in these words: *an infringement of the law of God.* That is why the fault of the first man, symbolizing humanity, is itself symbolized by an act of disobedience.

20. By telling Adam that he will draw his food from the ground by the sweat of his face. God symbolizes the obligation of work; but why is work a punishment? What would human intelligence be if we did not develop it through work? What would the Earth be, if it were not fertilized, transformed, sanitized by the intelligent work of human beings?

It was written: "When no bush of the field was yet in the land and no small plant of the field had yet sprung up-for the LORD God had not caused it to rain on the land ... then the LORD God formed the man of dust from the ground (Gen 2:5, 7)." These words, which are close to "fill the earth," prove that humans were from the beginning destined to occupy all the earth and to cultivate it; and, moreover, that paradise was not a place circumscribed on a corner of the globe. If the cultivation of Earth were to be a consequence of Adam's fault, it would have resulted that if Adam had not sinned, the Earth would not have been cultivated, and God's views would not have been accomplished.

Why does God tell the woman that, because she has committed the fault, she will give birth in pain? How can the pain of childbirth be a punishment, since it is a consequence of the organism, and it is proved physiologically that it is necessary? How can something that is according to the laws of Nature be a punishment? This is what the theologians have not yet explained, and what they would not be able to do until they come out of the point of view in which they have placed themselves. Yet these words, which seem so contradictory, may be justified.

21. Let me first remark that if, at the moment of the creation of Adam and Eve, their souls had been drawn from nothingness, as it is taught, they must have been novices in all things; they did not have how to know what it was to die. Since they were alone on Earth, as long as they lived in earthly paradise, they had not seen anyone die; how could they understand what was the threat of death that God was giving them? How could Eve have understood that to be in pain would be a punishment, since having just been born, she had never had children and was the only woman in the world?

The words of God, therefore, should have no meaning for Adam and Eve. Hardly out of nothing, they knew neither why nor how they came out of it; they were to understand neither the Creator nor the purpose of the prohibition It was imposing on them. Without any experience of the conditions of life, they have sinned as children who act indiscriminately, which makes even more incomprehensible the terrible responsibility that God has placed on them and on the whole of humanity.

22. What is an impasse for theology, Spiritism explains it without difficulty and in a rational way by the earlier existence of the soul and the plurality of existences; a law without which everything would be mystery and anomaly in human life. Indeed, let us admit that Adam and Eve had already lived before, then everything is justified: God does not speak to them as to children, but as beings able to understand It and who do understand It, an obvious proof that they have an early acquired knowledge. Let us admit, moreover, that they lived in a more advanced and less material world than ours, where the work of the spirit made up for any bodily work; and from where, by their rebellion to the law of God, referred to as disobedience, they have been excluded and exiled to earth as punishment, where humans, as a result of the globe's nature, are bound to bodily labor. God was right to say to them: In the world where you will live henceforth, you shall cultivate the earth and "By the sweat of your face"; and to the woman, "In pain you shall bring forth children," because such is the condition of this world. (See chapter **XI** above, items **31** et seq.)

The earthly paradise, whose trace has been searched for on earth, was therefore the figure of the happy world in which Adam had lived, or rather the group of spirits of which he is the personification. The expulsion from paradise marks the moment when these spirits came to incarnate themselves among the inhabitants of planet Earth, and the change of situation which followed it. The angel armed with a flaming sword defending the entrance to paradise symbolizes the impossibility of spirits of the lower worlds to enter the higher worlds before having deserved it through their purification. (See chapter **XIV**, item **9** *et seq.* below.)

23. "Cain said to the LORD, 'My punishment is greater than I can bear. Behold, you have driven me today away from the ground, and from your face I shall be hidden. I shall be a fugitive and a wanderer on the earth, and whoever finds me will kill me.' Then the LORD said to him, 'Not so! If anyone kills Cain, vengeance shall be taken on him sevenfold.' And the LORD put a mark on Cain, lest any who found him should attack him (Gen 4:13-15)."

"Then Cain went away from the presence of the LORD and settled in the land of Nod, east of Eden. Cain knew his wife, and she conceived and bore Enoch. When he built a city, he called the name of the city after the name of his son, Enoch (Gen 4:16-17)."

24. If we refer to the letter of Genesis, here are the consequences: Adam and Eve were alone in the world after their expulsion from earthly paradise; it was only later that they had children, Cain and Abel. But Cain, having killed his brother and having retired to another country, did not see again his father and his mother, who were alone again. It was only long afterwards, at the age of one hundred and thirty years, that Adam had a third son named Seth. After the birth of Seth, he lived, according to the biblical genealogy, eight hundred years, and had sons and daughters.

When Cain came to the east of Eden, there were only three people on earth: his father and his mother, and he alone on his side. Yet he had a wife and a child; what could this woman be and where could he have taken her? He built a city; but a city supposes inhabitants, for it is not to be presumed that he did it all himself, his wife, and his son, or that he could build it all by himself.

It must therefore be inferred from this very story that the country was peopled; but it could not be by the descendants of Adam, who then had none other than Cain.

The presence of other inhabitants is also apparent from this saying of Cain: "I shall be a fugitive and a wanderer on the earth, and whoever finds me will kill me," and God's answer to him regarding whoever he feared might kill him; after all what good was the mark that God put on Cain to preserve him, if he were to meet no one? If there were other humans on Earth besides Adam's family, it was because they were there before him; hence this consequence, taken from the very text of Genesis, that Adam is neither the first nor the only father of the human race. (See chapter **XI**, item **34** above.)

To shed light on all parts of spiritual Genesis, it was required the knowledge that Spiritism has brought concerning the relations of the spiritual principle and the material principle, and the nature of the soul, its creation in the state of simplicity and ignorance, its union to the body, its gradual progress, through successive existences during an indefinite time, and through different worlds which are so many echelons in the path to perfection, its gradual liberation from the influence of matter by the use of its free will, the cause of its good or bad inclinations, and its aptitudes, the phenomena of birth and death, the state of the spirit in erraticity; and finally the future which is the reward of a soul's efforts to improve itself and its perseverance in good.

Thanks to this light, humans know henceforth where they come from, where they are going, why they are on Earth and why they suffer. They know that their future is in their hands, and that the duration of his captivity here below depends on themselves. Thus Genesis, coming out of narrow and petty allegory, appears to them as great and worthy of the Creator's majesty, goodness, and justice=. Considered from this point of view, Genesis will confuse unbelief and vanquish it.

Part two

Miracles

according to Spiritism

Chapter XIII
Characteristics of miracles

1.   In its etymological sense, the word miracle (from Latin *miraculum* 'object of wonder,' from *mirari* 'to wonder') means: wonderful, admirable, extraordinary, surprising. The French Academy defines this word as, "An act of divine power contrary to the known laws of nature."

In its usual sense, this word has lost, like so many others, its original meaning. Generally speaking, it was restricted to a particular order of facts. In the minds of the general public, a miracle implies the idea of a preternatural fact, whereas in the liturgical sense, it is a derogation from the laws of Nature, by which God manifests Its power. Such, indeed, is its usual meaning, which has become its accepted meaning, and it is only by comparison and metaphor that it can be applied to the ordinary circumstances of everyday life.

One of the characteristics of a miracle, properly speaking, is to be inexplicable, by the very fact that it is accomplished outside natural laws; and this is the idea attached to it, that if a miraculous fact can eventually be explained, it is said that it is no longer a miracle, however surprising it may be.

Another characteristic of a miracle is to be unusual, isolated and exceptional; the moment a phenomenon recurs, either spontaneously or by an act of the will, is that it is subject to a law, and therefore, whether this law is known or not, it cannot be a miracle.

2. Science does miracles every day in the eyes of the ignorant. That a truly dead person is summoned back to life by divine intervention is a true miracle, because it is a fact contrary to the laws of Nature. But if this person has only the appearance of being dead, if there is still in him/her a remnant of *latent vitality* – and science, or a magnetic action, succeeds in reviving this person – for enlightened people it is a natural phenomenon, but in the eyes of the ignorant, the fact will pass for miraculous. That in the middle of certain countries, a physicist flies an electric kite, making lightning strike on a tree, this new Prometheus will certainly be regarded as armed with a diabolical power; yet Joshua, stopping the movement of the Sun, or rather of the Earth, if we admit the fact, would be a veritable miracle, for there is no magnetizer endowed with such power to effect a prodigy of this magnitude.

The centuries of ignorance have been fruitful in miracles, because everything whose cause was unknown was considered miraculous. As science has revealed new laws, the circle of the marvelous has become restricted; but as it had not explored the whole field of Nature, there still remained a fair share of the marvelous.

3. The marvelous, expelled from the realm of materiality by science, has entrenched itself in that of spirituality, which has been its last refuge. Spiritism, by demonstrating that the spiritual element is one of the living forces of Nature, a force incessantly acting concurrently with the material force, brings the phenomena which emerge from it into the circle of natural effects, since, like the others, they are all subject to laws. If the marvelous is expelled from spirituality, it has no more reason to be, and only then can it be said that the time of miracles has passed.[70]

4. Spiritism therefore comes, in its turn, to do what every science has failed to do at its arrival, namely, to reveal new laws, and to consequently explain the phenomena which fall within the jurisdiction of these laws.

---

70 The word *element* is not taken here in the sense of a *simple elementary body*, of *primitive molecules*, but in the sense of *constituent part of a whole*. In this sense, it can be said that the *spiritual element* has an active part in the economy of the universe, as it is said that both the *civilian element* and the *military element* figure in the number of a population; that the *religious element* enters into education; such as, for example, in Algeria, the *Arab element* must be taken into account, and so on.

It is true that these phenomena are connected with the existence of spirits and their intervention in the material world; hence, it is said, they are supernatural. But then it would be necessary to prove that spirits and their manifestations are contrary to the laws of Nature; that this is not and cannot be one of these laws.

The spirit is none other than the soul that survives the body; it is the main being since it does not die, while the body is only an accessory which is destroyed. Its existence is therefore just as natural after the one during the incarnation; it is subject to the laws which govern the spiritual principle, as the body is subject to those which govern the material principle; but since these two principles have a necessary affinity, they react incessantly upon each other, and from their simultaneous action result the movement and harmony of the whole, it follows that spirituality and materiality are the two parts of the same whole, one being as natural as the other, and that the first part is not an exception, an anomaly in the order of things.

5. During its incarnation, the spirit acts upon matter through its fluidic body: the perispirit. The same occurs outside incarnation. It does, as spirit and to the extent of its abilities, what it did as an incarnate person; only, as it no longer has its fleshly body as an instrument, it makes use, when necessary, of the material organs of an incarnate who becomes the so-called *medium*. The spirit does as one who, unable to write by oneself, borrows the hand of a secretary; or who, not knowing a language, uses an interpreter. A secretary and an interpreter act as mediums of an incarnate, the same way that a medium is the secretary or interpreter of a spirit.

6. The environment in which the spirits and their means of execution act are no longer the same as they were in the state of incarnation: the effects are different. These effects seem supernatural only because they are produced by agents who are not the ones we normally use; but from the moment that these agents are in Nature, and the facts of manifestations are accomplished by virtue of certain laws, there is nothing supernatural or wondrous. Before the properties of electricity were known, electrical phenomena were considered prodigies in the eyes of certain people. As soon as their cause became known, the marvelous disappeared. It is the same with the phenomena of spirituality, which are not more extraneous to the order of natural laws than the electrical, acoustic, luminous and other phenomena, which once have been the source of a host of superstitious beliefs.

7. Yet, it will be said, you admit that a spirit can lift a table and maintain it suspended in the air without any point of support. Is this not a departure from the law of gravity? Indeed, to the known law; but do we know the entire laws? Before we experienced the ascending force of certain gases, who would have said that a heavy machine carrying several people can triumph over the force of attraction? In the eyes of the general public, should that not look wondrous, even diabolical? Anyone who had proposed a century ago to send a message 1,500 miles away, and receive an answer in a few minutes, would have passed for a mad person – and if this person had actually done so, one would have thought that he/she had the devil at his/her command, for at that time the devil alone was able to go so fast. However, today, the thing is not only recognized as possible, but it seems quite natural. Why, then, should not an unknown fluid have the property, under given circumstances, of counterbalancing the effect of gravity, like hydrogen counterbalances the weight of a balloon? This is indeed what happens in the case of lifted tables. (See A. KARDEC, *The Mediums' Book*, chapter IV.)

8. Spiritual phenomena, being part of Nature, have occurred in all epochs; but precisely because their study could not be done by the material means available to common science, they have remained longer than others in the realm of the supernatural; whence Spiritism has brought them out of superstition today.

The supernatural, based on unexplained appearances, gives free rein to the imagination which, by wandering in the unknown, gives birth to superstitious beliefs. A rational explanation based on the laws of Nature, bringing humans back to the realm of reality, puts a stop to the vagaries of imagination, and destroys superstitions. Far from expanding the domain of the supernatural, Spiritism restricts it to its limits and takes away its last refuge. If it makes one believe in the possibility of certain facts, it prevents belief in many other things, because it demonstrates in the circle of spirituality, as science in the circle of materiality, what is possible and what is not. However, as it does not pretend to have the last word on all things, even on those which are within its competence, it does not pose as an absolute regulator of what is possible, staying open instead to future disclosures.

9.   Spiritual phenomena consist in the different modes of manifestation of the soul or spirit, either during incarnation or when discarnate, in the state of erraticity. It is through its manifestations that the soul reveals its existence, its survival and its individuality; it is judged by its effects. Since the cause is natural, so is the effect. It is these effects which are the special object of research and study of Spiritism, in order to arrive at the fullest possible knowledge of the nature and attributes of the soul, as well as the laws which govern the spiritual principle.

10.   For those who deny the existence of the independent spiritual principle, and hence that of the individual surviving soul, all Nature is in tangible matter. All phenomena connected with spirituality are, in their eyes, supernatural, and consequently chimerical. By not admitting the cause, they cannot admit the effect; and when the effects are obvious, they attribute them to the imagination, to an illusion, to hallucination, and refuse to examine them deeper. Hence a preconceived opinion which makes them unfit to judge soundly, because they start from the precept of negating all that is not material.

11.   From the fact that Spiritism admits the effects which are the consequence of the existence of the soul, it does not follow that it accepts all the effects described as wondrous, and that it intends to justify and accredit them; or that it should be the champion of all dreamers, all utopias, all systematic eccentricities, all miraculous legends: one would have to know very little to think so. Its opponents believe that it makes an unanswerable argument when, after doing scholarly research on the convulsionaries of Saint-Médard, the Camisards of Cévennes, or the nuns of Loudun, they came to discover the obvious instances of deceit that no one can deny; but are these stories the gospel of Spiritism? Did its supporters ever deny that charlatans exploited for their benefit certain facts created by imagination; and that fanaticism has exaggerated them a lot? Spiritism is not more supportive of any extravagances that can be committed in its name, since true science is not the abuse of ignorance, nor is true religion built on the excesses of fanaticism. To judge Spiritism based only on fairy tales and popular legends which are nothing but fictions, would be worth the same as judging history through historical novels or theatrical plays.

12. Most often Spiritual phenomena are spontaneous, and occur without any preconceived idea in persons who think of it the least. In certain circumstances, there are some that may be induced by agents referred to as mediums. In the first case, the medium is unaware of what is happening through himself/herself; in the second case, he/she acts knowingly; hence the distinction between conscious mediums and unconscious mediums. The latter are the most numerous and are often among the most obstinate skeptics, who thus practice Spiritism unknowingly and unintentionally. Spontaneous phenomena have, by this very fact, an important value, for no one would doubt the good faith of those who obtain them. It is here like somnambulism (i.e., trance mediumship), which, in certain individuals, is natural and involuntary, and in others, induced by magnetic action.[71]

But whether or not these phenomena are the result of an act of the will, the first cause is exactly the same, and in no way departs from natural laws. The mediums, therefore, produce absolutely nothing supernatural; thus they do no miracles – cases of instantaneous healing are themselves no more miraculous than the other effects, because they are all due to the action of a fluidic agent acting as a therapeutic agent, whose properties are no less natural for remaining unknown to this day. The epithet of thaumaturges given to certain mediums by ignorant critics of the principles of Spiritism, is therefore utterly improper. By comparison, the description of miracles given to these kinds of phenomena can only mislead people about their true character.

13. The intervention of occult intelligences in Spiritist phenomena does not make them more miraculous than all the other phenomena that are due to invisible agents, because these occult beings who populate spaces are one of the powers of nature, a power

---

71 See A. KARDEC *The Mediums' Book*, ch. V. See also examples in *The Spiritist Review – 1865*, December and August [Trans. note: English version of the latter will go to press after the year 2019].

whose action is incessant upon the material world, as well as on the moral world.

By enlightening us about this power, Spiritism offers the key to a multitude of things hitherto unexplained, and inexplicable by any other means; and which may have been regarded, in the distant past, as prodigies. It reveals, as well as magnetism, a law, if not unknown, at least poorly understood; or, to put it better, we knew the effects, because they have always happened, but we did not know the law, and it is the ignorance of this law which engendered superstition. Once this law becomes know, the marvelous disappears and the phenomena return to the order of natural things. This is why Spiritists do no miracles by turning a table or writing from the deceased, than the doctor by reviving a dying person, or the physicist by dropping a lightning bolt. Whoever claims to work miracles by means of this science would be either ignorant of it, or a dupe maker.

14. Since Spiritism repudiates all claims to miraculous things, apart from it, are there miracles in the usual sense of the word?

Let me first say that among the reputedly miraculous facts which occurred before the advent of Spiritism, and which are still happening today, most, if not all, find their explanation in the new laws which Spiritism has come to reveal. These facts occur again, albeit under another name, in the order of Spiritist phenomena, and as such are not supernatural. It is understood, of course, that these include only authentic facts, and not those which, under the name of miracles, are the product of underhanded trickery in order to exploit credulity; no more than certain legendary facts which may have had, in the beginning, a vestige of truth, but which superstition has amplified to the point of absurdity. It is about these facts that Spiritism has come to throw light, by giving the means to discern the error from the truth

15. As to miracles, properly speaking, since nothing is impossible to God, It can undoubtedly do them; but did God do them? In other words: does God derogate from the laws established by Itself? It does not behoove to humans to prejudge the acts of the Divinity and to subordinate them to the weakness of their understanding. Yet we have as a criterion of our judgment, with regard to divine things, the very attributes of God. To Its sovereign power, Its sovereign wisdom should be joined; whence it must be concluded that God does nothing useless.

Why then would God work miracles? To attest to its power, it is said; but is not the power of God manifested in a manner otherwise quite striking by the grand array of the works of creation, by the farsighted wisdom which presides over the tiniest up to the largest parts, and by the harmony of the laws that govern the universe? Would God be able to prove Its power only by some small and childish departures from the law that any trickster would know how to imitate? What to say about a knowledgeable mechanic who, to prove his/her skill, would break the clock he/she has built, a masterpiece of science, to show that he/she can undo what he/she has done? On the contrary, does the mechanic's knowledge not come from the regularity and precision of the clock movement?

The question of miracles, properly speaking, is not the responsibility of Spiritism; yet, relying on this reasoning, namely, that God does nothing useless, Spiritism expresses this opinion that, since miracles are not necessary for the glorification of God, nothing in the universe departs from the general laws. If there are phenomena that we do not understand, it is because we still lack the necessary knowledge.

16. By admitting that God could, for reasons which we cannot fathom, accidentally derogate from the laws It has established, these laws would no longer be immutable; yet at least it is rational to think that God alone has this power. However, it cannot be admitted, without denying God's omnipotence, that it is given to a spirit to undo the work of God, while doing wonders to deceive even the elect, which would imply the idea of a power equal to God's – this is what has been taught. If Satan has the power to interrupt the course of natural laws, which are the divine work, without having the authority of God, he is more powerful than God: therefore God does not have omnipotence. If God delegates this power, as it is claimed, to more easily induce humans to evil. God does not possess supreme kindness. In either case, this is the negation of one of the attributes without which God would not be God.

Besides, the Church[72] distinguishes the good miracles that come from God, the bad miracles that come from Satan; but how to tell the difference? Whether a miracle is official or not, it nonetheless remains a departure from the laws that emanate from God alone. If an individual is cured miraculously, whether by God or Satan, he is no less cured. One must have a very poor idea of human intelligence to hope that such doctrines can be accepted today.

As there is the possibility of certain facts considered miraculous to be recognized, it must be concluded that, whatever the source attributed to them, they are natural effects which spirits or incarnate individuals can use, as all the others coming from their own intelligence and their scientific knowledge, for good or for evil, according to their goodness or their perversity. A perverse being, making use of his/her knowledge, can therefore do things which are considered as prodigies in the eyes of the ignorant; but when these effects result in some good, it would be illogical to attribute a diabolical origin to them.

17. But, it is said, religion relies on facts that are neither explained nor explainable. Unexplained, perhaps, but inexplicable, that is another matter completely. Do we know the discoveries and the knowledge that the future holds for us? Without talking of the miracle of Creation, which is the greatest of all without contradiction, and which has now returned to the domain of universal law, do we not already witness again and again, under the influence of magnetism, somnambulism (i.e., trance mediumship), and Spiritism, ecstasies, visions, apparitions, remote sight, instantaneous healing, levitations, oral and other types of communications with the beings of the invisible world, in short, phenomena known from time immemorial, formerly considered as wondrous, but demonstrated today to belong to the order of natural things, according to the constituent law of beings? The sacred books are full of facts of this kind classed as supernatural; but, as we find analogous and still more wonderful ones in all pagan religions of antiquity, if the truth of a religion depended on the number and nature of these facts, it is not too clear which of them would prevail.

---

72 [Trans. note] In KARDEC's time it was customary for many European writers to refer to the dominant religion of their country as the Church (with a capital C). In France, it was the Roman Catholic church.

18.   To pretend that the supernatural is the necessary foundation of all religions, and that it is the keystone of the Christian edifice, is to sustain a dangerous thesis. If the truths of Christianity are rested on the sole basis of the wondrous, it is to give it a fragile support whose stones are plucked out every day. This thesis, of which eminent theologians have made themselves the defenders, leads right to the conclusion that, in a given time, there will be no more religion possible, not even the Christian religion, if what is regarded as supernatural is demonstrated to be natural; for, in vain, we will persist in maintaining the belief that a fact is miraculous, when it is proved that it is not. The proof that a fact is no exception to the natural laws is when it can be explained by these same laws, and that, it can be reproduced through the intervention of any individual, thus ceasing to be the privilege of the saints. It is not the *supernatural* that is necessary for religions, but rather the *spiritual principle* which is wrongly confused with the wondrous, and without which no religion is possible.

Spiritism considers the Christian religion from a higher point. It gives it a more solid foundation than miracles: it is the immutable laws of God, which govern the spiritual principle as well as the material principle. This foundation defies time and science, because time and science will eventually corroborate it.

God is nonetheless worthy of our admiration, of our gratitude, and of our respect, for not having departed from Its laws, especially for their immutability. There is no need for the supernatural to render to God the worship which is due to It. Is Nature not sufficiently imposing by itself to need anything else be added to itself to prove God's supreme power? Religion will find less unbelievers, as it is corroborated by reason in all respects. Christianity has nothing to lose from this corroboration; on the contrary, it can only win from it. If anything has damaged it in the opinion of certain people, it is precisely the abuse of the wondrous and the supernatural.

19.   If we take the word *miracle* in its etymological sense, which is an *admirable thing*, we constantly have miracles under our eyes. We breathe them in the air and tread on them under our feet, since everything is a miracle in Nature.

So, do they wish to give the masses, the ignorant, the poor-minded, an idea of the power of God? Then show It to them in the infinite wisdom which presides over everything, in the admirable organism of all that lives, in the fructifying of plants, in the suitability of all the parts of each being to its needs, according to the environment in which it is called to live. It is necessary to show them the action of God in the blade of grass, in the flower which blooms, in the Sun which vivifies everything. It is necessary to show them God's goodness in Its solicitude toward all created beings, however small they may be; Its foresight regarding the raison d'être of each thing, of which none is useless; the good which always emerges from a momentary, apparent evil. Make them understand, above all, that the real evil is the work of humans, not that of God; and do not try to frighten them by depicting eternal flames, in which they no longer believe, and which make them doubt the goodness of God, but instead encourage them by the certainty of being able to redeem themselves one day, and repair the evil they have done. Show them the discoveries of science as the revelation of divine laws, and not as the work of Satan. And finally, teach them to read in the book of Nature which is incessantly open before them, in this inexhaustible book where the wisdom and the goodness of the Creator are written on every page. Then they will understand that a Being so great, which is taking care of each and every one, of everything, and foreseeing everything, must be supremely powerful. The plowman will see it by tracing his furrow, and the unfortunate will bless God in his/her afflictions, for he/she will say to themselves: If I am unfortunate, it is my fault. They will be really religious, especially religiously rational, which is much better than trying to make them believe that there are stones that sweat blood, or statues that blink and shed tears.

Chapter XIV
Fluids

NATURE AND PROPERTIES OF FLUIDS

1. Science has given the key to miracles that are more particularly apparent from the material element, either by explaining them, or by demonstrating their impossibility by the laws that govern matter. However, the phenomena in which the spiritual element has a preponderant part, which cannot be explained solely by the laws of matter, escape the investigations of science. That is why they have, more than the others, the apparent character of being wondrous phenomena. It is therefore in the laws that govern spiritual life that we can find the key to miracles of this category.

2. The universal cosmic fluid is, as has been demonstrated, the primitive elementary matter, whose modifications and transformations constitute the innumerable variety of the bodies of Nature. As a universal elementary principle, it offers two distinct states, namely: ethereality or imponderability, which can be considered as the primitive normal state, and that of materialization or ponderability, which is only a sort of consecutive state. The intermediate point is that of the transformation of fluid into tangible matter; but, again, there is no abrupt transition, for imponderable fluids can be considered as an intermediate between the two states. (See chapter **IV**, item **10** *et seq.* above)

Each of these two states necessarily gives rise to special phenomena: to the second one belongs those of the visible world, and to the first one those of the invisible world. Some, called *material phenomena*, are the domain of science, properly speaking; others, classed as *spiritual or psychical phenomena*, because they are more especially bound to the existence of spirits, are within the attributions of Spiritism. But, as the spiritual life and the bodily life are in incessant contact with each other, phenomena of these two orders often occur simultaneously. Humans, in the state of incarnation, can only have the perception of the psychical phenomena that are related to bodily life, whereas those which are of the exclusive domain of spiritual life escape the material senses, and can be perceived only in the state of spirit.[73]

3. In the state of ethereality, the cosmic fluid is not uniform; without ceasing to be ethereal, it undergoes modifications as varied in their kind, and perhaps more numerous than in the state of tangible matter. These changes constitute distinct fluids which, although proceeding from the same principle, are each endowed with special properties, and give rise to particular phenomena of the invisible world.

Since all is relative, these fluids have for spirits, which are themselves fluidic, an appearance as material as that of tangible objects for the incarnate souls; and are for spirits the same that earthly substances are for us in the material world. They develop and combine them to produce definite effects, as we do with our materials, albeit through different methods.

But there, as here below, only the most enlightened spirits can understand the role of the constituent elements of their world. The ignorant of the invisible world are also as incapable of explaining the phenomena they witness, and to which they often contribute mechanically, as the ignorant of the Earth are unable to explain the effects of light or electricity, in order to tell how they can see and hear.

4. The fluidic elements of the spiritual world are not detectable by our instruments of analysis and the perception of our senses, made for tangible matter and not for ethereal matter. There are some who belong to a milieu so different from ours, that we can only judge them through comparisons as imperfect as those with

---

73 Calling them a *psychical* phenomenon conveys the idea more accurately than the expression *spiritual* phenomenon, since these phenomena are based on the properties and attributes of the soul, or better, the perispiritual fluids which are inseparable from the soul. This qualification ties them more closely to the order of natural facts governed by general laws. We can therefore admit them as psychical effects, without classing them as miracles. [Trans. note: The term soul was usually applied by KARDEC to denote an incarnate spirit.]

which a person blind from birth would attempt to form an idea of the theory of colors.

Nevertheless, among these fluids, some are closely related to bodily life, and belong in some way to the earthly environment. In the absence of direct perception, one can observe their effects, and acquire knowledge of a certain precision about their nature. Such study is essential because it is the key to a host of phenomena inexplicable by the laws of matter alone.

5. The starting point of the universal fluid is a degree of absolute purity, of which nothing can give us an idea. The opposite point is its transformation into tangible matter. Between these two extremes, there are innumerable transformations, which are more or less similar to each other. As fluids come the closest to materiality, they are the least pure, therefore composing what may be called the Earth's spiritual atmosphere. It is from this milieu, where we also find different degrees of purity, that Earth's incarnate and discarnate spirits draw the necessary elements for managing the resources of their existence. These fluids, subtle and impalpable as they are for us, are nonetheless of a coarse nature when compared to the ethereal fluids of higher regions.

It is the same on the surface of all the worlds, except for differences in constitution and the conditions of life specific to each one. The less material life is there, the less the spiritual fluids have affinity with matter, properly speaking.

Their qualification as *spiritual fluids* is not rigorously exact, since, in the end, it is always more or less quintessentiated matter. They have nothing truly *spiritual* except for the soul or the intelligent principle. They are thus designated by comparison, and especially because of their affinity with spirits. We could say that they are the matter of the spiritual world; that is why they are called *spiritual fluids*.

6. Besides, who knows the innermost constitution of tangible matter? It is perhaps compact only in relation to our senses, and what would prove it is the ease with which it is traversed by the spiritual fluids and spirits to which it offers no more obstacles than transparent bodies offer to light.

Tangible matter, having as a primitive element the ethereal cosmic fluid, must be able, by disintegrating, to return to the state of ethereality, as the diamond, the hardest of bodies, can volatilize into intangible gas. The solidification of matter is in reality only a transitory state of the universal fluid, which can return to its primitive state when the conditions of cohesion cease to exist.

Who knows even if, in the state of tangibility, matter is not likely to acquire a sort of etherealization which would give it special properties? Certain phenomena which seem authentic lead to this supposition. We still only have milestones of the invisible world, but the future undoubtedly reserves to us the knowledge of new laws that will enable us to understand what still remains a mystery.

7.   The perispirit, or fluidic body of the spirits, is one of the most important products of the cosmic fluid; it is the condensation of this fluid around a focus of intelligence, the soul. It also has its principle in the same fluid transformed and condensed in tangible matter, in the perispirit: only that the molecular transformation takes place differently, because the fluid retains its imponderability and its ethereal qualities. Both the perispiritual body and the corporeal body have their source in the same primitive element: both are matter, though in two different states.

8.   Spirits draw their perispirits from the environment in which they are, that is to say, this envelope is formed of ambient fluids; it follows that the constituent elements of the spirit must vary according to the worlds. Jupiter, being described as a very advanced world compared to Earth, and where bodily life does not have the materiality of ours, the perispirit envelopes on that planet must be of an infinitely more quintessentiated nature than on Earth. Now, just as we could not exist in this world with our fleshly body, our spirits could not penetrate Jupiter with their earthly perispirit. When leaving Earth, the spirit leaves its fluidic envelope, and puts on another one appropriate to the world to where it must go.

9.   The nature of the fluidic envelope is always related to the spirit's degree of moral advancement. Lower-order spirits cannot change them at will, and therefore cannot, at will, move from one world to another. There are some whose fluidic envelope, though

ethereal and imponderable in relation to tangible matter, is still too heavy – if we can express it this way – in relation to the spiritual world, which prevents them to escape their environment. It is necessary to include in this category those whose spirits are coarse enough to confuse them with their fleshly bodies, and which, for that reason, still believe they are physically alive. These exist in great number, and they remain on the surface of the Earth like the incarnated, always believing that they are going on with their routine occupations. Others, a little more dematerialized, are however not sufficiently so to rise above earthly regions.[74]

Higher-order spirits, on the other hand, can come into lower worlds and even incarnate in them. They draw from the constituent elements of the world into which they enter the materials of the fluidic and fleshly envelopes appropriate to the environment in which they are found. They do as the great lord who leaves his gilded clothes to put on temporary clothing, without ceasing to be a great lord.

Thus spirits of the highest order can manifest themselves to the inhabitants of the Earth, or incarnate in mission amidst them. These spirits bring with them, not the envelope, but their past memory by intuition of the regions whence they come, and which they see through thought. They are seers among the blind.

10. The layer of spiritual fluids that surrounds the Earth can be compared to the lower layers of the atmosphere: heavier, more compact, less pure than the upper layers. These fluids are not homogeneous; they form a mixture of molecules of various qualities, among which are necessarily the elementary molecules which form the base, albeit more or less altered. The effects produced by these fluids will be depend on the *sum* of pure parts that they contain. Such is, by comparison, the alcohol when rectified or mixed, in different proportions, with water or other substances: its specific weight increases by this mixture, at the same time as its strength and inflammability diminish, although in the whole pure alcohol is still present.

Spirits called to live in this environment draw their perispirit from it; but as the spirit itself becomes more or less purified, its perispirit

---

74 For examples of spirits which believe they are still physically alive on Earth, see *The Spiritist Review – 1859*, December; – *1864*, November; and – *1865*, April.

is formed of the purest or coarsest parts of this environment. There the spirit produces, by comparison, and not by assimilation, the effect of a chemical reagent which attracts to itself molecules that are assimilable to its nature.

The result of this capital fact is that the inner constitution of the perispirit is not identical in all incarnate or discarnate individual spirits that inhabit the Earth or the surrounding space. It is not so with the corporeal body, which, as has been shown, is formed of the same elements, whatever the superiority or inferiority of the spirit. So, for all, the effects produced by the body are the same, with the same needs, while they differ for all that is inherent in the perispirit.

Again, it follows that the perispirit shell of the same spirit is modified with the moral progress of the latter with each incarnation, although incarnating in the same milieu. Higher-order spirits, incarnating exceptionally in mission in an a lesser evolved world, have a less coarse perispirit than that of the natives of this world.

11. The environment is always related with the nature of the beings that must live in it: the fish are in the water; terrestrial beings are in the air; spiritual beings, even on Earth, are in the spiritual or ethereal fluid. The ethereal fluid is for the needs of the spirit what the atmosphere is for the needs of the incarnate. Now, just as fish cannot live in the air, and terrestrial animals cannot live in an atmosphere too rarefied for their lungs, lower-order spirits cannot endure the brilliance and impact of the most ethereal fluids. They would not die there, because the spirit does not die, but an instinctive force keeps them away, just like one would move away from a blazing fire or from an extremely dazzling light. That is why they cannot leave the environment that is appropriate to their nature. To change of environment, they must first change their nature so that they are stripped of the material instincts which retain them in material environments. In a word, they must first purify and transform themselves morally; then, gradually, they identify themselves with a more refined environment, which for them becomes a necessity, like the eyes of someone who has long lived in darkness gradually become accustomed to daylight and the brightness of the Sun.

12.   Thus everything is connected, everything is linked in the universe; everything is subject to the great and harmonious law of unity, from the most compact materiality to the purest spirituality. The Earth is like a vessel from which a thick smoke escapes, which becomes clearer as it elevates itself, and whose rarefied particles are lost in infinite space.

Divine power breaks out in all parts of this grand ensemble, and there are those who still would like it to better testify to its power. God, not satisfied with what It did, would come to disturb this harmony! And lower Itself to the role of magician, by resorting to puerile effects worthy of a conjurer! And moreover, one dares to give God as Its rival in skills, Satan himself! Never, indeed, has divine majesty been so abased, and yet some people are astonished at the progress of incredulity!

People are right to say, "Faith is vanishing!" But it is the faith in everything that shocks common sense and reason that is vanishing. Faith like that which once, in ancient times, said, "The gods are vanishing!" But faith in serious things, faith in God and immortality is always alive in the heart of humans, and if it has been stifled under the puerile stories that overburdened it, it will rise strong again as soon as it is cleared, as the withered plant rises as soon as it sees the Sun!

Indeed, everything is miraculous in Nature, because everything is admirable and bears witness to divine wisdom! These miracles are for everyone, for all who have eyes to see and ears to hear, and not for the benefit of the few. But no! There are no miracles in the sense that has been attached to this word, because everything springs from the eternal laws of creation.

13.   Spiritual fluids, which constitute one of the states of the universal cosmic fluid, are therefore the atmosphere of spiritual beings; they are the element from which they draw the materials upon which they operate. The environment in which special phenomena occur, perceptible to the sight and hearing of the spirit, escaping the material senses which are impressed only by tangible matter. Finally, they are the vehicle of thought, like air is the vehicle of sound.

14.   Spirits act upon spiritual fluids, they do not manipulate them as humans manipulate gases, but by means of thought and will. To spirits, thought and will are what hands are to humans. Through thought, they impress this or that direction upon these fluids: they gather them, combine them or disperse them, forming sets with a certain appearance, shape, and color. They change the fluids' properties like a chemist changes those of gases or other bodies by combining them according to certain laws. It is the great workshop or laboratory of spiritual life.

Sometimes these transformations are the result of an intention; often they are the product of an unconscious thought; it is enough for the spirit to think of something for this thing to happen.

Thus, for example, a spirit that enters the vision field of an incarnate person gifted with spiritual sight, bearing the appearance that he/she had during a lifetime when he/she was known, would have had several other incarnations since. The spirit presents itself with the garments, the outward signs, infirmities, scars, amputated limbs, etc., which he/she had then. A decapitated person will come headless. This is not to say that the individual has kept such an appearance; certainly not, for, as spirit, it is neither lame, nor one-handed, nor one-eyed, nor decapitated. Yet the spirit's *thought* is focused on the time when he/she looked so, making its perispirit instantly take the appearance, which can be abandoned instantly. If, then, a spirit was once a black man, and at another time white man, it will present itself as being one or another, depending on which of these two incarnations is evoked, focusing its thought on either one accordingly.

By a similar effect, the thought of the spirit creates through fluids the objects which it used to carry; a miser will handle gold, a soldier will have his/her weapons and uniform, a smoker his/her pipe, a plowman his/her plow and oxen, an old woman her distaff. These fluidic objects are as real to the spirit as they were in the material state during its lifetime as an incarnate; but, for the same reason that they are created by thought, their existence is as fleeting as thought itself.[75]

15. The action of spirits upon spiritual fluids has consequences of direct and capital importance for the incarnate. From the moment that these fluids are the vehicle of thought, and that thought can

---

75 See *The Spiritist Review – 1859*, July. See also A. KARDEC, *The Mediums' Book*, ch. VIII.

modify their properties, it is evident that they must be impregnated with the good or evil qualities of the thoughts which put them into vibration, modified by the purity or the impurity of feelings. Bad thoughts corrupt the spiritual fluids, same as deleterious miasmas corrupt breathable air. The fluids surrounding or projected by evil spirits are therefore vitiated, while those that receive the influence of good spirits will be as pure as the latter's degree of moral perfection.

It would be impossible to enumerate or classify good and bad fluids, or to specify their respective qualities, since their diversity is as great as that of thought.

16. If the ambient fluids are modified by the projection of thoughts of the spirit, its perispiritual envelope; which is a constituent part of its being, receiving directly and permanently the impression of its thoughts; must still bear the imprint of its qualities, whether good or bad. The fluids vitiated by the efforts of evil spirits can be purified by distancing oneself from these, but one's perispirit will always be what it is, as long as the spirit does not change itself.

17. Since humans are incarnate spirits, they have in part the attributes of spiritual life, because they live from this life as well as from bodily life, first during sleep, and often in the waking state. The spirit, while incarnated, preserves its perispirit with the qualities which are proper to it, and which, as we know, are not circumscribed by the body, but radiate all around and envelop it like a fluidic atmosphere.

By its intimate connection with the body, the perispirit plays a preponderant role in the organism; whereas, by its expansion, it puts the incarnate spirit in more direct relation with the discarnate spirits.

The thought of an incarnate spirit emits spiritual fluids like that of discarnate spirits. They are transmitted from spirit to spirit through the same way, and, according as it is good or bad, it cleanses or vitiates the surrounding fluids.

18. The perispirit of the incarnate being of a nature identical to that of spiritual fluids, it assimilates them with ease, like a sponge imbibes liquid. These fluids have on the perispirit an action all the more direct as, by its expansion and its radiation, it merges with them.

Since these fluids act upon the perispirit, this latter, in turn, reacts on the physical organism with which it is in molecular contact. If the emanation is of good nature, the body feels a salutary impression; if they are bad, the impression is painful. If the bad ones are permanent and vigorous, they can generate physical disorders: certain diseases have no other cause.

The environments in which evil spirits abound are thus impregnated with bad fluids which are absorbed by all the pores of the perispirit, just like pestilential miasmas are absorbed by the pores of the body.

19.   It is the same when incarnates meet. A gathering is a focal point where various thoughts radiate. Since thought acts upon fluids as sound acts upon the air, these fluids bring us thoughts as the air brings us sound. We can thus say, in all truth, that there are in these fluids thought waves and rays which intersect without merging themselves, as in the air there are sound waves and rays.

A gathering of people is, like an orchestra, a chorus of thoughts where each one produces his/her note. The result is a multitude of fluidic currents and emissions, of which everyone receives the impression by the spiritual sense, same as in a musical chorus each receives the impression of sounds by the sense of hearing.

But just as there are harmonic or discordant sound rays, there are also harmonic or discordant thoughts. If the whole is harmonic, the impression is pleasant; if it is discordant, the impression is painful. For this reason, there is no need for thought to be formulated in words; the fluidic radiation does not exist less, whether expressed or not; but if some bad thoughts are involved, they produce the effect of an icy stream of air in a warm environment.

Such is the cause of the feeling of satisfaction which one experiences in a sympathetic gathering, animated by good and benevolent thoughts. There one finds a salubrious moral atmosphere, where people can breathe comfortably and come out of it comforted, because it is impregnated with beneficial fluidic emissions. This also explains the anxiety, the indefinable discomfort that one feels in an unpleasant environment, where malicious thoughts produce something like nauseating currents of air.

20.   Thus thought produces a kind of physical effect which reacts upon the moral one – this is what Spiritism alone could make one understand. Humans feel it instinctively, since they seek homogeneous and sympathetic gatherings where they know they can draw new moral forces. It could be said that one recovers the fluidic losses one makes every day by the radiation of thought, same as one recovers through food the losses of the material body. This is because thought is indeed an emission that causes a real loss of spiritual fluids, and consequently of material fluids; therefore humans need to be reinvigorated by emissions they receive from outside.

When one says that a doctor cures his patient with good words, one is absolutely right, because benevolent thoughts bring with them restorative fluids which act both physically and morally.

21.   It is undoubtedly possible, some will say, to avoid humans who are known to be malicious. Yet how to escape the influence of evil spirits that swarm around us and creep everywhere without being seen?

The means is very simple, because it depends on the will of the individuals themselves, who carry in them the necessary protection. Fluids unite because of the similarity of their nature; hence dissimilar fluids repel each other; there is incompatibility between good and bad fluids, just as between oil and water.

What do you do when the air is stale? It is sanitized, it is purified, by destroying the focus of miasmas, expelling the unhealthy effluvia by stronger currents of salubrious air. To the invasion of bad fluids, it is therefore necessary to oppose good fluids; and, as each person has in his/her own perispirit a permanent fluidic source, one carries the remedy in oneself. It is only a question of purifying this source and of giving it such qualities that are a *repellent* to bad influences, instead of being an attracting force. The perispirit is therefore a cuirass to which one must give the best possible toughness. Now, as the qualities of the perispirit are due to the qualities of the soul, it is necessary to work for its own improvement, for it is the imperfections of the soul that attract evil spirits.

Flies go where pockets of decay attract them; destroy these focuses, and the flies will disappear. Similarly, evil spirits go where evil attracts them; destroy the evil, and they will depart. Truly good spirits, whether incarnate or discarnate, have nothing to fear from the influence of evil spirits.

22. The perispirit is the link between the corporeal life and the spiritual life: it is through it that the incarnate spirit is in constant contact with the spirits. Finally, it is through it that special phenomena, which do not have their primary cause in tangible matter, are produced in humans; and which, for this reason, seem supernatural.

It is in the properties and the radiation of the perispiritual fluid that we must look for the cause of *second sight*, or *spiritual sight*, which may also be called *psychical sight*, with which many people are endowed, often without their knowledge, as well as *somnambulistic sight.*[76]

The perispirit is the *sensory organ* of the spirit; it is through it that the incarnate spirit has the perception of spiritual things which escape the corporeal senses. Through the organs of the body, our sight, hearing, and various sensations are located in and limited to the perception of material things; whereas by the spiritual senses, they are not localized: the spirit sees, hears and feels all over its being what is in the sphere of radiation of its perispiritual fluid.

In humans, such phenomena are the manifestation of spiritual life; it is the soul that acts outside the organism. In second sight, or perception by the spiritual sense, one does not see through the eyes of the body, though often, by habit, one will direct them to the point where one's attention is drawn. The person sees through the eyes of the soul, and the proof is that he/she can see just as well with eyes shut, beyond the range of the visual field.[77]

23. Although, during a lifetime, the spirit is riveted to the body by the perispirit, it is not so much a slave, that it cannot stretch

76 [Trans. note] *Somnambulistic sight* is an old term referring to visions perceived by certain mediums during a state of trance.

77 For cases of second sight and somnambulistic lucidity, see *The Spiritist Review – 1858*, January & November; – *1861*, July; – *1865*, November.

its chain and carry itself away, either on Earth or to any point in space. The spirit is only reluctantly attached to its body, because its normal life is in liberty, while the bodily life is that of a serf bound to feudal land.

The spirit is therefore happy to leave its body, like a bird leaving its cage. It seizes every opportunity to free itself from it, and takes advantage of it for every moment that its presence is not necessary to the life of relation. This is the phenomenon referred to as *the emancipation of the soul*; it always takes place during sleep. Whenever the body rests and the senses are inactive, the spirit emerges. (See A. Kardec, *The Spirits' Book*, ch. VIII.)

In these moments, the spirit lives a spiritual life, while the body lives only a vegetative life. The spirit leaves in the state it will be after death. It travels space, talks to its friends and other spirits either free or incarnate like it.

The fluidic link that holds the spirit to the body is only finally broken at death. Complete separation takes place only by the absolute extinction of any activity of the vital principle. As long as the body lives, the spirit, whatever distance it may be from the body, is instantly recalled to it as soon as its presence is necessary. Then it resumes the course of the outer life of relation. Sometimes, on awakening, it retains from its peregrinations a memory, a more or less precise image, which constitutes the dream. In any case, it brings back with itself intuitions which suggest new ideas and thoughts, justifying the proverb: The night brings counsel

Thus are also explained certain phenomena characteristic of natural and magnetic somnambulism, catalepsy, lethargy, ecstasy, etc., which are but manifestations of spiritual life.[78]

24. Since spiritual sight is not performed by the eyes of the body, this happens because the perception of things does not take place by the ordinary light. In fact, such spiritual light is made for the material world: for the spiritual world, there is a special light whose nature is unknown to us, but which is undoubtedly one of the properties of the ethereal fluid assigned to the visual perceptions of the soul. There is therefore material light and spiritual light. The first has its focus circumscribed in luminous bodies; the second has

---

78 Examples of lethargy and catalepsy: *The Spiritist Review – 1858*, September, "Mrs. Schwabenhaus"; – *1866*, January, "The young cataleptic of Swabia."

its focus everywhere. This is the reason why there are no obstacles to the spiritual sight: it is not stopped by the distance or the opacity of matter; for it, darkness does not exist. The spiritual world is therefore lighted by spiritual light, which has its own effects, as the material world is lighted by sunlight.

25. The soul, enveloped in its perispirit, thus bears in itself its luminous principle. Penetrating matter by virtue of its ethereal essence, there is no opaque body for its sight.

However, spiritual view has neither the same extent nor the same penetration in all spirits. Pure spirits alone possess it in all its power; in lower-order spirits it is weakened by the relative coarseness of their perispirit, which interposes itself like a sort of fog.

It manifests itself in varying degrees in incarnate spirits through the phenomenon of second sight, either in natural or magnetic somnambulism,[79] or in the waking state. According to the degree of this faculty, lucidity is said to be lesser or greater. It is with the help of this faculty that some people can see the inside of the body and describe the cause of diseases.

26. Therefore spiritual sight gives special perceptions which, not being located in the physical organs, operate in conditions quite other than the corporeal sight. For this reason, one cannot expect identical effects and experience the same processes. Achieved outside the body, it has a mobility that defies any anticipation. It has to be studied in its effects and causes, and not by assimilating it to the ordinary eyesight, which it is not destined to provide except in exceptional cases, and which cannot be taken as a rule.

27. The spiritual sight is necessarily incomplete and imperfect in incarnate spirits, and therefore subject to anomalies. Having its seat in the soul itself, a soul's state must influence the perceptions it gives. According to the degree of its development, the circumstances, and the moral state of the individual, it can give, either during sleep or in the waking state: 1ST) Perception of certain real material facts, such as the knowledge of events occurring in the distance, the descriptive details of a locality, the causes of a disease and appropriate remedies. 2ND) Perception of equally real things in the spiritual world, such as the sight of spirits. 3RD) Fantastic images

---

79 [Trans. note] Trance mediumship.

created by the imagination, analogous to the fluidic creations of thought (see item **14** above). These creations are always related to the moral dispositions of the spirit that is generating them. Thus the thought of persons strongly imbued and preoccupied with certain religious beliefs introduces them to hell, its furnaces, its tortures and its demons, as they appear to them: it is sometimes quite an epic; the pagans saw Olympus and Tartarus, as Christians see Hell and Paradise. If, on awakening, or coming out of ecstasy, these people retain a clear memory of their visions, they take them for realities and confirmations of their beliefs, whereas this is only a product of their own thoughts.[80] There is therefore a very rigorous choice to make of ecstatic visions before accepting them. The remedy for too much credulity in this respect is the study of the laws that govern the spiritual world.

28.   Dreams themselves contain the three natures of visions described above. It is to the first two that dreams belong to predictions, forebodings and warnings; it is in the third category, that is to say, in the fluidic creations of thought, that we can find the cause of certain fantastic images which have nothing real in relation to material life, but which sometimes have, for the spirit, such vividness and seem so real, that the body suffers their impact, as we have seen a case of hair whitening under the impression of a dream. These creations can be induced by exalted beliefs; by retrospective memories; by tastes, desires, passions, fear, remorse; by the usual concerns; by the needs of the body, or a gene in the functions of the organism; and finally, by other spirits, with a benevolent or malicious intention, according to their nature.[81]

29.   Inert matter is insensible; so is the perispiritual fluid, but it transmits sensations to the sensory center which is the spirit. The painful lesions of the body are thus reflected in the spirit as an electric shock, by means of the perispiritual fluid whose nerves

---

80 This possibly explains the visions of Sister Emerich, a German nun who, referring to the time of the Passion of Christ, says that she saw material things which have never existed except in the books which she has read. Also those of Mrs. Cantianille B, (*The Spiritist Review – 1866*, August), and a part of those of Emanuel SWEDENBORG.

81 See *The Spiritist Review – 1866*, June & September. See also A. KARDEC, *The Spirits' Book*, ch. VIII, item 400.

appear to be its conducting wires. It is the so-called nervous impulse of physiologists, who, not knowing the relations of this fluid with the spiritual principle, have not been able to explain all its effects.

This interruption can take place by the separation of a limb, or the sectioning of a nerve; but also partially or generally, and without any lesion, in moments of emancipation, great excitement or preoccupation of the soul. In this state, the spirit no longer thinks of the body, and it draws from its feverish activity, so to speak, the perispiritual fluid which, by withdrawing from the surface, causes a momentary insensibility in it; such as, in the heat of combat, a soldier often does not notice that he/she is wounded; or when a person, whose attention is absorbed in a work, does not hear the noise that is made around him/her. It is an analogous but more pronounced effect the one that occurs in certain somnambulists, in lethargy and catalepsy; and thus it is possible to explain the insensibility of convulsionaries and certain martyrs. (*The Spiritist Review – 1868*, January, "Study on the Aïssaouas.")

Paralysis does not have the same cause at all; here the effect is entirely organic; it is the nerves themselves, the conducting wires, which are no longer capable of fluidic circulation; it is like the strings of the instrument which have been altered.

30. In certain pathological states, while the spirit is no longer in the body, and the perispirit only adheres to it at a few points, the body has all the appearance of death, and we are absolutely right when saying that life hangs by a thread. This state may last longer or shorter; some parts of the body can even decay, without life being permanently extinguished. As long as the last wire is not broken, the spirit can, either by an energetic action of its own will, or by an equally powerful, extraneous fluidic influx, be recalled into the body. Some prolongations of life against all probability, and certain supposed resurrections, can thus be explained. It is like the plant that sometimes is able to thrive by putting forth only a single sprout from its root; yet when the last molecules of the fluidic body are detached from the fleshly body, or when the latter is in a state of irreparable decay, any return to life becomes impossible.[82]

---

82 Examples in *The Spiritist Review – 1863*, August, "Dr. Cardon"; – *1866*, May, "The Corsican woman."

31. The universal fluid is, as we have seen, the primitive element of both the corporeal body and the perispirit, which are only transformations. According to the modality of its nature, this fluid can provide the body with restorative principles. Being condensed in the perispirit, the propellant is the spirit, whether incarnate or discarnate, which injects into a deteriorated body a part of the substance of its fluidic envelope. Healing takes place by substituting a healthy molecule for an unhealthy molecule. The healing power will therefore be due to the purity of the inoculated substance; it still depends on the energy of the will, which causes a more abundant fluid emission, and gives the fluid a greater force of penetration. Finally, intentions that animate the one who wants to heal, *whether an incarnate human or a discarnate spirit.* Fluids that emanate from an impure source are like adulterated medical substances.

32. The effects of the fluidic action on patients are extremely varied according to circumstances. This action is sometimes slow and calls for a continued treatment, as in ordinary magnetism; at other times, it is fast as an electric current. There are persons endowed with such power, that they operate upon certain patients instantaneous cures by the mere laying on of hands, or even by a single act of the will. Between the two extreme poles of this faculty there are an infinite number of nuances. All cures of this kind are varieties of magnetism, and differ only in the power and speed of action. The principle is always the same, it is the fluid which acts as a therapeutic agent, whose effect is subordinated to its quality and to special circumstances.

33. ([83]) Magnetic action can occur in several ways:

1ST) By the very fluid of the magnetizer; it is magnetism properly speaking, or human magnetism, whose is subordinated to the power and especially to the quality of the fluid.

2ND) By the fluid of spirits acting directly and without intermediary on an incarnate, either to heal or soothe some specific sorrow, or to provoke spontaneous somnambulic sleep, or to exert on the individual any physical or moral influence. This is spiritual magnetism, whose quality is due to the qualities of the spirit.[84]

---

83 [Trans. note] A typographical error in the 1868 French original numbering this item as 32 was duly corrected above to **33** with no further changes.

84 Examples in *The Spiritist Review –1863*, February; – *1865*, April & September.

3RD) By the fluid that spirits pour on the magnetizer and of which he/she acts as a conductor. This is *mixed* magnetism, *semi-spiritual* or, if you will, *spiritual-human*. The spiritual fluid, combined with the human fluid, gives the latter the qualities it lacks. The participation of spirits, in such a circumstance, is sometimes spontaneous, but most often it is induced by a request of the magnetizer.

34. The ability to heal by fluidic action is very common, and can be developed through exercise, but that of healing instantly by the laying on of hands is rarer, and at its apex it can be considered exceptional. At various times, however, and almost among all peoples, we have seen individuals possessing it to an eminent degree. In recent times, we have seen several remarkable examples, whose authenticity cannot be disputed. Since these kinds of cures are based on a natural principle, and the power to operate them is not a privilege, it is because they do not come out of Nature and are miraculous only in appearance.[85]

35. The perispirit is invisible to us in its normal state, but, as it is formed of ethereal matter, the spirit may, in certain cases, subject it, by an act of its will, to a molecular modification which renders it momentarily visible. It is thus that *apparitions* occur, which, like the other phenomena, are not outside the laws of Nature, not being more extraordinary than vapor, which is invisible when it is very rarefied, and becomes visible when condensed.

Depending on the condensation degree of the perispiritual fluid, an apparition is sometimes vague and vaporous; at other times it is more clearly defined. Finally, at other times, it has all the appearance of tangible matter; it can even go as far as actual tangibility, to the point that one can be mistaken about the nature of the being that one has in front of oneself.

Vaporous apparitions are frequent, and it happens quite often that individuals present themselves after their death to persons whom they have loved. Tangible apparitions are rarer, though there are quite a few perfectly authentic examples. If the spirit wishes to be recognized, he will impart to its envelope all the external signs that it had during its lifetime as an incarnate.

85 Examples of instant cures in *The Spiritist Review – 1866*, December. "Prince Hohenlohe"; October & November, "Jacob"; – *1867*, October & November, "Jacob"; August, "Simonet"; October, "Caïd Hassan"; November, "the priest Gassner."

36. It is to be noted that tangible apparitions have only the appearance of fleshly matter, but cannot have its qualities, because of their fluidic nature, They cannot have the same cohesion because, in reality, it is not flesh. They form instantly and disappear, or evaporate by the disintegration of fluid molecules. The beings that present themselves in these conditions do not came into view or die like other humans; now we see them, and now we no longer see them, without knowing where they come from, how they came, or where they go. They could not be killed, chained, or incarcerated, since they have no physical body; any blows struck against them would actually hit the void.

Such is the character of the so-called *ageners*,[86] with whom one can converse without ever suspecting who they really are, but who never make long stays, and cannot become an ordinary guest at a house, nor figure among the members of a family.

There is, moreover, in their whole person, in their peculiarities, something strange and unusual, which is both material and spiritual. Their gaze, vaporous and penetrating at the same time, does not have the clearness of the eyes of flesh. Their short and almost always laconic language has nothing of the brilliancy and volubility of human language. Their approach makes one feel an indefinable sensation of surprise which inspires a kind of fear, and, while taking them for individuals like everybody else, one says to oneself involuntarily: This is a peculiar individual.[87]

37. The perispirit being the same in the incarnate and the discarnate, through a completely identical effect, an incarnate spirit can appear, in a moment of freedom, at a place other than that where his/her body is resting, with his/her usual features and with all the signs of his/her identity. It is this phenomenon, of which there are authentic examples, that gave rise to the belief in the *doppelgänger* (i.e., a double of a living person).[88]

---

86 [Trans. note] From the French *agénère*, also translated as 'agenerate,' an *agener* is an extremely realistic apparition which can easily pass for a normal human being.

87 Examples of vaporous or tangible apparitions, and of ageners: *The Spiritist Review* – *1858*, January & October; – *1859*, February, March, January, November and August; – *1860*, April & May; – *1861*, July; – *1866*, April, "the plowman Martin introduced to King Louis XVIII, complete details"; December.

88 Examples of apparitions of living persons: *The Spiritist Review* – *1858*, December; – *1859*, February & August; – *1860*, November.

38. An effect typical of these kinds of phenomena is that vaporous and even tangible apparitions are not perceptible indistinctly by everybody; spirits only show themselves when they want and to whom they want. A spirit could therefore appear in an assembly to one or more people, and not be seen by anyone else. This comes from the fact that these kinds of perceptions are effected by spiritual sight, and not through corporeal sight, for not only is spiritual sight not given to everyone, but it can also be withdrawn by the will of a spirit, if necessary, momentarily granted to someone, if the spirit deems it necessary.

The condensation of the perispiritual fluid in the apparitions, even to the point of tangibility, does not, therefore, have the properties of ordinary matter; otherwise the apparitions, if perceptible by the eyes of the body, would be visible to all present.[89]

39. The spirit being able to effect transformations in the fabric of its perispiritual envelope, and this envelope radiating around the human body like a fluidic atmosphere, a phenomenon analogous to that of apparitions can occur on the very surface of the body. Under the fluidic layer, the real figure of the body may fade more or less completely and take on other features; or the primitive features seen through the modified fluidic layer, as through a prism, taking another expression. If the spirit, casting aside earthly concerns, identifies itself with the things of the spiritual world, the expression of an ugly countenance can become beautiful, radiant, and sometimes even luminous. If, on the contrary, the spirit is exalted by evil passions, a beautiful countenance may take a hideous aspect.

This is how *transfigurations* take place, which are always a reflection of the predominant qualities and feelings of the spirit. This phenomenon is therefore the result of a fluidic transformation; it is a kind of perispiritual apparition which is produced on the body itself while still alive and sometimes at the moment of death, instead of occurring in the distance, as in apparitions properly speaking. What distinguishes apparitions of this kind is

---

89 One must accept with extreme reserve stories of purely individual apparitions which, in certain cases, could be the subject of exaggerated imagination, and sometimes an invention made for an interested purpose. It is therefore necessary to keep a scrupulous account of the circumstances, of the good repute of the person, as well as of his/her interest in abusing the credulity of overconfident individuals.

that they are generally perceptible by all persons present, and to the eyes of the body, precisely because they are based on visible fleshly matter, whereas, in purely fluidic appearances, there is no tangible matter.[90]

40. The turning and talking tables' phenomena, of the ethereal suspension of bodies from the grave, of mediumistic writing, as old as the world, but much more frequent today, give the key of some spontaneous analogous phenomena to which, in the ignorance of the law that governed them, had been attributed a supernatural and miraculous character. These phenomena are based on the properties of the perispiritual fluid of either incarnate or free spirits.

41. It is with the help of its perispirit that the spirit acted on its living body. It is again with this same fluid that it manifests itself by acting on inert matter, producing noises, moving tables and other objects that it lifts, overturns, or transports. This is not surprising if we realize that, among us, the most powerful engines lie in the most rarefied and even imponderable fluids, such as air, steam and electricity.

It is also with the aid of its perispirit that the spirit makes mediums write, speak or draw; since it has no tangible body to act ostensibly when it wants to manifest itself, it uses the body of a medium, from which it borrows the organs, which then it makes act as if it were its own body, by the fluidic emission that it pours on the latter.

42. It is by the same means that the spirit acts on the table, either to make it move without a definite meaning, or to make it emit intelligent raps indicating the letters of the alphabet, so as to form words and sentences – a phenomenon referred to as *typtology*. The table is in this case only an instrument which it uses as a pencil for writing; the spirit gives it a momentary vitality by the fluid with which it acts upon it, although *it does not identify with it*. People that, overcome with emotion when they see a being who is dear to them, embrace the table, make a ridiculous act, for it is absolutely as if they are kissing the stick which a friend uses to strike blows. It is the same with those who speak to the table, as if the spirit were concealed in the wood, or as if the wood had become spirit.

---

90 Example and theory of transfiguration: *The Spiritist Review – 1859*, March. See also A. KARDEC, *The Mediums' Book*, ch. VII.

When communications take place through this means, the spirit must be represented, not within the table, but by the side, *as it was during its lifetime as an incarnate*, and as it would be seen if, at that moment, it could make itself visible. The same thing takes place in communications by writing: we would see the spirit beside the medium, directing the latter's hand or transmitting its thought to the medium through a fluidic current.

43. When the table detaches itself from the floor and floats in the air without any support, the spirit does not lift it with the force of arms, but envelops and penetrates it with a sort of fluidic atmosphere which neutralizes the effect of gravitation, as air does for balloons and kites. The fluid that penetrates it momentarily gives it a greater specific lightness. When it is nailed to the ground, then it is in a situation analogous to that of a pneumatic bell, under which a vacuum is created. These are only comparisons to show the analogy of the effects, and not an absolute similarity of causes. (See also A. KARDEC, *The Mediums' Book*, ch. IV.)

From this it is understood that it is not more difficult for the spirit to lift a person than to lift a table, to transport an object from one place to another, or to throw it somewhere: these phenomena occur by the same law.[91]

When the table chases someone, it is not the spirit which runs, because it can remain quietly at the same place, but it gives the table the impetus by a fluidic current with which it moves it at will.

When blows are heard in the table or elsewhere, the spirit strikes neither with its hand, nor with any object: it directs on the point

---

91 Such is the principle behind the phenomenon of *apportation* [Trans. note: *teleportation*]; a very real phenomenon, but one which must be accepted with the greatest reserve, for it is one of those which most lend themselves to simulation and trickery. An irrefutably good reputation on the part of the person who obtains them, his/her complete disinterestedness – both materially and *morally* – and the convergence of accessory circumstances, must be taken into serious consideration. Above all, it is necessary to watch out for the extreme ease with which such effects are imitated, and to hold suspicious those which are renewed too frequently and at will, so to speak. Magicians can do more extraordinary things.

The lifting of a person is no less real, but much rarer perhaps, because it is more difficult to emulate. It is well known that Mr. D. D. Home more than once climbed to the ceiling as he walked around the room. It is said that Saint Cupertino had the same faculty, which was no more miraculous for one than for the other.

where the noise starts a jet of fluid which produces the effect of an electric shock. It modifies the noise, as one can modify the sounds produced by the air.[92]

44. A very frequent phenomenon in mediumship is the aptitude of certain mediums to write in a language which is unknown to them; and to discuss, with the spoken word or through writing, topics and subjects which are well beyond their scope and formal education. It is not uncommon to find mediums who can write fluently without having learned how to write; and others who make poetry without having ever been able to make a verse in their life, Others still can draw, paint, sculpt, compose music, play an instrument, without knowing drawing, painting, sculpture or music. Very often, a medium is able to reproduce the handwriting and the signature that spirits communicating through him/her had in their lifetime, even though the medium never knew them.

This phenomenon is no more marvelous than seeing a child writing when leading his/her hand; thus we can make the child do whatever he/she wants. An absolute beginner can be made to write in any language by dictating the words letter by letter. We understand that this can be the same in mediumship, if we refer to the way in which the spirits communicate themselves with the mediums, which actually are for them, only passive instruments. But if the medium has the mechanism, if he/she has overcome the practical difficulties, if the expressions are familiar to him/her, and finally, if the medium has in his/her brain the elements of whatever the spirit wants him/her to perform, he/she is in a position of reading and writing fluently. Work becomes easier and faster; then the spirit has only to transmit the thought that its interpreter will reproduces by the means at his/her disposal.

---

92 Examples of material manifestations and disturbances in *The Spiritist Review* – *1858*, January, the girl from the "Passage des Panoramas"; February, "Mademoiselle Clairon"; May, June and July, "The Rapping Spirit of Bergzabern," a complete report; August, "The Rapping Spirit of Dibbelsdorf"; – *1860*, March, "Baker of Dieppe"; April, "Manufacturer of St. Petersburg"; August, "Rue des Noyers"; – *1861*, January, "The Rapping Spirit of Aube"; – *1864*, January, "Fontenelle and the Rapping Spirits"; May, "Poitiers" (also in – *1865*, May); June, "The Rapping Spirit of Sister Marie"; – *1865*, April, "Marseille"; August, "Manifestations of Fives, near Lille"; – *1866*, February, "The rats of Équihen."

A medium's aptitude for things unknown to himself/herself is often also due to the knowledge that the medium possessed in a previous existence, and of which his/her soul has preserved intuition. If the medium had once been a poet or a musician, for example, he/she will have more ease in assimilating the poetic or musical thought that a spirit wants him/her to reproduce. The language a medium does not know today may have been familiar to him/her in another existence; hence, for the medium, there may be a greater ability to write mediumistically in that language.[93]

45. Evil spirits abound around the Earth because of the moral inferiority of its inhabitants. Their evil action is one of the scourges against which humanity has to struggle here below. Obsession, which is one of the effects of this action, as well as diseases and all life tribulations, must therefore be regarded as a trial or an atonement, and be accepted as such.

Obsession is the persistent action that an evil spirit can exert over an individual. It comes in quite different varieties, from a simple moral influence without sensible external signs, to a complete disturbance of one's organism and mental faculties. Furthermore, it obliterates all the mediumistic faculties; related to one's auditory and psychographic mediumship, resulting in the obstinacy of a single spirit to manifest itself to the exclusion of all others.

46. Just as illnesses are the result of physical imperfections which make the body accessible to external pernicious influences, an obsession is always due to a moral imperfection which opens rifts to an evil spirit. To a physical cause, a physical force is opposed; whereas, to a moral cause, we must oppose a moral force. To preserve from illnesses, one fortifies the body; to avoid obsession one must strengthen one's soul. Hence, for the obsessed, the need to work on their own improvement, which is usually enough to get rid of the obsessor, without the help of strangers. The latter's help becomes necessary when the obsession degenerates into subjugation

---

93 The aptitude of certain persons for languages which they know, so to speak, without having learned them, has no other cause than an intuitive memory of what they knew in another existence. The example of the French poet Méry, reported in *The Spiritist Review – 1864*, November, "Memory of Past Lives," is proof of that. It is evident that if Mr. Méry had been a medium in his youth, he would have written in Latin easily, as well as in French, and would have been acclaimed as a prodigy.

and possession, because then sometimes the patient loses his/her volition and free will.

Obsession is almost always the result of a vengeance exerted by a spirit, and which most often has its source in the relationships that the obsessed had with the spirit in an earlier existence.

In cases of serious obsession, the obsessed is like enveloped and impregnated with a pernicious fluid that neutralizes the action of beneficial fluids and repels them. It is of this fluid that the person must be rid, but a bad fluid cannot be pushed back by another bad fluid. By an action identical to that of a healing medium in cases of disease, *it is necessary to expel the bad fluid with the help of a better fluid.*

This is a mechanical action, but that is not always enough: above all, it is necessary to *act upon the intelligent being* to which one must have the right to *speak with authority.* This authority is only granted by moral superiority; the larger it is, the greater the authority.

That is not all: to secure deliverance, the evil spirit must be led to renounce its evil designs. Repentance and the desire for good must be born in the spirit, by means of cleverly directed instructions, and evocations made for the purpose of its moral education. Thus one can have the double satisfaction of delivering an incarnate and converting an imperfect spirit.

This task is made easier when the obsessed, understanding his/her situation, brings the help of his/her will and prayer; not so when the latter, seduced by the deceiving spirit, deludes himself/herself as to the qualities of the obsessor, and delights in the error in which the latter plunges them. Then, far from endorsing it, the obsessed rejects all assistance. This typifies cases of fascination, which are always infinitely more rebellious than the most violent subjugation. (See A. KARDEC, *The Mediums' Book*, ch. XXIII,)

In all cases of obsession, prayer is the most powerful auxiliary in acting against the obsessing spirit.

47. In obsessions, the spirit acts externally with the help of its perispirit, which it associate with that of the incarnate. The latter is then entwined as in a network and forced to act against its will.

In possessions, instead of acting externally, the discarnate spirit substitutes itself, so to speak, with the incarnate spirit, taking domicile in the latter's body, however without the incarnate leaving the body definitively, which can only happen at death. Possession is therefore always temporary and intermittent, since a discarnate spirit cannot definitively invade and take place of an incarnate spirit, because the molecular union of the perispirit to the body can only take place at the moment of conception. (See cb, **XI**, item **18** above.)

The spirit, momentarily in possession of the body, uses it as if it were its own. It speaks through the body's mouth, sees through the body's eyes, acts with the body's arms, as it would have done in its lifetime. This is no longer as in speaking mediumship, where the incarnate spirit speaks by transmitting the thought of a discarnate spirit; it is the latter himself/herself who speaks and acts, and if the discarnate spirit has been known during its lifetime, it is recognized by its language, its voice, its gestures, and even the expression of its physiognomy.

48. An obsession is always the action of a malicious spirit. Possession may be the action of a good spirit which wants to speak and, to make a stronger impression on its listeners, borrows the body of an incarnate person, which is lent to it voluntarily, as one lends one's coat. This is done without any disturbance or discomfort, and during this action the incarnate spirit regains liberty as in the state of emancipation, and most often he/she stands beside its substitute to listen to it.

When the possessing spirit is evil, things are different; it does not borrow the body, it seizes it if the holder has no moral strength to resist him. It does this by malice towards the incarnate victim, whom it tortures and disturbs in every possible way, even to the point of destroying him/her, either by strangulation, or by pushing its victim into the fire or other dangerous places. Using the limbs and organs of the unfortunate person, it blasphemes, insults and mistreats those who happen to be around it. It lends itself to eccentricities and actions which have all the characteristics of furious madness.

Facts of this order, at different degrees of intensity, are very numerous, and many cases of madness have no other cause. Often pathological disorders are connected, which are only consecutive and against which medical treatment is powerless, as long as the primary cause remains undiscovered. Spiritism, by making known this source of part of human miseries, indicates the means of remedying it, which means to act on the author of the evil, which, being an intelligent being, must be intelligently treated.[94]

49. Most often, obsession and possession are individual, yet sometimes they are epidemic. When a swarm of evil spirits falls on a locality, it is like when a troop of enemies comes for an invasion. In this case, the number of individuals affected can be considerable.[95]

---

94 Examples of obsession and possession cures; *The Spiritist Review – 1863*, December; – *1864*, January & June; – *1865*, January & June; – *1866*, February; – *1867*, June.

95 An epidemic of this kind erupted for some years in the French village of Morzine, in Savoy (see a complete report of this epidemic in *The Spiritist Review* – *1862*, December; and – *1863*, January, February, April and May).

Chapter XV
Miracles in the Gospel

PRELIMINARY OBSERVATIONS · DREAMS · STAR OF THE WISE MEN ·
SECOND SIGHT · CURES · POSSESSED INDIVIDUALS ·
RESURRECTIONS · JESUS WALKS OVER THE WATER ·
TRANSFIGURATION · APPEASING A TEMPEST · WEDDING
IN CANA · MULTIPLICATION OF BREAD · THE TEMPTATION
OF JESUS · PRODIGIES AT THE DEATH OF JESUS · APPARITIONS OF
JESUS AFTER HIS DEATH · DISAPPEARANCE OF THE BODY OF JESUS

PRELIMINARY OBSERVATIONS

1.   Facts reported in the Gospel, and which have hitherto been considered miraculous, for the most part belong to the order of *psychical phenomena*, that is to say, of those whose primary cause is the faculties and attributes of the soul. By bringing them closer to those described and explained in the preceding chapter, it is easy to see that there is an identity of cause and effect between them. History shows analogous ones in all epochs and among all peoples, for the reason that, since there have always been incarnate and discarnate souls, the same effects must have occurred. One can dispute, it is true, the veracity of history on this subject; but today they occur before our eyes, so to speak, at will, and by individuals who are not at all exceptional. The mere fact of the reproduction of a phenomenon under identical conditions is enough to prove that it is possible and subject to a law; and therefore from that moment it is not miraculous.

The principle of psychical phenomena rests, as we have seen, on the properties of the perispiritual fluid which constitutes the magnetic agent on manifestations of spiritual life during a lifetime and after death, and finally on the constituent state of spirits and their role as an active force of Nature. These known elements and their effects, as observed, have the consequence of making one admits the possibility of certain facts which one would reject when attributing to them a supernatural origin.

2. Without prejudging the nature of Christ, which is not within the scope of this book to examine, yet considering him, through hypothesis, to be a higher-order spirit, one cannot fail to recognize him to be one of the highest order, and that he is placed by his virtues well above earthly humanity. Talking of the immense results he has obtained, his incarnation in this world could only be one of those missions which are entrusted only to the direct messengers of the Divinity for the accomplishment of its designs. Assuming that he was not God himself, but rather an envoy of God to transmit Its word, he would be much more than a prophet, for he was a divine Messiah.

As a human being, he had the organization of fleshly beings; but as a pure spirit, detached from matter, he had to live spiritual life rather than bodily life, of which he possessed no weaknesses. His superiority over humans was not due to any particular qualities of his body, but to those of his spirit, which dominated matter in an absolute way, and those of his perispirit drawn from the most quintessential part of Earth's fluids (see ch. **XIV**, item **9** above). His soul was to hold on to the body only through the strictly necessary links: being constantly released, it had to give it a second sight, not only permanent, but of exceptional penetration, which was well in excess of the one found in ordinary human beings. They same applied to all phenomena that depend on the perispirit or psychical fluids, and the higher quality of these fluids gave him an immense magnetic power seconded by an unceasing desire to do good.

In the cures he operated, did he act as a medium? Can we consider him a powerful healer? No; for a medium is an intermediary, an instrument used by discarnate spirits. But Christ did not need help, it was he who assisted others; he who acted thus by himself, by virtue of his personal power, like the incarnate can do in certain cases to the extent of their strength. Moreover, which spirit would have dared to infuse its own thoughts with his and instruct him to transmit them? If he received any extraneous influx, it could only be from God. According to the definition given by a spirit, he was a medium of God Itself.

DREAMS

3. Joseph, says the Gospel, was warned by an angel that appeared to him in a dream and told him to flee to Egypt with the child (MATTHEW 2:19–23).

Warnings through dreams play a great role in the sacred books of all religions. Without guaranteeing the accuracy of all the reported facts, and without discussing them, the phenomenon itself is not anomalous when we know that the time of sleep is when the spirit, freeing itself from the bonds of matter, enters momentarily into the spiritual life where it meets with those it has known. Often this is the moment that protector spirits choose to manifest themselves to their protégés and give them more direct advice. Authentic examples of warnings through dreams are numerous, but it should not be inferred that all dreams are warnings, and still less that all that one sees in dreams has a meaning. Among superstitious and absurd beliefs is the art of interpreting dreams. (See ch. **XIV**, items **27** and **28** above.)

STAR OF THE WISE MEN

4. It is said that a star appeared to the Wise Men[96] who came to adore Jesus, that it moved before them to show them the way and stood still when they arrived (MATTHEW 2:1–12).

The question is not whether the fact reported by MATTHEW is real, or if it is only figurative, indicating that the Wise Men were guided in a mysterious way to the place where the newborn Child was, bearing in mind that there is no way of verifying it, but whether a fact of this nature can actually happen.

One thing is certain, that in this circumstance the light could not have been a star. We could believe it at the time when it was thought that the stars were luminous points attached to the firmament and which could fall on the ground; but not today that we know their nature.

Setting aside the cause usually attributed to it, the fact of the appearance of a light with the aspect of a star is nonetheless possible. A spirit may appear in a luminous form, or transform part of its perispiritual fluid into a luminous point. Several facts of this kind,

---

96 [Trans. note] Also referred to as the three Magi.

recent and perfectly authentic, have no other cause, and this cause is not supernatural.

SECOND SIGHT

Jesus' entry in Jerusalem

5.   Now when they drew near to Jerusalem and came to Bethphage, to the Mount of Olives, then Jesus sent two disciples, saying to them, 'Go into the village in front of you, and immediately you will find a donkey tied, and a colt with her. Untie them and bring them to me. If anyone says anything to you, you shall say, 'The Lord needs them,' and he will send them at once.' This took place to fulfill what was spoken by the prophet, saying, 'Say to the daughter of Zion, 'Behold, your king is coming to you, humble, and mounted on a donkey, and on a colt, the foal of a beast of burden.'

The disciples went and did as Jesus had directed them. They brought the donkey and the colt and put on them their cloaks, and he sat on them." (MATTHEW 21:1–7 ESV)."

The Judas kiss

6.   "'Rise, let us be going; see, my betrayer is at hand.' While he was still speaking, Judas came, one of the twelve, and with him a great crowd with swords and clubs, from the chief priests and the elders of the people. Now the betrayer had given them a sign, saying, 'The one I will kiss is the man; seize him.' And he came up to Jesus at once and said, 'Greetings, Rabbi!' And he kissed him. Jesus said to him, 'Friend, do what you came to do.' Then they came up and laid hands on Jesus and seized him (MATTHEW 26:46-50 ESV)."

The miraculous fishing

7.   On one occasion, while the crowd was pressing in on him to hear the word of God, he was standing by the lake of Gennesaret, and he saw two boats by the lake, but the fishermen had gone out of them and were washing their nets. Getting into one of the boats, which was Simon's, he asked him to put out a little from the land. And he sat down and taught the people from the boat.

And when he had finished speaking, he said to Simon, 'Put out into the deep and let down your nets for a catch.' And Simon answered, 'Master, we toiled all night and took nothing! But at your word I will let down the nets.' And when they had done this, they enclosed a large number of fish, and their nets were breaking. They signaled to their partners in the other boat to come and help them. And they came and filled both the boats, so that they began to sink (LUKE 5:1–7 ESV)."

Vocations of Peter, Andrew, James, John, and Matthew

8. "While walking by the Sea of Galilee, he saw two brothers, Simon (who is called Peter) and Andrew his brother, casting a net into the sea, for they were fishermen. And he said to them, 'Follow me, and I will make you fishers of men.' Immediately they left their nets and followed him.

And going on from there he saw two other brothers, James the son of Zebedee and John his brother, in the boat with Zebedee their father, mending their nets, and he called them. Immediately they left the boat and their father and followed him (MATTHEW 4:18–22)."

"As Jesus passed on from there, he saw a man called Matthew sitting at the tax booth, and he said to him, 'Follow me.' And he rose and followed him (MATTHEW 9:9)."

9. These facts are not surprising when we know the power of second sight and the quite natural cause of this faculty. Jesus possessed it to the highest degree, and it can be said that it was his normal state, which is attested by a great number of actions in his life, and by what is explained magnetic phenomena and Spiritism today.

The fishing episode described as miraculous is also explainable by second sight. Jesus did not spontaneously produce fish where none existed; he saw, as someone lucid in the waking state could have done by the sight of his/her soul, the place where the fish were, and thus was able to say with assurance to the fishermen where to throw their nets.

The penetration of thought, consequently resulting in certain predictions, are the consequence of spiritual sight. When Jesus called to himself Peter, Andrew, James, John, and Matthew, he had to be aware of their inner dispositions in order to know that they would follow him and that they were capable of fulfilling the mission which he would assign to them. Furthermore, it was necessary that they themselves had the intuition of this mission so as to surrender themselves to him. It was the same when, on the day of the Last Supper, he announced that one of the twelve will betray him and that designates him by saying that the traitor was the one who was going to put his hand in the dish with him; and also when he said that Peter would deny him.

In many passages of the Gospel, we read, "But Jesus, knowing their thought, said to them..." Yet how could he know their thought, if not both by the fluidic radiation that brought him this thought and the spiritual sight that allowed him to read inwardly all individuals?

So often we believe in a thought deeply buried in the folds of our soul, that we have no doubt that we carry in ourselves a reflecting mirror, a revelator impregnated with its own fluidic radiation. If we could see the mechanism of the invisible world around us, the ramifications of these threads of thought that connect all intelligent beings, both corporeal and incorporeal; the fluidic emissions charged with the imprints of the moral world like currents as they pass through space; we would be less surprised by certain effects which ignorance ascribes to chance. (See ch. **XIV**, items **22** *et seq.* above.)

CURES

Loss of blood

10. "And there was a woman who had had a discharge of blood for twelve years, and who had suffered much under many physicians, and had spent all that she had, and was no better but rather grew worse. She had heard the reports about Jesus and came up behind him in the crowd and touched his garment. For she said, 'If I touch even his garments, I will be made well.' And immediately the flow of blood dried up, and she felt in her body that she was healed of her disease.

And Jesus, *perceiving in himself that power had gone out from him,* immediately turned about in the crowd and said, 'Who touched my garments?' And his disciples said to him, 'You see the crowd pressing around you, and yet you say, 'Who touched me?' And he looked around to see who had done it.

But the woman, knowing what had happened to her, came in fear and trembling and fell down before him and told him the whole truth. And he said to her, 'Daughter, your faith has made you well; go in peace, and be healed of your disease' (MARK 5:25–34 ESV)."

11. These words, *"Perceiving in himself that power had gone out from him,"* are significant; they express the fluidic movement that operated from Jesus to the sick woman. Both felt the action that had just occurred. It is remarkable that the effect was not provoked by any act of Jesus' will; there had been neither magnetization nor imposition of hands. Normal fluidic radiation was sufficient to effect healing.

Yet why did this radiation come to this woman rather than to others, since Jesus did not think of her, and was surrounded by a crowd?

For a very simple reason: The fluid, being given as therapeutic material, must reach an organic disorder to repair it; it can be directed to the ailment by the will of the healer, or attracted by the ardent desire, the confidence, in a word, the faith of the patient. With respect to the fluidic flow, the first has the effect of a pressure pump and the second of a suction pump. Sometimes simultaneity of the two actions is necessary, other times only one is enough; it is the second that took place in this circumstance.

Jesus was right to say, "Your faith has made you well." It is understood that here faith is not the mystical virtue as some people understand it, but a real attractive force of one who has not opposed to the fluidic current a repulsive force, or at least a force of inertia that would paralyze the action. It is understood from this that two patients with the same disease, in presence of a healer, one can be cured, and the other not. This is one of the most important principles of healing mediumship, and explains, by a very natural cause, certain apparent anomalies. (See ch. **XIV**, items **31**, **32** and **33** above.)

The blind man of Bethsaida

12. "And they came to Bethsaida. And some people brought to him a blind man and begged him to touch him.

And he took the blind man by the hand and led him out of the village, and when he had spit on his eyes and laid his hands on him, he asked him, 'Do you see anything?' And he looked up and said, 'I see men, but they look like trees, walking.' Then Jesus laid his hands on his eyes again; and he opened his eyes, his sight was restored, and he saw everything clearly.

And he sent him to his home, saying, 'Do not even enter the village' (MARK 8:22–26)."

13. Here the magnetic effect is obvious; the healing has not been instantaneous, but gradual, and as a result of a sustained and repetitive action, though more rapid than in ordinary magnetization. The first sensation of this man is that experienced by the blind when recovering sight; by an optical effect, objects appear to be of a disproportionate size to them.

A paralytic

14. "And getting into a boat he crossed over and came to his own city. And behold, some people brought to him a paralytic, lying on a bed. And when Jesus saw their faith, he said to the paralytic, 'Take heart, my son; your sins are forgiven.'

And behold, some of the scribes said to themselves, 'This man is blaspheming.' But Jesus, knowing their thoughts, said, 'Why do you think evil in your hearts? For which is easier, to say, 'Your sins are forgiven,' or to say, 'Rise and walk'? But that you may know that the Son of Man has authority on earth to forgive sins' – he then said to the paralytic – 'Rise, pick up your bed and go home.'

And he rose and went home. When the crowds saw it, they were afraid, and they glorified God, who had given such authority to men (MATTHEW 9:1–8)."

15. What could these words mean: "Your sins are forgiven"; and what could they do for healing? Spiritism gives the key, as of an infinity of other words misunderstood to this day; it teaches us, by the law of the plurality of existences, that the evils and afflictions of life are often atonements of the past, and that we suffer in the current life the consequences of the faults that we have committed in an earlier existence. Different existences are closely linked to one another until the debt of one's imperfections has been paid.

If, then, this man's illness was a punishment for the evil he might have committed, saying to him, "Your sins are forgiven," was to say to him; "You have paid your debt; the cause of your illness is effaced by your current faith; as a result, you deserve to be delivered from your illness." This is why he says to the scribes, "'Why do you think evil in your hearts? For which is easier, to say, 'Your sins are forgiven,' or to say, 'Rise and walk'?" Once the cause ceases, its effect must also cease. The case is the same as for a prisoner who would be told, "Your crime is atoned for and pardoned," which would be tantamount to saying, "You can now get out of prison."

The ten lepers

16. "On the way to Jerusalem he was passing along between Samaria and Galilee. And as he entered a village, he was met by ten lepers, who stood at a distance and lifted up their voices, saying, 'Jesus, Master, have mercy on us.' When he saw them he said to them, 'Go and show yourselves to the priests.' And as they went they were cleansed.

Then one of them, when he saw that he was healed, turned back, praising God with a loud voice; and he fell on his face at Jesus' feet, giving him thanks. Now he was a Samaritan.

Then Jesus answered, 'Were not ten cleansed? Where are the nine? Was no one found to return and give praise to God except this foreigner?' And he said to him, 'Rise and go your way; your faith has made you well' (LUKE '7:11–19 ESV)."

17. The Samaritans were schismatics, almost like Protestants to Catholics in recent times, and were despised by the Jews as heretics. Jesus, by indiscriminately healing Samaritans and Jews, gave at the same time a lesson and an example of tolerance; and pointing out that the Samaritan alone had returned to give glory to God, he showed that there was in that man more true faith and gratitude than among those who called themselves orthodox. By adding, "Your faith has made you well," he shows that God looks deep inside one's heart and not into the outward form of worship. However the others were healed; it was necessary for the lesson he wished to give, and to prove their ingratitude, but who knows what will have happened later, and if they have been favored? By saying to the Samaritan, "Your faith has made you well," Jesus suggests that it would not be the case for the others.

Withered hand

18. "Again he entered the synagogue, and a man was there with a withered hand. And they watched Jesus, to see whether he would heal him on the Sabbath, so that they might accuse him. And he said to the man with the withered hand, 'Come here.' And he said to them, 'Is it lawful on the Sabbath to do good or to do harm, to save life or to kill?' But they were silent. And he looked around at them with anger, grieved at their hardness of heart, and said to the man, 'Stretch out your hand.' He stretched it out, and his hand was restored.

The Pharisees went out and immediately held counsel with the Herodians against him, how to destroy him. Jesus withdrew with his disciples to the sea, and a great crowd followed, from Galilee and Judea and Jerusalem and Idumea and from beyond the Jordan and from around Tyre and Sidon. When the great crowd heard all that he was doing, they came to him (MARK 3:1–8 ESV)."

A woman with a disabling spirit

19. "Now he was teaching in one of the synagogues on the Sabbath. And there was a woman who had had a disabling spirit for eighteen years. She was bent over and could not fully straighten herself. When Jesus saw her, he called her over and said to her, 'Woman, you are freed from your disability.' And he laid his hands on her, and immediately she was made straight, and she glorified God.

But the ruler of the synagogue, indignant because Jesus had healed on the Sabbath, said to the people, 'There are six days in which work ought to be done. Come on those days and be healed, and not on the Sabbath day.'

Then the Lord answered him, 'You hypocrites! Does not each of you on the Sabbath untie his ox or his donkey from the manger and lead it away to water it? And ought not this woman, a daughter of Abraham whom Satan bound for eighteen years, be loosed from this bond on the Sabbath day?'

As he said these things, all his adversaries were put to shame, and all the people rejoiced at all the glorious things that were done by him (LUKE 13:10–17)."

20. This fact proves that at that time most diseases were attributed to the devil, and that, as today, we confuse the possessed with the sick, but in the opposite direction; that is to say, today, those who do not believe in evil spirits confuse obsessions with pathological diseases.

The paralytic at the pool

21.　"After this there was a feast of the Jews, and Jesus went up to Jerusalem. Now there is in Jerusalem by the Sheep Gate a pool, in Aramaic called Bethesda, which has five roofed colonnades. In these lay a multitude of invalids, blind, lame, and paralyzed.

One man was there who had been an invalid for thirty-eight years. When Jesus saw him lying there and knew that he had already been there a long time, he said to him, 'Do you want to be healed?' The sick man answered him, 'Sir, I have no one to put me into the pool when the water is stirred up, and while I am going another steps down before me.' Jesus said to him, 'Get up, take up your bed, and walk.' And at once the man was healed, and he took up his bed and walked. Now that day was the Sabbath.

So the Jews said to the man who had been healed, 'It is the Sabbath, and it is not lawful for you to take up your bed.' But he answered them, 'The man who healed me, that man said to me, 'Take up your bed, and walk.' They asked him, 'Who is the man who said to you, 'Take up your bed and walk'?' Now the man who had been healed did not know who it was, for Jesus had withdrawn, as there was a crowd in the place.

Afterward Jesus found him in the temple and said to him, 'See, you are well! Sin no more, that nothing worse may happen to you.'

The man went away and told the Jews that it was Jesus who had healed him. And this was why the Jews were persecuting Jesus, because he was doing these things on the Sabbath. But Jesus answered them, 'My Father is working until now, and I am working.' (JOHN 5:1–17).".

22.　Pool (*piscine* in the original Latin, from *piscis*, fish) was understood in Roman times as reservoirs or fishponds where fish were fed. Later, the meaning of this word was extended to basins where people bathed together.

The pool of Bethsaida in Jerusalem was a cistern near the Temple, fed by a natural spring, whose water appears to have had healing properties. It was undoubtedly an intermittent source, which at times erupted with force and stirred the water. According to popular belief, this moment was the most favorable to cures; perhaps in reality, at the moment of its release, the water had a more active property, or that the agitation produced by the gushing water stirred up the salutary mud in certain diseases. These effects are quite natural and perfectly known today; but then the sciences were little advanced, and a supernatural cause was seen in most misunderstood phenomena. The Jews, therefore, attributed the agitation of this water to the presence of an angel, and this belief seemed to them all the better founded, that at that moment the water was more salutary.

After having healed this man, Jesus said to him, "Sin no more, that nothing worse may happen to you." With these words, he makes him understand that his illness was a punishment, and that, if he does not improve, he may be punished again more rigorously. This tenet is entirely in conformity with that taught by Spiritism,

23. Jesus seemed to be taking on the task of healing on the Sabbath, because he had occasion to protest against the rigor of the Pharisees concerning the observance of that day. He wanted to show them that true piety does not consist in the observance of external practices and formalities, but that it lies in the feelings of the heart. He justifies himself by saying: "My Father is working until now, and I am working." That is to say, God does not suspend Its works or Its action upon the things of Nature on the Sabbath, It continues to produce what is necessary for your food and your health, and I am Its example.

A born-blind man

24. "As he passed by, he saw a man blind from birth. And his disciples asked him, 'Rabbi, who sinned, this man or his parents, that he was born blind?'

Jesus answered, 'It was not that this man sinned, or his parents, but that the works of God might be displayed in him. We must work the works of him who sent me while it is day; night is coming, when no one can work. As long as I am in the world, I am the light of the world.'

Having said these things, he spat on the ground and made mud with the saliva. Then he anointed the man's eyes with the mud and said to him, 'Go, wash in the pool of Siloam' (which means Sent). So he went and washed and came back seeing.

The neighbors and those who had seen him before as a beggar were saying, 'Is this not the man who used to sit and beg?' Some said, 'It is he.' Others said, 'No, but he is like him.' He kept saying, 'I am the man.' So they said to him, 'Then how were your eyes opened?' He answered, 'The man called Jesus made mud and anointed my eyes and said to me, 'Go to Siloam and wash.' So I went and washed and received my sight.' They said to him, 'Where is he?' He said, 'I do not know.'

They brought to the Pharisees the man who had formerly been blind. Now it was a Sabbath day when Jesus made the mud and opened his eyes.

So the Pharisees again asked him how he had received his sight. And he said to them, 'He put mud on my eyes, and I washed, and I see.' Some of the Pharisees said, 'This man is not from God, for he does not keep the Sabbath.' But others said, 'How can a man who is a sinner do such signs?' And there was a division among them.

So they said again to the blind man, 'What do you say about him, since he has opened your eyes?' He said, 'He is a prophet.' The Jews did not believe that he had been blind and had received his sight, until they called the parents of the man who had received his sight and asked them, 'Is this your son, who you say was born blind? How then does he now see?'

His parents answered, 'We know that this is our son and that he was born blind. But how he now sees we do not know, nor do we know who opened his eyes. Ask him; he is of age. He will speak for himself.' (His parents said these things because they feared the Jews, for *the Jews had already agreed that if anyone should confess Jesus to be Christ, he was to be put out of the synagogue.*) Therefore his parents said, 'He is of age; ask him.'

So for the second time they called the man who had been blind and said to him, 'Give glory to God. We know that this man is a sinner.' He answered, 'Whether he is a sinner I do not know. One thing I do know, that though I was blind, now I see.' They said to him, 'What did he do to you? How did he open your eyes?' He answered them, 'I have told you already, and you would not listen. Why do you want to hear it again? Do you also want to become his disciples?' And they reviled him, saying, 'You are his disciple, but we are disciples of Moses. We know that God has spoken to Moses, but as for this man, we do not know where he comes from.'

The man answered, 'Why, this is an amazing thing! You do not know where he comes from, and yet he opened my eyes. We know that God does not listen to sinners, but if anyone is a worshiper of God and does his will, God listens to him. Never since the world began has it been heard that anyone opened the eyes of a man born blind. If this man were not from God, he could do nothing.'

They answered him, 'You were born in utter sin, and would you teach us?' And they cast him out (JOHN 9:1–34)."

25. This story, so simple and so naive, bears in itself an evident truth. Nothing fantastic or wondrous; it is a scene of real life taken as the fact occurred. The language of this blind man is that of those simple people in whom knowledge is supplemented by common sense, and who retort the arguments of their adversaries with good humor, and with reasons which are neither lacking in justice nor in purpose. Is the tone of the Pharisees that of proud individuals who admit nothing beyond their intelligence and are indignant at the mere thought that a man of the people can question their authority? Except for the local color of names, it is like our time.

To be driven out of the synagogue meant to be put out of the Church; it was a form of excommunication. Spiritists, whose tenets are those of Christ interpreted according to the progress of current enlightenment, are treated as the Jews who recognized Jesus as the Messiah. By excommunicating them, they are put out of the Church, as the scribes and Pharisees did to Jesus' followers. So, here is a man who is driven out because he cannot believe that the one who healed him is a sinner and possessed by the devil; and for glorifying God for his healing! Is this not similar to what is being done to Spiritists nowadays? Whatever they get, wise counsel from the spirits, gratitude to God and goodness, cures, everything is the work of the devil and for these anathema is proclaimed upon them. Have we not seen priests say, from the pulpit, that it was better to remain incredulous than to return to the faith through Spiritism? Have we not seen it said to the sick that they should not be healed by Spiritists because their gift is satanic? And what did the Jewish priests and the Pharisees say and do? Besides, it is said that everything must happen today as it was in the time of Christ.

This question of the disciples: Is it the sin of this man that caused him to be born blind? It indicates the intuition of an earlier existence, otherwise it would have no meaning; for the sin which would be the cause of a birth infirmity should necessarily have been committed before birth and, consequently, in a previous existence. If Jesus had deemed to be a wrong idea, he would have said to them, "How could this man have sinned before he was born?" Instead, he tells them that if this man is blind it is not that he has sinned, but that the power of God would break out in him; that is to say, he had to be the instrument of a manifestation of the power of God. If it was not an atonement for the past, it was a test that was to be used for its advancement, because God, who is righteous, could not impose suffering on him without compensation.

As to the means employed to cure it, it is evident that the specific kind of mud made with saliva and earth could have virtue only by the action of the healing fluid with which it was impregnated. Thus the most insignificant substances, such as water, for example, can acquire powerful and effective qualities under the action of the spiritual or the magnetic fluid to which they serve as a vehicle, or, if you will, a *repository*.

Several cures performed by Jesus

26. "And he went throughout all Galilee, teaching in their synagogues and proclaiming the gospel of the kingdom and healing every disease and every affliction among the people. So his fame spread throughout all Syria, and they brought him all the sick, those afflicted with various diseases and pains, those oppressed by demons, epileptics, and paralytics, and he healed them. And great crowds followed him from Galilee and the Decapolis, and from Jerusalem and Judea, and from beyond the Jordan (MATTHEW 23–25)."

27. Of all the facts which bear witness to the power of Jesus, the most numerous are indisputably the cures. He wished to prove by this that true power is that which does good, that its object is to render itself useful, and not to satisfy the curiosity of the indifferent by extraordinary things.

By relieving sorrow and suffering, he touched people in the heart, which gained him proselytes more numerous and more sincere than if they had only been struck by what their eyes could see. By this means he made himself loved, whereas if he had limited himself to producing surprising material effects, as the Pharisees demanded, most would have seen in him only a sorcerer or a skillful wizard, whom *idle individuals would go to see for entertainment.*

So when John the Baptist sends his disciples to ask him if he is the Christ, he does not say, "I am," for any impostor could have said the same thing. He does not speak to them of wonders or marvelous things, instead simply replying: "Go and tell John what you have seen and heard: the blind receive their sight, the lame walk, lepers are cleansed, and the deaf hear, the dead are raised up, the poor have good news preached to them (LUKE 7:22 ESV)." It was like telling John: "Recognize me through my works, judge the tree for its fruit," for that was the true character of his divine mission.

28.   It is also by the good it does that Spiritism proves its providential mission. It cures physical ailments, but it also cures especially moral diseases – and these are the greatest prodigies through which it asserts itself. Its most sincere followers are not those who have been struck only by the sight of extraordinary phenomena, but those who have been touched in the heart by consolation; those who have been delivered from the tortures of doubt; those whose courage has been reassured in afflictions, who have drawn strength from the certainty of the future which it has come to bring to them, with the knowledge of their spiritual being and their destiny. In a word, those whose faith is unshakable, because they can feel and understand.

Those who see in Spiritism only material effects cannot understand its moral force; and the incredulous who know it only by phenomena whose primal cause they do not admit, see in the Spiritists only tricksters and charlatans. It is not by wonders that Spiritism will triumph over incredulity, it is by multiplying its moral benefits, in view of the fact that, if unbelievers do not admit prodigies, they experience, like everyone else, suffering and afflictions, and no one would refuse relief and consolation. (See ch. **XIV**, item **30** above.)

POSSESSED INDIVIDUALS

29.   "And they went into Capernaum, and immediately on the Sabbath he entered the synagogue and was teaching. And they were astonished at his teaching, for he taught them as one who had authority, and not as the scribes. And immediately there was in their synagogue a man with an unclean spirit. And he cried out, 'What have you to do with us, Jesus of Nazareth? Have you come to destroy us? I know who you are, the Holy One of God.' But Jesus rebuked him, saying, 'Be silent, and come out of him!' And the unclean spirit, convulsing him and crying out with a loud voice, came out of him.

And they were all amazed, so that they questioned among themselves, saying, 'What is this? A new teaching with authority! He commands even the unclean spirits, and they obey him' (MARK 1:21–27 ESV)."

30. "As they were going away, behold, a demon-oppressed man who was mute was brought to him. And when the demon had been cast out, the mute man spoke. And the crowds marveled, saying, 'Never was anything like this seen in Israel.'

But the Pharisees said, 'He casts out demons by the prince of demons' (MATTHEW 9:32–34 ESV)."

31. "And when they came to the disciples, they saw a great crowd around them, and scribes arguing with them. And immediately all the crowd, when they saw him, were greatly amazed and ran up to him and greeted him.

And he asked them, 'What are you arguing about with them?' And someone from the crowd answered him, 'Teacher, I brought my son to you, for he has a spirit that makes him mute. And whenever it seizes him, it throws him down, and he foams and grinds his teeth and becomes rigid. So I asked your disciples to cast it out, and they were not able.'

And he answered them, 'O faithless generation, how long am I to be with you? How long am I to bear with you? Bring him to me.' And they brought the boy to him. And when the spirit saw him, immediately it convulsed the boy, and he fell on the ground and rolled about, foaming at the mouth.

And Jesus asked his father, 'How long has this been happening to him?' And he said, 'From childhood. And it has often cast him into fire and into water, to destroy him. But if you can do anything, have compassion on us and help us.'

And Jesus said to him, 'If you can! All things are possible for one who believes.' Immediately the father of the child cried out and said, 'I believe; help my unbelief!'

And when Jesus saw that a crowd came running together, he rebuked the unclean spirit, saying to it, 'You mute and deaf spirit, I command you, come out of him and never enter him again.' And after crying out and convulsing him terribly, it came out, and the boy was like a corpse, so that most of them said, 'He is dead.' But Jesus took him by the hand and lifted him up, and he arose.

And when he had entered the house, his disciples asked him privately, 'Why could we not cast it out?' (MARK 9:14–28 ESV)."

32. "Then a demon-oppressed man who was blind and mute was brought to him, and he healed him, so that the man spoke and saw. And all the people were amazed, and said, 'Can this be the Son of David?'

But when the Pharisees heard it, they said, 'It is only by Beelzebul, the prince of demons, that this man casts out demons.'

Knowing their thoughts, he said to them, 'Every kingdom divided against itself is laid waste, and no city or house divided against itself will stand. And if Satan casts out Satan, he is divided against himself. How then will his kingdom stand? And if I cast out demons by Beelzebul, by whom do your sons cast them out? Therefore they will be your judges. But if it is by the Spirit of God that I cast out demons, then the kingdom of God has come upon you. (MATTHEW 12:22–28 ESV)."

33. The deliverance of the possessed appears, with the cures, among the most numerous acts of Jesus. Among the facts of this nature there is, like the one mentioned above, in item 30, where possession is not evident. It is probable that at that time, as it still happens today, the influence of demons was attributed to all diseases whose cause was unknown, mainly mutism, epilepsy, and catalepsy. But there is one where the action of evil spirits is not doubtful; with those of which we have been witnesses, they have an analogy which is so striking that we recognize in them all the symptoms of this kind of affliction. The proof of the participation of a hidden intelligence in such a case, emerges from a concrete fact, namely, the numerous radical cures obtained at some Spiritist Centers, solely by the evocation and the moral counseling of the obsessing spirits, without using any magnetization or drugs, and often in the absence of the patient who is at a distant location. The immense superiority of Christ gave him such authority over imperfect spirits, then called demons, that it was sufficient for him to command them to go away for them to leave, since they could not resist such an order. (See ch. **XIV**, item **46** above.)

34. The fact of evil spirits being sent into the body of swine is contrary to all probability. An evil spirit is nonetheless a human spirit still imperfect enough to do evil after death, as it did before, and it is against the laws of Nature that it would be able to animate the body of an animal. We must therefore see in this passage one of those amplifications of a real fact common in times of ignorance and superstition; or perhaps an allegory to characterize the foul inclinations of certain spirits.

35. The obsessed and the possessed appear to have been very numerous in Judea, in the time of Jesus, which gave him the opportunity to heal many. The evil spirits had undoubtedly invaded this country and caused an epidemic of possessions. (See ch. **XIV**, item **49** above.)

Without being an epidemic, individual obsessions are extremely frequent and appear in very different modalities, which a thorough knowledge of Spiritism makes easily recognizable. They can often have unfortunate consequences for one's health, either by aggravating or determining organic afflictions. They will undoubtedly one day rank among the pathological causes requiring, by their special nature, special healing means. Spiritism, by making known the cause of evil, opens a new path to the art of healing, and provides science with the means to succeed where it often unsuccessful for failing to attack the root cause of the evil. (See A. KARDEC, *The Mediums' Book*, ch. XXIII.)

36. Jesus was accused by the Pharisees of casting out demons by means of other demons; the good itself that he did was, according to them, the work of Satan, without thinking that Satan himself chasing himself would be an act of foolishness. This doctrine is still the one that the Church seeks to make prevail today against Spiritist manifestations.[97]

RESURRECTIONS

Jairus's daughter

37. "And when Jesus had crossed again in the boat to the other side, a great crowd gathered about him, and he was beside the sea. Then came one of the rulers of the synagogue, Jairus by name, and seeing him, he fell at his feet and implored him earnestly, saying, 'My little daughter is at the point of death. Come and lay your hands on her, so that she may be made well and live.'

And he went with him. And a great crowd followed him and thronged about him.

And there was a woman who had had a discharge of blood for twelve years, and who had suffered much under many physicians, and had spent all that she had, and was no better but rather grew worse. She had heard the reports about Jesus and came up behind him in the crowd and touched his garment. For she said, 'If I touch even his garments, I will be made well.' And immediately the flow of blood dried up, and she felt in her body that she was healed of her disease. And Jesus, perceiving in himself that power had gone out from him, immediately turned about in the crowd and said, 'Who touched my garments?' And his disciples said to him, 'You see the crowd pressing around you, and yet you say, Who touched me?' And he looked around to see who had done it. But the woman,

---

97 The following passage was extracted from *Conférences sur la Religion* [*Conferences on Religion*], by Monseigneur FRAYSSINOUS, bishop of Hermopolis, vol. II, page 341, Paris, 1825, whose value cannot be disputed by the clergy:

"If Jesus had worked his miracles by virtue of the demon, the devil would have worked to destroy his empire, and he would have used his power against himself. *Certainly, a demon who seeks to destroy the reign of vice to establish that of virtue, would be a strange demon.* This is why Jesus, to reject the absurd accusation made by the Jews, said to them: 'If I perform wonders in the name of the devil, the devil is divided with himself; he seeks, therefore, to destroy himself'; an answer which received no retort."

This is precisely the argument that Spiritists oppose to those who attribute to the devil the good counseling they receive from the spirits. The demon would act like a professional thief that would return all that he stole, and commit the other thieves to become good and honest individuals.

knowing what had happened to her, came in fear and trembling and fell down before him and told him the whole truth. And he said to her, 'Daughter, your faith has made you well; go in peace, and be healed of your disease.'

While he [Jairus] was still speaking, there came from the ruler's house some who said, 'Your daughter is dead. Why trouble the Teacher any further?' But overhearing what they said, Jesus said to the ruler of the synagogue, 'Do not fear, only believe.' And he allowed no one to follow him except Peter and James and John the brother of James.

They came to the house of the ruler of the synagogue, and Jesus saw a commotion, people weeping and wailing loudly. And when he had entered, he said to them, *'Why are you making a commotion and weeping? The child is not dead but sleeping.'* And they laughed at him. But he put them all outside and took the child's father and mother and those who were with him and went in where the child was. Taking her by the hand he said to her, *'Talitha cumi,'* which means, 'Little girl, I say to you, arise.' And immediately the girl got up and began walking (for she was twelve years of age), and they were immediately overcome with amazement. (MARK 5:21–42)."

Son of Nain's widow

38. "Soon afterward he went to a town called Nain, and his disciples and a great crowd went with him. As he drew near to the gate of the town, behold, a man who had died was being carried out, the only son of his mother, and she was a widow, and a considerable crowd from the town was with her. And when the Lord saw her, he had compassion on her and said to her, 'Do not weep.' Then he came up and touched the bier, and the bearers stood still. And he said, 'Young man, I say to you, arise.' And the dead man sat up and began to speak, and Jesus gave him to his mother.

Fear seized them all, and they glorified God, saying, 'A great prophet has arisen among us!' and 'God has visited his people!' And this report about him spread through the whole of Judea and all the surrounding country (LUKE 7:11–17)."

39. The fact of returning to bodily life an individual who is truly dead would be contrary to the laws of Nature, and therefore miraculous. Now, it is not necessary to resort to this order of facts to explain the resurrections made by Christ.

Since among us the appearance of death sometimes deceive even well reputed doctors, accidents of this nature would be much more frequent in a country where no precaution was taken, and where the burial was immediate.[98] There is, therefore, every probability that in the two examples above there was only syncope or lethargy. Jesus himself says so positively about Jairus's daughter: *The child is not dead but sleeping.*

Due to the fluidic power possessed by Jesus, it is not surprising that the vivifying fluid directed by a strong will has revived the numb senses; allowing him even to call back in the body the spirit which was ready to leave it, as long as the perispiritual link had not been definitively broken. For the people of that time, who believed the individual was dead as soon as he/she was no longer breathing, there was resurrection, and they could affirm it in very good faith. But, actually, there was healing and not resurrection in the correct sense of the word.

40. The resurrection of Lazarus, whatever may be said, in no way invalidates this principle. For four days, he was in the sepulcher, it is said; but we know that there are cases of lethargy that last eight days or more. We should add that it smelled bad, which is a clear sign of decomposition. This allegation proves nothing either, because in some individuals there is partial decomposition of the body even before death, and they exhale an odor of rottenness. Death only happens when the organs essential to life are attacked.

And who could know if he smelled bad? It is his sister Martha who says it, but how did she know? Lazarus having been buried for

---

98 A proof of this custom is found in the Acts of the Apostles 5:5 *et seq.*:

"When Ananias heard these words, he fell down and breathed his last. And great fear came upon all who heard of it. The young men rose and wrapped him up and carried him out and buried him. After an interval of about three hours his wife came in, not knowing what had happened. And Peter said to her, 'Tell me whether you sold the land for so much.' And she said, 'Yes, for so much.' But Peter said to her, 'How is it that you have agreed together to test the Spirit of the Lord? Behold, the feet of those who have buried your husband are at the door, and they will carry you out.' Immediately she fell down at his feet and breathed her last. When the young men came in they found her dead, and they carried her out and buried her beside her husband."

four days, she could have supposed it, but not been certain of it. (See ch. **XIV**, item **29** above.)[99]

41. "Immediately he made the disciples get into the boat and go before him to the other side, while he dismissed the crowds. And after he had dismissed the crowds, he went up on the mountain by himself to pray.

When evening came, he was there alone, but the boat by this time was a long way from the land, beaten by the waves, for the wind was against them. And in the fourth watch of the night he came to them, walking on the sea.[100] But when the disciples saw him walking on the sea, they were terrified, and said, 'It is a ghost!' and they cried out in fear. But immediately Jesus spoke to them, saying, 'Take heart; it is I. Do not be afraid.'

And Peter answered him, 'Lord, if it is you, command me to come to you on the water.' He said, 'Come.'" So Peter got out of the boat and walked on the water and came to Jesus. But when he saw the wind, he was afraid, and beginning to sink he cried out, 'Lord, save me.' Jesus immediately reached out his hand and took hold of him, saying to him, 'O you of little faith, why did you doubt?' And when they got into the boat, the wind ceased. And those in the boat worshiped him, saying, 'Truly you are the Son of God' (MATTHEW 14:22–33)."

42. This phenomenon finds its natural explanation in the principles outlined above, in ch. **XIV**, item **43**.

---

99 The following fact proves that decomposition sometimes precedes death. In the Couvent du Bon-Pasteur (Convent of the Good Shepherd), founded in Toulon by the abbot Marin, chaplain of prisons, for repentant girls, was a young woman who had endured the most terrible sufferings with the calm and impassibility of an expiatory victim. In the midst of the pains, she seemed to smile at a celestial vision. Like St. Teresa, she asked to suffer again, her flesh went to pieces, gangrene gained her limbs; by wise foresight, the doctors had recommended that the body be buried immediately after death. Strange thing! Scarcely had she last breathed, that all work of decomposition stopped; the cadaverous exhalations ceased; for thirty-six hours she remained exposed to the prayers and veneration of the community.

100 Lake Genesareth or Tiberias.

Similar examples prove that this is neither impossible nor miraculous since it is in the laws of Nature. It may have occurred in two ways.

Jesus, though alive, could appear on water in a tangible form, while his corporeal body was elsewhere; this is the most probable hypothesis. One can even recognize in the narrative certain characteristic signs of tangible apparitions. (See ch. **XIV**, items **35**, **36** and **37** above.)

On the other hand, his body could have been supported somehow, and its gravity be neutralized by the same fluidic force that lifts a table in the air without any apparent support. The same effect has occurred several times on human bodies.

TRANSFIGURATION

43. "And after six days Jesus took with him Peter and James and John, and led them up a high mountain[101] by themselves. And he was transfigured before them, and his clothes became radiant, intensely white, as no one on earth could bleach them. And there appeared to them Elijah with Moses, and they were talking with Jesus.

And Peter said to Jesus, 'Rabbi, it is good that we are here. Let us make three tents, one for you and one for Moses and one for Elijah.' For he did not know what to say, for they were terrified.

And a cloud overshadowed them, and a voice came out of the cloud, 'This is my beloved Son; listen to him.'

And suddenly, looking around, they no longer saw anyone with them but Jesus only.

And as they were coming down the mountain, he charged them to tell no one what they had seen, until the Son of Man had risen from the dead (Mark 9:1–9)."

44. It is still in the properties of the perispiritual fluid that we can find the reason for this phenomenon. Transfigurations, explained in ch. **XIV**, item **39** above, are rather ordinary facts which, by reason of fluidic radiation, can modify the appearance of an individual. Yet the purity of Jesus' perispirit has allowed his spirit to give him an exceptional brilliance. As for the appearance of Moses and Elijah,

---

101 Mount Thabor or Tabor, about 1,000 meters high, SW of Lake Tabarich, 11 km SE of Nazareth.

it falls entirely within phenomena of the same order. (See ch. **XIV**, item **35** *et seq.* above.)

Of all the faculties that have been revealed in Jesus, there is none that is outside the conditions of humanity, and that we do not find in common people, because they are all in Nature, yet by the superiority of his moral essence and of his fluidic qualities, he attained proportions above those of ordinary people. He represented to us, apart from his corporeal envelope, the state of pure spirits.

APPEASING A TEMPEST

45. "One day he got into a boat with his disciples, and he said to them, 'Let us go across to the other side of the lake.' So they set out, and as they sailed he fell asleep. And a windstorm came down on the lake, and they were filling with water and were in danger. And they went and woke him, saying, 'Master, Master, we are perishing!' And he awoke and rebuked the wind and the raging waves, and they ceased, and there was a calm. He said to them, 'Where is your faith?' And they were afraid, and they marveled, saying to one another, 'Who then is this, that he commands even winds and water, and they obey him?' (LUKE 8:22–25 ESV)."

46. We do not yet know enough the secrets of Nature to categorically affirm whether there are occult intelligences that preside over the action of the elements. In this hypothesis, the phenomenon in question could be the result of an act of authority over these same intelligences, and would prove a power which no human is allowed to exercise.

In any case, Jesus, sleeping quietly during the storm, attests to a security that can be explained by the fact that his spirit saw that there was no danger, and that the storm was going to subside.

WEDDING IN CANA

47. This miracle, mentioned solely in JOHN's Gospel, is indicated as being the first that Jesus did, and as such it should have been all the more noticed. However, it must have produced very little sensation, since no other evangelist has spoken about it. Such an extraordinary thing ought to have astonished the guests, and especially the master of the house, who do not even seem to have noticed it.

Considered in itself, this fact is of little importance compared to those who truly testify to the spiritual qualities of Jesus. Admitting that things have happened as they are reported, it is remarkable that it is the only phenomenon of this kind that he has produced; he was of a nature too elevated to attach himself to purely material effects peculiar only to stimulate the curiosity of the crowd, which would have likened him to a magician. He knew that truly useful things would conquer him more sympathy and bring him more adherents than those who could pass for special tricks and did not touch the heart.

Although to a certain extent the fact can in part be explained by a fluidic action which, as magnetism offers similar examples, would have changed the properties of water by giving it the taste of wine, this hypothesis is unlikely, because in such a case the water, having only the taste of wine, would have preserved its color, which would not have failed to be noticed. It is more rational to see in it one of those parables so common in the teachings of Jesus, such as the Prodigal Son, the Wedding Feast, and so many others. He will have made during the meal an allusion to wine and water, from which he would have drawn a teaching. What justifies this opinion are the words addressed to him on this subject by the master of the feast: "Everyone serves the good wine first, and when people have drunk freely, then the poor wine. But you have kept the good wine until now (JOHN 2:9–10 ESV)."

MULTIPLICATION OF BREAD

48. The multiplication of the loaves is one of the miracles which have most intrigued the commentators, at the same time that it has baffled the incredulous. Without bothering to probe the allegorical meaning, the latter saw in it only a puerile tale; but most serious people have seen in this narrative, though in a form different from the ordinary one, a parable comparing the spiritual nourishment of the soul with the nourishment of the body.

One can, however, see in it more than a figure of speech, and admit, from a certain point of view, the reality of a material effect, without resorting to any prodigy. We know that a great concern of one's mind, the constant attention given to something, make us forget hunger. Now, those who followed Jesus were eager to hear him: so it is not surprising to me that engrossed by his word and perhaps also by the powerful magnetic action he exerted upon them, they did not feel the material need to eat.

Jesus, foreseeing this result, was able to reassure his disciples by saying, in the usual figurative language, admitting that they had actually brought some bread, that these breads would be enough to satiate the crowd. At the same time he was giving them a lesson: "You give them something to eat (LUKE 9:13 ESV)," he said; teaching them that they too could feed on the word.

Thus, beside the allegorical moral sense, a well-known natural physiological effect has been produced. The prodigy, in this case, is in the ascendancy of the word of Jesus, powerful enough to captivate the attention of an immense crowd to the point of making them forget to eat. This moral force bears witness to the superiority of Jesus, far more than the purely material fact of the multiplication of the loaves which must be considered as an allegory.

This explanation is confirmed by Jesus himself, in the following delightful passages:

The leaven of the Pharisees

49. "When the disciples reached the other side, they had forgotten to bring any bread. Jesus said to them, 'Watch and beware of the leaven of the Pharisees and Sadducees.' And they began discussing it among themselves, saying, 'We brought no bread.'

But Jesus, aware of this, said, 'O you of little faith, why are you discussing among yourselves the fact that you have no bread? Do you not yet perceive? Do you not remember the five loaves for the five thousand, and how many baskets you gathered? Or the seven loaves for the four thousand, and how many baskets you gathered? How is it that you fail to understand that I did not speak about bread? Beware of the leaven of the Pharisees and Sadducees.'

Then they understood that he did not tell them to beware of the leaven of bread, but of the teaching of the Pharisees and Sadducees (MATTHEW 16:5–12 ESV)."

The bread of heaven (or the bread of life)

50. "On the next day the crowd that remained on the other side of the sea saw that there had been only one boat there, and that Jesus had not entered the boat with his disciples, but that his disciples had gone away alone. Other boats from Tiberias came near the place where they had eaten the bread after the Lord had given thanks. So when the crowd saw that Jesus was not there, nor his disciples, they themselves got into the boats and went to Capernaum, seeking Jesus.

When they found him on the other side of the sea, they said to him, 'Rabbi, when did you come here?' Jesus answered them, 'Truly, truly, I say to you, you are seeking me, not because you saw signs, but because you ate your fill of the loaves. Do not labor for the food that perishes, but for the food that endures to eternal life, which the Son of Man will give to you. For on him God the Father has set his seal.'

Then they said to him, 'What must we do, to be doing the works of God?' Jesus answered them, 'This is the work of God, that you believe in him whom he has sent.'

So they said to him, 'Then what sign do you do, that we may see and believe you? What work do you perform? Our fathers ate the manna in the wilderness; as it is written, He gave them bread from heaven to eat.' Jesus then said to them, 'Truly, truly, I say to you, it was not Moses who gave you the bread from heaven, but my Father gives you the true bread from heaven. For the bread of God is he who comes down from heaven and gives life to the world.' They said to him, 'Sir, give us this bread always.'

Jesus said to them, '*I am the bread of life; whoever comes to me shall not hunger, and whoever believes in me shall never thirst.* But I said to you that you have seen me and yet do not believe' (JOHN 6:22–36 ESV)."

"Truly, truly, I say to you, whoever believes has eternal life. I am the bread of life. Your fathers ate the manna in the wilderness, and they died. This is the bread that comes down from heaven, so that one may eat of it and not die (JOHN 6:47–50 ESV)."

51. In the first passage, Jesus, recalling the effect produced above, makes it clear that there was no material bread; otherwise, his comparison with the leaven of the Pharisees would have been moot. "Do you not yet perceive," said he, "and do you not remember the five loaves for the five thousand, and how many baskets you gathered? Or the seven loaves for the four thousand, and how many baskets you gathered? How is it that you fail to understand that I did not speak about bread? Beware of the leaven of the Pharisees and Sadducees." This comparison had no reason to be in the hypothesis of a material multiplication. The fact would have been extraordinary enough in itself to have struck the imagination of his disciples, who, however, did not seem to recall it.

This is no less clear from Jesus' discourse on the bread of heaven, in which he endeavors to explain the true meaning of spiritual nourishment. In other words, Jesus said: "Work not to have the food that perishes, but the one that dwells for everlasting life, and that the Son of Man will give you. This food is his word, which is the bread that comes down from heaven and gives life to the world." "I am," he says, "the bread of life; *whoever comes to me shall not hunger*, and whoever believes in me shall never thirst."

However these distinctions were too subtle for these brusque natures, which included only tangible things. The manna that had nourished the bodies of their ancestors was for them the true bread of heaven – that was the miracle. If, then, the fact of the multiplication of bread had taken place materially, how could these same people, for whose benefit it would have occurred a few days before, have been so little impressed as to say to him, "Then what sign do you do, that we may see and believe you? What work do you perform?" What are you doing that is extraordinary? It was because they understood as miracles the wonders which the Pharisees demanded, that is to say, signs in the sky performed at one's command, as by the wand of an enchanter. What Jesus did seemed too simple and did not deviate enough from the laws of Nature; the cures themselves did not have a strange, extraordinary character; in short, spiritual miracles did not have enough momentum for them.

THE TEMPTATION OF JESUS

52. Jesus, transported by the devil to the summit of the Temple, then on a mountain, and tempted by him, is one of those parables so typical of Jesus, which public credulity has transformed into material facts.[102]

53. "Jesus was not lifted away, but he wanted to make human beings understand that humanity is prone to fail, and that it must always be on guard against the evil inspirations to which its weak nature surrenders – a figure of speech, and one would have to be blind to take it literally. How would you like the Messiah, the Word of God incarnate, to be subjected for a time, however short, to the suggestions of the devil, and as the Gospel of LUKE says, the devil had left him *for a time*, which would suggest that he will still be subject to his power. No, you should better understand the teachings given to you. The spirit of evil could do nothing about the essence of good. Nobody said that they had seen Jesus on the mountain or at the top of the Temple; a fact that, should it have been true, would certainly have spread through narratives of all peoples. Therefore the temptation was neither a physical or material act. As for the moral side, can you admit that the spirit of darkness could say to Jesus who knew his origin and power: 'Adore me, and I will give you all the kingdoms of the earth'? So the demon would have ignored who Jesus was making such offers, which is not likely. If he knew Jesus, his proposal was nonsense, because he knew he would be rejected by the one who was coming to ruin his empire over humans."

"Understand, then, the meaning of this parable, for it is one, just as well as those of the Prodigal Son and the Good Samaritan. One shows us the dangers that humans run, if they do not resist this inner voice that cries to them incessantly: 'You can be more than you are; you can possess more than you own; you can grow, acquire; just yield to the voice of ambition, and all your wishes will be fulfilled.' It shows you the danger and the way to avoid it, saying to the bad inspirations: *Get thee behind me, Satan!* – or in other words: *Be gone, temptation!*"

"The other two parables that I have mentioned show you what an individual who was too weak to ward off the devil, having succumbed to his temptations, can still hope for. They show you the mercy of the father of the family extending his hand on the repentant son's forehead, and granting him, with love, the pardon he had implored.

---

102 The following explanation is taken textually from a communication given on this subject by a spirit.

They show you the culprit, the schismatic, the man repulsed by his own brothers, better in the eyes of the supreme judge than those who despise him, because he has been practicing the virtues taught by the law of love."

"Weigh well the teachings offered in the Gospels; know how to distinguish between what is literal and what is figurative, and the errors that have blinded you for so many centuries will gradually fade away to make way for the dazzling light of truth." (Bordeaux, 1862, spirit of John the Evangelist.)

PRODIGIES AT THE DEATH OF JESUS

54. "Now from the sixth hour there was darkness over all the land until the ninth hour (MATTHEW 27:45 esv)."

"And behold, the curtain of the temple was torn in two, from top to bottom. And the earth shook, and the rocks were split. The tombs also were opened. And many bodies of the saints who had fallen asleep were raised, and coming out of the tombs after his resurrection they went into the holy city and appeared to many (MATTHEW 27:51–53 esv)."

55. It is strange that such prodigies, being accomplished at the very moment when the attention of the city was fixed on the torment of Jesus, which was the event of the day, have not been noticed, since no historian makes mention of them. It seems impossible that an earthquake, and *all the earth covered with darkness for three hours,* in a country where the sky is always perfectly clear, may have gone unnoticed.

The duration of this darkness is pretty much that of an eclipse of the Sun, but these kinds of eclipses only occur at the new moon, and the death of Jesus took place during the full moon on the 14th of the month of Nissan, Passover day of the Jews.

The obscuration of the Sun can also be produced by the spots that are noticeable on its surface. In this case, the brightness of the light is noticeably weakened, but never to the point of producing obscurity and darkness. If such a phenomenon had taken place at that time, it would have had a perfectly natural cause.[103]

---

103 There are constantly fixed spots on the surface of the Sun, which follow its rotation and serve to determine the duration. But these spots sometimes increase in

As for the dead risen, it may be that some people had visions or apparitions took place, which is not unusual; but, as we did not know the cause of this phenomenon then, we can suppose that some individual apparitions came out of the sepulcher.

Jesus' disciples, deeply moved by the death of their master, have undoubtedly attached to it some particular facts to which they would have paid no attention in other occasions. It was enough for a fragment of rock to be detached at that moment, to make people predisposed to the wondrous see a prodigy in it, and that, by amplifying the fact, said that the stones had split.

Jesus' greatness resides in his works, and not in the fantastic tales with which a poorly enlightened enthusiasm seemed to surround him.

APPARITIONS OF JESUS AFTER HIS DEATH

56. "But Mary [Magdalene] stood weeping outside the tomb, and as she wept she stooped to look into the tomb. And she saw two angels in white, sitting where the body of Jesus had lain, one at the head and one at the feet. They said to her, 'Woman, why are you weeping?' She said to them, 'They have taken away my Lord, and I do not know where they have laid him.'

Having said this, she turned around and saw Jesus standing, but *she did not know that it was Jesus.* Jesus said to her, 'Woman, why are you weeping? Whom are you seeking?'

Supposing him to be the gardener, she said to him, 'Sir, if you have carried him away, tell me where you have laid him, and I will take him away.'

Jesus said to her, 'Mary.' She turned and said to him in Aramaic, 'Rabboni!' (which means Teacher). Jesus said to her, 'Do not cling to me, for I have not yet ascended to the Father; but go to my brothers and say to them, 'I am ascending to my Father and your Father, to my God and your God.'

---

number, in extent, and in intensity, and it is then that there is a diminution in the light and in the heat. This increase in the number of spots seems to coincide with certain astronomical phenomena and the relative position of some planets, which brings about its periodical return. The duration of obscuration is very variable; sometimes it is only two or three hours, but in the year 535 there was one that lasted fourteen months.

Mary Magdalene went and announced to the disciples, 'I have seen the Lord' – and that he had said these things to her (JOHN 20:11–18)."

57. "That very day two of them were going to a village named Emmaus, about seven miles from Jerusalem, and they were talking with each other about all these things that had happened. While they were talking and discussing together, Jesus himself drew near and went with them. *But their eyes were kept from recognizing him.* And he said to them, 'What is this conversation that you are holding with each other as you walk?'

And they stood still, looking sad. Then one of them, named Cleopas, answered him, 'Are you the only visitor to Jerusalem who does not know the things that have happened there in these days?' And he said to them, 'What things?' And they said to him, 'Concerning Jesus of Nazareth, a man who was a prophet mighty in deed and word before God and all the people, and how our chief priests and rulers delivered him up to be condemned to death, and crucified him. But we had hoped that he was the one to redeem Israel. Yes, and besides all this, it is now the third day since these things happened. Moreover, some women of our company amazed us. They were at the tomb early in the morning, and when they did not find his body, they came back saying that they had even seen a vision of angels, who said that he was alive. Some of those who were with us went to the tomb and found it just as the women had said, but him they did not see.' And he said to them, 'O foolish ones, and slow of heart to believe all that the prophets have spoken! Was it not necessary that the Christ should suffer these things and enter into his glory?' And beginning with Moses and all the Prophets, he interpreted to them in all the Scriptures the things concerning himself.

So they drew near to the village to which they were going. He acted as if he were going farther, but they urged him strongly, saying, 'Stay with us, for it is toward evening and the day is now far spent.' So he went in to stay with them. When he was at table with them, he took the bread and blessed and broke it and gave it to them. *And their eyes were opened, and they recognized him. And he vanished from their sight.*

They said to each other, 'Did not our hearts burn within us while he talked to us on the road, while he opened to us the Scriptures?'

And they rose that same hour and returned to Jerusalem. And they found the eleven and those who were with them gathered together, saying, 'The Lord has risen indeed, and has appeared to Simon!' Then they told what had happened on the road, and how he was known to them in the breaking of the bread.

As they were talking about these things, Jesus himself stood among them, and said to them, 'Peace to you!' But they were startled and frightened and thought they saw *a spirit*.

And he said to them, 'Why are you troubled, and why do doubts arise in your hearts? See my hands and my feet, that it is I myself. Touch me, and see. For a spirit does not have flesh and bones as you see that I have.' And when he had said this, he showed them his hands and his feet.

And while they still disbelieved for joy and were marveling, he said to them, 'Have you anything here to eat?' They gave him a piece of broiled fish, and he took it and ate before them. Then he said to them, 'These are my words that I spoke to you while I was still with you, that everything written about me in the Law of Moses and the Prophets and the Psalms must be fulfilled.'

Then he opened their minds to understand the Scriptures, and said to them, 'Thus it is written, that the Christ should suffer and on the third day rise from the dead, and that repentance and forgiveness of sins should be proclaimed in his name to all nations, beginning from Jerusalem. You are witnesses of these things. And behold, I am sending the promise of my Father upon you. But stay in the city until you are clothed with power from on high' (LUKE 24:13–49 ESV)."

58. "Now Thomas, one of the Twelve, called the Twin, was not with them when Jesus came. So the other disciples told him, 'We have seen the Lord.' But he said to them, 'Unless I see in his hands the mark of the nails, and place my finger into the mark of the nails, and place my hand into his side, I will never believe.'

Eight days later, his disciples were inside again, and Thomas was with them. Although the doors were locked, Jesus came and stood among them and said, 'Peace be with you.'

Then he said to Thomas, 'Put your finger here, and see my hands; and put out your hand, and place it in my side. Do not disbelieve, but believe.' Thomas answered him, 'My Lord and my God!'

Jesus said to him, 'Have you believed because you have seen me? Blessed are those who have not seen and yet have believed' (JOHN 20:24–29 ESV)."

59. "After this Jesus revealed himself again to the disciples by the Sea of Tiberias, and he revealed himself in this way. Simon Peter, Thomas (called the Twin), Nathanael of Cana in Galilee, the sons of Zebedee, and two others of his disciples were together. Simon Peter said to them, 'I am going fishing.' They said to him, 'We will go with you.' They went out and got into the boat, but that night they caught nothing.

Just as day was breaking, Jesus stood on the shore; yet the disciples did not know that it was Jesus. Jesus said to them, 'Children, do you have any fish?' They answered him, 'No.' He said to them, 'Cast the net on the right side of the boat, and you will find some.' So they cast it, and now they were not able to haul it in, because of the quantity of fish. That disciple whom Jesus loved therefore said to Peter, 'It is the Lord!' When Simon Peter heard that it was the Lord, he put on his outer garment, for he was stripped for work, and threw himself into the sea. The other disciples came in the boat, dragging the net full of fish, for they were not far from the land, but about a hundred yards off (JOHN 21:1–8 ESV)."

60. "Then he led them out as far as Bethany, and lifting up his hands he blessed them. While he blessed them, *he parted from them and was carried up into heaven.*

And they worshiped him and returned to Jerusalem with great joy, and were continually in the temple blessing God (LUKE 24: 50–53 ESV)."

61. Apparitions of Jesus after his death are reported by all the evangelists in a profusion of details that does not allow to doubt the reality of the fact. They are, moreover, perfectly explainable by the fluidic laws and the properties of the perispirit; and present nothing anomalous compared with the phenomena of the same kind, of which ancient and contemporary history offers many examples, without excluding the tangibility of the apparition. If we observe the circumstances which accompanied his various apparitions, we recognize in him, at these moments, all the characteristics of a fluidic being. He appears unexpectedly and disappears in the same way; he is seen by some and not by others under appearances which do not make him promptly recognizable by his disciples; he shows himself in enclosed spaces where a corporeal body could not penetrate; his very language does not have the verve of that of a bodily being; he has the brief and sententious tone peculiar to the spirits that manifest themselves in this manner; all of these traits, in a word, have something which is not of the earthly world. The sight of him causes both surprise and fear; his disciples, on seeing him, do not speak to him with the same freedom; they feel that it is no longer the incarnate human they knew.

Jesus therefore showed himself with his perispiritual body, which explains that he was only seen by those he wanted to see him. If he had had his fleshly body, he would have been seen by anyone, as in his lifetime. His disciples, ignoring the primary cause of the phenomenon of apparitions, were not aware of those peculiarities; they probably did not notice, they were convinced it was Jesus and touched him. For them it must have been his resurrected body (See ch. **XIV**, items **14**, and **35** to **38**, above.)

62. While incredulity rejects all the facts accomplished by Jesus, due to their supernatural appearance; and considers them, without exception, as legends, Spiritism offers to most of these facts a natural explanation. It proves their possibility, not only by the theory of fluidic laws, but by their identity with analogous facts produced by a multitude of persons in the most ordinary conditions. Since these facts are somehow in the public domain, they prove nothing, in principle, concerning the exceptional nature of Jesus.[104]

63. The greatest of the miracles that Jesus has done, which truly testifies to his superiority, is the revolution that his teachings have made in the world, despite the smallness of his means of action.

---

104 The various contemporary facts of cures, apparitions, possessions, second sight and others, which are related in several issues of *The Spiritist Review*, and recalled in some notes above, offer, even in the circumstances of detail, such an striking analogy with those related by the Gospel, that the similarity of effects and causes remains obvious. Hence, one wonders why the same fact would have a natural cause today and formerly a supernatural one; diabolical in some and divine in others. If it had been possible to place them here opposite each other, the comparison would have been easier; but their number and the developments that most of them require, have not allowed it.

Indeed, Jesus, being obscure, poor, born in the most humble condition, in a small nation almost ignored and without political, artistic or literary significance, preached for only three years. During this short space of time, he was misunderstood and persecuted by his fellow citizens, slandered, treated as an impostor. He was obliged to flee so as not to be stoned; he was betrayed by one of his apostles, denied by another, abandoned by all at the moment when he fell into the hands of his enemies. He did only good, and that did not protect him from malevolence, which turned against him the very services he rendered. Condemned to the torment reserved for criminals, he died unknown to the world, for contemporary history is silent about him.[105] He wrote nothing, and yet, helped by some obscure men like himself, his word has sufficed to regenerate the world; his tenets have killed all-powerful paganism, and have become the torch of civilization. He had then against him all that can make humans fail, that is why we say that the triumph of his teachings is the greatest of his miracles, at the same time that it proves his divine mission. If, instead of social and regenerative principles, founded on the spiritual future of humanity, he had only a few wondrous facts to offer to posterity, hardly would we know him by name today.

DISAPPEARANCE OF THE BODY OF JESUS

64. The disappearance of Jesus' body after his death has been the subject of many controversies. It is attested by the four evangelists, on the account of the women who presented themselves at the sepulcher on the third day, and did not find it there. Some saw in this disappearance a miraculous fact, others supposed a clandestine abduction.

According to another opinion, Jesus would not have invested with a fleshly body, but only with a fluidic body. He would have been, throughout his life, only a tangible apparition; in a word, a sort of *agener*.[106] His birth, his death, and all the material events of his life would have been but an appearance. It is thus – it is said – that his

---

105 The Jewish historian Josephus is the only one who speaks of Jesus, yet he wrote very little about him.

106 [Trans. note] See footnote 86 above.

body, once returned to the fluidic state, could have disappeared from the sepulcher; and it is with this same body that he would have shown himself after his death.

Undoubtedly such a fact is not radically impossible, from what we know today about the properties of fluids; but it would be at least entirely exceptional and in formal opposition to the characteristics of ageners (see ch. **XIV**, item **36** above). The question is therefore whether such a hypothesis is admissible, whether it is confirmed or contradicted by the facts.

65. Jesus' stay on Earth has two periods: the one that preceded and the one that followed his death. In the first, from the moment of conception to birth, everything takes place, in the womb, as in the ordinary conditions of life. From birth to death, everything in his acts, language, and the various circumstances of his life presents the unequivocal characteristics of corporeality. The phenomena of psychical order which occur in him are accidental, and have nothing anomalous, since they are explained by the properties of the perispirit, and are found in different degrees in other individuals. After his death, on the contrary, everything reveals in him the fluidic being. The difference between the two states is so marked that it is not possible to assimilate them.[107]

The fleshly body has the properties inherent in matter, properly speaking, and which differ essentially from those of the ethereal fluids. Disintegration is effected by the rupture of the molecular cohesion. A sharp instrument, penetrating into the material body, divides the tissues; if the organs essential to life are attacked, their functioning stops, and death follows, that is, the death of the body. Since this cohesion does not exist in fluidic bodies, life does not rest on the action of special organs, and similar disorders cannot occur in them. A sharp instrument, or whatever, would enter it as into a vapor, without causing any injury. That is why these kinds of bodies *cannot die*, and the reason why the fluidic beings designated under the name of *ageners* cannot be killed.

After the torment of crucifixion, Jesus' body remained there, inert and lifeless. He was buried like ordinary bodies, and everyone could see him and touch him. After his resurrection, when

---

107 I am not referring the mystery of his incarnation, which I have not dealt with here, and will be discussed later.

he wants to leave Earth, he does not die: his body rises, vanishes, and disappears without leaving a trace – an evident proof that this body was of a different nature from the one that perished on the cross. Hence it must be concluded that if Jesus could die, he had a fleshly body.

As a result of its material properties, the fleshly body is the seat of sensations and physical pains that are reflected in the sensory center or spirit. It is not the body that suffers; it is the spirit that receives the feedback of the lesions or alterations of the organic tissues. In a body deprived of spirit, sensation is absolutely null; for the same reason, the spirit, which has no material body, cannot experience the sufferings which are the result of the changes of matter – from which it must also be concluded that if Jesus suffered physically, as we cannot doubt, it was because he had a material body of a nature similar to that of everyone else.

66. To material facts it should be added overwhelming moral considerations.

If Jesus had been, during his life, in the conditions of a fluidic being, he would have felt neither the pain nor any of the needs of the body. To suppose that it has been so, is to deprive him of all the merit of the privation and suffering he had chosen as an example of resignation. If all in him was only appearance, all the acts of his life, the repeated announcement of his death, the painful scene of the Garden of Olives, his prayer to God to take away the chalice from his lips, the Passion, his agony, all the way to his last cry at the moment of rendering his spirit, would have been nothing but a vain simulacrum to change his nature and to make believe in the illusory sacrifice of his life – a comedy unworthy of a simple honest man, let alone of a being so superior. In a word, he would have abused the good faith of his contemporaries and posterity. These are the logical consequences of this system, consequences which are not admissible, because they are morally belittling, instead of elevating Jesus.

Jesus, like everyone else, had a fleshly body and a fluidic body, attested by both the material phenomena and the psychical phenomena that marked his life.

67. What has become of his fleshly body? It is a problem whose solution can only be deduced, until further notice, by hypotheses, for want of sufficient elements to establish a conclusive answer. This solution, moreover, is of secondary importance, and would add nothing to the merits of Christ, nor to the facts which prove, in a far more commanding manner, his superiority and his divine mission.

There can be no question of the manner in which this disappearance has occurred except personal opinions, which would have no value unless they were sanctioned by rigorous logic, and by the general teaching of spirits. However, so far, none of those which have been formulated have received the corroboration of this double verification.

If the spirits have not yet solved this issue by a unanimous decision, it is because the moment of solving it has not yet come, or perhaps we still lack the knowledge by means of which we can solve it ourselves. In the meantime, if we exclude the supposition of a clandestine abduction, we might find, by analogy, a probable explanation in the theory of the double phenomenon of apportation[108] and invisibility. (See A. KARDEC, *The Mediums' Book*, ch. IV and V.)

68. This idea about the nature of the body of Jesus is not new. In the fourth century, Apollinaris of Laodicea (4th century AD), leader of the sect of Apollinarians, claimed that Jesus had not taken a body like ours, but an impassible body, which had come down from heaven in the bosom of the Blessed Virgin, and was not born of her: according to him Jesus was born, had suffered, and died only in appearance. The Apollinarians were anathematized as heretics at the Council of Alexandria in 362; the Synod of Rome in 374; and the Council of Constantinople in 381.

---

108 [Trans. note] *Apportation* is the same of *teleportation*, in modern, non-Spiritist parlance.

PART THREE

Predictions

according to Spiritism

Chapter XVI
Theory of prescience

1. How is knowledge of the future at all possible? One understands the prediction of events which are the consequence of the present state, but not of those which have no relation to it; and still less of those which are attributed to chance. Future things, it is said, do not exist; they are still in nothingness; so how can anyone know that they will happen? Examples of predictions made are, however, quite numerous, from which it must be concluded that there is a phenomenon of which we have no key. Since there is no effect without a cause, it is this cause that we will try to find; and again, it is Spiritism– itself the source of so many mysteries – that will provide an explanation to us, moreover showing us that the very fact of predictions does not occur outside natural laws.

Let us take, as a comparison, an example from ordinary things, which will help to explain the principle that will then be developed below.

2. Let us imagine an individual placed on a high mountain, and consider the vast expanse of the plain. In this situation, the space of three miles will look short, and it will be easy to see at a glance all the accidents on the ground, from the beginning to the end of the road. The traveler who follows this road for the first time knows that by walking he/she will eventually arrive at the end: this is a mere forecast of the consequence of his/her march; but accidents on the ground, climbs and descents, rivers to cross, woods to pass through, precipices where one can fall, thieves ready to rob the traveler, hostels where he/she can take a rest; all this is independent of his/her person. For the traveler these are the unknown, the future, because his/her sight does not reach beyond the little circle that surrounds him or her. As for duration, the traveler measures it by the time he/she spends on the road; take away the landmarks and the duration will disappear. For the observer standing higher up on the mountain, who follows the traveler with his/her eyes, all this is present time. Suppose this observer comes down to warn the traveler, by saying: "At such and such moment you will meet such a thing, you will be attacked and rescued." The observer will thus have predicted the future; that is, the future for the traveler. For the observer from the top of the mountain, this future is the present.

3.   If we now come out of the circle of purely material things, and if we enter, through thought, into the realm of spiritual life, we will see this phenomenon occur on a larger scale. The dematerialized spirits are like that person observing on the top of the mountain: space and duration are effaced for them. But the extent and penetration of their sight are proportional to their purification and elevation in the spiritual hierarchy. They are, in relation to lower-order spirits, like an individual armed with a powerful telescope, in comparison to others who have only their eyes. In these latter, sight is circumscribed, not only because they can only hardly depart from the globe to which they are attached, but because the coarseness of their perispirit veils distant things from them, as a fog would do for their bodily eyes.

We can therefore understand that, according to its degree of perfection, a spirit can embrace a period of a few years, a few centuries and even several thousand years, for what is a century in presence of the infinite? Events do not unfold successively before such a spirit, like the incidents on the traveler's road: it sees the beginning and the end of the period simultaneously; all the events which, in this period, are the future for the traveler on Earth, are for the spirit the present. It could therefore come and tell us with certainty, "Such a thing will happen at such a time," because it can see the whole situation, just as the observer on the top of the mountain sees what awaits the traveler on the road; if he does not do it, it is because the knowledge of the future would be harmful to humans: such knowledge would hinder their free will, it would paralyze them in the work they must accomplish for their progress; the good and the evil that await us, being in the unknown, are for us a trial.

If such a faculty, restricted as it is, can be in the attributes of the created being, to what degree of power would it rise in the Creator, which embraces the infinite? For God, time does not exist: the beginning and the end of the worlds are the present. In this immense panorama, what is the duration of the life of an individual, a generation, a nation?

4. However, since humans must contribute to general progress, and certain events must result from this cooperation, it may be useful, in certain cases, for us to be forewarned of these events so that we can prepare the way for them, and be ready to act when the time is right – that is why God sometimes allows a corner of the veil to be lifted; albeit always for a useful purpose, and never to satisfy vain curiosity. This mission can therefore be given, not to all spirits, since there are some that know no better about the future than incarnate humans, but to some spirits sufficiently advanced to carry it on. It should be pointed out that these kinds of revelations are always made spontaneously, and never, or very rarely, in answer to a direct request.

5. This mission can also be entrusted to certain incarnate human beings, and here is how:

A person entrusted with the task of revealing a hidden thing may receive, without his/her knowledge, the inspiration of the spirits that know it, and then transmit it mechanically, without realizing it. It is furthermore known that, either during sleep or in the waking state, during ecstasies of second sight, the soul emerges and regains to a greater or lesser degree the faculties of a free spirit. If this person is an advanced spirit; and if, above all, like the prophets, he/she has received a special mission for this purpose; this person will enjoy, in the moments of emancipation of the soul, the faculty of embracing, by himself/herself, a more or less extended time period, and see, as if happening at the present, all the events of such period. He/she can then reveal them at the same moment, or keep their memory when he/she wakes up. If these events are to remain secret, this person will have lost all memory of them; otherwise a vague intuition will remain, sufficient to guide him/her instinctively.

Thus we see this faculty developing providentially in certain occasions, such as imminent dangers, great calamities, revolutions – and that most persecuted religious groups have had many *seers*. It is also thus that we see great commanders march resolutely against the enemy, with the certainty of victory; and individuals of genius, like Christopher Columbus for example, pursue a goal by predicting, as it were, the moment when they will reach it. It is because they all have seen this goal, which is not unknown to their spirit.

The gift of prediction is therefore no more supernatural than a plethora of other phenomena; it rests on the soul's prerogatives and the law of the relations between the visible and the invisible worlds that Spiritism has come to make known. But how can we admit the existence of an invisible world, if we do not admit the existence of the soul, or if we admit it without its individuality after death? The unbeliever who denies prescience is consistent with himself/herself; it remains to be seen whether they themselves are consistent with natural law.

6. This theory of prescience may not resolve in an absolute way all cases that the revelation of the future can present, but it cannot be denied that it posits its fundamental principle. If we cannot explain everything, it is because of the difficulty, for us humans, of placing ourselves in this point of view away from the earthly sphere. Spring out of this very inferiority, our thought incessantly bring us back to the path of material life, and is often powerless to detach itself from the ground. In this respect, some humans behave like young birds whose wings are still too weak to allow them to rise in the air; or like those whose sight is too short for them to see far; or finally like those who lack the sense for some perceptions.

7. To understand spiritual things, that is to say, to get as clear an idea as we can of a landscape that is before our eyes, we really lack a sense, exactly as a blind person lacks the necessary sense to understand the effects of light, colors and sight without contact. It is only by an effort of imagination that we reach it, and with the help of comparisons drawn from the things we are familiar with. Yet material things can only give a very imperfect idea of spiritual things; that is why we should not take these comparisons literally, and believe, for example, in the case at hand, that the extent of the perceptive powers of the spirits is due to their actual altitude, and that they need to be on a mountain or above the clouds in order to encompass time and space.

This faculty is inherent in the state of spiritualization, or, if you will, dematerialization. In other words, spiritualization produces an effect that can be compared, albeit very imperfectly, with that of the general view of the person who is on a mountain. This comparison was simply intended to show that events that are in the future for some, are in the present for others, and can thus be predicted, which does not imply that the actual effect occurs in the same way.

Therefore, to enjoy this perception. A spirit does not need to be transported to any point of space. The spirit that is on the ground, beside us, may possess such perception in its fullness, just as well as if it were a thousand miles away, while we see nothing outside our visual horizon. Since sight in spirits does not occur in the same manner or with the same elements as in incarnate humans, their visual horizon is quite different. This is precisely the sense that we lack in order to perceive it. *Next to the incarnate, a spirit is like a seeing person next to a blind person.*

8. Moreover, it must be understood that this perception is not limited to extents, but includes the penetration of all things. It is, I repeat, an inherent faculty proportional to the degree of one's dematerialization. This faculty is *attenuated* by incarnation, but it is not completely annulled, because the soul is not concealed in the body as in a box. The incarnate still possesses the faculty, though always to a lesser degree than when it is entirely free. That is what gives some individuals a power of penetration that is totally lacking in others, a greater accuracy in their moral views, an easier understanding of things beyond the material realm.

Not only does the spirit perceive, but it remembers what it has seen in the state of spirit; and this memory is like a picture that repeatedly comes to his/her thought. During a lifetime as an incarnate, one sees, but vaguely and as though through a veil; in the state of freedom, as spirit, one sees and discerns clearly. *The principle of sight is not outside but within the individual;* that is why one does not need external light. Through moral development, the circle of one's ideas and conceptions widens; by the gradual dematerialization of the perispirit, it purifies itself, getting rid of coarse elements that alter the delicacy of perceptions;. Hence it is easy to understand that the extent of all one's faculties follows the progress of the spirit.

9. It is the degree and extent of the faculties of the spirit which, during its lifetime as an incarnate, allows it to have a broader or narrower conception of spiritual things. However, this aptitude is not the necessary consequence of the development of intelligence; ordinary science does not grant it. This is why we see individuals of great knowledge as blind to spiritual things as others are to material things; they are refractory because they do not understand them. This happens because they have not yet accomplished progress in this particular sense, whereas we see persons of average education and intelligence grasp spiritual things with the greatest ease, which proves that they had the intuition of these beforehand. It is a retrospective memory of what they have seen and known, either in the erraticity[109] or in their previous lives, as others have the intuition of the languages and sciences they once knew.

10. The faculty of changing one's point of view and taking it from higher above does not only provide the solution to the problem of prescience; it is also the key to true faith, to solid faith; it is also the most powerful element of strength and resignation, because, from there, with earthly life appearing as a mere point in the immensity, we can understand the little value of the things which, seen from below, seem so very important. The incidents, the miseries, the vanities of life diminish as the immense splendid horizon of the future unfolds. Those who thus see the things of this world are scarcely concerned by vicissitudes, and for this very reason, they are as happy as they can be here below. We must therefore pity those who concentrate their thoughts on the narrow earthly sphere, because they feel, in all their might, the counterblow of all tribulations, which, like so many other goads, torment them incessantly.

11. As for the future of Spiritism, the spirits, as we know, are unanimous in asserting that triumph is forthcoming, in spite of the obstacles which are opposed to it. This prediction comes easy to them; first of all, because the propagation of Spiritism is their personal work. By contributing to the movement or directing it,

---

109 [Trans. note] As said before, *erraticity* (meaning errant or wandering state) is a Spiritist term for the period in which a spirit is free, between incarnations.

they know what they must do. Secondly, it is enough for them to embrace a short period of time, and in this period they see in their path the powerful auxiliaries that God has raised up for it, and those which will soon manifest themselves.

Without being discarnate spirits, let Spiritists move on mentally only thirty years ahead, to the middle age of the current generation, and from there, consider what is happening today. Let them follow the path of what is happening, and they will see the vain efforts of those who think they got a call to overthrow Spiritism. They will gradually see those adversaries disappear from the scene, by the side of this growing tree whose roots expand more and more every day.

12. The ordinary events of private life are, most often, the consequence of the manner of acting of each one of us. Some will succeed according to their abilities, their skills, their perseverance, their common sense and energy, while others will fail on account of their insufficiency. Therefore we can say that everyone is the architect of his/her own future, which is never subject to blind fatality independent of his/her person. Knowing the character of an individual, one can easily predict the fate that awaits him or her down the road they take.

13. Events affecting the general interests of humanity are regulated by Providence. When a thing is in God's plan, it must be accomplished anyway, either by one means or another. Human beings participate in its execution, but no one is indispensable, otherwise God Itself would be at the mercy of Its created beings. If the one who has the mission to execute it is missing, another is put in charge of it. There is no inescapable mission; the individual is free to fulfill or not the one entrusted to him/her, which they have voluntarily accepted. If he/she does not, he/she loses the benefit and takes responsibility for any delays that may occur due to such negligence or ill-will. If this person becomes an obstacle to its fulfillment, God can, in a manner of speaking, blow him/her down with a breath.

14. The end result of an event can therefore be certain because it is in God's designs; but since, most often, the details and the mode of execution are subordinate to the circumstances and to the free will of humans, the ways and means may vary. The spirits can presage us on the whole, if it is useful for us to be forewarned; yet in order to specify the place and the date, it would be necessary for them to know in advance the determination which this or that individual will take. Now, if this determination is not yet in its thought, according to what it will be, it can hasten or delay the denouement and modify the secondary means of action, while achieving the same result. It is thus, for example, that the spirits can, by all the circumstances, foresee that a war is more or less near, and that it is inevitable, without being able to predict the day when it will start, nor the incidents of detail that can be changed by the will of humans.

15. For establishing the time of future events, a circumstance must also be taken into account, which is inherent in the very nature of spirits.

Time as well as space can only be evaluated by means of points of comparison or benchmarks that divide it into periods that can be counted. On Earth, the natural division of time in days and years is marked by the rising and setting of the Sun, and by the duration of the translational motion of the Earth. The subdivision of days into twenty-four hours is arbitrary; it is indicated by means of special instruments, such as hourglasses, clepsydras, clocks, sundials, etc. The units of time measure must vary according to different worlds, since the astronomical periods are different. For example, in Jupiter the days are equivalent to ten of our hours, and the years to almost twelve terrestrial years.

Hence there is for each world a different way of calculating duration according to the nature of the astral revolutions which take place there. It would already be difficult for spirits that would not know our world to determine our local dates; but, outside the worlds, these means of measurement do not exist. For a spirit, in space, there is neither sunrise nor sunset marking the days, nor a periodic rotation marking the years: for it, there is only infinite duration and space (see ch. VI, items 1 et seq. above). Therefore a spirit which would never have come to Earth would have no knowledge of our time calculations, which, moreover, would be completely useless to it. There is more: a spirit that would never have been incarnated on any world would have no notion of fractions of the duration. When a spirit foreign to Earth comes to manifest itself, it can assign dates to events only by identifying with our uses, which is undoubtedly in the spirit's power, but which, more often, it does not consider it useful to do.

16. The mode of calculating duration is an arbitrary convention made among the incarnate for the needs of the life of relation in the physical world. To measure the duration like us, spirits could only do it with the aid of our precision instruments, which do not exist in the spiritual life.

But spirits that make up the invisible population of our globe, where they have lived and where they will continue to live among us, are naturally identified with our habits, of which they carry the memory when discarnate in the spiritual world. They have less difficulty than other spirits in getting to our point of view with regard to earthly uses: in ancient Greece they counted the passage of time by Olympiads; elsewhere, by lunar or solar periods, according to different epochs and places. They could, therefore, more easily assign a date to future events when they knew it. However, it is not always permissible for them to do it. They are prevented by the following reason: whenever the circumstances of detail are subordinated to free will and to possible human intervention, the precise date does not really exist until the actual event is accomplished.

Hence, circumstantial predictions cannot offer absolute certainty and should only be accepted as probabilities, even though they would not bear the stamp of any legitimate suspicion. Therefore truly wise spirits never predict anything as happening at fixed times. They limit themselves to anticipating the outcome of things which are useful for us to know. To insist on precise details is to expose oneself to the mystification of frivolous spirits, which predict all that one inquires about, without any concern for truth; and then amuse themselves with the fears and disappointments they cause.

The most likely predictions are those of a general and humanitarian nature; we must rely on others only when they are accomplished. Depending on the circumstances, they may be accepted as a warning, but it would be imprudent to act prematurely with a view to their implementation on a fixed date. It may be considered certain that the more detailed they are, the more suspicious they become.

17. The form generally used so far for predictions turns them into real puzzles, often indecipherable. This mysterious and Kabbalistic form, of which Nostradamus offers the most complete example, gives them a certain prestige in the eyes of the general public, who gives them all the more value as they are more incomprehensible. By their ambiguity, they lend themselves to quite different interpretations, so that, according to the meaning attributed to certain allegorical or convention words, the way of calculating the oddly complicated setting of dates; and with a little imagination, one encounters in them almost everything one may fancy.

Be that as it may, it cannot be denied that some predictions have a serious character, and confound by their truthfulness. It is probable that this veiled form had, for a time, its reason for being and even its necessity in the past.

Today, circumstances have greatly changed; the positivism of the 19th century would hardly accommodate Sibylline language. So the predictions of our days no longer bear these strange forms; those made by spirits are not mystical and spirits speak the language of everyday people, as they would have done in their lifetime, because they have not ceased to belong to humanity. They have presentiments of future things, whether personal or general, when these may be useful, and to the extent of insight with which each of them are endowed. They behave as advisers or friends would do. Their forecasts are therefore rather warnings which do not detract from anyone's free will, rather than predictions, properly speaking, which would imply an absolute and inescapable result. Moreover, their opinion is almost always well justified, because they do not want incarnate humans to annihilate their own reasoning and accept it in blind faith, therefore making it possible to evaluate its accuracy.

18.   Contemporary humanity also has its prophets; more than one writer, poet, scholar, historian or philosopher has foreseen in their writings the future course of things that we see happening today.

This aptitude is often due, without a doubt, to the rectitude of judgment which deduces the logical consequences of the present; yet often it is also the result of a special, unconscious clairvoyance, or to an extraneous inspiration. What these individuals did in their lifetime, they can do with even more forceful reason and more accurately in the state of spirit, when their spiritual view is no longer obscured by matter.

Chapter XVII
Predictions in the Gospel

NO ONE IS A PROPHET IN HIS/HER OWN COUNTRY

1. "And coming to his hometown he taught them in their synagogue, so that they were astonished, and said, 'Where did this man get this wisdom and these mighty works? Is not this the carpenter's son? Is not his mother called Mary? And are not his brothers James and Joseph and Simon and Judas? And are not all his sisters with us? Where then did this man get all these things?' And they took offense at him. But Jesus said to them, 'A prophet is not without honor except in his hometown and in his own household.' And he did not do many mighty works there, because of their unbelief (MATTHEW 13:54–58 ESV)."

2. Here Jesus was proclaiming a proverbial truth, which is of all time, and which could be extended by adding that *no one is a prophet while still alive.*

In today's language, this saying refers to the credit which a person enjoys among his/her own relatives and those amidst whom he/she lives; of the trust inspired in them by his/her superiority of knowledge and intelligence. If there are exceptions to the rule, these are rare, and in every case they are never absolute. The principle of this truth derives from a natural consequence of human weakness, and can be explained in this way;

The habit of seeing oneself from childhood, in the ordinary circumstances of life, establishes among human beings a sort of material equality which makes us often refuse to recognize moral superiority in a person who has been our acquaintance or companion, emerging from our same environment and whose first weaknesses have been seen. Pride is hurt by the position of ascendancy such a person occupies, to which one eventually has to submit. Whoever rises above the average level is always exposed to jealousy and envy. Those who feel unable to reach this person's height will strive to belittle him/her by denigration, gossip, and slander. They shout louder the smaller they see themselves, thinking they will thus grow and eclipse the other by the noise they make. Such has been and will be the history of humanity until humans have understood their spiritual nature and expanded their moral horizon. This prejudgment is therefore characteristic of narrow and vulgar spirits, who relate everything to their own personality.

On the other hand, humans generally make of an individual known only through their minds and imagination, an ideal image that grows with the distance of time and place. Such personages end up stripped of almost all human traits; it seems that they must neither speak nor feel like everyone else, that their language and their thoughts must be constantly in tune with sublimity, without considering that the mind cannot be incessantly concentrated, and in a perpetual state of exaltation.. In the daily contact of everyday life, we see too much of the material human being, which in nothing differs from the ordinary. The bodily human, who strikes the senses, almost obliterates the spiritual one, who strikes only the spirit: *From a distance, we only see flashes of genius; closely, one can see the mind at rest.*

After death, the comparison no longer exists, only the spiritual being remains, which seems all the greater because the memory of the corporeal human is farther away. This is why individuals who have marked their journey on Earth with works of real value are more appreciated after their death than during their lifetime. They are judged with more impartiality because, once the envious and jealous adversaries disappear, personal antagonisms no longer exist. Posterity is a disinterested judge which appreciates the work of the spirit, accepting it without blind enthusiasm if it is good, rejecting it without hatred if it is bad, regardless of the individuality that produced it.

Jesus could no less escape the consequences of this principle, inherent in human nature, since he lived in a environment that was little enlightened, and among people who were entirely steeped in material life. His compatriots saw in him only the carpenter's son, the brother of people as ignorant as they were; and they wondered what could make him superior to them and give him the right to reproach them. Also, seeing that his word had less credit among his own people, who despised him, than among foreigners, he went to preach among those who listened to him and in the midst of those in whom he found sympathetic support.

One can judge this situation from the feelings his relatives had toward him. Once his own brothers, accompanied by his mother, came to a gathering where he was, with the intent of *seizing* him, saying that *he had lost his mind.* (MARK, 3:20–21, and 31–35 ESV. And A. KARDEC, *The Gospel according to Spiritism*, ch. XIV.)

On the one hand, the priests and Pharisees accused Jesus of acting by influence of the devil; on the other, he was labeled mad by his closest relatives. Is this not the way which is used today with regard to Spiritists, and should they complain of being treated no better by their fellow citizens than Jesus was? What was not surprising, two thousand years ago, amidst an ignorant people, is stranger now in the 19th century AD, within civilized nations.

DEATH AND PASSION OF JESUS

3. (After curing a lunatic.) "While they were all marveling at everything he was doing, Jesus said to his disciples, 'Let these words sink into your ears: The Son of Man is about to be delivered into the hands of men.' But they did not understand this saying, and it was concealed from them, so that they might not perceive it. And they were afraid to ask him about this saying (LUKE 9:44–45 ESV)."

4. "From that time Jesus began to show his disciples that he must go to Jerusalem and suffer many things from the elders and chief priests and scribes, and be killed, and on the third day be raised (MATTHEW 16:21 ESV)."

5. "As they were gathering in Galilee, Jesus said to them, 'The Son of Man is about to be delivered into the hands of men, and they will kill him, and he will be raised on the third day.' And they were greatly distressed (MATTHEW 17:21–23 ESV)."

6. "And as Jesus was going up to Jerusalem, he took the twelve disciples aside, and on the way he said to them, 'See, we are going up to Jerusalem. And the Son of Man will be delivered over to the chief priests and scribes, and they will condemn him to death and deliver him over to the Gentiles to be mocked and flogged and crucified, and he will be raised on the third day' (MATTHEW 20:17–19 ESV)."

7. "And taking the twelve, he said to them, 'See, we are going up to Jerusalem, and everything that is written about the Son of Man by the prophets will be accomplished. For he will be delivered over to the Gentiles and will be mocked and shamefully treated and spit upon. And after flogging him, they will kill him, and on the third day he will rise.'

But they understood none of these things. This saying was hidden from them, and they did not grasp what was said (LUKE 18:31–34 ESV)."

8. "When Jesus had finished all these sayings, he said to his disciples, 'You know that after two days the Passover is coming, and the Son of Man will be delivered up to be crucified.'

Then the chief priests and the elders of the people gathered in the palace of the high priest, whose name was Caiaphas, and plotted together in order to arrest Jesus by stealth and kill him. But they said, 'Not during the feast, lest there be an uproar among the people' (MATTHEW 26:1–5 ESV)."

9. "At that very hour some Pharisees came and said to him, 'Get away from here, for Herod wants to kill you.' And he said to them, 'Go and tell that fox, Behold, I cast out demons and perform cures today and tomorrow, and the third day I finish my course' (LUKE 13:31–32 ESV)."

PERSECUTION OF THE APOSTLES

10. "'Behold, I am sending you out as sheep in the midst of wolves, so be wise as serpents and innocent as doves. Beware of men, for they will deliver you over to courts and flog you in their synagogues, and you will be dragged before governors and kings for my sake, to bear witness before them and the Gentiles' (MATTHEW 10:16–18 ESV)."

11. "'They will put you out of the synagogues. Indeed, the hour is coming when whoever kills you will think he is offering service to God. And they will do these things because they have not known the Father, nor me. But I have said these things to you, that when their hour comes you may remember that I told them to you' (JOHN 16:2–4 ESV)."

12. "'You will be delivered up even by parents and brothers3 and relatives and friends, and some of you they will put to death. You will be hated by all for my name's sake. But not a hair of your head will perish. By your endurance you will gain your lives' (LUKE 21:16–19 ESV)."

13. (*Martyrdom of Peter.*) "'Truly, truly, I say to you, when you were young, you used to dress yourself and walk wherever you wanted, but when you are old, you will stretch out your hands, and another will dress you and carry you where you do not want to go.' (This he said to show by what kind of death he was to glorify God.) ... (JOHN 21:18–19 ESV)."

IMPENITENT CITIES

14. "Then he began to denounce the cities where most of his mighty works had been done, because they did not repent.

'Woe to you, Chorazin! Woe to you, Bethsaida! For if the mighty works done in you had been done in Tyre and Sidon, they would have repented long ago in sackcloth and ashes. But I tell you, it will be more bearable on the day of judgment for Tyre and Sidon than for you.

And you, Capernaum, will you be exalted to heaven? You will be brought down to Hades. For if the mighty works done in you had been done in Sodom, it would have remained until this day. But I tell you that it will be more tolerable on the day of judgment for the land of Sodom than for you' (MATTHEW 11:20–24 ESV)."

THE RUIN OF THE TEMPLE AND
THE FALL OF JERUSALEM

15. "Jesus left the temple and was going away, when his disciples came to point out to him the buildings of the temple. But he answered them, 'You see all these, do you not? Truly, I say to you, there will not be left here one stone upon another that will not be thrown down' (MATTHEW 24:1–2 ESV)."

16. "And when he drew near and saw the city, he wept over it, saying, 'Would that you, even you, had known on this day the things that make for peace! But now they are hidden from your eyes. For the days will come upon you, when your enemies will set up a barricade around you and surround you and hem you in on every side and tear you down to the ground, you and your children within you. And they will not leave one stone upon another in you, because you did not know the time of your visitation' (LUKE 19:41–44 ESV)."

17. "'Nevertheless, I must go on my way today and tomorrow and the day following, for it cannot be that a prophet should perish away from Jerusalem.

O Jerusalem, Jerusalem, the city that kills the prophets and stones those who are sent to it! How often would I have gathered your children together as a hen gathers her brood under her wings, and you would not! Behold, your house is forsaken. And I tell you, you will not see me until you say, Blessed is he who comes in the name of the Lord!' (LUKE 13:33–35 ESV)."

18. "'But when you see Jerusalem surrounded by armies, then know that its desolation has come near. Then let those who are in Judea flee to the mountains, and let those who are inside the city depart, and let not those who are out in the country enter it, for these are days of vengeance, to fulfill all that is written. Alas for women who are pregnant and for those who are nursing infants in those days! For there will be great distress upon the earth and wrath against this people. They will fall by the edge of the sword and be led captive among all nations, and Jerusalem will be trampled underfoot by the Gentiles, until the times of the Gentiles are fulfilled' (LUKE 21:20–24 ESV)."

19. (*Jesus walking to the crucifixion.*) "And there followed him a great multitude of the people and of women who were mourning and lamenting for him. But turning to them Jesus said, 'Daughters of Jerusalem, do not weep for me, but weep for yourselves and for your children. For behold, the days are coming when they will say, Blessed are the barren and the wombs that never bore and the breasts that never nursed! Then they will begin to say to the mountains, Fall on us, and to the hills, Cover us. For if they do these things when the wood is green, what will happen when it is dry?' (Luke 23:27–31 esv)."

20. The faculty of sensing future things is one of the attributes of the soul, and is explained by the theory of prescience. Jesus possessed it, like all the other faculties, to an outstanding degree. He was therefore able to foresee the events that would follow his death, without involving anything supernatural, since this fact is displayed before our eyes in the most ordinary conditions. It is not uncommon for individuals to announce precisely the moment of their death: it is because their soul, in out-of-body state, is like the individual on the top of the mountain given earlier as an example (see ch. **XVI**, item **1** above): the observer's view encompasses the full road ahead and see its end.

This would be even more so in Jesus, who, being aware of the mission he was about to fulfill, knew that death by torture was a necessary consequence. The spiritual sight, which was permanent in him, as well as the penetrating insight of his thought, would show him the circumstances and its fatal development. For the same reason, he could foresee the ruin of the Temple, the fall of Jerusalem, the misfortunes that were going to strike its inhabitants, and the dispersion of the Jews.

21. Unbelief, which does not admit the existence of spiritual life independent of matter, cannot be aware of prescience. That is why it denies it, attributing to chance any authentic facts that are accomplished under its eyes. It is remarkable that it recoils before the examination of all psychical phenomena which occur everywhere, undoubtedly for fear of seeing the soul arise and negate unbelief itself.

CURSE ON THE PHARISEES

22. (John the Baptist.) "But when he saw many of the Pharisees and Sadducees coming to his baptism, he said to them, 'You brood of vipers! Who warned you to flee from the wrath to come? Bear fruit in keeping with repentance. And do not presume to say to yourselves, We have Abraham as our father, for I tell you, God is able from these stones to raise up children for Abraham. Even now the axe is laid to the root of the trees. Every tree therefore that does not bear good fruit is cut down and thrown into the fire' (MATTHEW 3:7–10 ESV)."

23.   "'But woe to you, scribes and Pharisees, hypocrites! For you shut the kingdom of heaven in people's faces. For you neither enter yourselves nor allow those who would enter to go in.

'Woe to you, scribes and Pharisees, hypocrites! For you travel across sea and land to make a single proselyte, and when he becomes a proselyte, you make him twice as much a child of hell as yourselves.

'Woe to you, blind guides, who say, If anyone swears by the temple, it is nothing, but if anyone swears by the gold of the temple, he is bound by his oath.' You blind fools! For which is greater, the gold or the temple that has made the gold sacred? And you say, If anyone swears by the altar, it is nothing, but if anyone swears by the gift that is on the altar, he is bound by his oath. You blind men! For which is greater, the gift or the altar that makes the gift sacred? So whoever swears by the altar swears by it and by everything on it. And whoever swears by the temple swears by it and by him who dwells in it. And whoever swears by heaven swears by the throne of God and by him who sits upon it.

'Woe to you, scribes and Pharisees, hypocrites! For you tithe mint and dill and cumin, and have neglected the weightier matters of the law: justice and mercy and faithfulness. These you ought to have done, without neglecting the others. You blind guides, straining out a gnat and swallowing a camel!

'Woe to you, scribes and Pharisees, hypocrites! For you clean the outside of the cup and the plate, but inside they are full of greed and self-indulgence. You blind Pharisee! First clean the inside of the cup and the plate, that the outside also may be clean.

'Woe to you, scribes and Pharisees, hypocrites! For you are like whitewashed tombs, which outwardly appear beautiful, but within are full of dead people's bones and all uncleanness. So you also outwardly appear righteous to others, but within you are full of hypocrisy and lawlessness.

'Woe to you, scribes and Pharisees, hypocrites! For you build the tombs of the prophets and decorate the monuments of the righteous, saying, 'If we had lived in the days of our fathers, we would not have taken part with them in shedding the blood of the prophets.' Thus you witness against yourselves that you are sons of those who murdered the prophets. Fill up, then, the measure of your fathers. You serpents, you brood of vipers, how are you to escape being sentenced to hell? Therefore I send you prophets and wise men and scribes, some of whom you will kill and crucify, and some you will flog in your synagogues and persecute from town to town, so that on you may come all the righteous blood shed on earth, from the blood of innocent Abel to the blood of Zechariah the son of Barachiah, whom you murdered between the sanctuary and the altar. Truly, I say to you, all these things will come upon this generation. Lament over Jerusalem' (MATTHEW 23:13–36 ESV)."

MY WORDS WILL NOT PASS AWAY

24. "Then the disciples came and said to him, 'Do you know that the Pharisees were offended when they heard this saying?' He answered, '*Every plant that my heavenly Father has not planted will be rooted up.* Let them alone; they are blind guides. And if the blind lead the blind, both will fall into a pit' (MATTHEW 15:12–14 ESV)."

25. "'Heaven and earth will pass away, but my words will not pass away' (Matthew 24:35 esv)."

26. Jesus' words will not pass away, because they will continue to be true in all eras. This moral code will be eternal because it contains the requirements for good which leads humans to their eternal destiny. But have his words reached us in a state of purity from any alloy and false interpretations? Have all Christian religions grasped them? Has none of them distorted their true meaning due to prejudices and ignorance of the laws of Nature? Has any of them made these words an instrument of domination to serve one's ambition and material interests – a step, not to rise to heaven, but to rise on earth? Has any of them proposed to practice the virtues of which Jesus made the express condition of salvation? Are all of them free from the reproaches he addressed to the Pharisees of his day? And finally, are all of them, in theory as well in practice, the pure expression of his tenets?

Truth, being one, cannot be found in contradictory affirmations, and Jesus could not wish to give a double meaning to his words. If, then, different Christian religions contradict one another; if some regard as true what others condemn as heresies, it is impossible that they are all in the truth. If all had taken the true meaning of the Gospel teachings, they would have met on the same ground, and there would have been no sects.

What will *never pass away* is the true meaning of Jesus' words; whereas what *will pass away* is what humans have built on the false meaning they have given to these very words.

Entrusted with the mission of bringing the thought of God to humankind, Jesus with his pure tenets alone can be the expression of this thought. That is why he said: *Every plant that my heavenly Father has not planted will be rooted up.*

THE CORNERSTONE

27. "Jesus said to them, 'Have you never read in the Scriptures: 'The stone that the builders rejected has become the cornerstone; this was the Lord's doing, and it is marvelous in our eyes'?

'Therefore I tell you, the kingdom of God will be taken away from you and given to a people producing its fruits. And the one who falls on this stone will be broken to pieces; and when it falls on anyone, it will crush him.'

When the chief priests and the Pharisees heard his parables, they perceived that he was speaking about them. And although they were seeking to arrest him, they feared the crowds, because they held him to be a prophet (MATTHEW ch. 21:42–46 ESV)."

28. The word of Jesus became the cornerstone, that is to say, the principal stone which forms the foundation of the new edifice of faith, raised on the ruins of the old one. The Jews, the chief priests, and the Pharisees having rejected this word, it has crushed them, as it will crush anyone who has since misunderstood it, or those who have misrepresented its meaning for the benefit of their ambition.

PARABLE OF THE TENANTS

29. "There was a master of a house who planted a vineyard and put a fence around it and dug a winepress in it and built a tower and leased it to tenants, and went into another country.

When the season for fruit drew near, he sent his servants to the tenants to get his fruit. And the tenants took his servants and beat one, killed another, and stoned another. Again he sent other servants, more than the first. And they did the same to them. Finally he sent his son to them, saying, 'They will respect my son.' But when the tenants saw the son, they said to themselves, 'This is the heir. Come, let us kill him and have his inheritance.' And they took him and threw him out of the vineyard and killed him.

When therefore the owner of the vineyard comes, what will he do to those tenants?' They said to him, 'He will put those wretches to a miserable death and let out the vineyard to other tenants who will give him the fruits in their seasons' (MATTHEW ch. 21:33–41 ESV)."

30. The master of the house is God; the vine he has planted is the law It has established; the vine growers to whom It has rented Its vineyard are humans who must teach and practice Its law; the servants whom It sends to them are the prophets who perished in their hands; Its son whom It sends at last is Jesus, whom they likewise killed. How, then, will the Lord deal with the predatory agents of Its law? It will treat them as they have treated Its messengers, and will call others who will give It a better account of Its property and fittingly take care of Its flock.

Thus were those scribes, chief priests, and Pharisees; thus will it be when the master comes again and asks each one of them what have they made of God's teachings. Authority will be taken away from anyone who has abused it, because God wants Its field to be administered according to Its will.

After eighteen centuries humankind, having come into adulthood, is now ripe to understand what Christ has only touched upon, because, as Jesus himself says, he would not have been understood. Now, to what result have those who, during this long period, were entrusted with his religious enlightening? To see indifference succeed to faith, and unbelief to turn into a doctrine. In fact, at no other time have skepticism and an attitude of negation become so prevalent as today, in all segments of society.

Yet if some of the words of Christ are veiled under allegory, for all that concerns rules of conduct, the relations of person to person, the principles of morality of which he has made the express condition of salvation (see A. KARDEC, *The Gospel according to Spiritism*, ch. XV), his words are clear, explicit and unambiguous.

What has been done of his maxims of charity, love, and tolerance; the recommendations he made to his apostles to convert people through gentleness and persuasion; of simplicity, humility, selfless-ness, and all the virtues of which he has given the example? In his name, humans threw anathema and curses upon one another; and slaughtered one another in the name of him who said: All humans are brothers and sisters. We have made a jealous, cruel, vindictive and partial entity out of God which Jesus proclaimed to be infinitely just, good, and merciful. More than a thousand victims were sacrificed to this God of peace and truth on flaming pyres, by tortures and persecutions, that even the Gentiles themselves had never sacrificed for their false gods. Prayers and favors of heaven were sold in the name of him who drove out the sellers out of the Temple, and said to his disciples: Give freely what you have received freely.

What would Christ say if he lived today among us? If he saw his representatives aspire to honors, riches, power, and the splendor of the princes of the world, while he, who was more than all kings of the Earth, entered Jerusalem on a donkey? Would he not be right in saying to them: What have you done of my teachings, you who adore the golden calf; who reserve in your prayers a large share for the rich and a small share for the poor, whereas I have said: The first will be the last and the last will be the first in the kingdom of heaven? But if he is not here in flesh and blood, he is here in spirit, and, like the master of the parable, he will come to ask his tenants for the yield of his vineyard, when harvest time has come.

ONE FLOCK, ONE SHEPHERD

31. "'And I have other sheep that are not of this fold. I must bring them also, and they will listen to my voice. So there will be one flock, one shepherd' (JOHN 10:16 ESV)."

32.   With these words, Jesus clearly announces that one day, human beings will rally behind a single belief; but how could this unification be done? This seems difficult, considering the differences among religions, the antagonism they maintain between their respective followers, their obstinacy in believing themselves to be in exclusive possession of the truth. All want unity, but at the same time all flatter themselves by saying that it will be to their advantage, since none is willing to make concessions regarding their beliefs.

However, unification will be attained in religion as it tends to be socially, politically, commercially, that is, by lowering the barriers that separate the nations, by the assimilation of traditions, uses, language. Nations of the whole world already fraternize, like those of the provinces of the same empire. We urge for unity, we desire it. It will happen by force of circumstances, because it will become a necessity to strengthen the bonds of fraternity among nations. This will be achieved by the development of human reason which will make us understand the puerility of dissidences; also by the progress of science, which daily demonstrates the material errors on which these conflicts are based, gradually detaching worm-eaten stones from their foundations. If science demolishes in religions that which is the work of humans and the fruit of their ignorance of the laws of Nature, it cannot destroy, despite the opinion of some, that which is the work of God and eternal truth. By clearing the accessories, it prepares the way for the unification.

To reach unity, religions must meet on a neutral ground common to all. For that to happen, each of them will have to make concessions and greater or smaller sacrifices, according to the profusion of their particular dogmas. Yet, by virtue of the principle of immutability which they all profess, the initiative of making concessions cannot come from the official camp. Instead of taking their point of departure from above, they will take it from below by individual initiative. For some time there has been a movement of decentralization which tends to acquire an irresistible force. The principle of immutability, which religions have hitherto regarded as a conservative aegis, will become a destructive element as their cults come to a standstill. While society moves forward, they will first be overwhelmed, then absorbed in the course of time by progressive ideas.

Among the persons who detach themselves wholly or in part from the main official religions, and whose number is constantly increasing, some want nothing to replace them. Yet the vast majority, who in no way accede to nothing, will still want something. This something is not yet defined in their minds, but they can foresee it; they tend to the same end by different ways, and it is through them that the movement of concentration toward unity begins.

In the current state of opinion and knowledge, the religion which will one day rally all humans under the same flag, will be the one which will best satisfy one's intellect and the legitimate aspirations of one's heart and spirit; which will on no account be contradicted by hard science; and which, instead of coming to a halt, will follow humanity in its gradual march, without ever allowing itself to be overtaken. A religion which will not be exclusive or intolerant; which will be emancipatory for the intellect by admitting only reasoned faith; one whose moral code will be the purest, the most rational, the most harmonious with social needs; and the most suitable to establish on earth, at last, the reign of good, by the practice of universal charity and fraternity.

Among existing religions, those which come closest to these normal conditions will have the least concessions to make. If one of them filled such requirements completely, it would naturally become the pivot of future unity; this unity will be around the one that will leave the less to be desired for one's reasoning, not by any official decree – because one does not regulate the conscience – but by individual and voluntary allegiance.

What maintains the antagonism among religions is the idea that each of them have their particular god, and their claim of having the only true and the most powerful one, which is in constant hostility with the gods of other beliefs, while busy fighting their influence. When they become convinced that there is only one God in the universe – and in the end it is the same that they worship under the names of Jehovah, Allah or Deus – they will eventually agree on its essential attributes, they will understand that a single Being can have only one will; they will stretch out their hands as servants of the same Master and children of one and same Parent; and thus they will have taken a great step toward unification.

THE ADVENT OF ELIJAH

33.   "And the disciples asked him, 'Then why do the scribes say that first Elijah must come?' He answered, 'Elijah does come, and he will restore all things.

But I tell you that Elijah has already come, and they did not recognize him, but did to him whatever they pleased. So also the Son of Man will certainly suffer at their hands.'

Then the disciples understood that he was speaking to them of John the Baptist (MATTHEW 17:10–13 ESV)."

34.   He had already returned in the person of John the Baptist (see A. KARDEC, *The Gospel according to Spiritism*, ch. IV, item 10). His new advent is announced in an explicit manner. Now, since he can only have returned with a new body, this is the formal confirmation of the principle of the plurality of existences (*The Gospel according to Spiritism*, ch. IV).

ANNOUNCING THE COMFORTER[110]

35.   "'If you love me, you will keep my commandments. And I will ask the Father, and he will give you another Helper, to be with you forever, even the Spirit of truth, whom the world cannot receive, because it neither sees him nor knows him. You know him, for he dwells with you and will be in you.' ... But the Helper, the Holy Spirit, whom the Father will send in my name, *he will teach you all things and bring to your remembrance all that I have said to you'* (JOHN 14:15–17 and 26 ESV. See also A. KARDEC, *The Gospel according to Spiritism*, ch. VI)."

36.   "'Nevertheless, I tell you the truth: it is to your advantage that I go away, for if I do not go away, the Helper will not come to you. But if I go, I will send him to you. And when he comes, he will convict the world concerning sin and righteousness and judgment: concerning sin, because they do not believe in me; concerning righteousness, because I go to the Father, and you will see me no longer; concerning judgment, because the ruler of this world is judged.

---

110 [Trans. note] The Comforter or the Helper in the *English Standard Version* (ESV) of the Bible used above.

'I still have many things to say to you, but you cannot bear them now.'

'When the Spirit of truth comes, he will guide you into all the truth, for he will not speak on his own authority, but whatever he hears he will speak, and he will declare to you the things that are to come. He will glorify me, for he will take what is mine and declare it to you' (JOHN 16:7–14 ESV)."

37. This prediction is unquestionably one of the most important from a religious point of view, because it shows in unequivocal terms that Jesus did not say everything he had to say, because it would not have been understood even by his apostles, since he is addressing himself to them. If he had given them secret instructions, they would have mentioned them in the Gospel. Since he did not tell his apostles everything, their successors could not know more than they did and could therefore misunderstand the meaning of his words, giving a false interpretation to his thoughts, often veiled in parabolic form. Therefore religions based on the Gospel cannot be in possession of the whole truth, since Jesus has left to complete his instructions at a later date. Hence the so-called principle of immutability is in direct contradiction to the very words of Jesus.

He announces, under the names of *Comforter* (or Helper) and the *Spirit of Truth*, the one who *will teach us all things and bring to our remembrance all that Jesus has said to us.* Therefore his teaching was not complete. Moreover, he foresees that people will have forgotten what he said, and that it will have been distorted, since the Spirit of Truth must make everyone *remind*, recollect it; and together with Elijah, *re-establish all things*; that is, according to the true thought of Jesus.

38. When will this new revelator come? It is obvious that if, at the time of Jesus' prediction, humans could not understand the things that remained to be said, it was not going to be in a matter of few years that they would acquire the necessary light. For fully understanding certain parts of the Gospel, with the exception of the precepts of morality, it was necessary to have the knowledge that the progress of science alone could give, and which would take the work of time and of many generations. If therefore a new Messiah had come shortly after Christ, he/she would have found the human milieu just as unfit, and would not have done more than Jesus had done. Now, from Christ to this day, there has been no great revelation that has completed the Gospel, and that has elucidated its obscure parts, which certainly indicates that the messenger had not yet come.

39. Who should this envoy be? By saying, "I will ask the Father, and he will give you another Helper [Comforter]," Jesus makes it clear that this envoy is not himself; otherwise he would have said; "I will come back to complete what I taught you." Then he adds: "To be with you forever, ... *for he dwells with you and will be in you.*" This cannot be understood as an incarnated individuality which would not be able to remain eternally with us, let alone be in us; but can be perfectly understood from the viewpoint of a doctrine which, in fact, once we have assimilated it, may be eternally in us. The *Comforter* lies, therefore, in the thought of Jesus, the personification of a supremely comforting tenet, whose inspiration must be the *Spirit of Truth*.

40. As has been shown, *Spiritism* fulfills (see ch. **I**, item **30** above) all the conditions of the *Comforter* promised by Jesus. It is not conceived by one sole individual, a human conception – no one can claim to be its creator. It is the product of the collective teaching of the spirits presided by the Spirit of Truth. It removes nothing from the Gospel, but rather completes and elucidates it. By means of the new laws which it reveals, together with those of science, it makes understandable what was hitherto unintelligible, and to admit the possibility of what unbelief regarded as inadmissible. It had precursors and prophets, who foresaw its coming. By its moralizing force, it has prepared the reign of good on earth.

The doctrine of Moses, incomplete, remained circumscribed to the Jewish people; whereas the one preached by Jesus, more complete, spread over the Earth through Christianity, but it did not convert the entire world. Spiritism, even more complete, having its roots in all beliefs, will eventually convert humanity.[111]

---

111 All philosophical and religious doctrines bear the name of their founding individual. They are called Mosaism, Christianity, Muhammadanism (i.e., Islam), Buddhism, Cartesianism, Fourierism, Saint-Simonianism, etc. The word Spiritism, on the contrary, does not denote any individual founder; it contains a general idea, which indicates both the character and the multiple source of its tenets.

41.   By saying to his Apostles: "I still have many things to say to you, but you cannot bear them now, when another comes, "He will guide you into all the truth," Christ proclaimed the necessity of reincarnation. How could these individuals benefit from the more complete teaching that would be given later; how could they become better able to understand him, if they were not to be born again? Jesus would have said something inconsistent if future humans were to be, according to common belief, new individuals, souls created from nothingness at birth. Conversely, if one admits that the apostles, and the people of their time, have reincarnated since, and that they live again today, Jesus' promise is justified. Their intelligence, which must have developed in contact with social progress, can now comprehend what it could not bear then. Without reincarnation, the promise made by Jesus would have been an illusion.

42.   It is said that this promise was fulfilled on the day of Pentecost by the Holy Spirit descending from heaven and inspiring them; and that this entity was able to open their intelligence and develop in them the mediumistic faculties that would facilitate their mission. However, as nothing new, other than that which Jesus had taught them, has been given to them, one can find no trace of a special teaching. Therefore the Holy Spirit did not accomplish what Jesus had said of the Comforter, otherwise the apostles would have elucidated, still in their lifetime, all that has remained obscure in the Gospel to this day, and whose contradictory interpretations gave rise to countless sects that divided Christianity since the first century.

SECOND ADVENT OF CHRIST

43.   "Then Jesus told his disciples, 'If anyone would come after me, let him deny himself and take up his cross and follow me. For whoever would save his life will lose it, but whoever loses his life for my sake will find it.

For what will it profit a man if he gains the whole world and forfeits his soul? Or what shall a man give in return for his soul? For the Son of Man is going to come with his angels in the glory of his Father, and then he will repay each person according to what he has done.

Truly, I say to you, there are some standing here who will not taste death until they see the Son of Man coming in his kingdom' (MATTHEW 16;24–28 ESV)."

44. "And the high priest stood up in the midst and asked Jesus, 'Have you no answer to make? What is it that these men testify against you?' But he remained silent and made no answer. Again the high priest asked him, 'Are you the Christ, the Son of the Blessed?' And Jesus said, 'I am, and you will see the Son of Man seated at the right hand of Power, and coming with the clouds of heaven.'

And the high priest tore his garments and said, 'What further witnesses do we need?' (MARK 14;60–63 ESV)."

45. Jesus announces his second advent, but he does not say that he will return to Earth in a corporeal body, nor that the *Comforter* will be personified in him. He presents himself as having to come in spirit, in the glory of his Parent, to judge merit and demerit, and to render to each according to his/her works when times are fulfilled.

These words, "There are some standing here who will not taste death until they see the Son of Man coming in his kingdom," seem to be a contradiction, since he was certain that he would not come alive during the lifetime of any of those who were present. Jesus could not, however, be mistaken in a prediction of this importance, and especially one regarding a contemporary event which concerned him personally. One must first ask whether his words have always been faithfully reproduced. Bearing in mind that he himself wrote nothing and that his words were collected only after his death, one may doubt their accuracy – and when one sees one same speech be almost always rendered in different terms by each evangelist, it is an evident proof that they are not the textual expressions of Jesus. Moreover, it is probable that the meaning must sometimes have been altered after undergoing successive translations.

On the other hand, it is certain that, if Jesus had said all he could have said, he would have spoken of all such things in a clear and precise manner which would not have given rise to any ambiguity, as was the fact when he spoke of moral principles, whereas he had to conceal his thought on subjects that he did not deem opportune to deepen. The apostles, persuaded that their own generation was to witness what he proclaimed, had to interpret the thought of Jesus according to they idea; they had, therefore writing it in the sense of their current time in a more absolute sense than he may actually have expressed. Anyway, the facts are there to prove that things did not happen the way they believed.

46. There is a crucial point that Jesus could not develop, because people of his time were not sufficiently prepared for this order of ideas and its consequences – but of which he nevertheless laid down the basic principle, as he had done for all things – which is the great and important law of reincarnation. This law, studied and brought to light today by Spiritism, is the key to many passages of the Gospel which otherwise appear to make no sense.

It is in this law that one can find the rational explanation of the words above, if we admit them to be textual. Since they cannot apply to the persons of the apostles, it is evident that they refer to the future reign of Christ, that is, to the time when his tenets, better understood, will be the universal law. By telling them that *some of those present would see his advent*, could only be understood in the sense that they would live again at a future time. But the Jews figured that they were going to see all that Jesus was announcing within their lifetime, and took his allegories literally.

Besides, some of his predictions have been fulfilled in their lifetime, such as the fall of Jerusalem, the misfortunes that followed, and the dispersion of the Jews. Yet he takes his view further, and while talking of the present, he is constantly referring to the future.

PRECURSORY SIGNS

47. "'And you will hear of wars and rumors of wars. See that you are not alarmed, for this must take place, but the end is not yet. For nation will rise against nation, and kingdom against kingdom, and there will be famines and earthquakes in various places. All these are but the beginning of the birth pains' (MATTHEW 24:6–8 ESV)."

48. "'And brother will deliver brother over to death, and the father his child, and children will rise against parents and have them put to death. And you will be hated by all for my name's sake. But the one who endures to the end will be saved' (MARK 13:12–13 ESV).

49. "'So when you see the abomination of desolation spoken of by the prophet Daniel, standing in the holy place (let the reader understand), then let those who are in Judea flee to the mountains. Let the one who is on the housetop not go down to take what is in his house, and let the one who is in the field not turn back to take his cloak. And alas for women who are pregnant and for those who are nursing infants in those days! Pray that your flight may not be in winter or on a Sabbath. For then there will be great tribulation, such as has not been from the beginning of the world until now, no, and never will be. And if those days had not been cut short, no human being would be saved. But for the sake of the elect those days will be cut short' (MATTHEW 24:15–22 ESV).'"

50. "'Immediately after the tribulation of those days the sun will be darkened, and the moon will not give its light, and the stars will fall from heaven, and the powers of the heavens will be shaken.

Then will appear in heaven the sign of the Son of Man, and then all the tribes of the earth will mourn, and they will see the Son of Man coming on the clouds of heaven with power and great glory.

And he will send out his angels with a loud trumpet call, and they will gather his elect from the four winds, from one end of heaven to the other.'

'From the fig tree learn its lesson: as soon as its branch becomes tender and puts out its leaves, you know that summer is near. So also, when you see all these things, you know that he is near, at the very gates.

Truly, I say to you, this generation will not pass away until all these things take place' (MATTHEW 24:29–34 ESV)."

"'For as were the days of Noah, so will be the coming of the Son of Man. For as in those days before the flood they were eating and drinking, marrying and giving in marriage, until the day when Noah entered the ark, and they were unaware until the flood came and swept them all away, so will be the coming of the Son of Man' (MATTHEW 24:37–39 ESV)."

51. "'But concerning that day or that hour, no one knows, not even the angels in heaven, *nor the Son*, but only the Father' (MARK 13:32 ESV)."

52. "'Truly, truly, I say to you, you will weep and lament, but the world will rejoice. You will be sorrowful, but your sorrow will turn into joy. When a woman is giving birth, she has sorrow because her hour has come, but when she has delivered the baby, she no longer remembers the anguish, for joy that a human being has been born into the world. So also you have sorrow now, but I will see you again, and your hearts will rejoice, and no one will take your joy from you' (JOHN 16:20–22 ESV)."

53. "'And many false prophets will arise and lead many astray. And because lawlessness will be increased, the love of many will grow cold. But the one who endures to the end will be saved. And this gospel of the kingdom will be proclaimed throughout the whole world as a testimony to all nations, and then the end will come' (MATTHEW 24:11–14 ESV)."

54. This depiction of the end of times is obviously allegorical, like most of those presented by Jesus. The scenes that it contains are, by their energy, devised to impress intelligences that were still coarse. To strike these imaginations which lacked much subtlety, it was necessary to paint vigorous images, in vivid colors. Jesus addressed specially the people, the least enlightened individuals, incapable of understanding metaphysical abstractions, and of grasping any delicacy of forms. To reach the hearts, it was necessary to speak to the eyes by means of material signs, and to the ears by using vigorous language.

As a natural consequence of this mindset, the supreme power, according to the belief of the time, could only be manifested by extraordinary, supernatural things: the more impossible they were, the better they were accepted as probable.

The Son of Man coming on the clouds of heaven, with great majesty, surrounded by his angels and the sound of trumpets, seemed to them far more imposing than a being invested only with moral power. So the Jews, who were expecting in the Messiah a sort of king of the Earth, mighty among all kings, to put their nation up in the first rank, and to raise again the throne of David and Solomon, would not recognize him in the humble carpenter's son, without material authority, treated as mad by some, and by others as the surrogate of Satan. They could not understand a king without refuge or retreat, and whose kingdom was not of this world.

However, this poor proletarian from Judea became the greatest among the great; he has conquered more kingdoms for his sovereignty than the most powerful potentates. With his word and a few impoverished fishermen, he revolutionized the world, and it is to him that the Jews owe their rehabilitation.

However, this poor proletarian from Judea became the greatest among the great; he has conquered more kingdoms for his sovereignty than the most powerful potentates. With his word and a few impoverished fishermen, he revolutionized the world, and it is to him that the Jews owe their restoration.

55. It should be remarked that among ancient populations, earthquakes and the obscuration of the Sun were obligatory symbols of all dire omens and events. They are found at the death of Jesus, at the death of Caesar, and in a host of circumstances in the history of paganism. If these phenomena had been produced as often as it is told, it would seem impossible that people should not have preserved their memory through tradition. To these we should add the stars that supposedly fell from the sky, as to testify to more enlightened future generations that it is fiction, since we now know that stars cannot fall.

56. However, great thruths lie beneath these allegories: They announce first of all calamities of all kinds that will strike humanity and decimate it; and also calamities engendered by the supreme struggle between good and evil, faith and unbelief, progressive ideas and retrograde ideas. Secondly, the diffusion throughout the Earth of the restored gospel in its primitive purity; then, the reign of good, in which there will be peace and universal fraternity, as a result of the Gospel moral code put into practice by all peoples. It will be truly the reign of Jesus, since he will preside at its establishment, and all humans will live under his law. A reign of happiness, for he says that *after the days of affliction will come those of joy.*

57. When will these things happen? "No one knows," said Jesus, "*not* [even] *the Son.*" But when the time comes, all humans will be warned by precursory signs. These signs will be neither in the Sun nor in the stars, but in the social state and in more moral than physical phenomena, as may be inferred from his allusions.

It is quite certain that this change could not take place during the lifetime of the apostles, a fact of which Jesus could not have been unaware, and besides, such a transformation could not be accomplished in just a few years. Yet if he speaks to them as if they should be witnesses, it is because they will be able to reincarnate at a future time and participate themselves in the transformation. Sometimes he speaks of the coming fate of Jerusalem, and sometimes he takes this fact as a point of comparison for the future.

58. Is it the end of the world that Jesus announces by his new advent, and when he says, "And this gospel of the kingdom will be proclaimed throughout the whole world as a testimony to all nations, and then the end will come."

It is not rational to suppose that God will destroy the world precisely at the moment when the latter will enter the path of moral progress by the practice of the Gospel teachings. Moreover, nothing in the words of Christ indicates a universal destruction which, under such conditions, would not be justified.

This widespread practice of the Gospel, in order to bring about an improvement of the moral state of humans, will thus bring about the reign of good and the fall of evil. So it is to the end of the old world – the world ruled by prejudice, pride, selfishness, fanaticism, unbelief, greed and all evil passions – that Christ alludes when he says: "And this gospel of the kingdom will be proclaimed throughout the whole world as a testimony to all nations, and then the end will come." However, this end will bring about a struggle, and it is from this struggle that the tribulations that he foresees will come out.

YOUR SONS AND DAUGHTERS WILL PROPHESY

59. "'And in the last days it shall be, God declares, that I will pour out my Spirit on all flesh, and your sons and your daughters shall prophesy, and your young men shall see visions, and your old men shall dream dreams; even on my male servants and female servants in those days I will pour out my Spirit, and they shall prophesy' (ACTS 2:17–18 ESV)."

60. If we consider the present state of the physical world and the moral world, the tendencies, the aspirations, the intuitions of the masses, the decadence of old ideas which, for a century, have struggled in vain against new ideas, we cannot doubt that a new order of things is being prepared, and that the old world is coming to an end.

If now, by taking the deeper sense of the allegorical form of certain depictions, and scrutinizing the inner meaning of Jesus' words, we compare the current situation with the times described by him, as marking an era of renovation, it cannot be denied that nowadays many of his predictions are being fulfilled. Hence it must be concluded that we are touching the announced times, which is confirmed by spirits that manifest themselves at all points of the globe.

61. As we have seen (Ch. I, item 32 above), the advent of Spiritism, coinciding with other circumstances, fulfills one of the most important predictions of Jesus, by the influence it must necessarily exert over ideas. This is, moreover, clearly announced in the Acts of the Apostles, with these words: "And in the last days it shall be, God declares, that I will pour out my Spirit on all flesh, and your sons and your daughters shall prophesy."

This unequivocally announces a widespread popularization of mediumship, which is revealed nowadays in individuals of all ages, sexes, and walks of life, as a result of the universal manifestation of spirits – because without spirits there would be no mediums. This, it is said, will happen in the last days. Since we have not reached the end of the world but, on the contrary, the time of its regeneration, we must understand by these words, the end times of the moral world that is coming to a close. (See A. KARDEC, *The Gospel according to Spiritism*, ch. XXI.)

THE FINAL JUDGMENT

62. "When the Son of Man comes in his glory, and all the angels with him, then he will sit on his glorious throne. Before him will be gathered all the nations, and he will separate people one from another as a shepherd separates the sheep from the goats. And he will place the sheep on his right, but the goats on the left. Then the King will say to those on his right, 'Come, you who are blessed by my Father, ...' (MATTHEW 25:31–46 ESV. See also A. KARDEC, *The Gospel according to Spiritism*, ch. XV)."

63. For the good to reign on Earth, it is necessary that spirits that have hardened in evil, and which could bring trouble and turmoil, are banned from it. God has left them enough time for them to reform, But once the moment arrives when the globe must rise in the hierarchy of worlds, through the moral progress of its inhabitants, staying on Earth, whether for spirits or incarnate humans, will be forbidden to all those who have not benefited from the teachings they have been able to receive here. They will be exiled to lower worlds – as once were exiled to Earth those of the so-called Adamic race – at the same time that better spirits will come to replace them. It is this separation, which will be presided by Jesus, that is represented in these words of the Final Judgment: "And he will place the sheep on his right, but the goats on the left" (i.e., The good will pass to his right, and the wicked to his left). (See ch. **XI**, items **31** *et seq.* above.)

64. The religious doctrine of a final, unique and universal judgment, forever putting an end to humanity, is repugnant to reason, in the sense that it would imply the inactivity of God during the eternity that preceded the creation of the Earth, and the eternity that would follow its destruction. One wonders then what use would have the Sun, the Moon and the stars, which, according to Genesis, had been made to illuminate our world. It is astonishing that so immense a work would have been made to last such little time and for the sole benefit of beings, the majority of which was destined beforehand to eternal torments.

65. Materially, the idea of a single judgment was, up to a certain point, admissible for those who do not seek the reason of things, when one thought that the whole humanity was on Earth, and that everything in the universe had been made for its inhabitants. This became inadmissible since we learned that there are billions of similar worlds which perpetuate their human civilizations for eternity; next to which the Earth is an imperceptible tiny point in space,

It is evident from this fact that Jesus was right when he said to his disciples, "I still have many things to say to you, but you cannot bear them now," since the future progress of science was indispensable for a sound interpretation of some of his words. Assuredly the apostles, St. Paul and the first disciples, would have established certain dogmas quite differently had they had the astronomical, geological, physical, chemical, physiological and psychological knowledge that we possess today. Therefore Jesus postponed his complementary instructions and announced that all things would eventually be restored.

66.   Morally speaking, a definitive and irrevocable judgment is irreconcilable with the infinite goodness of the Creator, which Jesus continually presents to us as a kind Parent, always leaving a way open to repentance, and ready to extend Its arms to the prodigal son or daughter. If Jesus had understood the judgment in that sense, he would have contradicted his own words.

Besides, if the final judgment is to surprise humans unexpectedly, in the midst of their ordinary occupations, and even pregnant women, one wonders to what purpose God, which does nothing useless or unjust, would let them give birth to children and create new souls at this supreme moment of the fatal end of humanity, to submit them into judgment while still in the womb, before they could become conscious of themselves, while others have had thousands of years to recognize themselves. On which side, to the right or to the left, will pass those souls that are not yet good or bad, and to whom any further path to progress would henceforth be closed, since humanity would no longer exist? (See ch. **II**, item **19** above.)

May those whose reason is content with such beliefs keep them, as it is their undeniable right, and no one finds fault with it. However, by their turn, may they not find fault with anyone who is not of their opinion.

67.   The judgment by means of an emigration as defined above (63) is rational. It is founded on the most rigorous justice, since it leaves eternally to the spirit its free will; that it does not constitute a privilege for anyone; that an equal latitude is given by God to all Its created beings, without exception, to evolve; that the gates of heaven are always open to those who make themselves worthy of entering; and that the very annihilation of a world, resulting in the destruction of the body, would not bring any interruption to the progressive march of the spirit. Such is the consequence of the plurality of worlds and the plurality of existences.

According to this interpretation, calling it the final judgment is not accurate, since all spirits undergo similar judgments at each renovation of the worlds they inhabit, until they have reached a certain degree of perfection. So, strictly speaking, there is no final judgment, but there are general judgments at all periods of partial or total renovation of the population of the worlds, resulting in great emigrations and immigrations of spirits.

Chapter XVIII
The time has come

SIGNS OF THE TIMES

1. The time set by God has arrived – we are told on all sides – where great events will be accomplished for the regeneration of humanity. In what sense are these prophetic words to be understood? To unbelievers, they have no importance; being only the expression of a puerile belief without foundation; but to the majority of believers, they hold something mystical and supernatural which, in their view, seems to herald an upheaval of the laws of Nature. These two interpretations are equally erroneous. The first for implying the negation of Providence; the second for supposing that these words announce the disturbance of Nature's laws, when actually they denote their fulfillment.

2. All is harmony in creation; everything reveals a foresight which is never absent from the smallest or the greatest things. Therefore, first of all, we must reject any idea of caprice or chance which is irreconcilable with divine wisdom. Secondly, if our time is marked by the accomplishment of certain things, it is because they all have their raisons d'être in the overall progress.

This being said, it should be pointed out that our globe, like everything that exists, is subject to the law of progress. It evolves physically through the transformation of the elements that compose it; and morally, by the purification of incarnate and discarnate spirits. These two progresses follow each other and run parallel to each other, for the perfecting of the dwelling is always in keeping with that of its inhabitants. Physically, the globe has undergone transformations – a fact ascertained by science – and has successively been rendered habitable by increasingly perfected beings. Morally, humanity progresses by the development of intelligence, the moral sense, and by a general amelioration of manners. At the same time as the improvement of the globe is effected under the empire of material forces, humans contribute to it by the efforts of their intelligence. They cleanse unhealthy regions, make communications easier, and increases the productivity the world.

This dual progress is accomplished in two ways: one slow, gradual and imperceptible; the other by more abrupt changes, each of which corresponding to a more rapid upward movement which marks, by very clear signs, the progressive periods of humankind. These movements, subordinated *in the details* to human free will, are in a way inexorable as a whole, because they are all subject to laws – such as those which govern the germination, growth and maturity of plants – bearing in mind that the goal of humanity is progress, notwithstanding the dawdling march of some individuals. That is why the progressive movement is sometimes partial, that is, limited to a specific race or a nation, and general and wide-ranging at other times.

The progress of humanity is therefore effected by virtue of a law. Now, as all laws of Nature are the eternal work of divine wisdom and foreknowledge, anything that is the effect of these laws is the result of God's will, and not of an accidental and capricious will. But of an unchanging will. So when humanity is ripe to go up a degree, we can say that the times set by God have come, as we can also say that they have arrived in this season for the ripening of the fruit and the harvest.

3. Since the progressive movement of humanity is inevitable, and although it is part of Nature, it does not follow that God is indifferent to it, and that, after having established laws, the Creator has fallen back into inaction, letting things proceed on their own. God's laws are eternal and immutable, no doubt, but because Its will itself is eternal and constant, and Its thought animates all things uninterruptedly. God's penetrating thought is the intelligent and permanent force that keeps everything in harmony. Should this thought cease for a single moment to act, the universe would be like a clock without the regulating pendulum. God therefore constantly watches over the enforcement of these laws, and the spirits who inhabit the spiritual world are Its ministers in charge of the details, according to attributions relative to their degree of advancement.

4. The universe is at the same time an incommensurable mechanism led by a no less incommensurable number of intelligences, an immense government in which every intelligent being has its share of action under the eye of the Sovereign Master, whose *unique* will maintains *unity* everywhere. Under the influence of this vast regulating power everything moves, everything functions in perfect order. What we see as disturbances are the peculiar and isolated movements, which appear to us to be irregular only because our sight is circumscribed. If we could encompass all of them, we would see that these irregularities are only apparent and that they harmonize in the whole.

5. Predictions of the progressive movements of humanity are not surprising from dematerialized beings which see the goal to which all things are tending. Some of these beings possess the direct thought of God, and can estimate, from partial movements, the time at which a general movement will be accomplished, as we ourselves can estimate in advance the time it will take for a tree to bear fruit, and as astronomers are able to calculate the time of an astronomical phenomenon by the time it takes for a star to complete its rotation or orbit.

But all those who announce these phenomena, the authors of almanacs who predict eclipses and tides, are certainly not in a position to make the necessary calculations themselves, they are only echoes. The same occurs with secondary spirits whose sight is limited, and which merely repeats what the higher spirits have to reveal to them.

6. To this day, humanity has made indisputable progress; humans, by their intelligence, have achieved results never seen before in science, the arts, and the material well-being. We still have to accomplish a great deal of progress *in order to make: charity, fraternity and solidarity prevail, thus ensuring moral well-being*. We could neither with our beliefs, nor with our antiquated institutions, remnants of another age, good at a certain time, sufficient for a transitory state, but which, having given what they had to offer, would be a stopping point today. Like a child is stimulated by hanging mobiles, useless at one's mature age. It is no longer only the development of intelligence that human beings need, but rather the elevation of feeling; and for that it is necessary to destroy all that could excite in us selfishness and pride.

Such is the period in which we will enter henceforth, and which will mark one of the principal phases of humanity. This phase, which is being developed at this moment, is the necessary complement of the preceding state, just as adulthood is the complement of young age. It could therefore be foretold and predicted in advance, and that is why it is said that the time set by God has arrived.

7. This time it will not be a partial change, a renovation limited to a country, a nation, a race. It will be a universal movement which operates toward moral progress. A new order of things is being established, and the individuals that are most opposed to it are without their knowledge; actually working for it. The future generation, disentangled from the dross of the old world and formed of more refined elements, will find itself animated by ideas and feelings quite different from the current generation, which is passing away at giant strides. The old world will be dead, and will remembered in history, as today we regard the Middle Ages, with their barbaric customs and superstitious beliefs.

Besides, everyone knows that the current order of things leaves much to be desired After having, in a way, exhausted the material well-being which is the product of intelligence, we now begin to understand that the complement of this well-being can only be found in moral development. The more we advance, the more we feel what is lacking, without, however, being able to clearly define it. This is the effect of the inner work of regeneration which is taking place. We have desires, aspirations that are like an intuition of a better state or condition.

8. But a change as radical as that which is now in progress cannot be accomplished without turmoil. There is an inevitable struggle between different ideas. From this conflict will necessarily arise temporary disturbances, until the ground is cleared and balance restored. It is therefore from the struggle of ideas that the momentous events announced will arise, and not from cataclysms or purely material catastrophes. Widespread cataclysms were the consequence of the state of formation of the Earth. *Today it is no longer the entrails of the Earth which are in turmoil, but rather the entrails of humanity.*

9. Humanity is a collective being in which the same moral revolutions take place as in every individual being, with the difference that some are accomplished from year to year, while others from century to century. If one would follow these evolutions through time, one would see the life of the various races and civilizations being marked by periods which give to each epoch a particular character.

In addition to partial movements, there is a widespread, general movement which gives impetus to humanity as a whole; yet the progress of each part of the whole is relative to its degree of advancement. Let us imagine, for example, a family composed of several children, the youngest of whom still in the cradle, while the eldest is already ten years old. In ten years, the eldest will be twenty, becoming an adult, whereas the youngest will be ten years of age and, although more advanced than before, will be still a child, who, however, will also grow up to become an adult eventually. The same occurs with the different parts of humanity: the most backward advance, but cannot surge to the level of the most advanced ones,

10. Once grown up, humanity has new needs, wider and higher aspirations. It understands the emptiness of the ideas with which it had been swayed; the insufficiency of its institutions to bring happiness; and it no longer finds in the state of things legitimate satisfactions to which it feels called. That is why it shakes off its swaddling clothes, and rushes, driven by an irresistible force, toward unknown shores, so as to discover new, less limited horizons.

And it is when humanity is too cramped in its material sphere, that intellectual life overflows, that the feeling of spirituality blossoms, that individuals claiming to be philosophers hope to fill up the void with the doctrines of nothingness and materialism! Strange aberration! The same individuals who pretend to push humanity forward, strive to circumscribe it to the narrow circle of matter from which it aspires to emerge. They close to it the aspect of infinite life, and tell it, pointing to the grave: *Ne plus ultra*.[112]

11. The progressive march of humanity takes place in two ways, as said above. One gradual, slow, imperceptible, if we consider the

---

112 [Trans. note] Ancient Latin inscription meaning "nothing further." In the context above, "there is nothing after death."

already accomplished periods, reflected in successive improvements in morals, the laws, the manners and habits; like only in the long run one notices the changes which the currents of water bring to the surface of the globe. The other way, by relatively sudden, rapid movements, similar to those of a torrent breaking dikes, which, in just a few years, make it cross the range which it would have taken it centuries to traverse. It is then a moral cataclysm which engulfs for a few moments the institutions of the past, and which brings about a new order of things which gradually affirms itself, as peace is restored, and then becomes definitive.

To those who will live long enough to encompass the gentle slopes of the new phase, it will seem that a new world has emerged from the ruins of the old: character, manners, habits, everything will be changed; because these are newcomers to Earth's human race, or better regenerated souls. The ideas held by the generation that is extinguished will have given way to new ideas in the rising generation.

It is at one of these periods of transformation, or, if you will, of *moral growth*, that humanity has arrived. From adolescence it now goes into adulthood; the past can no longer suffice its new aspirations, its new needs. It can no longer be conducted by the same means; it no longer treats itself to illusions and hired prestige: it needs a more substantial food. The present is too ephemeral; humanity feels that its destiny is greater, and that corporeal life is too limited to enclose it in its entirety. That is why it looks into the past and toward the future, in order to discover the mystery of its existence and to draw from it a comforting sense of security.

12.   Whoever has meditated about Spiritism and its consequences, and does not circumscribe it to the production of certain phenomena, understands that it has opened to humanity a new way, and has unfolded the horizons of the infinite by introducing to human beings the mysteries of the invisible world, showing its true role in creation, a *perpetually active* role both in the spiritual state and in the physical state. Humans no longer walk blindly: we know where he we came from, where we are going, and why we are on Earth. The future is revealed to us in its reality, free from the prejudices of ignorance and superstition. It is no longer a vague hope, but a palpable truth, as certain for us as the succession of day and night. We know that one's being is not limited to a few moments of an ephemeral existence; that one's spiritual life is not interrupted by death; that we all have already lived before, and that we will live again together with all that we have acquired of perfection through our work and deeds. Nothing is lost; we find in our previous existences the reason for what we are today; and *from what we do of ourselves today, we can conclude what we will be someday.*

13. With the thought that individual activity and cooperation in the general work of civilization is supposedly limited to one's current lifetime, that were nothing before and will be nothing afterwards, what does it matter to humans whether there will be further progress of humanity? What does it matter to humans that, in future, people will be better governed, more friendly, more enlightened, and better for one another? Anyway, since one cannot draw any benefit from it, what good would be such progress for oneself? What is the point of working for those who come after us, if we should never know them, if they are new beings who will soon return to nothingness? Under the influence of such negation of any individual future, everything is necessarily reduced to the petty proportions of the fleeting moment and one's own personality.

But, on the contrary, what an amplitude is given to human thought by a certainty of the perpetuity of one's spiritual being! What could be more rational, more magnificent, more worthy of the Creator than this law according to which spiritual life and corporeal life are only two modes of existence which alternate in the accomplishment of progress! What could be more just and comforting than the idea of the same beings progressing incessantly, first through the generations of a same world, and then from world to world until reaching perfection, without any interruption? Then there is a goal, since, by working for all, one works for oneself, and vice versa; so that neither individual progress nor general progress is ever sterile. It benefits future generations and individuals, who are none other than past generations and individuals, who have attained a higher stage of advancement.

14. The spiritual life is the normal and eternal life of the spirit, and incarnation is only a temporary form of its existence. Except for their outer envelopes, there is identity between the incarnate and the discarnate spirits. They are the same individualities under two different aspects, belonging sometimes to the visible world, sometimes to the invisible one, inhabiting either one or the other, and contributing in one and the other to the same end, by means appropriate to their situation.

To this law follows that of the perpetuity of the relations among beings; death does not separate them, and does not put an end to their sympathetic relations and their reciprocal duties. Hence the solidarity of all for one and one for all; and also fraternity. Human beings will live happily on Earth only when these two feelings have entered their hearts and their manners, for only then will they conform to their laws and institutions. This will be one of the main results of the transformation which is taking place,

But how to reconcile the duties of solidarity and fraternity with the belief that death makes humans forever strangers to one another? By the law of the perpetuity of relations which bind all beings, Spiritism rests this double principle upon the laws of Nature, making it not only a duty, but a necessity. By that of the plurality of existences, humans are connected with what has been done and what will be done, with persons of the past and those of the future. Therefore, we can no longer say that we have nothing in common with those who died, since both meet one another constantly in this world and in the world beyond, to climb together the ladder of progress, and lend mutual support to one another. Fraternity is no longer circumscribed to some individuals brought together by chance during the ephemeral duration of a lifetime; it is as perpetual as the life of the spirit; as universal as humanity, which constitutes a great family of which all members are in solidarity with one another, *whatever the epoch in which they lived*

Such are the ideas that emerge from Spiritism, and that it will arise among all human beings, when it becomes universally spread, compiled, taught and practiced. With Spiritism, fraternity, synonymous with the charity preached by Christ, is no longer a vain word; it has its reason for being. From the feeling of fraternity springs that of reciprocity and social duties, from person to person, from nation to nation, from race to race. From these two well-understood feelings will necessarily emerge institutions which will prove to be the most advantageous to the well-being of all.

15.   Fraternity must be the cornerstone of the new social order; but there can not be a real, solid and effective fraternity, unless it is supported by an unbreakable base, which is faith. And not the faith in such and such particular dogmas, which changes according to time and people, and at which stones are thrown – because, by pronouncing anathemas against others, such dogmas will feed antagonism – but faith in the fundamental principles which everyone can accept, namely, *God, the soul, the future, **an unlimited individual progress, and the perpetuity of the relations among beings***. When all human beings become convinced that God is the same for each and every one, that God, supremely just and good, cannot wish or devise anything unjust, and that evil comes from humans and not from God, we will regard ourselves as children of one Parent and hold our hands out to our Creator.

It is this faith which Spiritism gives, and which will henceforth be the pivot on which the human race will move, whatever their individual modes of adoration and their particular beliefs, which Spiritism respects, but with which it does not wish to occupy itself.

From this faith alone can true moral progress emerge, because it alone gives a logical corroboration to legitimate rights and duties. Without it, the right is the one given by strength; and duty, a human code imposed by constraint. Without it, what is a human being? A small amount of matter that dissolves, an ephemeral being just passing by; even genius is only a spark that shines for a moment, only to die out forever – there is certainly not much there to raise one's self-esteem before one's own eyes.

With such a thought, where are the rights and duties really? What is the goal of progress? Only this faith can make humans feel their dignity by the perpetuity and progression of their beings, not into a petty and circumscribed future, but a magnificent and splendid one. This thought places human beings above the Earth; we feel ourselves growing up thinking that we all have our role in the universe; that this universe is our domain which we can travel one day, and that death will not reduce us to nothing, or a useless thing to ourselves and the others.

16.   The intellectual progress accomplished in greatest proportions nowadays has been a great step, and marks the first phase of humanity. But it alone is powerless to regenerate humanity. As long as humans are dominated by pride and selfishness, they will use their intelligence and knowledge for the benefit of their passions and personal interests. That is why humans apply their intelligence and skills for perfecting means of injuring others and destroying one another.

Moral progress alone can assure human happiness on Earth. By putting a brake on bad passions; it alone can bring harmony, peace, and true fraternity toward one another.

It will lower the barriers that separate peoples and nations, and also bring down prejudices of caste, and silence the antagonisms of sects, by teaching people to regard themselves as brothers and sisters, called upon to help one another and not to live at the expense of one another.

Moral progress is also seconded here by the progress of the intellect, which will join humans in one same belief based on the eternal truths, not subject to discussion and, by this very fact, accepted by all.

Unity of belief will be the most powerful bond, the most solid foundation of universal fraternity, which has been broken at all times by religious antagonisms that divide peoples and families, which make us see in our fellow human beings enemies we must flee, fight, or exterminate, instead of brothers and sisters who should be loved.

17. Such a state of affairs presupposes a radical change in the sentiment of the masses, a general progress which could only be accomplished by leaving the narrow circle of down-to-earth ideas which incite self-interest. At various times, a few select individuals have sought to push humanity in this direction, yet humanity, still too young, has remained deaf, and their teachings have been like good seed falling on stone.

Today, humanity is ripe to look higher than it did, to assimilate broader ideas and understand what it formerly did not understand.

The generation that is now disappearing will carry with it its prejudices and errors, while the rising generation, having drunk from a purer spring and imbued with healthier ideas, will impart upon the world an ascending movement, in the sense of moral progress, which should mark the new phase of humanity.

18. This phase is already being revealed by unambiguous signs, by attempts at useful reforms, by large and generous ideas which are emerging and beginning to find echoes. It is thus that a host of protective, civilizing and emancipatory institutions have been founded, under the impetus and initiative of individuals who are evidently predestined for the task of regeneration, that the penal laws are daily being replaced by more humane ones. Race prejudices are weakening, people are beginning to regard themselves as members of a large family. By the uniformity and facility of means of transaction, they remove the barriers which have divided them; from all parts of the world they gather in international events for peaceful tournaments of intelligence.

But these reforms still lack a basis for developing, completing, and consolidating a more general moral predisposition for propagating and gaining acceptance from the masses. They are nonetheless a characteristic sign of time, the prelude to what will be accomplished on a larger scale, as the terrain becomes more favorable.

19. A sign no less characteristic of the period which we are now entering is the evident reaction which takes place concerning spiritualistic ideas. An instinctive repulsion manifests itself against materialistic ideas. The mood of incredulity which had seized upon the masses, whether ignorant or enlightened, and made them reject, with the form, the very foundation of all beliefs, seems to have been a slumber at the end of which one feels the need to breathe a more invigorating air. Involuntarily, where the void has been made, one seeks something, a support, a hope.

20. In this great regenerative movement, Spiritism has a considerable role – not the ridiculous Spiritism invented by mocking criticism, but philosophical Spiritism, as understood by anyone who takes the trouble to seek the kernel under the surface.

By the proofs it brings of fundamental truths, Spiritism fills the void that unbelief has created in ideas and beliefs. By the certainty it gives of a future in conformity with the justice of God, and which the most strict reason can admit, it tempers the bitterness of life and prevents the fatal effects of despair.

By making known new laws of nature, Spiritism gives the key to misunderstood phenomena and to problems which were insoluble to this day, besides banishing both incredulity and superstition. For it, there is neither supernatural nor wondrous; everything is accomplished in the world under immutable laws.

Far from substituting one exclusivism for another, it poses itself as an absolute champion of freedom of conscience; also combating any form of fanaticism, and cutting it at its root by proclaiming salvation for all good human beings, and the possibility, for the most imperfect among them, of arriving, by their efforts, at atonement and reparation, and eventually to perfection which alone can lead to supreme bliss. Instead of discouraging the weak, Spiritism encourages them by showing the harbor they can reach.

It does not say, *Without Spiritism there is no salvation*, but instead, with Christ, *Without charity there is no salvation* – a principle of union and tolerance, which will rally all humans behind a common feeling of fraternity, instead of dividing them into mutually hostile sects.

By this other principle, namely, *Unshakable faith is only that which can stand face to face with reason in any period of human history*, it destroys the empire of blind faith that annihilates reason, of passive obedience that dazes and dumbs; while, at the same time, it emancipates human intelligence and elevates moral standards.

Consistent with itself, Spiritism is not imposed on anyone: it says what it is, what it wants, what it gives, and waits for people to come to it freely and voluntarily. It wants to be accepted by reason and not by force. It respects all sincere beliefs, and fights only incredulity, selfishness, pride, and hypocrisy, which are scourges of society and the most serious obstacles to moral progress. However, it does not throw anathema against anyone, not even its own enemies, because it is convinced that the path of good is open to the most imperfect individuals, and that sooner or later they too will enter it.

21. If one assumes that the majority of human beings are imbued with these sentiments, one can easily imagine the changes they would bring about in social relations. Charity, fraternity, benevolence toward all, and tolerance of all beliefs, will become their motto. This is the aim for which humanity, the object of its aspirations and desires, naturally strives, without being aware of the means of accomplishing them. It tries, it gropes around, but it is stopped by active resistance or the force of inertia engendered by prejudices and stationary beliefs refractory to progress. Such are the forms of resistance that must be overcome, and this will be the task of the new generation. If we follow the present course of things, we will recognize that everything seems predestined to prepare the way for it. The double power of number and ideas, and an increased experience of the past, will be on its side.

22. The new generation will therefore work toward the accomplishment of all humanitarian ideas compatible with the degree of advancement it has achieved. Spiritism, marching toward the same goal, and accomplishing its views, will meet with them on the same ground. Progressive individuals of this new generation will find a powerful lever in Spiritist ideas, whereas Spiritism will find in them spirits ready to welcome it. In view of this, what can those hell-bent on hindering and obstructing it do?

23. It is not Spiritism that creates social renovation, it is humanity reaching maturity that makes this renovation a necessity. By its moralizing force, by its progressive tendencies, by the extent of its views, by the wide scope of the questions it embraces, Spiritism is, more than any other philosophical or religious doctrine, truly apt to second the regenerative movement – that is why it is contemporary with it. It came at the moment when it could be useful, because for it times have arrived too. If it would have come earlier, it would have encountered insurmountable obstacles. It would inevitably have succumbed, because people, satisfied with what they had, did not yet feel a need for what it brings. Today, born with the movement of new ideas that are emerging, it finds the terrain ready to receive it. People's minds, weary of doubt and uncertainty, frightened at the void dug before them, welcome it as an anchor of salvation and supreme consolation.

24. To say that humanity is ripe for regeneration does not mean that all individuals are equal, but many of them intuitively have the seed of the new ideas that circumstances will bring about. After that, they will be more advanced than it was supposed, and they will eagerly follow the impetus of the majority.

There are, however, some people who are fundamentally refractory, even among the most intelligent individuals, and who, certainly, will never embrace it, at least in this existence – some, in good faith, out of conviction; others for interest. Those whose material interests are connected with the current state of things, and who are not advanced enough to abnegate them, and who good of all people touches them less than the good of their own person, cannot see even the least reforming movement without apprehension. *The truth is for them a secondary issue, or, rather, truth, for certain people, should be entirely limited to that which causes them no trouble.* All progressive ideas are, in their eyes, subversive ideas, which is why they nurture an implacable hatred and wage a bitter war against them. Too smart not to perceive in Spiritism an auxiliary of these ideas and of the elements of the transformation they dread – because they are not sufficiently advanced to receive it – they strive to bring it down. If they deemed it really worthless and without any reach, they would not care. As I once said elsewhere: *"The greater an idea is, the more adversaries it meets, and its importance can be measured by the violence of the attacks directed against it."*

25. The number of laggards is probably still great, but what can they do against the rising tide, if not throw some stones at it? This flood is the generation that rises, while they disappear with the generation that is going away every day. Until then, they will defend every inch of their territory. Therefore there is an inevitable struggle, but this is an unequal struggle between the decrepit past which is falling into tatters against the youthful future; between stagnation versus progress; between some created beings and the will of God; since the times set by God have come.

THE NEW GENERATION

26. For human beings to be happy on Earth, it must be populated only by good spirits whether incarnate or discarnate, that will wish only good. This time having arrived, a great emigration is being accomplished at this very moment among those that inhabit it. Since those which do evil for evil, and that the feeling of goodness *does not touch*, are no longer worthy of the transformed Earth, will be excluded from this planet, lest they again bring about trouble and turmoil, and be an obstacle to progress. They will atone for their hardening, some in lower-order worlds, others in backward earthly races that will be the equivalent of lower-order worlds, where they will carry their acquired knowledge and skills, and whom they will have the mission to advance. They will be replaced by better spirits that will make justice, peace and fraternity prevail.

The Earth, according to the spirits, should not be transformed by a cataclysm which would annihilate a generation. The current generation will gradually disappear, and a new one will succeed it without change in the natural order of things.

Therefore, as usual, everything will happen externally, with this difference alone, which is of utmost importance: some of the spirits that incarnated here there will no longer incarnate on Earth. In a child who will be born, instead of a backward spirit inclined to evil, the spirit that will incarnate will be more advanced and *inclined toward good*.

It is therefore much less a new corporeal generation than a new generation of spirits. Thus, those who would expect to see the transformation operate through supernatural and wondrous effects will be disappointed.

27. The current era is one of transition; in which elements of the two generations merge. Placed at the intermediate point, we witness the departure of one and the arrival of the other generation, and each one is already indicated in the world by their own characteristics.

These two succeeding generations have quite opposite ideas and views. Judging by the nature of moral dispositions, but especially by intuitive and innate dispositions, it is easy to distinguish to which of the two belongs each individual.

The new generation, having to establish the cause of moral progress, is distinguished by generally precocious intelligence and reason, together with an innate feeling of good and spiritualistic beliefs, which is an unmistakable sign of a certain degree of *previous* advancement. It will not be composed exclusively of eminently superior spirits, but of those which, having already progressed, are predisposed to assimilate all progressive ideas and able to endorse the regenerative movement.

What distinguishes, on the contrary, the backward spirits is, first of all, revolt against God by refusing to recognize any power superior to humanity; and also an instinctive propensity to degrading passions, to anti-fraternal sentiments of selfishness and pride, together with an attachment to all material things.

It is from these vices that Earth must be purged by exiling those souls which refuse to make amends, because they are incompatible with a reign of fraternity, and good souls would always suffer from their contact. When planet Earth is delivered from them, humans will walk unhindered to the better future which is reserved for them here below, as a reward for their efforts and their perseverance, until an even more complete purification opens to them the entrance to higher-order worlds.

28. By this emigration of spirits, we must not understand that all the laggards will be expelled from Earth and relegated to the lower-order worlds. On the contrary, many will come back to it, since many of them had succumbed to circumstances and bad examples; the surface was worse than the inner kernel. Once removed from the influence of matter and the prejudices of the corporeal world, most will see things in a very different light than in their lifetime, as attested by many cases. In this, they are helped by benevolent spirits that are interested in them and that hasten to enlighten them and show them the wrong course they have followed. Through prayers and exhortations, we ourselves can contribute to their improvement, because there is perpetual solidarity between the dead and the living.

The manner in which such transformation takes place is very simple, and, as we can see, it is entirely moral and in no way departs from the laws of Nature.

29. Whether the spirits of the new generation are new and better spirits, or old improved spirits, the result is the same. As soon as they bring better dispositions, there is always a renewal. Incarnate spirits thus comprise two categories, according to their natural dispositions: on the one hand, the laggard spirits which leave; and on the other hand the progressive spirits which arrive. Therefore the state of manners and habits, and of society, whether among a people, a nation, or the whole world, will depend on which of the two categories prevails.

To simplify the question, suppose that a people, at any degree of advancement, and composed of twenty million souls, for example;

undergoes a gradual renewal of spirits being as extinctions, either isolated or en masse. There must have been a moment when the generation of laggard spirits was greater in number than that of progressive spirits, which had only a few representatives without influence, and whose efforts to make good and progressive ideas predominate were paralyzed. Now, as some are leaving and others are arriving, after a given time, the two forces are balanced and so are their influence. Later, the newcomers are in the majority and their influence becomes preponderant, although still hindered by that of the other category. But since the latter continues to diminish while the others multiply, they will eventually disappear, and eventually there will come a time when the influence of the new generation will exclusively prevail. However, this cannot be understood if one does not admit the existence of a spiritual life independent of material life.

30.   We are witnessing this transformation, the conflict that results from the struggle of opposite ideas that seek to take root: some march with the flag of the past, others with that of the future. If we examine the current state of the world, we will recognize that, taken as a whole, earthly humanity is still far from the intermediate point where these forces would reach a balance; and that the different nations, considered in isolation, are at a great distance from one another on this scale; with some touching at this point, but none overtaking it as yet. Moreover, the distance which separates them from the extreme points is far from being equal in duration. Once the threshold limit is crossed, the faster will the new road be traversed, with a multitude of circumstances coming to smooth it out.

Thus the transformation of humanity is accomplished. Without emigration, that is to say, without the departure of laggard spirits that must not return, or that should not return until after having improved, earthly humanity would not necessarily remain indefinitely stagnant, since the most backward spirits will eventually advance in their turn. But it would have taken centuries, and perhaps thousands of years, to reach the result that half a century will suffice to achieve.

31.   A trivial comparison may clarify even better what takes place in this circumstance. Let us suppose a regiment composed for the most part of turbulent and undisciplined soldiers. These will incessantly carry with them a disorderly conduct which the severity of the penal law will often have difficulty in curbing. Suppose that these soldiers are also the strongest, because of their greater number. In addition, they support one another, encourage one another and stimulate one another through example. Meanwhile, the few good ones are without influence. Their advice is despised; they are flouted and abused by others, and suffer from this contact. Is not this the image of today's society?

Now suppose we remove these soldiers from the regiment, one by one, ten by ten, hundred by hundred, and replace them with an equal number of good soldiers, even by those who have been expelled but who will have seriously amended their mindset. After a while we will still have the same regiment, yet totally transformed: good order which will have succeeded to disorder. So will it be with regenerated humanity.

32. Great mass departures are not only intended to speed up exile, but also to transform the mood of the mass more quickly by ridding it of bad influences, and to give more ascendancy to new ideas.

It is because many, despite their imperfections, are ripe for this transformation, and leave in order to go back to a purer source. As long as they remained in the same milieu and under the same influences, they would have persisted in their attitudes and in their way of seeing things. A sojourn in the spiritual world should suffice to open their eyes, because there they will be able to see what they could not notice on Earth, and the unbeliever, the fanatic, the authoritarian, can come back imbued with innate ideas of faith, tolerance, and liberty. On their return they will find things changed, and will be submitted to the prevailing mood of the new environment in which they will be born; and instead of opposing new ideas, will assist in their propagation.

33. Therefore the regeneration of humanity does not absolutely require a complete renewal of spirits: a modification in their moral dispositions will suffice. This modification takes place in all those who are predisposed to it, when they are removed from the pernicious influences of the world. As a result, those who come back are not always other spirits, but often the same spirits thinking and feeling differently.

When this improvement is isolated and individual, it goes unnoticed, and it has no ostensible influence upon the world. However, the effect is quite different, when it operates simultaneously on large masses of people; because then, depending on its proportions, in one generation, the ideas of a people or a nation can be profoundly modified.

This is almost always noticed after big earthquakes and other catastrophes that decimate whole populations. Such destructive events annihilate the physical body, but do not reach the spirit. They activate the back-and-forth movement between the corporeal world and the spiritual world, and consequently the progressive movement of discarnate and incarnate spirits. It should also be noted that at all periods of history great social crises have been followed by an era of progress.

34. It is one of these widespread movements that is taking place at this moment, and which should bring about the reshaping of humanity. The multiplicity of causes of destruction is a characteristic sign of the times, because they must hasten the sprouting of new seeds. Autumn leaves are falling and will be replaced by new leaves full of life, because humanity has its seasons, as individuals have their ages. The dead leaves of humanity's autumn, swept away by gusts and gales, will be reborn even more alive under the same breath of life, which is not extinguished, but rather purifies itself.

35. For materialists, the destructive disasters are calamities without any compensation or useful results, since, according to them, *such events definitely and permanently annihilate living beings*. But for one who knows that death destroys only the physical envelope, they have not the same consequences, and do not cause him or her the least fright. Such people understand the purpose of these catastrophes, and also knows that humans do not lose more in dying together than in dying alone, since, in one way or another, we will all necessarily reach the point of departing from the physical world.

Unbelievers will laugh at these things and treat them as delusional fantasies; but whatever they say, they will not escape the common law. They will perish like all the others, and then what will happen to them? They say: absolutely nothing. Yet they will live on in spite of themselves, and one day will be compelled to open their eyes.

Bibliography

BOOKS BY ALLAN KARDEC PUBLISHED IN ENGLISH

KARDEC, Allan. *The Gospel According to Spiritism*. Trans. H. M. Monteiro. New York: USSF, 2020.

—————————. *Heaven and Hell*. Trans. D. W. Kimble, M. M. Saiz, I. Reis. 2nd ed. Brasília, DF (Brazil): ISC/Edicei, 2011.

—————————. *The Mediums' Book*. D. W. Kimble and M. M. Saiz. 2nd ed. Brasília, DF (Brazil): ISC/Edicei, 2010.

—————————. *The Spirits' Book*. Trans. N. Alves, J. Korngold, H. M. Monteiro. 3rd ed. New York: USSF, 2020.

—————————. *Spiritist Journey in1862*. Trans H. M. Monteiro. New York: USSF, 2019.

—————————. *The Spiritist Review –1858*. Trans L. A. V. Cheim, J. Korngold. New York: USSC/USSF, 2015.

—————————. *The Spiritist Review –1859*. Trans L. A. V. Cheim, J. Korngold, J. C. Madden. New York: USSC/USSF, 2015.

—————————. *The Spiritist Review –1860*. Trans L. A. V. Cheim, D. Caron, J. Korngold, J. C. Madden. New York: USSC/USSF, 2016.

—————————. *The Spiritist Review –1861*. Trans L. A. V. Cheim, D. Caron, J. Korngold. 2nd ed. New York: USSF, 2018.

—————————. *The Spiritist Review –1862*. Trans L. A. V. Cheim, J. Korngold, J. C. Madden. 2nd ed. New York: USSF, 2019.

Note: *In 2020 and following years, the six remaining volumes of The Spiritist Review, comprising all issues from years 1863–1868 are scheduled to be published in English, besides Heaven and Hell and The Mediums' Book, by the USSF in New York.*

**UNITED STATES
SPIRITIST FEDERATION**
New York – USA
Book portal: https://is.gd/ussf1

Made in the USA
Monee, IL
16 April 2022

94889839R00197